Community Mental Health

Community Mental Health

Challenges for the 21st Century

Foreword by Sylvia Nasar, author of *A Beautiful Mind*

Edited by Jessica Rosenberg and Samuel Rosenberg

Routledge
Taylor & Francis Group
New York   London

Published in 2006 by
Routledge
Taylor & Francis Group
270 Madison Avenue
New York, NY 10016

Published in Great Britain by
Routledge
Taylor & Francis Group
2 Park Square
Milton Park, Abingdon
Oxon OX14 4RN

Printed in the United States of America on acid-free paper
10 9 8 7 6 5 4 3 2

International Standard Book Number-10: 0-415-95010-4 (Hardcover) 0-415-95011-2 (Softcover)
International Standard Book Number-13: 978-0-415-95010-7 (Hardcover) 978-0-415-95011-4 (Softcover)
Library of Congress Card Number 2005016676

Library of Congress Cataloging-in-Publication Data

Community mental health : challenges for the 21st century / [edited by] Jessica Rosenberg & Samuel Rosenberg.
    p. cm.
    ISBN 0-415-95010-4 (hb : alk. paper) -- ISBN 0-415-95011-2 (pbk. : alk. paper)
    1. Community mental health services--United States. 2. Mentally ill--Care--United States. 3. Mental health policy--United States. I. Rosenberg, Jessica (Jessica Millet) II. Rosenberg, Samuel.

RA790.6.C592 2005
362.2'2--dc22
                                2005016676

Taylor & Francis Group
is the Academic Division of Informa plc.

Visit the Taylor & Francis Web site at
http://www.taylorandfrancis.com

and the Routledge Web site at
http://www.routledge-ny.com

TABLE OF CONTENTS

ABOUT THE AUTHORS

Jessica Rosenberg, Ph.D., LCSW, is assistant professor of social work, Long Island University, and director of its GranCare Center, a program for grandparent caregivers. She holds an MSW from Hunter College School of Social Work and a Ph.D. from Wurzweiler School of Social Work, Yeshiva University. She is the former assistant director of the New York City Chapter of the National Association of Social Workers, where she worked on passage of the licensing law and facilitated the NASW/1199-SEIU Alliance. Dr. Rosenberg has practiced for over 10 years with clients with serious mental illness in community mental health agencies. She has published on issues related to clinical work with serious mental illness and about culture and immigration. She has presented on numerous topics: grandparent caregivers; stigma, sexual orientation, and mental illness; and social workers and labor unions. Her current research is in the area of grandparent caregivers and the impact of mental illness on family functioning, intergenerational relationships, and immigration.

Samuel J. Rosenberg, Ph.D., LCSW, is professor of social work and sociology at Ramapo College of New Jersey. Dr. Rosenberg has been a scholar and direct practitioner for over 25 years. He has taught at the State University of New York, the City University of New York, Brooklyn College, and the New York State Office of Mental Health Intensive Case Manager Program. Dr. Rosenberg was the director of the Heights Hill Mental Health Service of the South Beach Psychiatric Center, New York State Office of Mental Health. He has written numerous articles on issues concerning providing mental health services and diversity, psychoeducation, immigration, and professional concerns of mental health professionals. Dr. Rosenberg was the recipient of a grant from the New York Community Trust for the production of the groundbreaking educational video *The Whole Family*, a psychoeducational film for Latino families and consumers. *The Whole Family* is used at colleges and universities throughout the United States, Europe, and Latin America.

FOREWORD

Along with many Princetonians who knew the face that flashed on CNN only as the Phantom of Fine Hall, I was astonished when John Nash won the Nobel prize. As a graduate student, I had studied Nash's theory of conflict and cooperation, but the "Nash equilibrium" has been part of the foundations of economics for far too long to make me suspect that the author could still be alive. At the *New York Times*, where I was a reporter, I heard Nash's tragic history and a rumor that he might be on the short list for the prize. But the notion that someone who had dropped out of academia thirty years earlier might actually win the world's most coveted honor seemed wildly romantic and highly improbable. So, seeing John's name more than a year later in an AP wire story literally took my breath away.

To tell the truth, however, I was actually more astounded and moved later on—after my biography of Nash was published and he and I became friends—by things that Nash did that were intensely, utterly ordinary: going to a Broadway play. Driving a car. Having lunch with friends. Caring for a child. Wearing a new fall sweater. Taking a trip. Struggling over an essay. Cracking a joke during his and Alicia's wedding ceremony. In other words, when John Nash got a life.

A psychiatrist at a conference once asked John if he thought his "triumph" over schizophrenia, a disease that many assume is a life sentence without parole, was a miracle. It's great not to be plagued by delusions, John agreed. But, frankly, he said, he wished he could work again. Another time a student asked what winning a Nobel meant to him. The prize signified "social rehabilitation," John answered, but, again frankly, it wasn't the same as being able to work again.

Watching Nash reach for "life's bright pennies" in his 60s, after more than 30 years, was truly thrilling. "Getting a life"—wanting what everyone else wants—is exactly what schizophrenia is supposed to rule out. The long overdue recognition of the Nobel and even aging out of an illness commonly regarded as a life sentence were fairy tales. This was real, this was happening as I watched, and, most of all, it was very much Nash's doing.

After my story about Nash ran in the *Times*, I got a letter from a man who, I learned from another reporter, had been a rising star at the paper in the 1970s before he began to display the symptoms of paranoid schizophrenia. He had been living on the streets of Berkeley for 25 years and called himself Berkeley Baby, a sad figure not unlike the Phantom. John Nash's story, he wrote, "gives me hope that one day the world will return to me too."

As the authors of this book make clear, that hope is close to becoming a reality for millions of people who suffer from one of the most common—and devastating—of mental illnesses. Two generations ago, a diagnosis of schizophrenia usually meant being locked away for life. One generation ago, it began to mean homelessness or jail in the worst cases, and depending on parents or siblings, disability checks, and odd jobs ("the messenger syndrome," as one mother put it) in the rest. As recently as 1983 when Fuller Torrey's self-help classic, *Surviving Schizophrenia*, was first published, he wrote that parents often told him they'd rather hear that their child had cancer than that their child had schizophrenia.

Such grimness is no longer justified, nor is mere survival the best that can be hoped for. Schizophrenia is on its way to becoming a condition that people can *live* with—the way people now live with a host of other serious conditions—diabetes, epilepsy, blindness—that once ruled out full lives or even staying alive. Living, as most of us think of it, involves getting an education, working at a job, driving a car, living on one's own, having a social life, finding a mate. Drugs like clozapine and Abilify and various drug cocktails are more compatible with having a life than older drugs. Promising new treatments are in the pipeline. Breakthroughs in basic research, including mapping the genome, have dramatically raised the odds that some will prove more successful than the existing ones. Diagnosis has gotten better. More people have access to treatment now. To be sure, only a minority of young adults with schizophrenia are working yet. But I believe that many more will be working in the near future. Meanwhile, the tens of thousands who do are living proof of what is possible. And success is the best antidote to stigma, as it has been for other scourges that have been tamed in the past century.

One of the most encouraging signs—very much evident in the essays in this important volume—is a sea change taking place among professionals who work with the mentally ill. As more and more individuals who suffer from conditions, physical or mental, that once meant invalidism or institutionalization insist on having fuller lives, the very concept of illness is changing. Focus is shifting from what isn't possible to what is, from deficits to capabilities, from differences with "normals" to shared aspirations and experiences. Professionals who stress the positive and seek to empower are no longer regarded as being in denial over the gravity of an illness.

I can't think of anything more important or rewarding than doing what the authors of this book do every day: encouraging young people to learn to *live* with their illnesses, helping them get the skills they need, whether it is how to cook a meal or how to study for a test, and supporting their efforts in large ways and small. Getting a life, as John Nash has shown, is a beautiful thing.

Sylvia Nasar
Professor, Graduate School of Journalism
Columbia University
Tarrytown, New York

PREFACE

This book is about the promises and failures of community mental health. It is also about hope and recovery. During the past 50 years, the treatment of persons with serious mental illness has undergone a radical transformation. Significant advances in research and the influence of a growing consumer advocacy movement are forcefully shaping a brave new world in community mental health. At the same time, tremendous suffering persists for those afflicted by serious mental illness.

A recent chance encounter on a New York City subway with a young woman speaks to the heart of what this book is about. She was seated across from me and recognized me as her former therapist in a community mental health center where she had been a client about 15 years ago. She recalled with gratitude and animation the help that she received from me. In fact, I remember her as a bright and vivacious person tortured by bouts of a psychotic mood disorder, and that I had to have her hospitalized due to a serious suicide attempt. Now, as we talked, she was open and insightful about the pernicious nature of her mental illness and recognized the need for ongoing treatment. She asked me for advice because she was having problems finding good mental health care due to her limited health insurance.

We consider that this anecdote exemplifies the promise and pitfalls confronting community mental health. This is a woman whose life hangs in the balance between recovery and relapse. She is full of potential yet exists one step away from homelessness and cyclical psychiatric hospitalizations. The difference for her, which is a difference between life and death, is community mental health. She is alive today because of community mental health, yet because community mental services are fragmented and access to care is often problematic, her future is in question.

This book outlines the substantial challenges facing contemporary community mental health. It contains a collection of 20 original chapters by leading scholars, consumers, and practitioners and offers a wealth of knowledge. Many of the chapters present original research. The book is intended for use with both undergraduate and graduate students in social work, psychology, sociology, psychiatry, and related disciplines. Practitioners will also find many chapters to be of great interest. It is a comprehensive text that addresses the following issues:

- Best practices
- Consumer perspectives
- Diversity
- Homelessness
- Substance abuse
- Policy

The book is divided into an introductory discussion, which provides an excellent overview, and five sections, each of which is introduced by a heading that outlines the major themes of the section.

Section I is composed of five chapters that examine one of the most exciting developments in community mental health today: recovery and the consumer movement. The chapters explicate the multidimensional nature of the recovery process. This new paradigm emphasizes hope, empowerment, and collaboration with consumers, who partner as experts in forging pathways to recovery. The chapters present original research, best practice treatment models, and vividly bring the consumer voice to life through anecdotal interviews. Students in policy and practice courses will find these chapters especially instructive. The chapters would also be of great interest to those working in the field or who have personal relationships with persons with serious mental illness.

Section II presents innovative research-based treatment approaches. In this section, readers will encounter the latest approaches in working with children and adolescents, clients with mental illness and substance abuse disorders, ethical guidelines for making involuntary interventions, and the most up-to-date review of psychiatric interventions and psychopharmacology. These chapters are appropriate for students in practice courses and for seasoned practitioners. The multidisciplinary focus of this section makes it particularly useful for courses in allied helping professions, such as psychology, nursing, and medicine.

Section III focuses on community mental health with populations that have traditionally been discriminated against by the community mental health field. An excellent overview by Drs. Page and Blau identifies how oppression and racism have been perpetuated in mental health care. Issues of race, class, and gender are tackled and strategies for "breaking the impasse" are presented. Readers will find the next four chapters to be complex and extremely useful for practitioners as well as students. The mental health needs of lesbian, gay, bisexual, and transgender clients with serious mental illness — an area that is often ignored — are fully examined. Readers will find a thoughtful discussion on cultural issues related to mental health care with Chinese Americans. A chapter is devoted to an excellent review of clinical interventions appropriate to Hispanics. In this section, readers will also find one of the most incisive and powerful discussions of the experiences of African Americans in the mental health system. The author explores the legacy of the slave experience and scientific racism, concluding that "mental health professionals face daunting challenges in the near future to ensure that all Americans have access to the full range of quality mental health services needed to lead self-fulfilled and productive lives." The selections in this section would fit well in courses about diversity, human behavior, and practice.

Section IV concerns one of the most serious issues in community mental health: homelessness. The three chapters in this section address this issue from different vantage points, including examining the role of the homeless shelter as part of the community mental health system. An excellent chapter reviews new research on best practice case management models for working with homeless persons with mental illness and substance abuse problems. A third selection by two seasoned practitioners who work with homeless mentally ill clients on the streets provides guidelines on effective ways to engage these clients in treatment, while presenting a moving portrayal of these individuals. This section would be most appropriate to courses in policy and practice.

Section V turns to policy and the organizational context for services. Dr. Segal's chapter on managed care deftly navigates the reader through the complex policies of managed care. His analysis examines both the positive and negative consequences of managed care, urging mental health professionals to seize the moment, that is, to not run from managed care, but rather to harness its potential. Themes related to organization challenges and government funding are explored from different perspectives. In the closing chapter by Professor Sullivan, readers will be fascinated and heartened by a masterful discussion of the role of leadership in charting a course through the turbulent waters of community mental health. This section is compelling and a primer for practitioners and students of public health policy.

The book represents a coherent and comprehensive presentation of the salient issues that constitute the manifold challenges for the improvement in the provision of community mental health services in the early years of the 21st century. As such, it supplies fundamental information for students, practitioners, and consumers in their quest to jointly construct an effective and humane mental health delivery system.

ACKNOWLEDGMENTS

The authors particularly acknowledge the staff at Routledge, who have helped us since the beginning of this project. Their responsiveness and professionalism have been so important to us.

Dr. Jessica Rosenberg thanks the Social Work Department of Long Island University: Glenn Gritzer, Amy Krentzman, Samuel Jones, and Susanna Jones, who have been wonderful sources of support and inspiration. Their consistent thoughtfulness and collegiality are tremendously appreciated.

Associate dean of Wurzweiler School of Social Work Dr. Camen Ortiz Hendricks was an extremely helpful reader, and her early comments helped shape the project. Dr. Jessica Rosenberg especially acknowledges the late Dr. Margaret Gibelman, former director of the doctoral program, Wurzweiler School of Social Work, for always insisting on the best and providing the encouragement to achieve it. She was truly an inspirational figure.

Dr. Samuel Rosenberg has had generous support from the Social Work Program at Ramapo College. Professors Mitch Kahn, Donna Crawley, and Yolanda Prieto have been a tremendous source of ideas and selflessly helped in reading proposals and manuscripts. In addition, Dr. Samuel Rosenberg benefited greatly from participation in the Scholar in Residence Program of the Center for Faculty Resources at New York University, and the generous support of the Ramapo College Foundation. In this connection, Dr. Samuel Rosenberg thanks Dr. Debra Szebinsky from NYU and Dr. Ron Kase and Ann Smith from Ramapo College.

We also thank all those individuals who had a significant impact in developing our interest and commitment to the field of community mental health: Jack O'Brien, Jean Okie, John McLaughlin, Dominick Scotto, David Horowitz, Diane Boyd Horowitz, David Graeber, Warren Gold, Paula Gold, Ron Hellman, Donna Corbett, and Silvia Rosenberg.

Finally, we dedicate this book to our children, Daniel and Adrienne, who bring so much love and joy into our lives.

Introduction
Conceptualizing the Challenges in Community Mental Health
JESSICA ROSENBERG AND SAMUEL J. ROSENBERG

DEINSTITUTIONALIZATION AND ITS DISCONTENTS

It is difficult to identify a single explanation for the community mental health movement and the drive for deinstitutionalization that culminated in the passage of the Community Mental Health Act of 1963. Cynics would underscore the government's motivation to cut costs for a population that did not constitute an organized force capable of influencing public policy. Others have attributed President Kennedy's commitment to issues of mental health treatment to his personal experience with his sister, a victim of a lobotomy. Psychopharmacology proponents would argue that the serendipitous discovery of psychotropic medications during the 1950s made it possible to stabilize psychiatric symptoms, thereby enabling the mentally ill to live in the community.

Within this multifaceted context that created the conditions for community mental heath, we would like to address two fundamental issues examined in this volume: the effect of deinstitutionalization on persons with mental illness, and the current challenges confronting community mental health today.

The evolution of deinstitutionalization of persons with major mental illness as it has developed over the past 50 years requires examination from a variety of perspectives. Prior to the development of community mental health, individuals experiencing severe and persistent psychiatric symptoms were typically confined to asylums. As such, their lives were highly regimented and routinized; their ability to move around freely was restricted; and they were socially marginalized. These total institutions were characterized by the isolation of the individual from the rest of society.

The rationale for institutionalization evolved historically as an attempt to protect society from the bizarre and sometimes violent behavior of mentally ill individuals, and to protect those very individuals from the social, political, and economic demands of industrial development. The results of this social marginalization generated a population of dependent, socially unskilled individuals who lived in a "protective" environment with rules and norms extraneous to the larger society.

By the 1970s, through deinstitutionalization, approximately 500,000 individuals were discharged to the larger society. As such, the simplicity of a constructed marginality offered by the total institution, call it state hospital or asylum, was replaced by the chaos and lack of social supports characteristic of society at large. It is indeed at this point that what we may call community mental health today experiences its greatest challenge. It has been repeatedly stated that the expulsion of hospital residents to the streets was not properly planned, and this is indeed the case. However, the distinctive characteristics of the transition from life in total institutions to society created multiple conditions that exacerbated the process. The point here is that whereas before deinstitutionalization planners, politicians, and especially mental health professionals worked with a confined and repressed population, after deinstitutionalization all those involved with mental health had to expand their understanding of the mentally ill within a context that includes what social workers have long advocated: human behavior is the result of the multifaceted and complex process of the interaction of person and environment. That is, mentally ill individuals are not immune to the psychosocial stressors that "normals" experience when living in the community. In addition, persons with mental illness have to struggle with the ill effects of multiple stigmas, and discrimination and lack of practical skills to survive in a society based on individualism and personal responsibility. Herein lies the challenge of community mental health. Providing services in communities requires an understanding of the person in an environment in a world that largely views persons with mental illness with, at best, suspicion and, at worst, hostility.

In the early years of deinstitutionalization, persons with mental illness lacked adequate housing; most of the housing was provided by inadequate nursing homes intent on maximizing Medicaid dollars and residences in the poorest sectors of cities, where drugs and crime ran rampant. Conceptually, the person in environment perspective shifts attention to addressing psychosocial needs of individuals no longer sheltered by total institutions, to individuals now susceptible to the same social problems experienced by members of the society at large, that is, substance abuse, lack of adequate housing, and access to medical care. Subsequently, the rapid rise in co-occurring disorders, the homeless mentally ill, and multiple health problems become dominant, and a community mental health system emerges unprepared without clear understanding of the new manifold challenges posed by this historical juncture.

CURRENT DIALOGUES IN COMMUNITY MENTAL HEALTH

For the past 50 years a number of constituencies have emerged that have tried to develop strategies to deal with the difficult task of providing effective services to a large group of individuals with severe mental illness whose potential for recovery runs the range from maintenance in a safe and humane environment to a complete recovery and the ability to lead fulfilling and productive lives. Community mental health practitioners, as demonstrated in this volume, have tirelessly tried to develop approaches that recognize the functional diversity in the population with mental illness, developing treatment models that correspond to a continuum of need, such as assertive community teams and peer-supported programs committed to psychiatric rehabilitation.

Another constituency is that composed of families and relatives of those with mental illness. The formation of the National Association of the Mentally Ill in 1979 has been instrumental in bringing the concerns of consumers and their families to a broad social stage and has influenced the thinking of planners. Perhaps the most important constituency currently is that composed of consumers of mental health services. The consumer movement, as it is currently called, has brought the perspective of consumers to the attention of practitioners, families, planners, and, most importantly, consumers themselves. The movement has generated an interest in issues related to work, housing, programming, and the development of peer programs. These constituencies in turn have evolved into lobbying groups and have significantly politicized the policy issues regarding the future of community mental health.

TOWARD RATIONAL COMMUNITY MENTAL HEALTH

To conclude, we believe, as this volume illustrates, that the treatment of the severely mentally ill is too often provided within a fragmented system of care. Coordinated and comprehensive systems of care require a unified approach wherein policy promotes treatment, which in turn is supported by funding. However, the history of community mental health illustrates that too often, public policy lags behind knowledge expansion and best practice treatment models, while funding is frequently inconsistent and inadequate.

Accordingly, we propose that a rational community mental health system requires a comprehensive and multifaceted conceptual framework to understand its structure and anticipate and develop future programs. In our estimation, such a conceptual framework must contain minimally, and not exclusively, a template composed of:

1. Cutting-edge treatments that emphasize recovery while recognizing the variability in potential functionality among individuals
2. Policy alternatives at the local and national levels
3. Funding streams and sources

These three elements of a rational community mental health system need to be coordinated in tandem with one another. Treatment models that work require policy initiatives that support them with adequate funding.

We hope that the present volume begins to integrate the challenges for all those involved in community mental health in the 21st century. An improvement in the life conditions of persons with mental illness constitutes an improvement for the society at large.

I

Recovery and the Consumer Movement

The chapters in Section I highlight one of the most promising and exciting developments in community mental health: a philosophical shift away from viewing treatment as managing chronically mentally ill patients to one that emphasizes recovery. Whereas heretofore persons with serious mental illness had been viewed as incapable of living independent and productive lives, current perspectives on mental illness emphasize growth and recovery. Central to this point of view is the development of the consumer movement, an advocacy movement that promotes consumer participation in mental health program design and delivery.

"Patient, Client, Consumer, Survivor: The Mental Health Consumer Movement in the United States," by Richard T. Pulice and Steven Miccio, provides an excellent discussion of the history of the consumer movement and examines the transition of persons suffering from mental illness from patient to advocate. Michael A. Mancini, in "Consumer-Providers' Theories about Recovery from Serious Psychiatric Disabilities," presents a unique qualitative research study of consumer-providers of mental health services, one that vividly portrays the voices of persons diagnosed with a serious mental illness who have become mental health providers.

In "Pursuing Hope and Recovery: An Integrated Approach to Psychiatric Rehabilitation," Lynda R. Sowbel and Wendy Starnes expand on the theme of empowerment in the recovery model and offer a treatment model that integrates cognitive strategies, motivational interviewing, and skills training. In "In the Community: Aftercare for Seriously Mentally Ill Persons from Their Own Perspectives," by Eileen Klein, presents a quantitative research study that examines consumer perceptions of what is needed to remain out of the hospital and in a community setting.

In the final chapter of this section, "The Wraparound Process: Individualized, Community-Based Care for Children and Adolescents with Intensive Needs," Janet S. Walker and Eric J. Bruns examine the extent to which it is possible to turn a "grassroots, value-driven movement into an evidence-based practice without destroying its soul." The authors provide a comprehensive analysis of wraparound treatment, which is an increasingly popular community-based method for treating children with severe emotional and behavioral disorders.

1

PATIENT, CLIENT, CONSUMER, SURVIVOR
The Mental Health Consumer Movement in the United States

RICHARD T. PULICE AND STEVEN MICCIO

Persons suffering from a mental illness have experienced different levels of social status, acceptance, and respect over the years. Originally viewed as inmates, they were often housed in prisons or prison-like environments and afforded the same level of treatment as criminals. Later, they assumed the role of hospital patient and were given treatments that ranged from lobotomies and sterilization to heavy doses of medication and electroshock therapy. Large, impersonal state facilities housed hundreds of thousands of people, often for their entire lives. The 1960s and 1970s ushered in an era of deinstitutionalization and with that the label of client, with the implication that they could make choices about the treatment they receive. Finally and most recently, persons suffering from a mental illness are now called consumers, who have a role in policy and program planning as well as advocacy and service delivery. This chapter examines the transition of persons suffering from mental illness from patient to client to consumer and then system survivor, and it furthermore considers the role of self-help and peer support as a model for continued positive change.

The mental health consumer movement that came to fruition in the 1970s is often viewed as a civil rights movement for people who have suffered from a serious mental illness and who were alleged to have been oppressed, overmedicated, incarcerated, and coerced for many years in mental health facilities in the United States and around the world. The movement was made up of people who believed that they were dehumanized by psychiatrists and other mental health providers due in large part to the belief that people with mental illness could not or would not recover to a life of independence and self-determination. The consumer movement put forward the theory that recovery was possible. The people that started the movement became more self-determined, independent, and were in fact recovering from what seemed to be a lifelong debilitating illness. Through the consumer movement people realized that they did not have to accept a life of low expectations and minimal achievements. People involved in the movement learned from each other how to become less reliant on the mental health system as it existed and moved to demand rights and respect

7

from a system that was created based on a foundation of long-term institutionalization and total dependence. The mental health consumer movement gave birth to self-help and peer support, which have been responsible for the growth of peer-operated services throughout the United States. It has also been a catalyst for the recovery of thousands of people who may have never achieved their full potential if the mental health system did not adapt to a more recovery-oriented structure. While the mental health system is far from perfect, it is better today than it was just 10 years ago, in a large part due to the efforts of the consumer movement of yesterday and today. The following pages trace the history of the consumer movement and the role that self-help and peer support play in the recovery of many.

A BRIEF HISTORY OF THE MENTAL HEALTH CONSUMER MOVEMENT

To understand the mental health consumer movement, one needs to go back in history to 1868, when Elizabeth Packard, a former psychiatric patient, founded the Anti-Insane Asylum Society. Packard wrote articles, books, and pamphlets that described her experiences while being committed to an Illinois insane asylum. As one of the first consumer advocates in mental health, she met great opposition during that time, as people had many fallacious beliefs about mental illness, including that it was the result of demonic possession. As a consequence, her activism was largely ignored.

In 1908, Clifford W. Beers, also a former psychiatric patient, founded the National Committee on Mental Hygiene. This committee later became what is known today as the National Mental Health Association, whose work was pioneering in supporting the causes of those with a mental illness. Beers's mission was to improve the life and treatment of people with mental illness, not through organizing people, but through connections and networks he developed in the community. Beers knew that the world was not ready for organized activism, and he knew that he could better serve the mentally ill by using the influence of other people in the community. Although Beers was relatively successful in his mission to improve the mental health system, he too continued to meet with great opposition. Despite some efforts to protect the rights of the mentally ill and to have services offered in the community, the 1920s and 1930s continued to be a time of significant growth of large psychiatric institutions.

In the 1940s, a group of former mental patients formed WANA (We Are Not Alone). Their goal was to help others make the transition from inpatient hospitalization to community living. These efforts led to the establishment of Fountain House. The members of Fountain House supported one another in a mutual setting and promoted meaningful work and social relationships. This model contributed greatly to peer support and self-help, which will be discussed later in this chapter. Fountain House still exists today in New York City as a model psychosocial rehabilitation program (Potter, 2001).

THE ERA OF DEINSTITUTIONALIZATION

The 1950s ushered in the era of deinstitutionalization. This led the way for what is today's current consumer movement. The impetus behind deinstitutionalization was an economic one designed to create cost savings for the states, disguised as a social movement whose stated aim was to put people back into community settings. However, the resources, both financial and programmatic, to serve those persons who were released from New York City institutions did not follow them into the community. This early effort resulted in many people falling through the cracks and promoted readmittance (recidivism) back into psychiatric hospitals and, some would hypothesize, has resulted in more people with mental illness ending up homeless or in jails and prisons. The money that was saved from reducing the cost of inpatient care did not get fully reinvested in the form of community services, resulting in service gaps in housing, clinical, social, and health services. One positive outcome of deinstitutionalization, however, was that some of the people who were released from the large institutions were witness to the civil rights movements taking place. Small groups began to gain a voice in regards to the treatment of people in the hospitals. Throughout the years, ex-patients began to find their voice and stood in opposition to the poor, inconsistent, and often inadequate treatment that they were receiving from the mental health community.

In the 1960s and 1970s the mental health consumer movement began to gain momentum. Interestingly, the movement made its mark inside psychiatric institutions in the United States, as patients began to protest the poor or disrespectful treatment that they were receiving. During this time, deinstitutionalization was in full swing. This furthered the mission of the consumer movement through the development of mutual support groups and the beginnings of consumer-run services in the community. The deinstitutionalization that occurred emphasized the need for community-based services to address reentry into the community in terms of adequate housing, meaningful work, effective treatment, and the development of social relationships.

As mental health services in the communities, they begged the need for public policy change to meet the demands put on community-based services. This public policy change fueled the consumer/survivor/ex-patient and mental patients to form mutual support groups in community settings. Sally Zinman, a self-described ex-mental patient and consumer leader, wrote a how-to book* with former patients, which educated others on how to start support groups (Clay, 2002).

The unrest among former mental patients in the United States gave root to several consumer support groups that developed unique and different philosophies and missions within each group. As the result of these differing opinions and philosophical differences, the antipsychiatry movement began. In fact, three distinct groups of ex-patients evolved. One group sought to abolish psychiatry and the mental health system due to alleged forceful coerciveness and poor treatment of people. A second group of ex-patients attempted to reform the mental health system in concert with concerned professionals and policy makers. Finally, a third group continued to believe in and rely on traditional mental health services. This group, which believes that the current mental health system is "okay," can best be described as follows: they are individuals who have been in the system for a very long time, have been told again and again that they will never recover, and consequentially believe that statement and are so fearful of the system that they will not stand up or voice opinions due to fear of retribution.

While this group is in decline today, there is still a presence of people that remain compliant to the system and lack self-determination and self-esteem. This is not a criticism of any particular group; it is just a reality of the perception that the antiquated mental health system continues to hold over people that could possibly have a better quality of life with improved education and greater self-esteem. This separation of philosophies among these three groups still continues today, yet one belief is clear: recovery from mental illness is possible if one has the proper supports in place.

---

* *Reaching Across* by Zinman et al., 1987.

On the other end of the spectrum, during the 1970s a social justice movement began that worked against forced treatment and promoted client self-determination. Groups emerged calling themselves by names such as Mad Pride, Network Against Psychiatric Assault, On Our Own, the Insane Liberation Front, and the National Association for Rights, Protection and Advocacy, to name a few. They were led by consumers that have been in the system and were now demanding "Nothing about us without us" from the policy makers of the mental health system. What this meant was that consumers believed that they knew what was best for them in their recovery from mental and emotional problems. Consumers wanted a place at the table of policy making and to reform the mental health system. Consumers insisted that the traditional model of mental health services did not take into account that people with mental illness were whole people and not just the symptoms recognized by many in the mental health system. This brought critical attention to how people were consistently and historically treated symptomatically with medication, psychotherapy, electroshock therapy, or long-term warehousing in large institutions or acute care settings.

As deinstitutionalization continued and advocacy groups continued to grow into the 1980s, consumer-operated groups began to organize in a more formal way. Many obtained official status as IRS 501(C)(3) not-for-profit organizations* and began to receive funding from federal and state governments. Services they provided included advocacy as well as peer support and mutual support groups. The consumer movement received recognition and support regarding the value of peer support, advocacy, and self-help. This was acknowledged by governments and policy makers. Today, many consumer-run organizations are "at the table" deeply involved in policy making and systems advocacy. Many have even become mental health service providers, offering housing, vocational assistance, and peer case management services. As a result of consumers becoming paraprofessionals in the mental health system, restlessness and disagreement have developed among consumers across the nation. Some groups feel that the consumer-providers have been co-opted by the mental health system and thus cannot promote change in the system that financially feeds them. The groups that are today called the more radical antipsychiatry movement refuse to accept funds from any government source and continue to fight at the grassroots level with limited support and organization. Consumer groups working within the mental health system accept local and government funding and work to partner with mental health professionals in changing the culture of managing mental illness to managing wellness. The approach is to create a more efficient and effective mental health system through self-help, person-centered treatment, and proactive treatment. While the consumer community continues to be fragmented at times, one thing is clear: consumer-operated services have been and continue to be a vital part of the mental health service system. As more research is completed that examines the efficacy of consumer-operated services, the mental health system should continue to promote a culture shift that will move from illness-based management to wellness-based management. The mental health system needs to be proactive in the recovery of individuals, and less reactive to the incidents of crisis that occur today. The majority of today's mental health consumer movement is focused on developing the partnership model between providers and consumers and creating change that is needed to infuse the philosophy of recovery. The consumer movement must work with policy makers at the state and federal levels to promote reform that will empower and promote consumers of services having a choice in treatment options.

---

* The IRS offers a number of not-for-profit designations, the most common of which is called 501(C)(3). This allows for exemption from taxes and for charitable donations to the organization to be tax deductible.

SELF-HELP AND PEER SUPPORT

Self-help and peer support, once called a partnership model, are processes by which people voluntarily come together to help each other in a group or individual setting by addressing common concerns and issues. Support groups are an intentional effort where people share their personal experiences with others to increase a person's understanding of a given situation. "Peer support is a system of giving and receiving help founded on key principles of respect, shared responsibility and mutual agreement of what is helpful" (Mead, Hilton, & Curtis, 2001). In the 1970s and 1980s, self-help and peer support began in the large psychiatric centers and concentrated on changing attitudes and behaviors on the psychiatric units. In California, a group called We C.A.N. (Client Advocacy Now) started support groups in the hospital units and began to play out real-life situations in the hospital by mimicking staff through acting out their perceptions of patient care. The first skits were born. Consumer groups got the attention of the hospital staff and became an integral part of staff training. This initiated a change in the attitudes of the staff and eventually became instrumental in getting the training out to the local county hospitals. This helped staff understand how they were being perceived and in turn changed behaviors of staff from seemingly insensitive treatment to respectful treatment of patients. As the skits continued, consumers began to return to the original model of support groups and more and more ex-mental patients wanted to learn more about self-help. This was the beginning of formalizing self-help support groups, which differed from the traditional medical model support groups that were run by professional therapists. One of the differences between professional support groups and groups run by peers is that consumer participation is completely voluntary. There is also no hierarchy in the peer support group and no one pretends to have all of the answers. Since there is no professional in a support group, it tends to promote independence, which in turn promotes higher self-esteem, stronger self-determination, and better recovery outcomes. Hope is elevated to a level that many professionals rarely attain with "patients."

While support is not therapy in the traditional sense, it can often result in better rewards either in concert with traditional therapy or, sometimes, other than therapy, as it offers comfort, support, and a friendly ear that will intently listen to and validate the feelings of fellow participants. It also builds relationships that in the traditional sense are often absent or limited, as today's therapists have very limited time to build healing relationships. In many cases, staff retention is a difficulty with therapists as a result of job movement or positions laid victim to funding cuts. It is difficult for a consumer to build a trusting relationship if therapists do not retain their positions and an individual may have two or several therapists in a single year. The support groups offer stability, time, and the ability to foster strong relationships, which often grow into natural social relationships. Support groups are very comforting to people that have experienced similar situations, and have been effective in helping people get beyond issues that have prevented forward progress toward recovery (Ralph, 2000).

There a few rules that most support groups follow. They include but are not limited to:

- No street drugs or alcohol may be used or carried on a person during scheduled activities.
- No violence, verbal or physical, will be permitted.
- Intolerance will not be tolerated.
- In return for support, members are expected to respect the needs of those supporting them and to be considerate of each other.

- Do not commit—unless expressly and freely told to do so by him or her in writing.
- Confidentiality is a must.

Peer support can be done in a group setting or one to one with individuals. Either way, it is effective. People can easily choose which format they would like that promotes recovery and comfort. Peer support is characterized by its promotion of mutual aid, and social and recreational companionship (Campbell & Leaver, 2003; Ministry of Health, 2001).

Support groups are usually the best means for individuals to learn new information on local programs, such as coping strategies or alternative treatments. Support groups educate individuals on local advocacy efforts, other support groups, and vital information related to entitlements. Support groups can include tasks that educate others on how to address problems and issues through modeling, teaching, learning, and problem-solving skills discussion.

In the traditional mental health system, the perceived focus according to many consumers is usually symptoms and symptom reduction. Consumers believe that this method of treatment does not take into account that people with mental illness are whole people. By only focusing on the symptoms, normative treatment is ignored. This results in limited discussion of personal interests, personal goals, and personal feelings beyond symptoms, and it limits social support networks. Support promotes personal interest discussion, as it promotes participants beyond symptomatic examination toward self-determination and empowerment, which are vital for successful recovery (Chamberlain, 1996). The traditional medical model also looks to reduce hospitalizations for individuals but does not take into account that a reduction of hospitalization does not necessarily mean a better quality of life. A person may be able to stay out of a hospital, but may be sitting in a room with a TV, chain-smoking cigarettes, and drinking large amounts of coffee (Deegan, 1992). These are topics that are often discussed in support groups, and these are the tools that help people get beyond illness and onto a road to recovery. This is not to say that there are no valid or acceptable traditional models of mental health care. It is to say that there needs to be a balance of treatment that looks at all aspects of one's life.

One of the more positive benefits of support groups is in the area of social integration. Support groups afford people the opportunity to participate in all aspects of community life. The groups promote voluntary relationships, valued social roles, and life-enriching activities. At a peer-operated organization called PEOPLE, Inc., many of the support groups have turned into additional groups that focus on recreational activities and community participation activities. Individuals from several support groups have started jewelry making, craft, and music groups. Some groups plan weekly shopping outings together or go to movies together or even plan cooking events, where each person brings ingredients and culinary delights are created. It is all self-perpetuated by participation in original support groups, and the participants drive the activities in a collaborative partnership. The longer a support group continues to meet, the stronger the relationships and the more valued the social networks become. Studies have shown (Corrigan & Jacobson, 1997) that continued group membership can result in improved self-esteem, better decision-making skills, and improved social functioning (Carpinello, Knight, & Janis, 1992).

In more recent years, support groups have become increasingly popular on the Internet, including many listservs, chat rooms, and bulletin boards. There are also national and local self-help clearinghouses that disseminate information about existing self-help groups. The bottom line to peer support and self-help is that these activities focus strongly on recovery outcomes and solutions for individuals. These groups are powerful tools in many aspects of one's life, yet remain underutilized and underresearched in the scientific field.

As new consumer leaders emerge in the consumer mental health movement, they are working to collaborate and partner with the mental health systems in their respective regions to reform the mental health system and develop better outcomes for individuals. It is more of a proactive approach that is different from the original advocates, who believed that they had to be adversarial to create change. As education is increasing, consumers and nonconsumers, providers, and family members understand the issues facing the mental health system a little better today, but there is a long way to go in reforming a system that is underfunded and underresearched. It is time to raise the bar on local state and federal accountability, and it is time to reform the vision of what mental health services should look like. Recovered consumers see the value in peer support and self-help and are demanding to not only sit at the table, but are also demanding to lead the way, or partner, in reforming services that are helpful for all individuals, and see individuals as whole people with needs, goals, and dreams.

SUMMARY

This chapter examined the history and development of the mental health consumer movement in the United States. It looked at the change in social status and acceptance of a disability group who, as a result of a lack of a strong advocacy base, often suffered from substandard and dehumanizing living conditions. As history has shown, mental health consumers have come forward to advocate for themselves and those who will need services in the future. This advocacy, coupled with the emergence of self-help groups and peer support efforts, has made great strides in bringing the needs and desires of those recovering from a mental illness to the forefront.

REFERENCES

Campbell, J. & Leaver J. (2003). *Emerging new practices in organized peer support.* Report from NTAC's National Experts Meeting, March 17–18. Available online at www.nasmhpd.org/ntac/reports/peersupportpracticesfinal.pdf

Carpinello, S.E., Knight, E.L., & Jatulis, L. (1992). *A study of the meaning of self-help, self-help groups processes and outcomes.* Proceedings of the 1992 NASMHPD Research Conference, Alexandria, VA, pp. 37–44.

Chamberlin, J. (1977). *On our own: patient controlled alternatives to the mental health system.* New York: McGraw-Hill.

Chamberlin, J. (1995). Rehabilitating ourselves: the psychiatric survivor movement. *International Journal of Mental Health, 24,* 323–346.

Chamberlin, J., Rogers, E., & Ellison, M.L. (1996). Self help programs: a description of their characteristics and their members. *Psychiatric Rehabilitation Journal, 19,* 33–42.

Clay, S. (2002). A personal history of the consumer movement. Available online at http://home.earthlink.net/_sallyclay/Z.text/history.html

Davidson, L., Chinman, M., Kloos, B., Weingarten, R., Stayner, D., & Tebes, J.K. (1999). *Peer support among individuals with severe mental illness: a review of evidence* (D12). New Haven, CT: Yale University, American Psychology Association, pp. 165–187.

Deegan, P.E. (1992). The independent living movement and people with psychiatric disabilities: taking back control over our own lives. *Psychosocial Rehabilitation Journal, 15,* 3–19.

Deegan, G. (2003). Recovery. *Psychiatric Rehabilitation Journal, 26,* 368–376.

Mead, S., Hilton, D., & Curtis, L. (2001). Peer support: theoretical perspective. *Psychiatric Rehabilitation Journal, 25,* 134–139.

Ministry of Health Services, British Columbia. (2001). *Peer support resource manual.* Author.

Potter, D. (2001). History of consumer operated services in the United States. Available online at http://www.hsri.org/ILRU/consumeroperatedservices/

Ralph, R.O. (2000). Recovery. *Psychiatric Rehabilitation Skills*, 4, 480–517.

2

CONSUMER-PROVIDERS' THEORIES ABOUT RECOVERY FROM SERIOUS PSYCHIATRIC DISABILITIES

MICHAEL A. MANCINI

Individuals diagnosed with serious psychiatric disabilities such as schizophrenia, bipolar disorder, and major depression have historically been assumed to suffer from lifelong dysfunction manifesting in a perceived need for high levels of care and surveillance in restrictive and coercive settings (American Psychiatric Association, 1994; Kraeplin, 1902). These and other enduring assumptions about the chronic, dangerous, and debilitating nature of psychiatric disabilities notwithstanding, research has shown that persons diagnosed with these disabilities are able to recover (USDHHS, 1999; Harding, Brooks, Ashikaga, Strauss, & Breier, 1987). These discoveries have led to a vision for mental health treatment that claims that with the right supports and the elimination of environmental barriers, individuals once thought to be chronically disabled are able to lead satisfying and productive lives (Anthony, 1993; Anthony, Cohen, Farkas, & Gagne, 2002).

Using first-person accounts, other research by psychiatric consumers, survivors and ex-patients, and their allies has found recovery to be a unique and dynamic process involving the development of a positive sense of self from an identity largely dominated by illness and brokenness (Estroff, 1989; Davidson, 2003; Davidson & Strauss, 1992).

For instance, Ralph (2004) developed a dynamic six-stage recovery model. This model was based on a combination of personal accounts, consumer and community mental health literature, and consensus among a number of consumer advocates that comprised the Recovery Advisory Group (Ralph, 2004). Their model suggests that recovery involves a progression from a sense of "anguish and despair" to a sense of "well-being, empowerment and recovery" via an "awakening" and development of "insight," engagement in "action" steps, and making a "determined commitment to be well" (Ralph, 2004).

In another study, Davidson and Strauss (1992) via semistructured interviews with 66 current and former consumers found that "rediscovery" and "reconstruction" of an agentic and capable sense of self were crucial in a person's recovery.

Other researchers using first-person accounts of recovery have identified several personal and environmental factors important to recovery. Applying dimensional analysis to

60 published and unpublished narratives of individuals who had recovered from psychiatric disability, Jacobson (2000) found that internal factors important to recovery included hope, healing, empowerment, and connection. External factors included human rights, a positive culture of healing, and recovery-oriented services (Jacobson, 2000; Jacobson & Greenley, 2001).

In a similar study, Ridgway (2001) used grounded theory to examine commonalities in four published accounts of recovery from serious psychiatric disabilities. She found that the stories conceptualized recovery as a nonlinear process in which individuals took control of their lives and developed identities that were no longer centered on their illness. This process was facilitated by support and encouragement from others and the development of enhanced social competencies, particularly in the area of employment (Ridgway, 2001).

These researchers and others have repeatedly confirmed that recovery is a multidimensional process that involves the development of a more healthy and agentic sense of self through positive, supportive, and empowering environments (Anthony, 1993; Davidson, 2003; Deegan, 1988, 1997; Estroff, 1989; Ralph, 2004). More research is needed in order to better understand the details of this process. To date, few studies have used qualitative interviews with consumer/survivors who have gone on to become leaders in the peer service field to understand the underlying mechanisms of the recovery process. By using established leaders who have personally experienced recovery and career success, this study sheds light on recovery via the perspective of unique experts.

This chapter will discuss the personal and environmental context via the personal stories of 15 consumer-providers. It will discuss their environmental realities prior to recovery, how their recoveries were initiated, and how they continued to maintain their recoveries. The chapter will conclude with how community mental heath practitioners can help develop recovery-oriented contexts in their work with consumers of community mental health services.

METHODOLOGY

Data Collection Methods

Semistructured interviews lasting approximately 1.5 to 2.0 hours were conducted with 15 persons diagnosed with a psychiatric disability that also provided consumer services in the form of advocacy, counseling, training, or research and self-identified as being in recovery. Participants were asked to reflect on their own experiences and discuss the factors that most impacted their recoveries from serious psychiatric disabilities. Participants represented a particularly rich source of information because of their backgrounds as both consumers and providers of mental health services and their theoretical and experiential understanding of the recovery process.

Sample Characteristics

Participants' ages ranged from 40 to 55 years. Six participants (40%) held administrative positions in community agencies, while six (40%) engaged in direct service provision. Three (20%) were involved in program development, policy, training, or research. Nine participants were women (60%) and thirteen (87%) were Caucasian. One participant (6%) was an African American woman and another (6%) was Latina.

Participants voluntarily reported diagnoses of schizophrenia, schizoaffective disorder, major depression, and bipolar disorder. In fact, many stated that they received several diagnoses over the course of their treatment histories. In addition, all participants reported at least one hospitalization for psychiatric reasons, while the majority reported more than one such incident.

Analysis

Interview transcripts were analyzed using a grounded theory approach (Charmaz, 2000; Glaser & Strauss, 1967). Grounded theory is an inductive method of cross-comparative analysis ideal for providing a "thick" description of complex phenomena (Glaser & Strauss, 1967). Interviews were closely analyzed for common codes that were collapsed into broader categories and subcategories. Themes were developed through a constant-comparative analysis across all interviews. Four main categories were generated: (1) personal factors facilitating recovery, (2) environmental factors facilitating recovery, (3) personal barriers to recovery, and (4) environmental barriers to recovery. Using the symbolic interactionism (Blumer, 1969) framework as a guide, key cruces within participants' accounts were examined in order to explore how the factors they identified as influencing recovery worked together to synthesize the recovery process.

Limitations

Due to their professional expertise and familiarity with the recovery concept as represented in the literature, participants may not be representative of the vast majority of individuals with psychiatric disabilities in recovery.

Furthermore, participants were asked specifically to discuss their *recovery*. Using this terminology may have led participants to unconsciously select experiences relevant to the concept of recovery in the literature, and neglect other experiences that may have also been relevant.

In addition, participants were not asked about psychiatric diagnoses. Through conversations with key informants it was determined that doing so might have inadvertently privileged the voice of professional paradigms rather than participants.

Finally, modifications were made to the grounded theory methodology in this study. Interviews were conducted close in time to one another and data were analyzed subsequent to completion of all interviews. This prevented simultaneous data collection and analysis and limited the ability to identify emerging themes during data collection.

METAPHORS OF PATIENTHOOD

All participants in this study gave succinct narratives of their recovery experiences that included aspects of their lives before they experienced recovery. Participants stated that prior to their recoveries they were isolated in negative environments that reinforced the message that they were sick, fragile, and incompetent. They were bombarded with diagnostic labels that reinforced their identities as "mental patients." This resulted in an overwhelming sense of despair found in similar studies and accounts (Deegan, 1997; Ralph, 2004; Ridgway, 2001). These messages were effectively communicated via professionals and treatment systems that were coercive, paternal, and indifferent, as illustrated in the following quotes:

> I don't know how many degrading hospitalizations I could have experienced…. It took me so long to get my self esteem back once I was in the hospital you just felt this degradation, this sense of non-person, it would take you so long to come back. (Kelly)

I was told I would never get better. That I would be in "remission." That I would be on medication for the rest of my life. I could never to go to school. I could never work. And I could never be a mother. (Cheryl)

Participants reported being trapped in "degrading hospitalizations" and outpatient programs described as "artificial communities." While in these environments participants were forced to engage in mind-numbing groups, prevented from engaging in any meaningful activities and exposed to cold, indifferent, and often brutal staff. In addition, while in these environments participants continued to experience debilitating psychiatric symptoms as well as side effects of psychiatric medication, electroshock, and insulin coma treatments.

I was a raging lunatic.… I mean each manic episode was a holocaust. There were messes all over the place with employers and friends and acquaintances and landlords … an entire world.… My life was blown to pieces, and I was not capable of mending it. (Nancy)

I had 40 insulin coma treatments.… I used to count 'em in terms of when I would get out, so that determined when I got out or not and you keep your mouth shut essentially … my mind was shot anyway, I had nothing to say. (Robert)

Identities are directly and indirectly shaped by the information we receive about ourselves from our external world (Blumer, 1969). How that information is perceived will largely determine our perception of ourselves and will then influence our behaviors accordingly. Participants' stories indicated that while isolated and sealed within coercive and paternal treatment systems they were bombarded by messages of illness and incompetence that were translated into identities dominated by metaphors of sickness and patienthood, as seen in the following quotes:

And it's very difficult, once you get lured in the system. It happens very gradually, where people internalize the self-stigma … it becomes your whole identity. If you lose your career, you're on disability, it becomes who you are. And then it's very difficult for a lot of people, giving that up. Your career becomes the career of the mental patient. It's all you start to see for yourself as. (Kelly)

Whenever you go into any institution … your identity is no longer your own.… What I found when I went into the institution was I was no longer Terry, I was the manic depressive, I was all the many labels they had given me [which I didn't believe in] … I did lose my identity … I was a number, I was a diagnosis … I didn't have a name. (Terry)

Participants' stories indicated that breaking out of these systems required a combination of active resistance, outside support, and opportunities to engage in meaningful activities.

CRITICAL INCIDENTS INVOLVING RISK AND RESISTANCE

Participants were specifically asked how their recoveries were initiated. As mentioned, participant stories often revealed that they were forced to endure coercive and paternal institutional treatments and practices prior to their recoveries. They were bombarded with diagnostic labels and messages reinforcing their identities as "mental patients" that often resulted in despair, apathy, and withdrawal from the world. However, many participants reported they resisted these professionally and institutionally imposed constraints and labels, and that this resistance was often described as the turning point that initiated their recoveries. Turning points consisted of critical incidents and people crucial to helping participants embark on a new direction toward living a satisfying and productive life.

Analysis revealed that the turning points participants described as initiating their recoveries contained common elements. For instance, participants identified a process by which they engaged in reflective decision making and action. This process has also been discussed in other studies examining the subjective aspects of recovery (Ralph, 2004). This process was initiated after they came to the realization that something in their lives had to change.

> I was sitting on a bench in front of a statue in the park, homeless, I had the clothes on my back … and I was sitting on this bench watching people walk by and it was a spiritual bottom. I realized that I just couldn't live this way anymore.… I didn't have the energy to live this way anymore … and I didn't want to die. (Vincent)

> I really felt that I had reached rock bottom.… I had nothing left to lose and I had only things to gain and I had to make choices and I had to get out of where I was at.… I just I remember thinking that this was not the life I wanted to have. (Sarah)

This resistance was often in the form of taking risks toward reestablishing their goals and expectations, such as engaging in work, school, volunteering, or social justice activities (protests, advocacy, etc.). This finding, also similar to Ralph (2004), indicated that participants were active participants in their own recoveries.

Although participants' recoveries were self-initiated, certain environmental conditions were necessary to facilitate the transition from illness to well-being. First, all participants cited the availability of supportive individuals as a necessary prerequisite for the initiation of recovery journeys. The people that participants stated were most important included professionals, family members, friends, and peers or other consumers. Although participating in different capacities, these individuals all provided a common element that helped participants take the first steps in their recoveries: they believed in them and supported them in their decisions and did not interfere in their plans to move forward.

> It was long — my longest hospitalization.… I'm doing really badly and I'm really confused and I'm really out of it and I looked at my mother and I said, "I'm gonna get a job, I've had it, I'm getting a job I'm so sick of this," and she said fine.… There was not a question in her mind that anything I wanted to do I was going to do. (Sarah)

Second, opportunities to engage in meaningful activities such as work, school, self-help, or volunteering needed to be available in order for participants to take the risks necessary to develop the "counter narratives" so important in the further development of their recoveries. As participants actively sought out and engaged in these activities, with the support of others surrounding them, they were able to develop a more hopeful view of themselves and of the future.

METAPHORS OF GROWTH AND TRANSFORMATION

Participants' initiation into the recovery process was followed by growth in various areas of social life. This development was spurred by continued engagement in meaningful activities, establishing supportive relationships, and active participation in treatment through the use of a combination of traditional and alternative approaches. Having begun their recovery journeys by actively resisting the institutional constraints and illness-dominated metaphors that isolated them in an ongoing cycle of despair and apathy, participants continued to take risks through employment and educational and volunteering activities. And as they continued to broaden their experiences, they were also able to expand their social network to include individuals who believed in their capacities to live satisfying and productive lives.

For instance, participants became involved in social action and advocacy activities within consumer- and peer-run organizations, using their experiences to assist others in their recovery journeys and eventually becoming leaders within the consumer movement. They were also able to take responsibility for their own wellness and break away from paternal and coercive professionals and replace them with empowering professionals instead. In fact, all participants stated that they continued to utilize the services of professionals. These supportive professionals worked collaboratively with participants and respected their self-determination by providing encouragement to take risks and information to make informed choices about their treatment.

> Counseling for me is a guided process where I'm the boss and I decide what's important to me and I need a counselor where I decide what's important to me. (Vincent)

Participants were fully involved in their own treatment and used a variety of tools to stay well. A key tension in this study centered on the role and importance of psychiatric medications in recovery. Some participants stated that getting the right type and dosage of medication(s) had a major impact on initiating and maintaining their recovery.

> I went from crazy to pretty much remission due to medication.... Clearly if I didn't take it I went crazy [and] if I did take it I was fine. (Nancy)

Others described engagement in alternative treatments such as meditation, yoga, acupuncture, exercise, or other hobbies as beneficial in maintaining wellness.

> A lot of us have explored and utilized the alternative therapies in our recovery. I have studied Tai Chi and that really just gave me the awareness [to] become conscious of the mind-body-spirit connection. (Kelly)

The type of treatment was not as important as having the ability to evaluate a variety of alternatives and having the self-determination to choose the method viewed as most effective (Jacobson & Greenley, 2001; Mead & Copeland, 2000). By being informed consumers and working collaboratively with their treatment providers, participants were able to select the right strategy for maintaining their physical and mental health and well-being.

Overall, participants most often described their recoveries as a journey using transformative and growth-oriented metaphors. Participants stated that before their recovery began they often thought of themselves as sick, damaged, worthless, hopeless, helpless, or strange. The development of an identity dominated by the notion of sickness was pervasive among participants. Recovery meant moving beyond this identity and developing a sense of hopefulness, agency, and competence, as illustrated in the following statements:

> [Recovery] its like I could say I'm all done having "mental patient" as my identity.... I know other people that probably feel that way too who have sort of gone beyond their identity of being a career mental patient. (Debbie)

> [Recovery is] a journey where I was able to not only reestablish my abilities, strengths and faith in myself but ... to go beyond any expectations I have of myself. (Karen)

Ever since I got into recovery I've started to grow way beyond the person that I believe I used to be…. I'm doing things in my life that I never dreamed I would be doing. (Brad)

Like many social processes, recovery was not linear or fixed, but rather was described as a slow and complex process marked by temporary, yet sometimes devastating setbacks, small steps forward, plateaus, and dramatic forward surges. In addition, recovery was not described as having an endpoint or as a destination, but was an ongoing movement forward into the future.

What is also important to note is that recovery was described as a unique and individual process. This study does not intend to develop a formula for recovery. Rather, its intent is to describe the overall context in which recovery may occur. The following section will use these contextual themes to outline some strategies that community mental health professionals can use in their own practices to assist others in embarking on their recovery journeys.

THE ROLE OF COMMUNITY MENTAL HEALTH WORKERS IN DEVELOPING RECOVERY CONTEXTS

Participants' stories supported the claim by others that coercion is the most detrimental factor to the recovery process and can significantly damage an individual's dignity, hope, and sense of self-worth (Deegan, 1988, 1997; Chamberlin, 1997; Mancini, Hardiman, & Lawson, 2005). Community mental health practitioners who engage in acts of implicit or explicit coercion are themselves barriers to recovery. Community mental health practitioners can assist their clients' recoveries by resisting traditional and hierarchical professional-patient relationships and, instead, strive to engage in collaborative partnerships with clients that embrace mutuality, compassion, and respect for human rights (Jacobson & Greenley, 2001). This finding reinforces the importance of collaborative treatment planning strategies whereby workers discuss with their clients all available possibilities and allow clients to make their own choices. Through these collaborative partnerships community mental health professionals can assist in repairing the damage inflicted by an often oppressive and judgmental treatment system and can help consumers develop the necessary skills to negotiate this system rather than be consumed by it.

The recovery process has been described as involving the transformation of illness-dominated identities to identities marked by competence, agency, and well-being (Estroff, 1989; Ralph, 2004; Davidson, 2003; Davidson & Strauss, 1992; Mancini et al., 2005). Participants confirmed this finding and stated that this transformation was significantly influenced by their participation in meaningful activities. Participants' stories indicated that they resisted becoming labeled as "chronically mentally ill" by resisting the advice of the professionals that worked with them to "play it safe" and, instead, engaged in activities previously thought impossible for them. They also developed supportive relationships with peer providers and self-help agencies. These peer role models communicated to participants that recovery was possible and helped participants develop and work toward recovery-related goals.

Community mental health providers can facilitate the recovery process by recognizing these forms of resistance as legitimate attempts to develop meaningful lives and not as desperate, unplanned, unrealistic, or uninsightful acts of noncompliance. Rather than discouraging these resistive acts, community mental health professionals can encourage and support their clients in taking risks and engaging in work, school, or volunteering activities. They can also encourage their clients to engage in activities and relationships that exist *out-*

side the formal treatment system, such as community churches, leagues, or organizations, so that they may develop identities separate from their diagnoses.

Furthermore, participants' stories repeatedly indicated that having access to the message that recovery was possible through peer role models was a vital aspect to their recoveries. Self-help support groups and peer-operated organizations provide recovery role models for people diagnosed with psychiatric disabilities and a level of compassion and understanding that traditional professional organizations can seldom match (Solomon, 2004). Community mental health workers can help their clients by establishing linkages with consumer self-help agencies in the community. For instance, clients could be made aware of self-help opportunities in their communities and be supported and encouraged to engage in those activities. Workers can facilitate the recovery process by becoming knowledgeable about self-help activities and options. They may do so by making it a practice to attend consumer conferences and workshops that are open to professionals in order to learn more about self-help approaches and paradigms.

Finally, participants reported that they relied on a wide variety of approaches to maintain their physical and mental well-being. Whether through the use of medications, therapy, lifestyle changes, nutrition, leisure and hobby interests, or other alternative approaches, all participants agreed that personal responsibility, self-determination, and informed *choice* were of primary importance (Jacobson & Greenley, 2001; Mead & Copeland, 2000).

Community mental health workers can assist their clients in their recoveries by working closely with clients and their prescribing psychiatrists in helping ensure that clients are fully educated about the various aspects of their psychiatric medications, including side effects and their management, long-term effects, interactions, contraindications, dosages, and alternatives to medication. Clients therefore should be well informed and supported in their decisions regarding their treatment regimen (Mead & Copeland, 2000; Mancini et al., 2005).

Workers can also assist clients in taking personal responsibility for their own well-being through education and support (Jacobson & Greenley, 2001). All participants in this study reported that taking responsibility for their health was a key factor in helping facilitate and maintain their recovery. Clients should not be overtly or covertly encouraged to maintain a passive stance in their treatment. Rather, workers can help clients learn wellness management strategies such as Mary Ellen Copeland's wellness recovery action plan (Copeland, 1997). These strategies are designed to help consumers understand their diagnosis, realize what helps and hinders their wellness, learn how to recognize when symptoms may be returning or escalating, and develop a crisis plan for action. Likewise, community mental health workers can educate and encourage clients with the help of legal counsel to develop advance directives in order that they may continue to exercise choice and self-determination in the event they become temporarily incapable of making decisions for themselves in times of crisis.

CONCLUSIONS

The findings of this study support four conclusions. First, people who recover from serious psychiatric disabilities develop, via autobiographical experiences, useful and important theories about the recovery process and are therefore a source of expert knowledge.

Second, for the consumer-providers in this study and others like them, traditional biomedical approaches to the treatment of psychiatric disabilities are, by themselves, inadequate to address the multidimensional nature of the recovery process. According to participants' theories, recovery may, in fact, be dependent on several environmental and personal factors. Environmental factors, including the presence of and engagement in supportive relationships, meaningful activities, and effective traditional and alternative treatments facilitated the recovery process. These factors often lead to participants' being able to develop identities marked by agency and competence.

Third, mental health professionals play a significant role in the recovery process. According to participants' accounts, how professionals treated them influenced their ability to successfully recover. The findings of this study suggest that warm, caring, genuine, trusting, and egalitarian relationships with mental health professionals provided participants with the support they needed to move forward in their recoveries.

Finally, identity appears to be a significant factor in understanding how people recover from serious psychiatric disability. In contrast to images of helpless, selfless patients, the findings of this study suggest that successful recovery from psychiatric disability may depend on the development of identities centered around agency, hope, and well-being.

ACKNOWLEDGMENTS

This chapter was based on the dissertation study of the author titled "Theories of Recovery from Serious Psychiatric Disabilities" (2003). Some information in this chapter was drawn from a previous article published by Mancini, M.A., Hardiman, E.R., and Lawson, H.A., *Psychiatric Rehabilitation Journal* (in press).

The author thanks the participants and key informants in this study for sharing their personal stories and theories about recovery and who further informed the research design, without which this project would have never occurred. Their thoughtful critique was invaluable to this study, and their stories of resilience and triumph have demonstrated the awesome power and complexity of the human spirit.

REFERENCES

American Psychiatric Association. (1994). *Diagnostic and statistical manual of mental disorders* (4th ed.). Washington, DC: Author.

Anthony, W.A. (1993). Recovery from mental illness: the guiding vision of the mental health service system in the 1990's. *Psychosocial Rehabilitation Journal, 16*, 11–23.

Anthony, W., Cohen, M., Farkas, M., & Gagne, C. (2002). *Psychiatric rehabilitation* (2nd ed.). Boston: Boston Psychiatric Center Press.

Blumer, H. (1969). *Symbolic interactionism: perspective and method.* Englewood Cliffs, NJ: Prentice Hall.

Chamberlin, J. (1997). Confessions of a non-compliant patient. *National Empowerment Center Newsletter.* Lawrence, MA: National Empowerment Center.

Charmaz, K. (2000). Grounded theory: objectivist and constructivist methods. In N. Denzin & Y. Lincoln (Eds.), *The handbook of qualitative research* (2nd ed., pp. 509–535). Thousand Oaks, CA: Sage Publications.

Copeland, M.E. (1997). *The wellness action recovery plan.* Peach Press., West Dummierston VT.

Davidson, L. (2003). *Living outside mental illness: qualitative studies of recovery in schizophrenia.* New York: New York University Press.

Davidson, L. & Strauss, J. (1992). Sense of self in recovery from severe mental illness. *British Journal of Medical Psychology, 65*, 131–145.

Deegan, P. (1988). Recovery: the lived experience of rehabilitation. *Psychosocial Rehabilitation Journal, 11*, 11–19.

Deegan, P. (1997). Recovery and empowerment for people with psychiatric disabilities. *Social Work and Health Care, 25*, 11–24.

Estroff, S.E. (1989). Self, identity and subjective experiences of schizophrenia: in search of the subject. *Schizophrenia Bulletin, 15*, 189–196.

Glaser, B.G. & Strauss, A.L. (1967). *Discovery of grounded theory: strategies for qualitative research.* Chicago: Aldine DeGruyter.

Harding, C.M., Brooks, G.W., Ashikaga, T., Strauss, J.S., & Breier, A. (1987). The Vermont longitudinal study of persons with severe mental illness. II. Long term outcome of subjects who retrospectively met DSM-III criteria for schizophrenia. *American Journal of Psychiatry, 144*, 727–735.

Jacobson, N. (2000). Experiencing recovery: a dimensional analysis of recovery narratives. *Psychiatric Rehabilitation Journal, 24*, 248–256.

Jacobson, N. & Greenley, D. (2001). A conceptual model of recovery. *Psychiatric-Services, 52*, 688.

Kraeplin, E. (1902). *Clinical psychiatry* (6th ed., A. Deffendorf, Trans.). New York: Macmillan.

Mancini, M.A., Hardiman, E.R., & Lawson, H.A. *Psychiatric Rehabilitation Journal, 29(1)*, 48–55.

Mead, S. & Copeland, M. (2000). What recovery means to us: consumer perspectives. *Community Mental Health Journal, 36*, 315–328.

Ralph, R. (2004). Verbal definitions and visual models of recovery: focus on the recovery model. In R. Ralph & P. Corrigan (Eds.), *Recovery in mental illness: broadening our understanding of wellness.* Washington, DC: American Psychological Association.

Ridgway, P. (2001). Re-storying psychiatric disability: learning from first person narrative accounts of recovery. *Psychiatric Rehabilitation Journal, 24*, 335–343.

Solomon, P. (2004). Peer support/peer provided services: underlying processes, benefits, and critical ingredients. *Psychiatric Rehabilitation Journal, 27*, 392–401.

U.S. Department of Health and Human Services (USDHHS). (1999). *Mental health: a report of the surgeon general.* Washington, DC: U.S. Government Printing Office.

3

PURSUING HOPE AND RECOVERY
An Integrated Approach to Psychiatric Rehabilitation

LYNDA R. SOWBEL AND WENDY STARNES

Although programs around the country have consistently described anecdotal evidence of the effectiveness of rehabilitation for people with serious mental disorders, few programs have been able to evince evidence-based outcomes to confirm the approaches they are using. This paper will explore a unique integrated practice model that reflects current trends in rehabilitation programming. This new framework encompasses motivational interviewing as well as a commitment to recovery principles and the instillation of hope for those who have been disenfranchised or marginalized as a result of serious mental illness.

BACKGROUND AND THEORETICAL UNDERPINNINGS

The vast majority of psychiatric rehabilitation programs that have emerged over the last decade have been associated with some variation of the Fountain House clubhouse model (Waters, 1994). Psychiatric rehabilitation prototypes have included hospital-based programs, sheltered workshops, assertive case management, psychosocial rehabilitation, including prevocational and transitional employment components, supported counseling and education, and supported employment (McReynolds, 2002).

Recently, however, programs for people with serious mental illness have begun paying more attention to outcomes evaluation data, as evidence-based practice has become the norm. The dialectic regarding the most effective model has become more widespread over the last three decades for two reasons. First, there have been many institutional changes, which have required more precise models. Some of those changes include service delivery criteria, programmatic goals, staff downsizing, finance mechanisms, larger programs, and perception of client capacity. The second reason is directly related to the state of the literature. Meaningful activity, the assumptions of real responsibility, feeling productive, hope, socialization, and inclusion have all been acknowledged as universal human needs (Young, 2001). Meeting the wide variety of needs and desires of stakeholders requires a comprehensive approach to intervention.

As a result, programs have begun to avoid the single-model trap by combining best practice models, which has contributed to the emergence of integrated approaches to psychosocial rehabilitation (Starks, Zahniser, Maas, & McGuirk, 2000). Multidimensional approaches to rehabilitation therefore might require more than one theoretical perspective. A social worker, occupational therapist, and rehabilitation specialist at an East Coast rehabilitation agency developed one such approach, and their model reflects the influence of empowerment theories and social cognitive career theory (Starnes, Van Ness & Rea, personal communication, 2003).

Empowerment is a central theme of the recovery model in psychiatric rehabilitation. Empowerment is "a process of increasing personal, interpersonal or political power so that individuals can take action to improve their life situations" (Gutierrez, 1990, p. 149). Lee (2001) describes empowerment as a process by which individuals or groups gain power and access to resources and control over their own lives, as well as reaping the benefits associated with greater access to power and resources to achieve their ultimate goals and collective aspirations. The recovery model stresses personal empowerment in confronting stigma and oppression and promotes integration into society. This model has become a popular paradigm for service providers of adults with chronic mental illness. Recovery is a process that focuses on developing new meaning in one's life as one transcends the catastrophic effects of psychiatric disability toward a satisfying, contributing, hopeful life (Anthony, 2000).

The second critical theory is social cognitive career theory (SCCT), which is a framework for integrating a person-in-environment approach with a cognitive-behavioral practice model in improving and individualizing rehabilitation services for people with serious mental disorders. The SCCT perspective stresses the effect that characteristics such as gender, disability, or socioeconomic status might have on "social cognitive variables, such as efficacy beliefs" (Fabian, 2000, p. 263). People with serious mental disorders like bipolar disorder or schizophrenia have unique disabilities that might interfere with enjoying a quality life relationally or vocationally. Some of these aspects of life may reflect cognitive difficulties such as problems processing stimuli, while others may represent the "effects of public stigma" (Corrigan, 2003, p. 347). It is the internal process resulting from the sociocultural response to the stigma attached to these status variables, self-stigma, that is believed to be an intractable barrier to employment for individuals with serious mental disorders (Caltaux, 2003). In concert with environmental responses to the disorders, functional deficits, and symptoms inherent in serious mental illness, self-stigma can have a debilitating effect on self-efficacy and quality of life (Caltaux, 2003). Prolonged suffering of marginalized people may prevent them from attaining their aspirations. It is important to understand that empowerment and cognitive-behavioral work are part of the process and content of the natural organic rehabilitation experience. Additionally, from the broader view of empowerment, knowledge is power when it comes to oppression (Lee, 2001). Empowerment and social cognitive theories provide a structure for maximizing quality and satisfaction of life for this population.

LITERATURE REVIEW

Cultural artifacts lead some researchers to date the beginning of the social construction of "madness" or the "mystery" of mental illness to around 1487. At that time madness began to be conceived of as something evil, as evidenced by *Mallelus Maleficarum*, a book by monks purporting that devils invading people's souls were responsible for deviant behaviors (Eaton, 2001, p. 34). The concept of demonic madness evolved over the centuries to witchcraft, to mysterious bizarre behavior of one's "odd" relatives, to boarding those with mental illness in asylums in the 20th century. Recently, the dominant culture has begun to see deviant behavior as more of a medical problem of pathology. Thus, the *medicalization* of mental illness evolved (Eaton, 2001). From the beginning, America adopted the legal and cultural standards of England, where the institutionalization of the "insane" was embedded into the natural order. This perspective persisted for the next 400 years until the Fountain House model emerged. The Fountain House perspective, on which most community psychosocial programs in the United States are based, is an intentional community creating a restorative milieu for people who were socially and vocationally disabled by severe psychiatric disability (Waters, 1994).

Eventually, other models began to develop that focused on community integration. In the 1980s professional providers focused on stabilization outside of the hospital through assertive community treatment models, which emphasized case management and community housing for people with serious mental disorders. Research later recognized employment as one of the primary goals identified by adults with serious mental illness, despite the fact that most were not working (McReynolds, 2002). This led to a shift in paradigm to one of facilitating adult role functions, represented by models such as supported employment. An often referenced study on supported employment in New Hampshire formed the basis for national policy implementation related to people with serious mental disorders (Young, 2001).

One way to examine the mental health delivery system in this country is using Lee's (2001) multifocal vision of empowerment. The empowerment vision of a dialectic process engaged in by client and worker incorporates historical, cultural, feminist, global, "ethclass" (integrated ethnic and class characteristics), and ecological issues into a broad critical perspective (Lee, 2001, p. 162). A cultural perspective includes the shared experiences and values of a specific marginalized group, in this case people diagnosed with serious mental disorders. For example, the "shared cognitive map" of the mentally ill subculture might include the experience of being on "meds," problems with the mental health system, and "spirit making/breaking" experiences (Deegan, 2003; Boydell, Gladstone, & Volpe, 2003, p. 423). This might lead to discussions of consumer choice or participatory treatment, which might facilitate advocacy or action.

THE RECOVERY MOVEMENT

Current policy shifts related to managed care, the political climate, and the rise of the consumer/recovery movement converged and amplified the need more than ever to create lasting partnerships among consumers, family clients, advocates, providers, government agencies, and communities toward a unified goal of improved mental health service delivery. Toward that end, in the true spirit of empowerment, the U.S. Department of Health and Human Services (DHHS) developed a detailed step-by-step guide for participatory dialogues between the aforementioned groups (U.S. DHHS, 2000). There was recognition by DHHS that individuals diagnosed with serious mental disorders share a historical heritage and positive identification, which has and hopefully will continue to lead to active self-advocacy. This individual and collective transformation, critical to success according to the empowerment theory, has been cited as a key component to the recovery process (Anthony, 2000; Lee, 2001).

Anthony (2000) outlined the components of an agency implementing the recovery model:

1. The organization must include "the language of recovery" in its design.
2. Program evaluation processes should identify consumer outcomes to be achieved. The organization should include outcomes geared toward improvement in role function, consumer satisfaction, and quality of life.
3. Effective training in recovery principles should be provided to and by organizational leadership.
4. Management must lay out a protocol for rehabilitation based on recovery.

Lee's (2001) critical perspective goes beyond description of social conditions and interactions and serves as an evaluation of many contextual factors related to oppression that must be considered in assisting disenfranchised consumers who are working toward personal empowerment. For example, from an ethclass perspective of the multifocal vision of empowerment, an African American consumer with a diagnosis of serious mental illness suffers from a double burden of discrimination, with its concomitant implications for mental health service. That is, an African American who has suffered negative valuations related to racism over a long period, and then receives a diagnosis of serious mental illness, has been conditioned to hopelessness, powerlessness, and low expectations externally and internally (Solomon, 1976, p. 12). Self-stigma and internalized oppression are natural consequences, which can only exacerbate an already challenging situation. This critical perspective, which underscores a multidimensional approach to mental health empowerment, is consistent with current policy trends that focus less on stabilizing or maintaining consumers and more on recovery.

The goals of critical consciousness in any empowerment process involve an increased awareness regarding political dynamics, which is comprised of several components: a reduction in self-blaming behavior, identification with the group, enhancement of one's sense of personal responsibility, and the ability to affect one's environment or situation (Freire, 2000). These are the same goals articulated for the recovery of those with serious mental illness (Anthony, 2000). The dialectic process whereby reflection leads to action, which leads to more reflection, is a central aspect of the critical consciousness, which precedes individual transformation or social change (Freire, 2000). The goal is therefore not that the client be a repository for the worker's plans, but rather an essential planner and implementer of the desired change (Lee, 2001).

Recent technological developments and major pharmaceutical advancements have helped to demystify mental illness and enhance functional performance but have not yet eliminated the persistent consequences of social, systemic, and internalized stigma. The recovery model, one steeped in the philosophy of hope, empowerment, and social connection, seems to be the obvious next step in the developmental process of mental health delivery systems. Just as clubhouse models flourished in the 1970s, community support programs in the early 1980s, and skills training models in the late 1980s, recovery prototypes have become the vanguard of the 1990s (Anthony, 2000).

There were two primary catalysts for the evolution of the 1990s' recovery movement. One was the consumer movement represented by advocacy groups like On Our Own and NAMI, which spawned recovery narratives to counter the "decline narrative," reflected in terms like *chronic mental illness* (Ridgway, 2001, p. 342). This was critical to a deeper understanding of the unique individual journey of each person with a psychiatric diagnosis (Deegan, 2003; Schiff, 2004). Secondly, in 1987 landmark longitudinal Vermont-Maine comparison research provided evidence of a domain-specific, heterogeneous course of serious mental illness (DeSisto, Harding, McCormick, Ashikaga, & Brooks, 1995). Prior to this time, there was the tacit assumption of a deteriorative course of illness, for people with a serious mental illness diagnosis. The Vermont subjects, participants in a model program, emphasized self-sufficiency, hope, and individualized collaborative planning prior to deinstitutionalization in the United States. These subjects consistently proved more productive, had fewer symptoms, better community adjustment, and better global functioning than their matched cohorts in a traditional setting. This shift toward a recovery philosophy led NAMI to proclaim in its annual report that "mental illness is no obstacle to a full life"(NAMI, 2003). The recovery model also resonated with social work researchers in their use of a strengths perspective toward the attainment of positive outcomes (Marty, Rapp, & Carlson, 2001).

THE NEW PHILOSOPHICAL APPROACH: AN INTEGRATED MODEL

The east coast agency, Way Station, has recently developed a distinct service model dedicated to recovery and hopefulness that integrates motivational interviewing, cognitive strategies, and skills training. Since its inception, the agency has adjusted and added services according to the needs of the clients. Early on, social work's self-determination and occupational therapy's perspective of health and healing through activity were reflected in agency ideology. Over time, however, the focus shifted to the more popular clinically oriented approach. Way Station is now moving toward a recovery model reminiscent of its original roots and principles. To say the agency has traveled a path of the clubhouse model to the medical model back to recovery is a simplified description of a rather arduous journey.

Recently a menu of popular services was offered: residential rehabilitation services, vocational services, and day programming. However, the only service guided by evidence-based practice was vocational programming, influenced by the well-known individual placement and support model. Stakeholders in the agency support an evidence-based approach throughout all programming. Research reflects several key components to effective recovery, including motivational interviewing and the stages of change (Rusch & Corrigan, 2002; Starks et al., 2000), as well as targeted skills training and cognitive-behavioral strategies (Wolpow, 2000).

For over a decade, Way Station's mission included the statement that the goal in working with clients was to promote community integration and purposeful life activity. In the spring of 2003, familiar complaints from clients continued to echo throughout the agency: "I'm tired of working here for free" or "I want to get paid for working in the units." When encouraged to utilize the vocational program and to seek community-based paid employment, many clients stated they could not tolerate "real work." Reasons given were "I can't work 40 hours," "I will lose my entitlements," or "I'm not ready." At the same time, clients were no longer viewing the clubhouse activities as purposeful.

A parallel process was taking place among frustrated and demoralized staff, which perceived a lack of progress with the clients. Staff made comments regarding clients' "noncompliance" with program guidelines or "manipulation of the system." Some went so far as to say clients were "lazy." There was a general sense from well-meaning staff that "we have to protect the clients" and "we don't want to set them up for failure." On the other hand, clients' comments reflected familiar themes in the literature: that the most commonly held goal was one of employment. All these dynamics indicated that the agency was experiencing forces antithetical to consumer recovery, those of internalized and externalized stigma.

Stigma, according to Goffman (1963), deals with a kind of discrediting or "shameful differentness" (p. 140) related to individuals and subgroups. For example, members might feel stigmatized as ex-mental patients when they enter a building clearly identified as an agency serving clients with mental illness, or they might feel stigmatized when others from their past are out in the community performing "normal" adults roles of being engaged in educational or vocational pursuits. Both kinds of stigma can be addressed through a recovery empowerment model of rehabilitation.

Perhaps the most difficult aspect of stigma is the internalized stigma suffered by individuals who have been demoralized by their experiences, their treatment, and their perceptions of their own abilities. Caltaux (2003) proposes that internalized stigma is a result of individuals taking the negative perceptions of mental illness and having an internal dialogue in which they incorporate these negative perceptions into their feelings about themselves, resulting in behaviors, interactions, and choices that reinforce the perceptions. A member in the program who disagrees with his boss at his supported employment placement or who needs more explicit instruction for a task may be afraid to voice his concern for fear that he will be dismissed as being overly emotional or "crazy." The individual begins a cycle of "I won't try because I'm mentally ill" or "I'll fail because I'm mentally ill" to "I knew I'd fail because I'm mentally ill." External stigma can also be self-perpetuating in that it is a ready-made excuse for everything one is dissatisfied with or has not accomplished (Goffman, 1963).

The best place to begin addressing systemic stigma is in one's *own home,* and in this case the agency may be a particularly comfortable *home.* The club had served its purpose in giving people a place to go where they felt included, needed, and safe. This, however, may have contributed to minimizing desire or ability of consumers to actively engage in the community. Van loads of clients could go out and attend social recreation events or even engage in volunteering, but few clients ventured out on their own. The idea of establishing a community with diverse activities was well intentioned, and the importance of mutuality experienced by the community of people diagnosed with serious mental disorders cannot be underestimated. At the same time, this safe community was limiting, almost a segregated haven, emphasizing the message that "your place is here, with other people with illness." "The community is too much for you."

The agency management explored the ambiguities of their current mission versus client goals, and staff perceptions. They began to recognize the need for a model with more structured, individualized intervention that was consistent with the mission and desired outcomes of the clients. The agency has shifted its emphasis from a clubhouse model of service delivery to one with recovery principles embedded in the approach as suggested by Anthony (2000). Paradigm, theory, and practice models of the new agency philosophy are summarized in Figure 1.

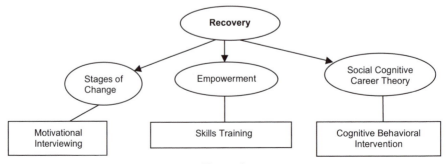

Figure 1

The agency adheres to the belief that recovery is facilitated through five life areas: regular activity/employment; safe, stable housing; integrated treatment; management of one's health; and positive relationships. Although Anthony (2000) indicated that the recovery model fits into any form of service delivery, there were no specific guidelines. The agency began an analysis of factors impacting successful community engagement. Issues identified were community acceptance, consumers' sense of preparedness, and adequate functional skills. The agency had historically achieved a level of acceptance due to ongoing social advocacy, lobbying, and consciousness-raising activities. Consumers and staff recognized that advocacy would continue under the new model.

In addressing consumers' sense of competence, the agency desired to shift the old messages to a gentle challenge to move ahead because "You can — you can be more than someone with mental illness who attends this program. You can contribute something to the community, but only if you get out there!" Contribution to the community and hope are part of a dialectic process. The illness is only one aspect of the individual, and deconstructing psychiatric labels contributes to successful recovery for people with serious mental disorders (Schiff, 2004). The agency decided to take a multifaceted approach to this issue.

First, they designed an updated program of activities and groups for the purpose of targeted skill building so consumers could choose between two tracks: the employment preparation program or the life skills program. If desired, consumers could design a hybrid program for themselves, choosing elements from both tracks. Employment preparation provides a work environment through the old clubhouse units where consumers focus on establishing and sustaining successful work habits. Life skills groups focus on educational training and the development of volunteer and social roles.

Skills training can enhance the "I can" attitude, which is essential for individual transformation. The facilitation of competitive employment by the worker, rather than the direction to work, promotes a client transition from "using service to providing a contribution." It has been well documented that prevocational services are no indication of consumer ability with respect to working, and therefore should not be set up as a prerequisite to working (Bond et al., 2001). Although this research has demonstrated that prevocational training has little impact on performance in actual employment settings, well-designed training, which closely replicates job site demands, can provide a vehicle for enhancing self-efficacy. Plans need to be individually tailored to meet needs and desires of individuals.

COGNITIVE-BEHAVIORAL TRAINING

In addition to skill development, structured activities can provide a vehicle for development of self-competence to combat self-stigma. Caltaux (2003) promotes a process of challenging and contradicting negative beliefs evidenced in Linehan's (1993) groundbreaking dialectic behavioral therapy (DBT), a cognitive-behavioral approach to enhancing self-competence. Linehan's dialectic behavioral program, distinguished in its effectiveness with people with a diagnosis of borderline personality, has been shown to be effective in a modified format for other populations, including people with eating disorders, bipolar disorder, and schizophrenia (Wolpow, 2000; Stromwall & Hurdle, 2003). In fact, Stromwall and Hurdle (2003) assert that cognitive-behavioral interventions should be included in the training of all social workers who plan careers with this population. The agency proffered the idea that a growing repertoire of successful experiences in work-related activities, along with essential discussion to articulate and draw attention to successes, can facilitate a change in cognition. This approach holds true to the recovery model providing individuals opportunities to identify aspects of who they are, to integrate the many dimensions of their personality and environment, and to reconstruct a view of the self as competent.

MOTIVATIONAL INTERVIEWING

The agency also incorporated the use of motivational interviewing. Miller and Rollnick (2002) define motivational interviewing as "a client-centered, directive method for enhancing intrinsic motivation to change by exploring and resolving ambivalence" (p. 25). They emphasize that the key to growth is exploring and resolving ambivalence that the individual feels about change, as well as perceived process and outcomes. Motivational interviewing is closely associated with the transtheoretical model of intentional behavior change, which asserts that individuals move through five stages of change, and that intervention is most effective when it matches the stage that the individual is experiencing (Miller & Rollnick, 2002; Rusch & Corrigan, 2002). The change stages are precontemplation, contemplation, preparation/planning, action, and maintenance.

Agency leaders realized that services and interventions were often located in the *action* stages; once a client identified a goal, staff immediately engaged in planning and encouraged the client to participate in specific activities or training. The client, while having interest in the goal, may actually still be in the phase of *contemplation*, and therefore did not engage in activities according to the plan. The client was struggling with ambivalence, and perhaps feared the uncertainty of change. The staff, however, perceived the client as "manipulative" or a "lost cause." Motivational interviewing is a strategy that guides staff and consumers in assessing individual attitudes and stage of change. Together, staff and clients explore and develop strategies for resolving ambivalence. Instead of jumping to action, staff and client work together to "start where the client is" and gear intervention toward support of the client change process. The goal is a more thorough, effective collaboration toward more recovery-related outcomes.

DISCUSSION AND PRACTICE IMPLICATIONS

Converting a philosophical shift to concrete program implementation involves multidimensional planning with maximum input from staff and clients. The clubhouse model promotes meaningful activity as an end in itself. The recovery model goes one step further in its proactive approach to moving consumers forward through purposeful activity. Anthony (2000) suggested that staff training is vital to implementation of the recovery approach. Lack of staff buy-in at any level of the organization could prevent successful implementation of the model's new emphasis.

Of particular focus in the training curriculum is the concept of hope and how to sustain it. Internalized and external stigmatization are powerful precipitants of hopelessness for people with serious mental illness. The cyclical and often unpredictable nature of mental illness also takes its toll on service providers, who can find themselves frustrated, disillusioned, and hopeless with respect to the functional possibilities of the people they are trying to serve. Yet Russinova (1999) outlined a critical role for service providers in facilitating recovery through the lending of hope to consumers, especially those newly diagnosed. The early stages in recovery when individuals with mental illness feel most hopeless is the time that extrinsic support and hopefulness are most critical.

Direct service staff involvement is essential in building hope and recovery (Anthony, 2000). Russinova (1999) suggests that "maintaining a generalized but stable belief that there is potential for a person struggling with a disabling mental illness to recover requires the practitioner to be able to contain his/her own feelings of helplessness, despair, and frustration with the slow improvement of clients" (p. 54). In other words, the ambivalence of staff, somewhat reminiscent of the ambivalence of clients, must be resolved beforehand if workers are to embrace a recovery model.

Deegan (2003) asks the quintessential question, "Can we make recovery a reality for as many people as possible while providing a diverse array of supports for a wide spectrum of needs?" (p. 374). The agency subscribes to the belief that it is possible, if we follow the recovery principle of listening to clients regarding their needs, fears, and desires. We must engage in a partnership and an ongoing dialogue, while offering structured programming that promotes self-competence. Guiding consumers to reframe their thinking and learn calming strategies and emotion-regulating techniques may be valuable tools in assisting consumers to achieve their goals.

Basic recovery beliefs have been adopted in the program. The blending of occupational and social work training programs over the last decade have led to a happy marriage within the confines of this particular agency. Therefore, it is not surprising that the model reflects social work and occupational knowledge and values. It is a synthesis of previously recognized practice strategies for skills training and employment with innovative approaches in motivational interviewing and cognitive-behavioral techniques that distinguish this integrated approach from those previously reviewed in the literature.

Research is under way to evaluate depression, self-esteem, employment, roles performed, and quality of life for consumers before the implementation of this new model. More information is obviously needed over time to evaluate the effectiveness of this new approach to pursuing recovery. Agencies on the front lines must be willing to subscribe to evidence-based research practice if they are to provide optimal service delivery. Providers of treatment must be willing to move outside their comfort zone of doing the same old thing and utilize outcomes clinically proven. Clients can claim much of the credit for this new model due to their demand for more relevant service provision and maximum consumer participation. In summary, there are three primary components to this hybrid model, which facilitate functioning as well as change and recovery: motivational interviewing, vocational and life skills training, and cognitive-behavioral strategies. The synthesis of these elements provides a rich foundation to foster dialogue and action among consumers, staff, and policy makers. These partnerships are essential for the emergence of a critical consciousness, which guides clients and providers toward recovery.

REFERENCES

Anthony, W. (2000). A recovery-oriented service system: setting some system level standards. *Psychiatric Rehabilitation Journal, 24*, 159–173.

Bond, G., Becker, D., Drake, R., Rapp, C., Meisler, N., Lehman, A., Bell, M., & Blyer, C. (2001). Implementing supported employment as an evidence-based practice. *Psychiatric Services Journal, 52*, 313–322.

Boydell, K., Gladstone, B., & Volpe, T. (2003). Interpreting narratives of motivation and schizophrenia: a biopsychosocial understanding. *Psychiatric Rehabilitation Journal, 26*, 422–426.

Caltaux, D. (2003). Internalized stigma: a barrier to employment for people with mental illness. *International Journal of Therapy and Rehabilitation, 10*, 539–543.

Corrigan, P. (2003). Towards an integrated, structural model of psychiatric rehabilitation. *Psychiatric Rehabilitation Journal, 26*, 346–358.

Deegan, G. (2003). Discovering recovery. *Psychiatric Rehabilitation Journal, 26*, 368–376.

DeSisto, M., Harding, C., McCormick, R., Ashikaga, T., & Brooks, G. (1995). The Maine and Vermont three-decade studies of serious mental illness. I. Matched comparison of cross-sectional outcome. II. Longitudinal course comparisons. *The British Journal of Psychiatry, 167,* 331–342.

Eaton, W. (2000). *The sociology of mental disorders* (3rd ed.). CT: Praeger Publishers: Westport, CT.

Fabian, E. (2000). Social cognitive theory of careers and individuals with serious mental health disorders: implications for psychiatric rehabilitation programs. *Psychiatric Rehabilitation Journal, 23,* 262–271.

Freire, P. (2000). *Pedagogy of the oppressed.* New York: Seabury.

Goffman, E. (1963). *Stigma: notes on the management of spoiled identity.* New York: Simon and Schuster.

Gutierrez, L. (1990). Working with women of color: an empowerment perspective. *Social Work, 35,* 149–153.

Lee, J. (2001). *The empowerment approach to social work practice* (2nd ed.). New York: Columbia University Press.

Linehan, M. (1993). *The cognitive-behavioral approach in working with borderline personality.* New York: Guilford Press.

Marty, D., Rapp, C., & Carlson, L. (2001). The experts speak: the critical ingredients of strengths model case management. *Psychiatric Rehabilitation Journal, 24,* 214–221.

McReynolds, C. (2002). Psychiatric rehabilitation: the need for a specialized approach. *The International Journal of Psychosocial Rehabilitation, 7,* 61–69.

Miller, W. & Rollnick, S. (2002). *Motivational interviewing: preparing people for change* (2nd ed.). New York: Guilford Press.

National Alliance for the Mentally Ill. (2003). *National Alliance for the Mentally Ill annual report.* Retrieved July 14, 2004, from http://www.NAMI.org

Ridgway, P. (2001). Restorying psychiatric disability: learning from first person narratives. *Psychiatric Rehabilitation Journal, 24,* 335–343.

Rusch, N. & Corrigan, P. (2002). Motivational interviewing to improve insight and treatment adherence in schizophrenia. *Psychiatric Rehabilitation Journal, 26,* 23–32.

Russinova, Z. (1999). Providing hope-inspiring competence as a factor in optimizing psychiatric rehabilitation outcomes. *Journal of Rehabilitation, 16,* 50–57.

Schiff, A. (2004). Recovery and mental illness: analysis and personal reflections. *Psychiatric Rehabilitation Journal, 27,* 212–218.

Solomon, B.B. (1976). *Black empowerment.* New York: Columbia University Press.

Starks, R., Zahniser, J., Maas, D., & McGuirk, F. (2000). The Denver approach to rehabilitation services. *Psychiatric Rehabilitation Journal, 24,* 59–67.

Stromwall, L. & Hurdle, D. (2003). Psychiatric rehabilitation: an empowerment-based approach to mental health services. *Health and Social Work, 28,* 206–213.

U.S. Department of Health and Human Services, Substance Abuse and Mental Health Services, Administration Center for Mental Health Services. (2000). *Participatory dialogues: a guide to organizing interactive discussions on mental health issues among consumers, providers and family clients.* Retrieved July 14, 2004, from http://www.NAMI.org

Waters, M. (1994). *Modern sociological theory.* Thousand Oaks, CA: SAGE Pub.

Wolpow, S. (2000). Adapting a dialectical behavior therapy (DBT) group for use in a residential program. *Psychiatric Rehabilitation Journal, 24,* 135–143.

Young, K.A. (2001). Working toward recovery in New Hampshire: a study of modernized vocational rehabilitation from the viewpoint of the consumer. *Psychiatric Rehabilitation Journal, 24,* 355–368.

4

IN THE COMMUNITY

Aftercare for Seriously Mentally Ill Persons from Their Own Perspectives

EILEEN KLEIN

Community aftercare has been an integral part of service provision to this population since 1906, when the first outpatient program opened in New York state (Trattner, 1999). However, despite policy and program changes, there is still a gap in service provision for the mentally ill, which has resulted in a great number of mentally ill persons living in shelters, jails, and on the streets. Since the closure and downsizing of large institutions there have been a wide variety of service systems put into place to meet the needs of the mentally ill. It is unfortunate that the majority of the interventions that have been initiated have been directed at producing services, rather than directed at meeting individual needs. "Effective reimbursement has taken precedence over matching services to the needs of patients" (McCrone & Strathdee, 1994, p. 83).

Current statistical data for the mentally ill is alarming. Using the criteria of serious and persistent mental illness, the number of homeless persons that are mentally ill is approximately 35% (Torrey, 1997). The number of mentally ill persons that are homeless or living in shelters is twice that of the number currently housed in public psychiatric hospitals (Isaac & Armat, 1990). Torrey reports that state mental hospital beds have decreased from 558,922 in 1955 to 72,000 in 1994. U.S. jails and prisons currently house persons suffering from serious psychiatric disorders in a greater number than public institutions. It is estimated that one in five prisoners are mentally ill, and that of 300,000 men and women in prison today that are mentally ill, approximately 70,000 are psychotic (Metzner et al., 1998). It has long been established that the closing of inpatient psychiatric beds has resulted in transinstitutionalization, or the transfer of care from hospital to other institutions, which have not been able to adequately deliver effective services to this population (Isaac & Armat, 1990).

Empirical literature has consistently described studies that have reported discharge planning has not been successful in having a long-range effect on rehospitalization (Caton et al., 1985; Smith et al., 1996; Castle, 1997). Even careful arrangements serve as a link, rather than a treatment, and outpatient services are often not adequate and poorly coordinated. This often results in treatment priorities that do not actually benefit the seriously and persistently mentally ill, and fails to provide meaningful services so they can remain in the community.

The following study was conducted in an effort to further the understanding of the outpatient treatment needs of mentally ill consumers that are clinically diagnosed with schizophrenia or schizoaffective disorder and meet the functional definition of serious and persistent mental illness. Need is a subjective concept and will be identified by participants in the study. Needs are defined as what the participants consider to be necessary for them to remain out of the hospital and in a community setting. These concepts will be expanded further in this study.

The study gathered information directly from the seriously and persistently mentally ill consumers about their perceived outpatient treatment needs. Information was obtained as to participants' assessment of needs in the areas of housing, finances, mental and physical health, and relationships. Participants in this study were outpatients currently receiving treatment services in a New York State-operated mental health center. The participants were surveyed using the Camberwell Assessment of Need–Research Version (CAN-R) and the Symptom Checklist-90–Revised (SCL-90-R). These are both survey instruments designed to gather quantitative information directly from mentally ill patients.

This results of this study can be instructive in developing staff training initiatives, treatment strategies, and services that will result in the provision of meaningful outpatient services that can serve to maintain this very vulnerable group in the community. This study's results can also be used as a tool for community education to dispel the myths of mental illness. Providing information to others of the basic issues and needs of this population may serve to help them be less prejudicial toward this group, reduce the stigma, and diminish negative responses to these individuals to allow them to integrate back into the community in a less stressful way (Penn et al., 1994).

METHODS

Subjects

This study employed a cross-sectional, correlational survey design. The cross-sectional survey design allowed for the collection of data from respondents in a relatively short period. The study participants were 133 self-selected seriously and persistently mentally ill adults currently living in Brooklyn or Staten Island and attending outpatient mental health centers that were affiliated with South Beach Psychiatric Center, a publicly funded program (APA, 1994). All participants met the DSM-IV criteria for an Axis I diagnosis of schizophrenia or schizoaffective disorder. Patients that had a primary substance abuse diagnosis, primary diagnosis of a mood disorder, organic brain syndrome, sensorimotor handicap, or severe mental deficiency were excluded from this study. This group was not included because their needs to live in the community are different as a result of their additional problems and present other significant treatment considerations, which may or may not be consistent with those of patients that have chronic mental illness alone (Hazel, Herman, & Mowbray, 1991).

Survey Design and Instruments

All participants responded to three survey instruments, a demographic questionnaire, the Camberwell Assessment of Need–Research Version (Slade, Thornicroft, Loftus, Phelan, &

Wykes, 1999), and the Symptom Checklist-90–Revised, developed by L.R. Derogatis. Both of these instruments have been used with psychiatric outpatients.

All participants were volunteers and had heard about the study from their therapist or through other participants. They all had a face-to-face interview with the researcher in which the demographic questionnaire and the CAN-R survey instrument were read to them. They had as much time as they needed to complete the SCL-90-R on their own, with the interviewer available for any questions. Individual self-reports are a major source of information, but there have been concerns raised about the ability of respondents with mental illness to reliably report their experiences (Cernovsky, Landmark, & O'Reilly, 1990). However, the literature indicates that there is evidence that these individuals can provide reliable responses, particularly when interviewed, rather than independently completing a questionnaire (Larson, Attkisson, Hargreaves, & Nguyen, 1979; McGlynn, 1996). In addition, individual self-reports derive data from the "experiencing self," and this cannot be the same as the data gathered from an external observer (Derogatis, 1994).

The Camberwell Assessment of Need–Research Version was selected because it is a self-report instrument that indicates a participant's subjective experience of his or her needs, if they are being met, by formal or informal sources, and into what areas these needs fall. The CAN-R is a tool designed to assess 22 domains of health and social needs. The CAN-R (Slade et al., 1999) uses a Likert scale design with four or five choices for each question, one of which is "unknown."

The 22 items of the CAN-R are accommodation, food, looking after the home, self-care, daytime activities, physical health, psychotic symptoms, information on condition and treatment, psychological distress, safety to self, safety to others, alcohol, drugs, company, intimate relationships, sexual expression, child care, education, telephone, transport, finances, and benefits. Phelan et al. (1995) state that at the end of the CAN-R there will be an identification of the needs of the participant in these domains, the help currently being received in these areas, and satisfaction with care.

The SCL-90-R is a 90-item instrument used to assess the participant's current symptoms and their intensity. The SCL-90-R is a multidimensional inventory that focuses on nine primary symptom dimensions. It is used to measure point in time, a broad range of psychological problems, usually in the past seven days. The SCL-90-R measures the current psychological symptoms of the participant. Each of the items on this instrument is rated on a five-point distress scale, ranging from "not at all" to "extremely." The GSI subscale of the SCL-90-R was used as a measure in this study since it is considered the best single indicator of a patient's current level of psychological disorder, and the depth of the disorder (Derogatis, 1994). The GSI is a single summary measure that combines the reported number of symptoms with the patient's perceived intensity of the distress. Assessing a participant's level of symptom distress can serve to validate the information collected on the CAN-R and as a basis of comparison of treatment needs.

A demographic and patient characteristic survey was designed for the purpose of the proposed study. Demographic information was collected and coded to ensure confidentiality. The participants were asked for their age, gender, ethnicity/race, highest level of education completed, date of last hospital discharge, date outpatient treatment began, and the number of times per week or month that they attend outpatient treatment. They were asked about their diagnosis.

RESULTS

Mental health consumers have expressed a clear interest in participating in research studies and having a chance to voice their preferences and concerns to clinicians and administrators. Consumers have consistently been willing participants in questionnaire and survey processes as a vehicle for expressing themselves. When this research project was discussed at staff meetings and the patients observed the posted flyers, volunteers began calling to sign up for participation in the study. Participants were quite forthcoming with information, and they clearly expressed their enthusiasm about their voice being heard for future program planning purposes. The researcher was often asked when the surveys would be completed, and many participants asked to be contacted about the results. It has been shown by other researchers that when patients are involved in data collection for treatment planning purposes, they may feel more positive about their treatment experience and become more engaged with staff (Eisen, Dickey, & Sederer, 2000).

Although participants were living in the community for at least six months and engaged in outpatient treatment, it was noted in the interview process that many of the consumer volunteers exhibited obvious symptoms. There was often evident pathology that was not captured in the data since it was not documented by their responses to the survey instruments. An example would be when a participant stated that he or she felt able to focus, but during the administration of one of the questionnaires he or she became tangential and digressed from the question to some aspect of his or her life or some other query. One possible explanation is that some of the participants wanted to please the researcher, or look healthy. Another possibility is that since the participants signed a consent, they were aware that their names were being recorded and some questioned this as contrary to their responses being confidential. Although assured that results would not be recorded by name, but by a numbered code, some consumers may have reacted anyway with the need to "do well" on the survey instruments. Further, it is also possible that they did not see themselves as not well, or symptomatic, and responded with their perceptions of self to the questions.

Wiedl (1992) studied coping, stress, and control in schizophrenic patients and found that there was a strong awareness of symptomatology and impairment in schizophrenics when there were a high level of negative symptoms. He noted that these patients were able to cope, but their methods were less cognitive and more emotionally oriented than in other patients in the study. He found that many patients tried to cope on their own with problems and stress. This could account for the observed lack of reporting of symptoms and needs in some of the participants in this study.

Since this was a survey of the consumer's perspective, this seemed to indicate that although the patient appeared to have a symptom, if it did not interfere with his or her functioning, it was not reported and not captured in this study. This finding could be reflective of some of the disparity of clinician and administrator responses to questionnaires of patient needs in terms of what the real issues are for treatment and service provisions. Studies have shown that often the therapist's focus is on clinical needs (Bengtsson-Tops & Hanson, 1999; Stansfield, Orrell, Mason, Nicholls, & D'Ath, 1998). Focusing only on clinical symptoms and not addressing social and relational issues has been shown to lead to psychiatric hospitalizations (Kent & Yellowlees, 1994). Studies indicate that patients have needs requiring interventions that may not be addressed by treatment providers. Clinicians should remain aware of the seriously and persistently mentally ill individual's ability to identify his or her treatment priorities and needs when engaging him or her.

Professionals should have a willingness to spend time with their clients to develop a shared understanding of need. This will ultimately help the engagement process and help to nurture the treatment alliance as well as help to define expectations (Bhui, 2001). Working on mutual goals can only enhance treatment and reduce resistance. There may be issues that a patient does not want to bring to treatment, and this should be respected by the clinician if it does not endanger the patient in the community. For example, a participant in this study expressed a fear of using public transportation in response to a survey question. He further stated that he had overcome this problem by using ambulette or car service and felt he didn't have any need, or want help in this area, as it was not interfering with his life. He said he did not want to discuss this with his therapist and felt his treatment should be focused on his inability to have enough to do during the day, or his need for social interaction. Therefore, he had a clearly defined treatment goal and expected this to be respected by his therapist.

The majority of the participants in this study were recipients of governmental benefits for financial support. Most of the participants (98%) did not indicate a need in this area, since their benefits were in place and they did not feel anything could be done to get more financial assistance. The majority (18.8%) also did not indicate a need for help with housing, since they were living in a safe place, often a supervised setting, such as an adult group home, or a supervised residence. The majority did, however, indicate a desire for daytime activity (76.7%) and company (77.3%). This was consistent with the finding of Tempier et al. (1998), who found that mentally ill patients were generally more satisfied with material domains and less satisfied with interpersonal relationships than welfare recipients. Many of the participants (48.9%) attended a day treatment program and reported that this was a very important connection for them. Many remarked how important it was to be with people and have a place to go each day.

This study found that there is often the expressed need to connect with others and have satisfying relationships. Interpersonal relationships are often difficult for many seriously and persistently mentally ill individuals, and they may need treatment in this area by a clinician. One of the relationships that may be very important to foster is the therapeutic alliance, and this can then serve as a way of helping the patient connect with others.

Trust and alliance are primary in any therapeutic relationship, and the participants in this study identified this as a need as well. While there is an awareness that schizophrenic behavior is more severe and disabling than neurotic behavior in degree, treatment is often seen as quite different. The need for interpersonal connections and relatedness, however, is quite similar for neurotic and psychotic patients, as is some of the etiology. Psychotics have factors in traumatic development that are similar to the neurotics, although they are often more severe and may occur earlier in life (London, 1973).

This study questioned if treatment needs were different for individuals based on their age, time out of the hospital, race, or gender. A literature review indicated that there may be differences based on these variables. This study did not find significant differences in these demographic variables. However, social needs, including the need for company and daytime activity, were identified as greater for all of those participants that had more clinical symptomatology. Those that defined themselves as having more psychological problems on the Symptom Checklist 90-R also identified the need for more help from formal and informal sources on the Camberwell Assessment of Need–Research Version.

DISCUSSION

The research study that was conducted was undertaken to add to the base of knowledge of understanding the needs of seriously and persistently mentally ill outpatients living in the community. Study results were to answer questions about whether or not patients have different needs for treatment and services based on their age, length of time out of the hospital, race, or gender; if the severity of a patient's clinical symptoms impact on his or her perception of social needs; if patients with more severe clinical symptoms report needing more help from clinical staff; and if patients with more severe clinical symptoms report receiving more help from informal sources, including family, friends, and clergy.

Studies have indicated that schizophrenics have the capacity to participate in their treatment by recognizing warning symptoms of psychotic episodes and communicating what they are experiencing to clinical staff (Boker, 1992). This study was conducted as a beginning for seriously and persistently mentally ill outpatients to indicate their areas of needs from clinical staff and informal networks of family and friends. The results indicate that they are clear about what needs they have, and which ones are met and unmet. Many indicated they wanted to bring certain specific issues to therapy, and which issues were not important to work on at this time in treatment.

It is also clear that this patient group wants to be involved in identifying their needs and expressed interest in being a part of future program planning and development. The results speak to joining with our clients in a therapeutic bond to work together on treatment issues, as well as life issues. It informs clinicians to view the seriously and persistently mentally ill patient as a person, not a cluster of symptoms. Therapeutic interventions should include the development of the patient's psychosocial environment to provide social support and structure for the most positive community integration. Inclusion of these areas will most likely keep the person in treatment longer and help him or her to develop a therapeutic partnership for recovery.

Inclusion of a patient in determining a treatment intervention and working together on mutual goals in the therapy can serve to work through the sense of estrangement many schizophrenics feel. This may come about through their deficiencies in object relationships that have been present since early developmental periods and have left the patient feeling disconnected to others. Jordan (1991) states that both the therapist and the patient grow when they are involved in a relationship that has mutuality. She finds that real caring can go both ways when there is mutual respect and that the therapist then becomes available for the healing process. The seriously and persistently mentally ill patient can often feel cutoff and out of touch with reality, which makes involvement in any relationship difficult.

Often staff find that working with this patient cohort is frustrating and stressful because of the patient's lack of capacity to connect or the patient's outward rejection of their attempts at help. One study found that the most rewarding aspect of work with schizophrenics was seeing some improvement, and the lack of progress caused significant burnout (Moore, Ball, & Kuipers, 1992). Helping therapists make the most meaningful connections with patients so that they could make positive interventions can only serve to help both the patient and staff to feel better about the therapeutic work.

One of the most difficult aspects of clinical work with the seriously and persistently mentally ill patient is to endure long periods of unrelatedness in the treatment session (Searles, 1969). There can be a psychotic transference in the therapy of a patient's distorted view of the world onto the therapist. The therapist can relate by working to keep his or her own view of reality in focus and becoming very responsible for "saving" the patient from his or her plight, which may include delusions, grief, isolation, and helplessness, and ultimately lead to guilt when this is not possible. This guilt may be the therapist's way of defending against ambivalent feelings about the patient. Countertransference can also lead the therapist to feel the need to be right and demonstrate competence to the patient, which can lead to the patient's communication not being addressed directly in the session for fear of saying the wrong thing (Spotnitz, 1969). Ultimately, not communicating openly and honestly will prevent the patient from maturing and growing through his or her own development of self-esteem by working out what is right for himself or herself. Therapists may be met in sessions with unpredictable and changeable symptoms. The relationship may have to sustain the patient's negative feelings, depression, or hostility. It is possible for the therapist to become more aware of unconscious aspects of himself or herself in the countertransference and use this in their work together. Therefore, it is possible to treat these patients and learn from them and grow as a therapist, rather than see the therapy as futile with few rewards. Agency supervisors should emphasize this aspect of the work in clinical, supervisory, and staff training.

The study results indicated that the development of a mutual and therapeutic relationship can positively impact on both male and female patients. Role development for males often includes a stress on being powerful, independent, and separated from emotional connectedness, while females are often encouraged to connect with others when they act and work (Surrey, 1991). Joining with a therapist will serve as a way to reduce barriers to accepting treatment interventions and ultimately will help patients function better within the context of their own roles and with others in their environment. They can use the therapeutic relationship to develop an understanding of interpersonal exchange that can be effective in making changes in their lives.

Having an honest and trusting relationship can help the schizophrenic cope more effectively with his or her illness. Sharing how one feels in an open dialogue can be instructive for the therapist in understanding the patient's prodromal signs of instability, and the clinician can work with the patient on self-monitoring and coping strategies. The identification and understanding of symptoms of the illness can lead to the development of ways for the patient to manage disabilities, improve ego functions, and improve social skills (Boker, 1992). Many of the participants in the study identified understanding of their illness as a need to be worked on with their therapist. When queried with the CAN-R, some participants indicated that they wished they knew more, but never thought to ask. They now understand that this is an appropriate discussion for the therapy session.

Therapists must keep in mind that patients have nonpsychotic aspects in their lives and thoughts, and this can then be the basis of the working alliance (Selzer & Carsky, 1990). Strauss (1992) suggests viewing a mentally ill person from a constructionist perspective. This view can allow us to view all aspects of a patient's experiences and to think of the normal functions that exist in very sick people. The mind can be considered as constructing experiences from the interaction of the world and the self, and these interactions take place on a continua across a range of normal and abnormal interactions. Therefore, the person can be normal and abnormal in his or her functioning and have a range of behaviors that require interventions based on varied mechanisms of the person's coping capacity and regulatory functioning. The treatment must flow from this exchange of ideas that flows along this range of behaviors and interactions. A patient may be able to accept a treatment goal when there is an ability to collaborate on the mode of treatment directed toward that goal in an established therapeutic alliance.

When there is an effective therapeutic alliance, staff are more likely to make treatment decisions that coincide with the patient's goals, and therefore will more likely be successful in meeting them. In community mental health agencies, the administrators and program planners often have a difficult task in planning for programs and interventions for the seriously and persistently mentally ill outpatient. There are financial, space, and staffing limitations to consider in designing outpatient treatments. Further, the patients present as a heterogeneous group in their levels of functioning and capacity. This makes development of programs and interventions that are individualized and meaningful even more difficult. Programs cannot be successful unless clinical staff are educated about the real needs of the mentally ill and how they can be most effective in providing relevant treatment interventions. Increasing staff knowledge about their role in the treatment process can ultimately benefit both the patients and the clinician, with better clinical outcomes.

Many studies have established that having a good client-therapist relationship has a significant impact on therapeutic outcome. Gehrs and Goering (1994) found that there was a significant correlation between the quality of the working alliance and psychosocial rehabilitation outcome and that the *therapist's perception* of the alliance had a stronger correlation than the patient's perception. This is further indication that education and training initiatives should reinforce with therapists the need to develop a collaborative relationship for treatment to be effective, and how they can promote this alliance. Increasing awareness of viable interventions and knowledge about psychosocial treatments that have been successful can raise hope in the clinicians that their work can be effective in treating the seriously mentally ill person. It can also raise hope and improve the satisfaction and overall quality of life for those treated (Rosenfeld & Neese-Todd, 1993).

This study indicates that although the symptomatology may differ, as well as their sociodemographics, treatment needs may be similar for those receiving outpatient mental health services. One participant put it succinctly, "We need someone to believe in us." This may be simplistic, but if there was more interaction between those that receive services and those that deliver the services, communication lines would be open for dialogue that could only improve the services delivered. Essentially, all participants in this study wanted to be connected with others, have a place to interact with others during the day, and have someone to listen to them when problems developed. This message could be communicated to all treatment staff so that they engage their patients in a meaningful exchange of their thoughts and feelings, rather than "take care" of the needs they define. Selzer and Carsky (1990) refer to a therapist's need to work through the internal tension of taking control of the patient's world versus giving control to the patient and flowing with different courses of action as they arise.

AREAS FOR FUTURE RESEARCH

This study was conducted in an attempt to understand what seriously and persistently mentally ill consumers need and what they want from their outpatient treatment providers. The survey instrument, the CAN-R, was used as an indicator of patients' needs based on their perceptions at a given point in time. The use of this instrument limited responses to those 22 needs identified in the survey instrument. The addition of a narrative section or a qualitative inquiry for a further study would enhance the results. It would help to expand our knowledge of patients' needs if they had a way of including all of their needs in a future study to evaluate if there are trends that have not been identified. Qualitative methods would complement the quantitative data that can be captured using a standardized survey instrument. Distinctions about the types of programs a patient attends, whether work, educational, or treatment oriented, could be captured using more descriptive methods of data collection. One area of interest not identified is the type of living arrangement the patient had and the amount of support and supervision the arrangement provided. This would have an impact on needs identified. It would be of interest to identify which treatment modalities have been helpful for managing different types of problems.

It would be interesting to assess the trends of needs and patient characteristics for participants in individual treatment settings. If the results of this study were analyzed by an individual clinician or clinic, this could be instructive for program managers and administrators to assess the need for staff development and program modifications to better serve their consumers. Agency leadership could also improve service delivery if they had data on what services the consumers feel could best meet their needs and what treatment modalities they have found to be most helpful.

Future research can also consider a longitudinal study of patients for the investigation of needs that may change over time. The participants' needs could be viewed along a continuum of services that can be offered as the patient has longer community tenure. Individual programs could be evaluated in relationship to needs that they address by the patients that attend to help to improve the programs offered and make them more effective in meeting their goals.

The literature indicates that there has been an insufficient attempt to gather information directly from the mental health consumer about what it is actually like to cope with this devastating malady. There is a need for mental health professionals to expand their knowledge about what methods of intervention have been most efficacious for the seriously and persistently mentally ill and the extent to which specific services are perceived as more appropriate for managing specific domains of their lives (Howard et al., 1996). Several cited studies have indicated that it is important that mental health professionals recognize the sociological aspects of patients' needs and the significance of, or their lack, of social networks. Social work partnership with mentally ill consumers can facilitate change in policy that can ensure their inclusion in treatment planning and resource development. It is important because they can provide insight into their own experience, and in the managed care environment existing resources are being rationed and carefully regulated.

The cited literature indicate that most studies have found this group to be reliable and capable of providing information to structured surveys and questionnaires that can inform practice and indicate preferences for service development and delivery. The researchers that included the input of the mentally ill showed that they had a clear preference to receive treatment interventions that promoted their independence and social functioning, as well as interventions in economic, family, and employment issues. These were seen as just as important as the treatment of their clinical symptoms, which were most often acknowledged by staff as requiring treatment.

There is a lack of a consensus in what determines appropriate outpatient treatment for the mentally ill. There is a lack of coordination and integration in assessing the needs of this population. Siegel, Attkisson, and Carson (1978) concluded that the assessment of service needs has been neglected and misunderstood, and that there must be a blending of consumer and professional participation in the planning of programs so that the programs will have relevance to human service needs. This study used a needs assessment tool for outpatients that are currently in treatment to express their needs. The results can be used as a beginning of identifying therapeutic services and interventions that are desirable for maintaining community tenure. If these services can be provided, and this population's needs met, the results should be an increase in their consistent use of outpatient services and compliance with treatment recommendations. This will lead to less rehospitalizations and a more satisfying life out of the hospital.

CONCLUSION

As a public health issue, it is essential to consider the delivery of relevant services as an important way of increasing treatment compliance and decreasing inpatient hospitalizations. The revolving door of readmission becomes an inevitable outcome when treatment programs are poorly conceived and do not match the needs of the seriously and persistently mentally ill patient, who often has no other support system in the community (Cohen, 1997). Both clinicians and patients feel a sense of failure when there is a clinical and systems mismatch that leads to a patient not improving and eventually dropping out of treatment. The patient is often seen as responsible for his or her treatment failure, and there is a blaming of the victim for becoming noncompliant. Frustration on the part of therapists can lead to a negative countertransference and result in an adversarial relationship with the patient.

It would be instructive for therapists to realize that patients have the capacity to grow further when they understand their illness as a way of controlling its effects on their functioning. This may lead to developing more psychoeducational groups for patients in existing treatment programs. It would also benefit family members and significant others to participate in these groups as a way of demystifying mental illness and its symptoms and reducing some of the fears and stigma that accompany it. It could also be helpful for staff to be reminded of the characteristics of the seriously and persistently mentally ill patient so that they can have realistic expectations of a patient's progress and not become frustrated with incremental changes that may occur, but experience them in a positive way. Psychoeducation can serve to educate the community at large about mental illness so that the seriously and persistently mentally ill person can be better understood and accepted when he or she attempts to be integrated into society. Enhancing the understanding of mental illness can be a means of tapping into existing social networks in the community as a means of improving the psychosocial adjustment of the seriously and persistently mentally ill.

REFERENCES

American Psychiatric Association, Committee on Nomenclature and Statistics. (1994). *Diagnostic and statistical manual of mental disorders (DSM-IV)* (4th ed.). Washington, DC: Author.

Bengtsson-Tops, A. & Hansson, L. (1999). Clinical and social needs of schizophrenic outpatients living in the community: the relationship between needs and subjective quality of life. *Social Psychiatry and Psychiatric Epidemiology, 34*, 513–518.

Bhui, K. (2001). Mental health needs assessment for ethnic and cultural minorities. In G. Thornicroft (Ed.), *Measuring mental health needs*. Glasgow, UK: Bell & Bain Ltd.

Boker, W. (1992). A call for partnership between schizophrenic patients, relatives and professionals. *British Journal of Psychiatry, 161*, 10–12.

Castle, L.N. (1997). Beyond medication: what else does the patient with schizophrenia need to reintegrate into the community? *Journal of Psychosocial Nursing, 35*, 18–21.

Caton, C.L.M. (1982). Effect of length of inpatient treatment for chronic schizophrenia. *American Journal of Psychiatry, 139*, 7.

Caton, C.L.M., Koh, S.P., Fleiss, J.L., Barrow, S., & Goldstein, J.M. (1985). Rehospitalization in chronic schizophrenia. *Journal of Nervous and Mental Disease, 170*, 139–147.

Cernovsky, Z.Z., Landmark, J.A., & O'Reilly, R.L. (1997). Symptom patterns in schizophrenia for men and women. *Psychological Reports, 80*, 1267–1271.

Cohen, N. (1997). Treatment compliance in schizophrenia: issues for the therapeutic alliance and public mental health. In B. Blackwell (Ed.), *Treatment compliance and the therapeutic alliance*. Australia: Harwood Academic Publishers.

Derogatis, L.R. (1994). *SCL-90-R: Administration, scoring and procedures manual* (3rd ed.). Minneapolis: National Computer Systems.

Eisen, S.V., Dickey, B., & Sederer, L.I. (2000). A self-report symptom and problem rating scale to increase inpatients' involvement in treatment. *Psychiatric Services, 51*, 349–353.

Gehrs, M. & Goering, P. (1994). The relationship between the working alliance and rehabilitation outcomes of schizophrenia. *Psychosocial Rehabilitation Journal, 18*, 43–54.

Hazel, K.L., Herman, S.E., & Mowbray, C.T. (1991). Characteristics of adults with serious mental illness in a public mental health care system. *Hospital and Community Psychiatry, 42*, 518–525.

Howard, K.I., Carnill, T.A., Lyons, J.S., Vessey, J.T., Lueger, R.J., & Saunders, S.M. (1996). Patterns of mental health service utilization. *Archives of General Psychiatry, 53*, 696–703.

Isaac, R.J. & Armat, V.C. (1990). *Madness in the streets*. New York: The Free Press.

Jeffrey, L., Metzner I.L., et al. (1998). Treatment in jails and prisons. In R.M. Wittstein (Ed.), *Treatment of offenders with mental disorders*. New York: Guilford Press.

Jordan, J.V. (1991). The meaning of mutuality. In J.V. Jordan, A.G. Kaplan, J.B. Miller, I.P. Stiver, & J.L. Surrey (Eds.), *Women's growth in connection: writings from the Stone Center*. New York: Guilford Press.

Kent, S. & Yellowlees, P. (1994). Psychiatric and social reasons for frequent hospitalization. *Hospital and Community Psychiatry, 45*, 347–350.

Larsen, D.L., Attkisson, C.C., Hargreaves, W.A., & Nguyen, T.D. (1979). Assessment of client satisfaction: development of a general scale. *Evaluation and Program Planning, 2*, 197–207.

London, N.J. (1973). An essay on psychoanalytic theory: two theories of schizophrenia. Part 1. Review and critical assessment of the development of the two theories. Part 2. Discussion and restatement of the specific theory of schizophrenia. *International Journal of Psychoanalysis, 54*, 169–193.

McCrone, P. & Strathdee, G. (1994). Needs not diagnosis: toward a more rational approach to community mental health resourcing in Britain. *International Journal of Social Psychiatry, 40*, 79–86.

McGlynn, E.A. (1996). Setting the context for measuring patient outcomes. In D.M. Steinwachs, L.M. Flynn, G.S. Norquist, & E.A. Skinner (Eds.), *Using client outcomes information to improve mental health and substance abuse treatment*. San Francisco: Jossey-Bass.

Metzner, I.L., Cohen, F., Grossman, L.S., & Wettstein, R.M. (1998). Treatment in jails and prisons. In R.M. Wettstein (Ed.). *Treatment of offenders with mental disorders*. (pp. 211–264.) New York: Guilford Press.

Moore, E., Ball, R.A., & Kuipers, L. (1992). Expressed emotion in staff working with the long-term adult mentally ill. *British Journal of Psychiatry, 161*, 802–808.

Penn, D.L., Guyan, K., Daily, T., Spaulding, W.D., Garbin, C.P., & Sullivan, M. (1994). Dispelling the stigma of schizophrenia: what sort of information is best? *Schizophrenia Bulletin, 20*, 567–577.

Phelan, M., Slade, M., Thornicroft, G., Dunn, G., Holloway, F., Wykes, T., Strathdee, G., Loftus, L., McCrone, P., & Hayward, P. (1995). The Camberwell Assessment of Need: the validity and reliability of an instrument to assess the needs of people with severe mental illness. *British Journal of Psychiatry, 167*, 589–595.

Rosenfeld, S. & Neese-Todd, S. (1993). Elements of a psychotherapy social clubhouse program associated with a satisfying quality of life. *Hospital and Community Psychiatry, 44*, 76–80.

Searles, H.F. (1979). *Countertransference and related subjects: selected papers*. Madison, CT: International Universities Press.

Seigel, L.M., Attkisson, C.C., & Carson, L.G. (1978). Need identification and program planning in the community context. In C.C. Attkisson, W.A. Hargreaves, M.J. Horowitz, & J.E. Sorensoen, J.E. (Eds.), *Evaluation of human service programs*. New York: Academic Press.

Selzer, M.A. & Carsky, M. (1990). Treatment alliance and the chronic schizophrenic. *American Journal of Psychotherapy, 44*, 506–515.

Slade, M., Thornicroft, G., Loftus, L., Phelan, M., & Wykes, T. (1999). *CAN: Camberwell Assessment of Need*. London: Gaskell.

Smith, T.E., Hull, J.W., MacKain, S.J., Wallace, C.J., Rattenni, L.A., Goodman, M., Anthony, D.T., & Kentros, M.K. (1996). Training hospitalized patients with schizophrenia in community reintegration skills. *Psychiatric Services*, *47*, 1099–1103.

Spotnitz, H. (1969). *Modern psychoanalysis of the schizophrenic patient*. New York: Grune & Stratton.

Stansfield, S., Orrell, M., Mason, R., Nicholls, D., & D'Ath, P. (1998). A pilot study of needs assessment in acute psychiatric inpatients. *Social Psychiatry and Psychiatric Epidemiology*, *33*, 136–139.

State Office of Mental Health. (2000). http://centrall.omh.state.ny.us/mis/mgtrpt

Strauss, J.S. (1992). The person-key to understanding mental illness: toward a dynamic psychiatry. III. *British Journal of Psychiatry*, *161* (Suppl. 18), 19–26.

Surrey, J.L. (1991). In J.V. Jordan, A.G. Kaplan, J.B. Miller, I.P. Stiver, & J.L. Surrey (Eds.), *Women's growth in connection: writings from the Stone Center*. New York: Guilford Press.

Tempier, R., Caron, J., Mercier, C., and Leouffre, P. (1998). Quality of life of severely mentally ill individuals: a comparative study. *Community Mental Health Journal*, *5*, 477–485.

Torrey, E.F. (1997). *Out of the shadows: confronting America's mental illness crisis*. New York: John Wiley & Sons.

Trattner, W. I. (1999). *From poor law to welfare state: a history of social welfare in America*. New York: The Free Press.

Wiedl, K.H. (1992). Assessment of coping with schizophrenia: stressors, appraisals and coping behavior. *British Journal of Psychiatry*, *161*, 114–122.

5

THE WRAPAROUND PROCESS

*Individualized, Community-Based Care for Children
and Adolescents with Intensive Needs*

JANET S. WALKER AND ERIC J. BRUNS

Collaborative consumer-provider teams have become an increasingly popular mechanism for creating and implementing individualized care plans for adults, children, and families with complex needs. This sort of team-based consumer- or family-driven planning is currently used in a wide variety of human service contexts, including special education, developmental disabilities, child welfare, and juvenile justice. Recently, much attention has been focused on such teams in the context of children's mental health, where an approach known as *wraparound* has become a primary strategy for planning and coordinating community-based care for children with severe emotional and behavioral disorders. One recent estimate put the number of children receiving wraparound at 200,000 (Burns & Goldman, 1999), and that number is likely increasing.

Wraparound's popularity stems from its philosophy for service delivery, which is appealing to a broad range of stakeholders, particularly the families of children and youth with severe mental health disorders. The philosophy begins from the idea that the perspectives of the family — including the child or youth — must be given primary importance during all phases and activities of wraparound. The philosophy further stresses that the wraparound planning process should be individualized, strengths based, and outcome oriented. Additionally, wraparound is intended to promote the use of community-based services and supports, thereby keeping families together while also decreasing the need for costly out-of-home placements. Finally, wraparound is intended to be a culturally competent process that is respectful of the family's values and beliefs, and that supports and builds on the strengths and assets of the family's culture, traditions, and community.

Despite widespread implementation of wraparound programs and the appeal of the philosophy, there is limited evidence for the effectiveness of the approach. This is a matter of concern among advocates of wraparound, because there is increasing pressure to allocate mental health resources to programs and interventions with demonstrated effectiveness. Accumulation of evidence for the effectiveness of wraparound has been hampered by the lack of any generally agreed-upon guidelines for wraparound practice. Although there is agreement about the philosophy that should guide wraparound, there currently exists no widely accepted model or manual for wraparound practice. Awareness of this difficulty has led to recent efforts to build theory for wraparound, define practice parameters, and develop measures of fidelity.

This chapter provides an overview of the development of wraparound, beginning from its roots in early practice and continuing up through ongoing efforts to build theory, define practice parameters, and study effectiveness. The "plot" of this wraparound story turns on the tension that arises between the desire to clearly define wraparound practice and the desire to maintain its flexibility both at the program level (so that wraparound programs can be tailored to fit within diverse communities) and at the team level (so that wraparound planning can be individualized to address the unique needs and goals of each child and family served). At a more general level, the plot hinges on the question of whether it is possible to turn a grassroots, value-driven movement into an evidence-based practice without destroying its soul.

Table 1 Wraparound and Its Roots

Ten Principles of Wraparound

1. **Family voice and choice**. Family and youth/child perspectives are intentionally elicited and prioritized during all phases of the wraparound process. Planning is grounded in family members' perspectives, and the team strives to provide options and choices such that the plan reflects family values and preferences.

2. **Team based**. The wraparound team consists of individuals agreed upon by the family and committed to them through informal, formal, and community support and service relationships.

3. **Natural supports**. The team actively seeks out and encourages the full participation of team members drawn from family members' networks of interpersonal and community relationships. The wraparound plan reflects activities and interventions that draw on sources of natural support.

4. **Collaboration**. Team members work cooperatively and share responsibility for developing, implementing, monitoring, and evaluating a single wraparound plan. The plan reflects a blending of team members' perspectives, mandates, and resources. The plan guides and coordinates each team member's work toward meeting the team's goals.

5. **Community based**. The wraparound team implements service and support strategies that take place in the most inclusive, most responsive, most accessible, and least restrictive settings possible, and that safely promote child and family integration into home and community life.

6. **Culturally competent**. The wraparound process demonstrates respect for and builds on the values, preferences, beliefs, culture, and identity of the child/youth and family, and their community.

7. **Individualized**. To achieve the goals laid out in the wraparound plan, the team develops and implements a customized set of strategies, supports, and services.

8. **Strengths based**. The wraparound process and the wraparound plan identify, build on, and enhance the capabilities, knowledge, skills, and assets of the child and family, their community, and other team members.

9. **Persistence**. Despite challenges, the team persists in working toward the goals included in the wraparound plan until the team reaches agreement that a formal wraparound process is no longer required.

10. **Outcome based**. The team ties the goals and strategies of the wraparound plan to observable or measurable indicators of success, monitors progress in terms of these indicators, and revises the plan accordingly.

The wraparound philosophy, as defined by its 10 principles, expresses a vision that has straightforward, commonsensical appeal. When a child or adolescent struggles with a severe mental health disorder, his or her family also struggles — to find adequate care and support, to stay safe, to stay together, and to maintain everyday life and functioning. The wraparound process begins by bringing a team together around the struggling child and family. Included on the team are people who have a stake in seeing the family succeed: family members, service providers, and members of the family's natural and community support networks. Guided by a wraparound facilitator, these people work to create, implement, and monitor a single, integrated plan that will maintain the child successfully in the community and help the family realize its vision for a better life. The plan typically includes formal services and interventions, together with community services and interpersonal support and assistance provided by friends, kin, and other people drawn from the family's social networks. The plan's components are measured against relevant indicators of success and are revised when outcomes are not being achieved. The planning process is family driven, culturally competent, and community and strengths based.

This vision for wraparound has evolved over the past 20 years in reaction to the typical experiences of children with severe emotional and behavioral disorders and their families. While recent years have seen some progress in transforming mental health service systems, families seeking help and support still typically encounter child-serving systems that are fragmented and uncoordinated, with a hodgepodge of providers, interventions, and payers. Community-based treatment options are often unavailable, and there is a continued overreliance on residential treatment and other restrictive placements. Such out-of-home placements can cause irreversible damage to family and community ties as the child or adolescent spends long periods distant from home or under conditions that prohibit or greatly restrict contact with family members. Even today, the lion's share of public dollars for children's mental health continues to be spent on residential and inpatient treatment, despite a near absence of evidence of effectiveness (U.S. Department of Health and Human Services, 1999). Meanwhile, families are often blamed for their children's difficulties and discouraged from participating in or directing their children's care.

The current vision of wraparound emerged gradually from the efforts of individuals and organizations committed to providing alternatives to the experiences of children, adolescents, and families, as described above. Building on program models drawn from Europe and Canada, the Kaleidoscope program in Chicago began implementing private agency-based individualized services as early as 1975. The term *wraparound* was first used in the early 1980s to describe the response to a class action lawsuit in North Carolina that resulted in development of an array of comprehensive, community-based services for individual children and their families. In 1985, the Alaska Youth Initiative was formed with the goal of returning to Alaska youth with complex needs who had been placed in out-of-state institutions. The initiative was successful in returning almost all youth from out of state, and the Alaska efforts were quickly followed by replications in Washington, Vermont, and elsewhere.

During the late 1980s and early 1990s, wraparound's growing popularity received added momentum from the development of a broader movement to build *systems of care* for children with serious emotional and behavioral disorders (Stroul & Friedman, 1988). The impetus for systems of care came from recognition of the ongoing problems listed above: uncoordinated and ineffective services, an overreliance on restrictive settings, and a lack of family participation and cultural competence. Proponents envision systems of care that provide a wide array of services and supports, with an emphasis on serving children and families in their home communities and in least restrictive environments. In systems of care, child-

and family-serving agencies collaborate and coordinate their efforts, providing individual-ized, culturally competent care. Systems of care encourage the full participation of families and youth consumers in planning, evaluating, and delivering services and supports.

Federal and foundation programs offered millions of dollars for states and communi-ties to plan and implement systems of care during the 1980s and 1990s. Over the past de-cade, federal grants administered by the Comprehensive Community Services for Children and Their Families Program have supported implementation of system of care principles in close to 100 communities across the country. While wraparound is certainly not the only means for implementing the systems of care philosophy for individual children with the most intensive needs, it has perhaps become the most commonly used means of doing so.

The growth of wraparound has also been fueled by the rapid expansion of the family advocacy movement within children's mental health. Local-, state-, and national-level fam-ily-run organizations grew in membership and visibility throughout the 1990s, using their increasing strength to advocate reforms consistent with both the wraparound and system of care philosophies. Family organizations are often strong supporters of wraparound because its philosophy of care stresses family empowerment and highlights the importance of fami-lies' social and community ties. Additionally, wraparound plans often build explicitly on the services and social support available from family advocacy organizations. Some wrap-around program models include formal roles for representatives from family organizations, who participate on teams as facilitators or family support partners, or in other roles.

The 1990s also saw increasing acknowledgment across child- and family-serving sys-tems — and within family advocacy organizations — of the importance of cultural com-petence. Wraparound's principles directly require cultural competence; however, within a well-implemented wraparound process there are multiple, reinforcing routes for promot-ing cultural competence in a manner that goes much deeper than lip service. The focus on family voice and choice throughout planning, the emphasis on individualization, the participation in planning of members drawn from the family's social support networks, and the emphasis on enhancing connections to community all work to promote service and support strategies that are respectful of, sensitive to, and based in family values and beliefs. What is more, family advocacy organizations have made concerted efforts to increase the diversity of their membership and their own level of cultural competence. This has enabled them to use their roles on wraparound teams and in wraparound programs to promote cultural competence. In turn, this gives legitimacy to claims for wraparound as a culturally competent process.

While the term *wraparound* came to be more and more widely used throughout the 1990s, there was still no formal agreement about exactly what wraparound was. Many wraparound programs shared features with one another, but there existed no consensus about how to define wraparound. Thus, in 1998, a group of stakeholders in wraparound gathered to clarify the essential features of wraparound. This meeting resulted in the defi-nition of 10 elements that provide the foundation for the wraparound process (Burns & Goldman, 1999). The principles of wraparound provided in Table 1 are based on these elements.

While the 10 elements provided a clear statement of the philosophy that guides wrap-around, they gave little information about the specific activities or skills necessary to imple-ment the process in a manner that reflects the philosophy. As experience with wraparound has accumulated, challenges arising from a lack of practice standards have become clearer. Alongside documented successes, it has become apparent that many teams and programs do not operate in a manner that reflects the wraparound principles (Bruns, Burchard, Suter,

Leverentz-Brady, & Force, 2004; Burchard, Bruns, & Burchard, 2002; Walker & Schutte, 2005). At the most basic level, it seems that many teams have difficulty adhering to a structured planning process that includes setting specific goals and monitoring progress toward outcomes. Additionally, wraparound plans often appear to be lacking in creativity and individualization. This may stem from policies and funding arrangements (e.g., lack of flexibility for funding unique or nontraditional services and supports, system incentives to fill program beds or slots, etc.) or a lack of knowledge about techniques for stimulating creativity during the planning process.

More profoundly, achieving true partnership with families and youth is an ongoing challenge within wraparound, just as it is in other human service contexts, where the perspectives and priorities of professionals are likely to dominate discussion and decision making. Even when professionals desire to act in partnership with youth and families, they often lack knowledge of skills and techniques to do so. What is more, youth and family members have often never had an opportunity to explore — and thus have difficulty expressing — their own perspectives regarding needs and goals, and the strategies that are likely to be successful in meeting them. Other challenges arise from the specification that wraparound be strengths based and culturally competent. While there seems to be little disagreement that traditional approaches within children's mental health tend to be deficit based and lacking in cultural sensitivity, much confusion remains about what exactly is meant by strengths-based and culturally competent practice.

Even when a wraparound team functions in a way that promotes family partnership, cultural competence, creativity, and a strengths orientation, other challenges often arise as the team strives to develop and implement plans that are truly coordinated, comprehensive, and community based (Walker, Koroloff, & Schutte, 2003). Many communities lack a true array of services and supports, making it difficult for wraparound teams to meet child and family needs using community-based options. Policies, agency cultures and mandates, and funding requirements often work against the use of a single comprehensive plan to coordinate services and supports across agencies. Moreover, the comprehensive wraparound plan is intended to extend beyond formal services by including roles for members of the family's community and informal support networks. Providers often lack knowledge, skills, and resources for accomplishing this.

In sum, wraparound originally developed as an alternative to systems that were viewed as fragmented, unfriendly to families, and overly restrictive. Wraparound's stock rose with the acceptance of system of care principles, the increasing influence of families, and the increasing importance of cultural competence in service delivery. Alongside this growth of enthusiasm for wraparound, however, were growing concerns about how to ensure its integrity.

RESEARCH ON WRAPAROUND

Despite the challenges described in the previous section, numerous individual wraparound programs have built impressive reputations that rest upon program evaluation and more formal studies (Burchard et al., 2002; Burns & Goldman, 1999). Among these programs, the most notable example is Wraparound Milwaukee (Kamradt, 2000), which was cited by the President's New Freedom Commission on Mental Health as a model program (New Freedom Commission on Mental Health, 2003). Meanwhile, findings from a number of published pre-post studies have provided evidence that most children receiving wraparound from the study programs were able to continue living in the community for months and even years after entry into wraparound. This is in contrast to studies showing that most children with severe emotional and behavioral problems who receive traditional services are eventually placed in more restrictive settings outside their home communities (Burchard et al., 2002).

Three quasi-experimental studies and two randomized clinical trials provide further encouraging support for the wraparound process. Among the five studies, four reported positive outcomes for children and youth receiving wraparound, in areas such as improved community adjustment, improved behavior, decreased functional impairment, fewer social problems, fewer placement changes, fewer days absent from school, and lower rates of delinquency (these results are summarized in Burchard et al., 2002). On the basis of results such as these, the Surgeon General's report on mental health characterized the available research as providing "emerging evidence" for the effectiveness of the approach (U.S. Department of Health and Human Services, 1999). The fifth study, published more recently, found no differences in outcomes for youth enrolled in wraparound versus a quasi-experimental comparison group; however, the study did not measure implementation and the author cautioned that there was little evidence youth in the two groups received services that differed meaningfully (Bickman, Smith, Lambert, & Andrade, 2003).

While these results are encouraging overall, they do not go very far in terms of building an evidence base for wraparound. The primary difficulty rests in the fact that none of the studies measured implementation or fidelity, making it impossible to determine how groups within a study differed, and the extent to which the wraparound that was delivered across the different studies was actually the same intervention. As is the case in communities overall, the wraparound that was implemented likely varied significantly from study site to study site.

Recognition of these difficulties provided a stimulus for the development of measures of wraparound fidelity during the late 1990s. Fidelity measures are intended to assess the extent to which a program *as implemented* is faithful to its prescribed protocol, standards, or model. Within wraparound, two approaches to the measurement of fidelity have been explored, one focusing on direct observation of fidelity to key elements of the wraparound process, and the other focusing on reported perceptions of fidelity to the wraparound principles. The best developed measure of process fidelity within wraparound is the Wraparound Observation Form (WOF; Nordness & Epstein, 2003), a structured observation form completed by an observer during a team meeting. The observer rates whether or not meeting participants engaged in certain types of activities that are presumed to reflect the principles of wraparound. In contrast, the Wraparound Fidelity Index (WFI; Bruns et al., 2004) uses structured interviews with family, youth, and care coordinators to assess perceptions of whether wraparound has been delivered in a way that reflects the philosophy expressed in the principles.

The development of these fidelity tools represents an important step forward for efforts to clarify expectations for wraparound practice. However, each approach also highlights obstacles that will need to be overcome in order for wraparound to be defined clearly enough to be replicated with fidelity and then evaluated at multiple sites. Because the WFI measures adherence to principles rather than practices, it can provide no definitive information about what sorts of practices are being implemented or how practices should be improved. The WOF measures practice directly, but only during wraparound team meetings. People with experience delivering wraparound are adamant that what happens during meetings represents only a small part of the activities and interactions that comprise wraparound.

CURRENT WORK AND FUTURE DIRECTIONS

As things stand now, there is widespread enthusiasm for wraparound, support from on-going funding initiatives, and evidence from program evaluation that the wraparound process has the potential to be effective. Most importantly, people who have participated on wraparound teams and implemented wraparound programs have accumulated a vast amount of practical knowledge about what makes wraparound successful. Yet there is also a growing realization that, given the current emphasis on evidence-based practices, it is unlikely that this positive momentum can continue unless wraparound practice can be more clearly defined. Such clarification will pave the way for replication and for accumulation of the research that is essential for establishing evidence of effectiveness.

One possible solution to this difficulty is that one well-regarded wraparound program or model will be replicated at several sites with a high degree of fidelity, and the replications will be studied sufficiently to produce the beginnings of an evidence base. The practices and elements of this program could evolve from there to become the *de facto* standard for wraparound. While this might be an expedient route to achieving a clear definition of wraparound, it also presents several drawbacks. First, by drawing exclusively from one program, there is the potential to lose much of the collective wisdom that has accumulated among practitioners, particularly knowledge that has grown out of efforts to implement wraparound within diverse communities and diverse policy and funding contexts. This presents a risk of sacrificing part of what has made wraparound successful, particularly in terms of being culturally competent, individualized, and community based. Picking one program as *the* model for wraparound would also seem to undercut the collaborative ethos that has been a central feature of wraparound's development, with wraparound developers freely sharing ideas and building their own practice models through incorporating tools and techniques used by others. More practically, it is quite possible that several programs would begin this evolution. If this happens, the stage is set for the development of rival wraparound models competing for legitimacy and for the resources that are required for the work of documenting effectiveness.

In response to such concerns, stakeholders from across the country came together in 2003 to work out a strategy for collaboratively defining wraparound and developing evidence for effectiveness. The idea that emerged from this meeting was to work as a group to refine the principles of wraparound and to specify the basic activities that are essential for wraparound. The activities would be defined in a manner that was sufficiently precise to permit measurement of process fidelity, but also sufficiently flexible to allow for diversity in the manner in which a given activity might be accomplished. The group also agreed that it was important to remedy the lack of a theory base for wraparound. While wraparound has always had implicit associations with various psychosocial theories (Burns, Schoenwald, Burchard, Faw, & Santos, 2000), a clear rationale has not been developed to explain why practice undertaken in accordance with wraparound's principles should produce the desired outcomes. This lack of theory has exacerbated difficulties in defining wraparound practice and conducting research. While recent work has begun the theory-building effort (Walker & Schutte, 2004), members of the group prioritized this for future work.

Between June 2003 and the end of 2004, the group of stakeholders, now called the National Wraparound Initiative (NWI; Bruns, Osher, Walker, & Rast, 2005), grew to more than 80 members, including family members and advocates, youth consumers, service providers, and administrators and policy makers from the agency level to the state and national levels. During that period, the initiative made significant progress on several of its top priorities using a range of collaborative and consensus-building strategies. For example, to refine the principles of wraparound, the group began with the existing elements produced in 1998. The intention was to rework these elements so that each one focused on a single theme and so that, together, they expressed a complete philosophy for wraparound practice at the team level. Using individual and small group open-ended feedback, the writing team prepared a revised version of the principles that then became the starting point for a structured communication and consensus-building process based on the Delphi technique (Woudenberg, 1991). Participants in the initiative provided quantitative ratings and comments on the proposed versions of each of the principles. Feedback was aggregated and the principles were resubmitted to respondents for a second round of quantitative and qualitative feedback. Results from the second round showed that the revised principles were acceptable to the large majority of participating experts. The percentage of respondents finding the current wording of each principle acceptable averaged 93%, and ranged from 87% for *family voice and choice* to 100% for *outcome oriented*.

More importantly, the feedback highlighted substantive problematic areas that have important implications for wraparound. These problematic areas, though widely discussed among stakeholders, had not been systematically acknowledged previously, since different interpretations of the wraparound philosophy had not been directly examined. In the area of family voice and choice, for example, the Delphi process illuminated difficulties that can arise around how the family's perspective should be balanced with the perspectives of other team members. Some comments expressed concern that the principle did not sufficiently emphasize the extent to which the wraparound process should prioritize the family members' perspectives over other team members' perspectives throughout collaboration. Others noted that there are times, such as when the child is in protective custody, that it is neither legal nor advisable for the family's perspective to drive the wraparound process. Taking all the feedback into account, the writing team produced a document that included a further-revised version of the principles, each with an extended commentary providing details about the principle's intended meaning and how it might apply in particular problematic situations.

A similar process, though with only one round of structured feedback, was used to develop a description of the essential phases and activities of the wraparound process (Table 2). Activities were grouped into four phases: engagement and preparation, initial plan development, implementation, and transition. Building on information from available descriptions of wraparound practice and open-ended feedback, a description of the phases and activities was submitted to initiative members for review using a Delphi-type technique similar to that used for the principles. The goals were to determine whether each of the proposed activities was essential for wraparound, whether the set of activities as a whole was sufficient for wraparound, and whether the description of each activity was acceptable.

Overall, the 30 respondents expressed a very high level of agreement with the proposed set of activities. For 23 of the 31 activities, there was unanimous or near-unanimous (i.e., one dissenter) agreement that the activity was essential. Respondents also found the proposed descriptions of the activities generally acceptable; in fact, all respondents rated the description acceptable for 20 of the 31 activities. The activities and descriptions were revised to reflect feedback, and a document was prepared that described the phases and activities along with notes about particular challenges and other considerations that might be associated with a given activity. Many of these notes were derived from the commentaries provided by respondents and focus on how to accomplish difficult yet crucial activities, such as defining and prioritizing needs and eliciting and using strengths.

Table 2 Phases and Activities of the Wraparound Process

Phase 1: Engagement and team preparation

1.1 Orient the family and youth to wraparound and address legal and ethical issues.

1.2 Stabilize crises: Elicit information from family members, agency representatives, and potential team members about immediate crises or potential crises, and prepare a response.

1.3 Explore strengths, needs, culture, and vision during conversations with child/youth and family, and prepare summary document.

1.4 Engage and orient other team members.

1.5 Make necessary meeting arrangements.

Phase 2: Initial plan development

2.1 Develop an initial plan of care: Determine ground rules, describe and document strengths, create team mission, describe and prioritize needs/goals, determine outcomes and indicators for each goal, select strategies, and assign action steps.

2.2 Create a safety/crisis plan to ameliorate risk and respond to potential emergencies.

2.3 Complete necessary documentation and logistics.

Phase 3: Implementation

3.1 Implement action steps for each strategy of the wraparound plan, track progress on action steps, evaluate success of strategies, and celebrate successes.

3.2 Revisit and update the plan, considering new strategies as necessary.

3.3 Maintain/build team cohesiveness and trust by maintaining awareness of team members' satisfaction and buy-in, and addressing disagreements or conflict.

3.4 Complete necessary documentation and logistics.

Phase 4: Transition

4.1 Plan for cessation of formal wraparound: Create a transition plan and a posttransition crisis management plan, and modify the wraparound process to reflect transition.

4.2 Create a "commencement" by documenting the team's work and celebrating success.

4.3 Follow up with the family.

The results from these two efforts from the NWI testify to a high level of preexisting — though not previously explicit — agreement regarding the guiding philosophy for wraparound and the overall structure of a practice model described by phases and their constituent activities. Equally important, the work highlighted areas of concern, regarding both situations that challenge the principles and particular activities that are viewed as critical to the wraparound process. Taken together, these documents provide a sense of the structure or framework within which the actual practice of wraparound occurs. In the next phases of its work, members of the initiative plan to flesh out this framework by providing inventories of tools, templates, and techniques that can be used as a basis for accomplishing the various activities in a manner consistent with the wraparound principles. Based on this foundation, critical supports to implementing high-quality wraparound will be available to programs and team facilitators, who can then select from various options — or tailor an existing option — for accomplishing an activity. As noted above, the goal is to retain flexibility within wraparound, so that it can be responsive to the needs of individual teams and diverse communities.

In addition, members of the initiative have stressed that merely accomplishing the activities does not mean that true wraparound is occurring. Accomplishing the activities in a manner that reflects the principles requires a great deal of skill in areas such as empathic listening, facilitation of collaboration, conflict resolution, management of logistics, and so on. Development of such skills would be facilitated by a set of training and support options that also remain to be developed. Finally, refined fidelity tools are needed that measure both adherence to the wraparound principles and accomplishment of specific activities. With these materials and tools in place, the potential for replication of and research on high-quality wraparound should be greatly enhanced.

SUMMARY

This chapter provided an introduction to wraparound, a widely attempted but poorly understood individualized planning process that is intended to meet the needs of children with severe emotional and behavioral challenges in their home communities. The story of wraparound is instructive given the current focus on evidence-based practice for mental health. Wraparound provides a case study of efforts to turn a value-based service process into an evidence-based practice that can be replicated and rigorously evaluated.

REFERENCES

Bickman, L., Smith, C.M., Lambert, E.W., & Andrade, A.R. (2003). Evaluation of a congressionally mandated wraparound demonstration. *Journal of Child and Family Studies, 12,* 135–156.

Bruns, E.J., Burchard, J.D., Suter, J.C., Leverentz-Brady, K., & Force, M.M. (2004). Assessing fidelity to a community-based treatment for youth: the Wraparound Fidelity Index. *Journal of Emotional and Behavioral Disorders, 12,* 79–89.

Bruns, E.J., Osher, T., Walker, J.S., & Rast, J. (2005). The National Wraparound Initiative: toward consistent implementation of high-quality wraparound. In C.C. Newman, C.J. Liberton, K. Kutash, & R.M. Friedman (Eds.), *The 17th annual research conference: a system of care for children's mental health* (pp. 129–133). Tampa, FL: University of South Florida, The Research and Training Center on Children's Mental Health.

Burchard, J.D., Bruns, E.J., & Burchard, S.N. (2002). The wraparound approach. In B.J. Burns & K. Hoagwood (Eds.), *Community treatment for youth: evidence-based interventions for severe emotional and behavioral disorders* (pp. 69–90). New York: Oxford University Press.

Burns, B.J. & Goldman, S.K. (Eds.). (1999). *Systems of care: promising practices in children's mental health, 1998 series,* Vol. IV, *Promising practices in wraparound for children with severe emotional disorders and their families.* Washington, DC: Center for Effective Collaboration and Practice, American Institutes for Research.

Burns, B.J., Schoenwald, S.K., Burchard, J.D., Faw, L., & Santos, A.B. (2000). Comprehensive community-based interventions for youth with severe emotional disorders: multisystemic therapy and the wraparound process. *Journal of Child and Family Studies, 9,* 283–314.

Kamradt, B. (2000). Wraparound Milwaukee: aiding youth with mental health needs. *Juvenile Justice, 7,* 14–23.

New Freedom Commission on Mental Health. (2003). *Achieving the promise: transforming mental health care in America: final report* (DHHS Publication SMA-03-3832). Rockville, MD: Author.

Nordness, P.D. & Epstein, M.H. (2003). Reliability of the Wraparound Observation Form–Second Version: an instrument designed to assess the fidelity of the wraparound approach. *Mental Health Services Research, 5,* 89–96.

Stroul, B.A. & Friedman, R.M. (1988). Caring for severely emotionally disturbed children and youth. Principles for a system of care. *Child Today, 17,* 11–15.

U.S. Department of Health and Human Services. (1999). *Mental health: a report of the surgeon general.* Rockville, MD: U.S. Department of Health and Human Services, Substance Abuse and

Mental Health Services Administration, Center for Mental Health Services, National Institutes of Health, National Institute of Mental Health.

Walker, J.S., Koroloff, N., & Schutte, K. (2003). *Implementing high-quality collaborative individualized service/support planning: necessary conditions.* Portland, OR: Research and Training Center on Family Support and Children's Mental Health.

Walker, J.S. & Schutte, K.M. (2004). Practice and process in wraparound teamwork. *Journal of Emotional and Behavioral Disorders*, 182–192.

Walker, J.S. & Schutte, K.M. (2005). Quality and individualization in wraparound planning. *Journal of Child and Family Studies 14*, 25–267.

Woudenberg, F. (1991). An evaluation of Delphi. *Technological Forecasting and Social Change, 40*, 131–150.

II

Best Practices in Community Mental Health

Evidence-based practice, practice that is based on research supporting its efficacy, is becoming the standard in program design and delivery. Section II presents innovative treatment approaches for persons with serious mental health problems and highlights the challenges in developing models that are, on the one hand, clearly defined and able to be replicated and, on the other hand, flexible enough to fit the unique needs of each individual.

"Evidence-Based Treatment for Adults with Co-Occurring Mental and Substance Use Disorders," by David E. Biegel, Lenore A. Kola, and Robert J. Ronis, is a critical review of current treatment models for adults with co-occurring mental illness and substance abuse disorders and provides the components of an integrated treatment model supported by research.

In "Putting Values into Practice: Involuntary Treatment Interventions in Mental Health," Melissa Floyd Taylor discusses one of the most difficult treatment interventions in working with mental illness: the use of coercion. The author points out that involuntary treatment is part of the history of mental health care and shows no signs of abating, despite the advocacy efforts of consumer groups. She outlines different types of involuntary treatment within a contextual analysis that includes personal and professional values.

The final chapter in this section, "Neuropsychiatry Perspectives for Community Mental Health Theory and Practice," by William H. Wilson, explores the contribution of neuropsychiatry and medication to community mental health. The use of medications to treat schizophrenia, mood disorders, anxiety disorders, and personality disorders is illustrated with case examples, with an emphasis on new and promising treatments.

6

EVIDENCE-BASED TREATMENT FOR
ADULTS WITH CO-OCCURRING MENTAL
AND SUBSTANCE USE DISORDERS*

DAVID E. BIEGEL, LENORE A. KOLA, AND ROBERT J. RONIS

Mental health and substance abuse providers, advocates, and policy makers across the country have become increasingly aware of the challenges related to the needs of clients with co-occurring mental and substance disorders. At the same time, there has been increasing attention concerning the importance of basing practice and service delivery on research-based evidence of effectiveness (evidence-based practice). This chapter discusses the characteristics and needs of adults with co-occurring mental and substance disorders, identifies problems with current treatment models, presents the components of an integrated treatment model and the research supporting its effectiveness, and discusses barriers to implementation of this model and support mechanisms that can address these barriers.

CHARACTERISTICS AND NEEDS OF ADULTS
WITH CO-OCCURRING MENTAL AND SUBSTANCE DISORDERS

A clinical awareness of the problem of dual disorders began in the early 1980s (Pepper, Krishner, & Ryglewicz, 1981; Caton, 1981). The terms *co-occurring disorders*, *dual disorders*, and *dual diagnosis*, as used here, indicate the presence of both severe mental illness and a substance use disorder. Data in the last two decades have established the fact that dual disorders are common. The Epidemiological Catchment Area (ECA) study, based on data collected from 1980 to 1985, showed that the lifetime rate of substance disorder for persons with severe mental illness was approximately half, with 48% of persons with schizophrenia and 56% of persons with bipolar disorder affected (Regier et al., 1990). Findings from the more recent National Comorbidity Study (NCS), with data collected from 1990 to 1992 from a nationally representative sample, also documents a high prevalence of co-occurring mental and addictive disorders. In the NCS, 41 to 65% of participants with a lifetime

* Research for this chapter was supported by grants from the Ohio Departments of Mental Health and Alcohol and Drug Addiction Services.

occurrence of addictive disorder also reported a lifetime occurrence of at least one mental disorder, and 51% of those with a lifetime occurrence of mental disorder reported a lifetime occurrence of at least one addictive disorder as well (Kessler et al., 1996). Studies have suggested that 25 to 35% of persons with a severe mental illness have an active or recent (within the last six months) substance disorder (Mueser, Bennett, & Kushner, 1995). Additionally, numerous studies report high rates of substance abuse among clients in treatment for severe psychiatric disorders (Mueser et al., 1990, 2000).

Dual diagnosis is associated with a variety of negative outcomes. These include higher rates of relapse (Swofford, Kasckow, Scheller-Gilkey, & Inderbitzin, 1996), hospitalization (Haywood et al., 1995), violence (Cuffel, Shumway, Chouljian, & Macdonald, 1994; Steadman et al., 1998), incarceration (Abram & Teplin, 1991; De Leon, Sacks, & Wexler, 2002), homelessness (Caton et al., 1994), and serious infections such as HIV and hepatitis (Compton, Cottler, Ben-Abdallah et al., 2000; Rosenberg et al., 2001) than are found for persons with only one diagnosis. Drug abusers with comorbid mental disorders are more likely to engage in risky behaviors, such as unprotected sex and needle sharing, that jeopardize their health (Leshner, 1999). Dually diagnosed bipolar patients experience more mixed episodes and rapid cycling, longer recovery times, greater resistance to lithium, and earlier and more frequent hospitalizations (Albanese & Khantzian, 2001).

Co-occurring disorders also pose special challenges for clients' treatment. There is strong evidence that substance abuse weakens the abilities of persons with a severe mental illness to develop and adhere to effective treatment plans and can shatter already fragile social networks. As a result, dually diagnosed individuals tend to use more psychiatric services than those with a single diagnosis, particularly such costly services as emergency room visits and inpatient hospitalizations (Dickey & Azeni, 1996). Similarly, substance abuse treatment seeking and adherence can be negatively impacted by symptoms and other effects of mental illness (Grant, 1997; Mueser, Drake, & Miles, 1997). For example, clinical depression may increase substance-abusing individuals' susceptibility to environmental influences that lead to relapse (Leshner, 1999).

THE NEED FOR INTEGRATED TREATMENT: THE PROBLEMS WITH CURRENT TREATMENT MODELS

Professionals working in the fields of mental health and addictions have increasingly recognized the simultaneous occurrence of mental and substance use disorders as presenting extensive problems. Individuals who suffer from this co-occurring disorder have problems in two areas: those arising within themselves as a result of their disorders, which result in clinical challenges and require multiple interventions and paradigm shifts in clinical services currently being offered, and those problems of external origins that derive from the conflicts, limitations, and clashing philosophies of the mental health and addiction treatment systems, which result in systemic challenges (Schollar, 1993).

Historically, services for individuals with co-occurring disorders have been either nonexistent or fragmented, and therefore ineffective in demonstrating positive outcomes for the psychiatric or substance use disorder (Drake, Mueser et al., 1996). Since the problem of dual disorders became more readily apparent in the early 1980s, researchers have demonstrated that parallel but separate mental health and substance abuse treatment systems, as well as sequential treatment, the most common model utilized, have not demonstrated effective outcomes (Drake et al., 1998).

Persons with dual disorders often find it difficult to access these parallel but separate mental health and substance abuse treatment systems so common in the United States (Ridgely, Goldman, & Willenbring, 1990; Ridgely, Osher, & Talbott, 1987; SAMHSA, 2002). For example, most severely mentally ill clients are unable to navigate between the separate systems, and their conflicting approaches to treatment often complicate or thwart their recovery. Individuals with co-occurring problems have typically responded poorly to traditional primary substance abuse treatment. Similarly, dually disordered individuals have not received maximum benefits from traditional psychiatric treatment programs, and their substance abuse often goes unrecognized, underdiagnosed, and untreated, thereby intensifying the negative consequences of their mental disorder (Singer, Kennedy, & Kola, 1998).

Clients' drug abuse may require adjustments in psychopharmacological treatments for mental illness (Carey, 1995; Leshner, 1999). Historically, each system has insisted that symptoms of the "other" disorder abate before treatment can be considered; i.e., substance abuse professionals require remission or control of psychiatric symptoms and mental health professionals require sobriety. Dually diagnosed clients may not have the wherewithal, perhaps due to transient or long-term cognitive impairment, to be readily aware of their substance disorder and its negative impact on their mental illness, and therefore may not be motivated to seek treatment for it.

Researchers have studied the use of traditional substance abuse treatments, such as 12-step programs in populations with serious mental disorders, since the early 1980s with disappointing results (Ridgely, Osher, & Goldman, 1987). However, a series of National Institute of Mental Health (NIMH)-funded demonstration projects in the late 1980s, incorporating assertive outreach and addictions interventions modified to meet the needs of mentally ill persons, began to show promise (Mercer-McFadden, Drake, & Brown, 1997). Programs began to incorporate motivational approaches and other comprehensive interventions in the context of multidisciplinary treatment teams in the 1990s, yielding initial positive outcomes, including remission of substance abuse, reductions in hospital utilization, and improved quality of life, as measured by uncontrolled studies (Drake, McHugo, & Noordsay, 1993).

As a result of these findings and the treatment barriers discussed above, there has been an accelerated movement to develop, refine, and evaluate comprehensive, integrated dual disorders treatment programs that meet the variety of clinical and service delivery challenges of this population (Drake & Wallach, 2000; Mueser, 2004; Drake, 2004; Sacks, 2000). However, today, integrated services are not the norm.

THE NEW HAMPSHIRE-DARTMOUTH INTEGRATED DUAL DISORDERS TREATMENT MODEL (IDDT)

The basic model for integrated dual disorders treatment involves cross-trained practitioners providing integrated, comprehensive services directed toward the two disorders simultaneously in the same venue, with the goal of recovery from both illnesses. It also assumes that treatment occurs in an orderly fashion geared to the motivation and readiness of the client and involves a long-term commitment on the part of both the practitioner and the client. A series of controlled studies of integrated interventions began to appear in the mid-1990s that demonstrated positive outcomes across client domains, including substance abuse, hospitalization rates, legal and functional status, and quality of life (Godley, Howeing-Roberson, & Godley, 1994; Jerrell & Ridgely, 1995; Drake, Yovetich, & Bebout, 1997; Carmichael et al.; Drake, McHugo, & Clark, 1998; Ho, Tsuang, & Liberman,

1999; Brunette et al., 2001; Barrowclough et al., 2001). Despite significant differences in the types of interventions offered in these integrated programs, several common components emerged as an evidence-based treatment for individuals with dual disorders, and have been incorporated into the integrated dual diagnosis treatment (IDDT) model developed by the New Hampshire-Dartmouth research group (Mercer-McFadden et al., 1998; Mueser et al., 2003). This integrated dual disorders treatment model has been demonstrated in controlled studies to be effective with significant reductions in client drug and alcohol use, hospitalizations, recidivism in the criminal justice system, homelessness, and improvement in symptom severity and overall life functioning (Mueser et al., 1997).

In order to develop effective treatment for clients with dual disorders, a cohesive, unitary system of care that is a seamless integration of psychiatric and substance abuse interventions is necessary (Mueser et al., 2003). This integrated service model overcomes many of the limitations of traditional approaches to intervening with these disorders. It combines philosophical, organizational, and treatment characteristics of both systems to provide co-ordinated interventions for individuals with co-occurring severe mental and substance use disorders. The model utilizes biopsychosocial treatments that combine pharmacological, psychological, educational, and social interventions that are directed to both clients and their families and friends. It promotes client and family involvement in service delivery, and stable housing and employment as a necessary condition for recovery. The focus of the model begins with the assertion that a core value is that of shared decision making, i.e., developing a collaborative relationship between the service provider and the client (Mueser et al., 2003).

Components of the IDDT model that have emerged as an evidence-based practice for the dually disordered population include the following characteristics.

Integrated Treatment

Effective dual disorders treatment programs combine mental health and substance abuse interventions at the clinical level. In the integrated treatment model, the same clinician or clinical team provides both mental health and substance abuse interventions, with the objective of motivating the patient toward a process of recovery (Mueser et al., 2003; Bellack et al., 1999). From the vantage point of the consumer, a consistent philosophy and set of recommendations guide the treatment, rather than the confusion of receiving mixed messages from multiple providers and systems with differing priorities and perspectives. An integrative perspective informs each aspect of the treatment from education about the disorders to counseling approaches and pharmacologic interventions.

Comprehensiveness

Effective programs recognize the need to integrate mental health and substance abuse treatment in all aspects of the service delivery system, and across all aspects of the client's living environment. Crisis intervention services, hospitalization and aftercare services, pharmacologic and psychotherapeutic treatments, physical health management, and housing and vocational services must be tailored to address the specific needs of the dual diagnosis patient. Healthy lifestyles are promoted through learning about diet and exercise, avoiding high-risk situations and behaviors, decreasing involvement in activities that adversely affect health and wellness, and developing friendships with people who do not abuse alcohol and drugs (Mueser, Noordsy, Drake, & Fox, 2003).

Stage-Wise Treatment

Incorporating the stages of change model of Prochaska and DiClemente (1984) and the stages of treatment (Osher and Kofoed, 1989), interventions are directed to where the client is with respect to his or her mental illness and substance abuse. The stages of treatment include *engagement*, forming a trusting relationship between provider and consumer; *persuasion*, developing motivation to define objectives and engage in treatment; *active treatment*, a process of acquiring skills and supports to achieve treatment objectives; and *relapse prevention*, enhancing the skills necessary to maintaining stable recovery (Mueser et al., 1995).

Assertive Outreach and Engagement Strategies

Effective integrated treatment programs engage clients through outreach services such as intensive case management or assertive community treatment (Mercer-McFadden et al., 1998; Meisler et al., 1997). Case managers may find clients at their residence or on the streets, and offer services, including assistance with housing and financial entitlements; linkages with general health care and social services providers; and transportation to community services or meetings. Interventions aim at improving access to services and fostering a trusting relationship with the provider. Without such efforts, engagement and adherence to treatment tend to be low (Hellerstein et al., 1995).

Motivational Interventions

Interventions such as motivational interviewing are intended to assist clients in understanding the impacts of their illness and drugs and alcohol on their lives, as well as to alert them to the hopeful possibility of recovery (Miller and Rollnick, 2002). Motivational interventions exploit underlying ambivalence to help move the individual to a state of readiness for treatment. Techniques such as expressing empathy, avoiding argumentation, and rolling with resistance allow the therapist to help the client identify discrepancies between current behaviors and future goals, and to develop strategies to begin to achieve them (Ziedonis & Trudeau, 1997).

Counseling

Successful IDDT programs incorporate several kinds of counseling aimed at developing skills and supports to pursue and maintain recovery from both mental illness and substance abuse (Mueser et al., 1998; Roberts, Shaner, & Eckman, 1999). Counseling may include individual, group, and family approaches, and may involve teaching cognitive and behavioral skills that help consumers to identify internal cues that may precede relapse and to cope more effectively with negative mood states or symptoms that in the past might have been addressed by using substances.

Social Support

Social supports may be enhanced by group treatments in which consumers may share strategies and experiences, by family interventions such as family psychoeducation (Lukens & McFarlane, 2004), and other techniques aimed at strengthening social networks (Drake & Mueser, 2000). Self-help groups provide support and companionship for individuals motivated to achieve and maintain abstinence, and include a range of options from traditional groups such as Alcoholics Anonymous (AA) and Narcotics Anonymous (NA) to groups tailored to special needs of the severely mentally ill dual diagnosis patient, such as Dual Recovery Anonymous (DRA) or Double Trouble. Each group has its own particular characteristics. Clinicians should assist consumers in selecting appropriate self-help groups as a means to enhance treatment and relapse prevention.

Long-Term Perspective

Research suggests that consumers with dual disorders may experience cycles of relapse and recovery throughout their lives and will achieve the highest quality of life when they have access to services at all times. Even in intensive treatment programs, people with co-occurring mental and substance use disorders rarely achieve stability and functional improvements quickly; rather, improvement occurs over months and years. Effective programs recognize the likelihood of relapse and provide time-unlimited services, including secondary interventions for treatment nonresponders, and incorporate effective rehabilitation activities intended to enhance and maintain gains (Alverson, Alverson, & Drake, 2000).

In summary, the IDDT model incorporates a number of components, including integrated treatment, stage-wise interventions, assertive outreach, motivational interventions, and counseling and social support services, organized within a comprehensive system of care that takes a long-term perspective to treatment. This model thus addresses the clinical as well as programmatic challenges of professionals working with this population.

EFFECTIVENESS OF INTEGRATED TREATMENT MODELS: OUTCOME RESEARCH STUDIES

There have been a number of research studies that have evaluated specific components of the IDDT model. In a review of 26 controlled studies of psychosocial interventions for people with severe mental illness and co-occurring substance use disorders reported or published since 1994, Drake and colleagues (Drake, Mueser, Brunette, & McHugo, 2004) identified 16 outpatient studies, including 12 experimental and 4 quasi-experimental designs. The experimental studies tended to focus on briefer clinical interventions, while comparisons of long-term interventions aimed at organizational aspects of care tended to utilize quasi-experimental designs. Seven studies (Godley et al., 1994; Jerrell & Ridgely, 1995; Drake et al., 1997; Carmichael et al., 1998; Drake, McHugo, Clark et al., 1998; Barrowclough et al., 2001; Penn & Brooks, 2000) compared integrated versus nonintegrated treatments in longer-term studies with treatment duration varying from a few months to three years. Most of these studies included motivational counseling and some form of active substance abuse counseling for clients in active treatment. In some of these studies, the intervention was structural (i.e., mental health and substance abuse clinicians were combined on the same team) rather than clinical (i.e., integration of specific clinical interventions was not specified).

Nearly all of these studies found some evidence that the more integrated form of treatment was superior in terms of abstinence or reductions in severity of alcohol or drug use, overall symptom reduction, hospital utilization, and other general outcomes. Although some studies showed no differences, none favored the less integrated programs. For example, Drake and colleagues (Drake et al., 1997) showed better outcomes in terms of progress toward recovery, reduced hospitalization, and reductions in alcohol abuse, but similar outcomes with respect to drug use, psychiatric symptoms, and quality of life. Mixed findings within two studies were partly explained by poor fidelity to implementing integrated treatment and to treatment drift (i.e., difficulties keeping the interventions separate for purposes of study) (Godley et al., 1994; Drake, McHugo, Clark et al., 1998). Still, persons with dual disorders were more likely to achieve full remissions on teams showing high fidelity to integrated treatment than low fidelity (43% vs. 15%) (McHugo, Drake, Teague, & Zie, 1999).

Studies focused on more limited integrated interventions, while generally supporting efficacy, were less robust, suggesting that successful integration may require the incorporation of multiple integrated elements. For example, Ho et al. (1999) found integrated day treatment plus assertive community treatment and skills training resulted in greater abstinence than integrated day treatment alone, while Hellerstein and colleagues (Hellerstein, Rosenthal, & Miner, 1995) found no differences between integrated and nonintegrated outpatient group treatment at four and eight months. James et al. (2004) found that a six-week group intervention based on motivational interviewing and tailored to subjects' stages of change and reasons for drug use showed greater reductions in psychopathology, alcohol and drug use, and hospitalization over usual care, while Burnham et al. (1995) found no group differences at six- and nine-month follow-ups to a comparison of three months' intensive integrated day treatment versus nonintegrated outpatient services. Of three studies comparing the impact of a single motivational interview in hospital versus usual care, two studies showed that the intervention group was more likely to attend their first outpatient visits and had a greater reduction in alcohol consumption at six months, while one study found no difference (Hulse & Tait, 2002; Baker et al., 2002; Swanson, Pantalon, & Cohen, 1999). Other studies looked at short- and long-term residential treatments, comparing integrated residential treatments with nonintegrated residential care. Despite large rates of attrition from all groups, integrated residential treatment appeared superior in almost all studies to treatment as usual with respect to treatment retention, abstinence or reduced relapse, and criminal activity.

In analyzing these studies, Drake and colleagues (Drake et al., 2004) have rated the level of evidence for each of these program characteristics, utilizing the Texas Psychosocial Rehabilitation Conference Criteria. Level 1, the highest level of evidence, requires at least five published studies with scientifically rigorous designs. Level 2 indicates evidence is supported by fewer than five published scientifically rigorous studies or studies using single-outcome measures or less rigorous independent variables. Level 3 indicates published studies of less rigorous design. Level 4 specifies multiple organizational "case studies" with outcomes published in peer-reviewed journals. Level 5 indicates the evidence is based on expert panel recommendations, but not including expert consensus (Cook, Toprac, & Shore, 2004).

Using these definitions, Drake and colleagues (Drake et al., 2004) rated the treatment characteristics of *integrated treatment, stage-wise treatments, outreach,* and *motivational counseling interventions* as meeting Level 1 criteria. *Counseling* and *social support* interventions, including cognitive and behavioral skills training, family and social network interventions, self-help and medications, and combinations of techniques for active treatment, are rated as Level 2 due to the lack of consistency across studies. As most dual diagnosis services are individualized according to patient needs, and are therefore difficult to evaluate due to the lack of specification of the intervention for research purposes, the level of evidence for *comprehensive services* as a critical element was rated as Level 3. However, although studies consistently show that clients who remain in treatment for longer intervals achieve better outcomes, the length of retention is not usually varied in a controlled fashion; therefore, evidence for the *long-term perspective* is rated as Level 2.

Thus, overall, research supports the effectiveness of integrated treatment and the evidence basis for each of the integrated treatment model's program components. Studies incorporating integration at multiple service levels and across multiple model components demonstrate efficacy more consistently than studies of more limited interventions. Further research is needed to better characterize the relative importance of fidelity to individual model elements, and to better understand the impact of model adaptations to meet the needs of specific subpopulations.

IMPLEMENTING THE MODEL: NEED FOR SYSTEM CHANGE AND IMPLEMENTATION SUPPORT

There are significant systemic challenges that must be addressed to successfully implement and maintain this evidence-based practice. Although many state mental health systems are attempting to implement integrated services for the dually disordered clients, barriers to the development of this integrated model are numerous and include changes required at all levels of the mental health and substance abuse service delivery systems. These include changes that involve organization and financing at the policy level, both structural and functional agency changes to support this innovative programming, training and supervision for clinicians at both the clinical and programmatic levels, and developing dissemination mechanisms to inform consumers so they may advocate for the development of these programs (Drake et al., 2001; Mueser, 2004). Many programs fail to meet all of these critical characteristics; however, research consistently supports that programs demonstrating high fidelity to the model described here — those that incorporate more of the core elements — produce better clinical outcomes (Ho et al., 1999; Jerrell & Ridgely, 1999; McHugo et al., 1999).

It is now recognized that barriers to implementation of evidence-based practices in the mental health and other fields cannot be achieved solely by traditional time-limited disseminating strategies of training of professionals and the provision of written materials. While these strategies may be a necessary component of bringing about program change, they are insufficient by themselves to bring about change in behavior (Torrey et al., 2001). In addition, successful implementation of evidence-based practices requires longer-term on-site implementation support involving programmatic and clinical consultation by experts in the model to be implemented and the creation of communication and support networks among providers implementing evidence-based practices.

Nationally, eight states are currently involved in a comprehensive approach to this issue as part of the Implementing Evidence-Based Practices for Severe Mental Illness Project, which is funded by the MacArthur, Johnson & Johnson, and Robert Wood Johnson Foundations, the U.S. Substance Abuse and Mental Health Services Administration, the National Alliance for the Mentally Ill, and state and local mental health organizations. This project involves promoting change in the use of evidence-based practices through three program elements: predisposing/disseminating strategies (educational materials and training), enabling methods (practice guidelines and decision support), and reinforcing strategies (practice feedback mechanisms) (Torrey et al., 2001).

In Ohio, the Ohio Departments of Mental Health (ODMH) and Alcohol and Drug Addiction Services (ODADAS) provide funding that supports a statewide coordinating center external to both the mental health and substance abuse service delivery systems (Biegel et al., 2003). Thus, the Ohio Substance Abuse and Mental Illness Coordinating Center of Excellence (SAMI CCOE) was created to facilitate the implementation and maintenance of high fidelity to the IDDT evidence-based treatment model in Ohio's mental health system. The SAMI CCOE is one of eight coordinating centers in Ohio developed over the past several years and funded by ODMH, whose purpose is to promote the use and maintenance of a variety of high-quality evidence-based mental health treatment modalities.

The SAMI CCOE is focused on assisting programs to implement and maintain high fidelity to the IDDT model in Ohio. The center accomplishes this purpose through the provision of training and technical assistance, dissemination, and research to mental health and substance abuse programs implementing this treatment model in Ohio. The goals of the SAMI CCOE are to:

1. Provide ongoing clinical training and direct clinical supervision for professional staff from mental health and substance abuse systems involved in the delivery of services or supervision and management of such services for persons with dual diagnosis
2. Provide administrative consultation on SAMI program design and implementation issues to administrators from mental health and substance abuse systems involved in the delivery, supervision, or management of such services for persons with a dual or co-occurring diagnosis
3. Disseminate evidence-based research about integrated treatment for persons with dual diagnosis
4. Conduct research focused on the assessment of program fidelity, model adaptations, and consumer, family, and systems performance outcomes for programs implementing the IDDT model

The SAMI CCOE supports fidelity to the IDDT model while appreciating the need for adaptations to the many service system and situational challenges existing in Ohio.

CONCLUSION

Policy makers, practitioners, consumers, and their families have reason to be optimistic about the future care of individuals with co-occurring substance and mental disorders given advances in the development of evidence-based treatments for this population, which provide hope for recovery from dual disorders. However as we have seen, to date, evidence-based treatment for adults with co-occurring disorders is not the norm, with significant barriers to both clinical and organizational issues still a significant issue. Ongoing state- and county-level collaborations are essential among currently parallel mental health, substance abuse, criminal justice, housing, and vocational rehabilitation systems in order for evidence-based treatments to be successfully implemented and maximally sustained with high fidelity.

REFERENCES

Abram, K.M. & Teplin, L.A. (1991). Co-occurring disorders among mentally ill jail detainees: Implications for public policy. *American Psychologist, 46*, 1036–1045.

Albanese, M. & Khantzian, E. (2001). The difficult-to-treat patient substance abuse. In M.J. Dewan (Ed.), *The difficult-to-treat psychiatric patient* (pp. 273–298). Washington, DC: American Psychiatric Publishing.

Alverson, H., Alverson, M., & Drake, R.E. (2000). An ethnographic study of the longitudinal course of substance abuse among people with severe mental illness. *Community Mental Health Journal, 36*, 557–569.

Baker, A., Lewin, T., Reichler, H., et al. (2002). Motivational interviewing among psychiatric in-patients with substance use disorders. *Acta Psychiatrica Scandinavica, 106*, 233–240.

Barrowclough, C., Haddock, G., Tarrier, N., Lewis, S.W., Moring, J., O'Brien, B., et al. (2001). Randomized controlled trial of motivational interviewing, cognitive behavior therapy, and family intervention for patients with comorbid schizophrenia and substance use disorders. *American Journal of Psychiatry*, 158 (10), 1706–1713.

Bellack, A.S., DiClemente, C.C., 1999. Treating substance abuse among patients with schizophrenia. *Psychiatric Services 50*, 75–80.

Biegel, D.E., Kola, L.A., Ronis, R.J., Boyle, P.E., Delos Reyes, C.M., Wieder, B., & Kubek, P. (2003). The Ohio Substance Abuse and Mental Illness Coordinating Center of Excellence: Implementation support for evidence-based practice. *Research in Social Work Practice, 13* (4), 531–545.

Brunette, M.F., Drake, R.E., Woods, M., et al. (2001). A comparison of long-term and short-term residential treatment programs for dual diagnosis patients. *Psychiatric Services 42*, 526–528.

Burnam, M.A., Morton, S.C., McGlynn, E.A., et al. (1995). An experimental evaluation of residential and nonresidential treatment for dually diagnosed homeless adults. *Journal of Addictive Diseases, 14*, 111–134.

Carey, K. (1995). Treatment of substance use disorders and schizophrenia. In A.F. Lehman & L.B. Dixon (Eds.), Double jeopardy: *Chronic mental illness and substance use disorders* (pp. 85–108). Chur, Switzerland: Harwood Academic Publishers.

Carmichael, D., Tackett-Gibson, M., Dell, O. et al. (1998). *Texas Dual Diagnosis Project Evaluation Report, 1997–1998*. College Station, Texas, Texas A&M University, Public Policy Research Institute.

Caton, C.L.M. (1981). The new chronic patient and the system of community care. *Hospital and Community Psychiatry, 32*, 475–478.

Caton, C.L.M., Shrout, P.E., Eagle, P.F., Opler, L.A., Felix, A., & Dominguez, B. (1994). Risk factors for homelessness among schizophrenic men: A case control study. *American Journal of Public Health, 84*, 265–270.

Compton, W.M., Cottler, L.B., Ben-Abdallah, A., Cunningham-Williams, R., & Spitznagel, E.L. (2000). The effects of psychiatric comorbidity on response to an HIV prevention intervention. *Drug and Alcohol Dependence, 58(3)*, 247–257.

Cook, J.A., Toprac, M., & Shore, S.E. (2004). Combining evidence-based practice with stakeholder consensus to enhance psychosocial rehabilitation services in the Texas Benefit Design Initiative. *Psychiatric Rehabilitation Journal, 27(4)*, 307–318.

Cuffel, B., Shumway, M., Chouljian, T., & Macdonald, T. (1994). A longitudinal study of substance use and community violence in schizophrenia. *Journal of Nervous Mental Disease, 182*, 704–708.

De Leon, G., Sacks, S., & Wexler, H.K. (2002). Modified prison therapeutic communities for the dual- and multiple- diagnosed offender. In C.G. Leukefeld & F. Tims (Eds.), *Treatment of drug offenders: Policies and issues*. New York, NY: Springer Publishing.

Dickey, B. & Azeni, H. (1996). Persons with dual diagnoses of substance abuse and major mental illness: Their excess costs of psychiatric care. *American Journal of Public Health, 87(7)*, 973–977.

Drake, R.E., Essock, S.M., Shaner, A., Carey, K.B., Minkoff, K., Kola, L., Lynde, D., Osher, F.C., Clark, R.E., Rickards, L. (2001). Implementing dual diagnosis services for clients with severe mental illness. *Psychiatric Services*, 52, 469–476

Drake, R.E., McHugo, G.J., Clark, R.E., et al. (1998). Assertive community treatment for patients with co-occurring severe mental illness and substance use disorder: A clinical trial. *American Journal of Orthopsychiatry 68*, 201–215.

Drake, R.E., McHugo, G., Noordsay, D.L. (1993). Treatment of alcoholism among schizophrenic outpatients: Four-year outcomes. *American Journal of Psychiatry, 150*, 328–329.

Drake, R.E., Mercer-McFadden, C., Mueser, K.T., et al (1998). Review of integrated health and substance abuse treatment for patients with dual disorders. *Schizophrenia Bulletin, 24*, 589–608.

Drake, R.E., Mueser, K.T., 2000. Psychosocial approaches to dual diagnosis. *Schizophrenia Bulletin, 26*, 105–118.

Drake, R.E., Mueser, K.T., Brunette, M.F., McHugo, G.J. (2004). A review of treatments for people with severe mental illnesses and co-occurring substance use disorders. *Psychiatric Rehabilitation Journal, 27*, 360–374.

Drake, R.E., Mueser, K.T., Clark, R.E., & Wallach, M.A. (1996). The course, treatment, and outcome of substance disorder in persons with severe mental illness. *American Journal of Orthopsychiatry, 66*, 42–51.

Drake, R.E., Yovetich, N.A., Bebout, R.R., et al. (1997). Integrated treatment for dually diagnosed homeless adults. *Journal of Nervous and Mental Disease, 18*, 298–305.

Godley, S.H., Hoewing-Roberson, R., Godley, M.D. (1994). *Final MISA Report*, Bloomington Lighthouse Institute.

Grant, B. (1997). The influence of comorbid major depression and substance use disorders on alcohol and drug treatment: Results of a national survey. In L. Onken, J. Blaine, S. Genser, & A. Horton, Jr. (Eds.), *Treatment of drug-dependent individuals with comorbid mental disorders* (NIDA Research Monograph 172, Publication No. 97-4172, pp. 4–15). Rockville, MD: National Institutes of Health.

Haywood, T.W., Kravitz, H.M., Grossman, L.S., Cavanaugh, J.L., Jr., Davis, J.M., & Lewis, D.A. (1995). Predicting the "revolving door" phenomenon among patients with schizophrenic, schizoaffective, and affective disorders. *American Journal of Psychiatry, 152*, 856–861.

Hellerstein, D.J., Rosenthal, R.N., Miner, C.R. (1985). A prospective study of integrated outpatient treatment for substance-abusing schizophrenic patients. *American Journal on Addictions 4*, 33–42.

Ho, A.P., Tsuang, J.W., Liberman, R.P., et al., 1999. Achieving effective treatment of patients with chronic psychotic illness and comorbid substance dependence. *American Journal of Psychiatry, 156*, 1765–1770.

Hulse, G.K., Tait, R.J. (2002). Six-month outcomes associated with a brief alcohol intervention for adult in-patients with psychiatric disorders. *Drug and Alcohol Review, 21*, 105–112.

James, W., Preston, N.J., Koh, G., Spencer, C., Kisely, S.R., & Castle, D.J. (2004) A group intervention which assists patients with dual diagnosis to reduce their drug use: A randomized controlled trial. *Psychological Medicine, 34*, 983–990.

Jerrell, J.M. & Ridgely, M.S. (1995). Comparative effectiveness of three approaches to serving people with severe mental illness and substance abuse disorders. *Journal of Nervous and Mental Disease 18*, 566–576.

Jerrell, J.M. & Ridgely, M.S. (1999). Impact of robustness of program implementation on outcomes of clients in dual diagnosis programs. *Psychiatric Services, 50*, 109–112.

Kessler, R.C., Nelson, C.B., McGonagle, K.A., Edlund, M.J., Frank, R.G., & Leaf, P.J. (1996). The epidemiology of co-occurring addictive and mental disorders: Implications for prevention and service utilization. *American Journal of Orthopsychiatry, 66*, 17–31.

Leshner, A. (1999). Drug abuse and mental disorders: Comorbidity is reality (Director's Column). *NIDA Notes, 14* (4), 1–3.

Lukens, E.P. & McFarlane, W.R. (2004). Psychoeducation as evidence-based practice: Considerations for practice, research, and policy. *Brief Treatment & Crisis Intervention, 4* (3), 205–225.

McHugo, G.J., Drake, R.E., Teague, G.B., Xie, H. (1999). Fidelity to assertive community treatment and client outcomes in the New Hampshire dual disorders study. *Psychiatric Services, 50*, 818–824.

Meisler, N., Blankertz, L., Santos, A., et al., 1997. Impact of assertive community treatment on homeless persons with co-occurring severe psychiatric and substance use disorders. *Community Mental Health Journal, 33*, 113–122.

Mercer-McFadden, C., Drake, R.E., Brown, N.B., et al (1997). The community support program demonstrations of services for young adults with severe mental illness and substance use disorders, 1987–1991. *Psychiatric Rehabilitation Journal 20(3)*, 13–24.

Mueser, K.T., Clinical interventions for severe mental illness and co-occurring substance use disorder. *Acta Neuropsychiatrica, 16*, 26–35.

Mueser, K.T., Bennett, M., & Kushner, M.G. (1995). Epidemiology of substance use disorders among persons with chronic mental illnesses. In A.F. Lehman & L.B. Dixon (Eds.), *Double jeopardy: Chronic mental illness and substance use disorders* (pp. 9–25). Chur, Switzerland: Harwood Academic Publishers.

Mueser, K.T., Yarnold, P.R., Levinson, D.F., Singh, H., Bellack, A.S., Kee, K., Morrison, R.L., & Yadalam, K.G. (1990). Prevalence of substance abuse in schizophrenia: Demographic and clinical correlates. *Schizophrenia Bulletin, 16*, 31–56.

Mueser, K.T., Yarnold, P.R., Rosenberg, S.D., Swett, C., Miles, K.M, & Hill, D. (2000). Substance use disorder in hospitalized severely mentally ill psychiatric patients: Prevalence, correlates, and subgroups. *Schizophrenia Bulletin, 26*, 179–192.

Mueser, K.T., Drake, R., & Miles, K. (1997). The course and treatment of substance use disorder in persons with severe mental illness. In L. Onken, J. Blaine, S. Genser, & A. Horton, Jr. (Eds.), *Treatment of drug-dependent individuals with comorbid mental disorders* (NIDA Research Monograph 172, Publication No. 97-4172, pp. 86–109). Rockville, MD: National Institutes of Health.

Mueser, K.T., Drake, R.E., Noorsdy, D.L. (2004). Integrated mental health and substance abuse treatment for severe psychiatric disorders. *Journal of Practical Psychiatry and Behavioral Health 4*, 129–139.

Mueser, K.T., Noorsdy, D.L., Drake, R.E., & Fox, L. (2003). *Integrated Treatment for Dual Disorders*. New York: Guilford Press.

Osher, F.C. & Kofoed, L.L. (1989). Treatment of patients with psychiatric and psychoactive substance use disorders. *Hospital and Community Psychiatry, 40*, 1025–1030.

Penn, P.E., Brooks, A.J. (2000). Five years, twelve steps, and REBT in the treatment of dual diagnosis. *Journal of Rational-Emotive and Cognitive-Behavioral Therapy, 18*, 197–208.

Pepper, B., Krishner, M.C., Ryglewicz, H. (1981). The young adult chronic patient:Overview of a population. *Hospital and Community Psychiatry, 32*, 463–469.

Prochaska, I.O., DiClemente, C.C. (1984). *The trans-theoretical approach: Crossing the traditional boundaries of therapy*. Homewood, IL: Dow-Jones/Irwin.

Regier, D.A., Farmer, M.E., Rae, D.S., Locke, B.Z., Keith, S.J., Judd, L.L., et al. (1990). Comorbidity of mental disorders with alcohol and other drug abuse. *Journal of the American Medical Association, 264*, 2511–2518.

Ridgely, M.S., Osher, F.C., Goldman, H.H., et al (1987). Executive Summary: *Chronic Mentally Ill young Adults with Substance Abuse Problems: A Review of Research, Treatment and Training Issues*. Baltimore: University of Maryland School of Medicine, Mental Health Services Research Center.

Ridgely, M.S., Goldman, H.H., & Willenbring, M. (1990). Barriers to the care of persons with dual diagnosis: Organization and financing issues. *Schizophrenia Bulletin, 16* (1), 123–132.

Roberts, L.J., Shaner, A., Eckman, T.A. (1999). *Overcoming addictions: Skills training for people with schizophrenia*. New York: Norton.

Rosenberg, S.D., Goodman, L.A., Osher, F.C., Swartz, M.S., Essock, S.M., Butterfield, M.I., et al. (2001). Prevalence of HIV, Hepatitis B and Hepatitis C in people with severe mental illness. *American Journal of Public Health, 91* (1), 31–37.

Sacks, S. (2000). Co-occurring mental and substance use disorders: Promising approaches and research issues. *Substance Use and Misuse, 35* (12–14), 2061–2093.

SAMHSA (2002). *Report to Congress on the prevention and treatment of co-occurring substance abuse disorders and mental disorders*. Rockville, MD: Substance Abuse and Mental Health Services Administration.

Singer, M.I., Kennedy, M., Kola, L. (1998). A conceptual model for co-occurring mental and substance-related disorders. *Alcoholism Treatment Quarterly, 16* (4), 75–89.

Steadman, H.J., Mulvey, E.P., Monahan, J., Robbins, P.C., Appelbaum, P.S., Grisso, T., et al. (1998). Violence by people discharged from acute psychiatric inpatient facilities and by others in the same neighborhoods. *Archives of General Psychiatry, 55 (5)*, 393–401.

Swanson, A.J., Pantalon, M.V., Cohen, K.R. (1999). Motivational interviewing and treatment adherence among psychiatric and dually diagnosed patients. *Journal of Nervous and Mental Disease, 187*, 630–635.

Swofford, C., Kasckow, J., Scheller-Gilkey, G., & Inderbitzin, L.B. (1996). Substance use: A powerful predictor of relapse in schizophrenia. *Schizophrenia Research, 20*, 145–151.

7

PUTTING VALUES INTO PRACTICE:
Involuntary Treatment Interventions in Mental Health

MELISSA FLOYD TAYLOR

Because of the nature of mental illness and the potential for individuals' insight into their illness to wax and wane, involuntary interventions have evolved to provide treatment to clients when they may not want treatment. Involuntary treatment can be defined as "mandated services, both inpatient and outpatient, that are provided to consumers, often despite their wishes to the contrary" (Taylor, 2002, p. 56). This chapter will outline different types of involuntary treatment for mental health clients in this country and explore value issues and social work roles. Recent developments in community mental health treatment, such as the advent and greater implementation of "assisted" outpatient treatment models, will be highlighted. Finally, possible future scenarios for a social work involvement in involuntary treatment interventions are offered.

Dennis and Monahan's (1996) *Coercion and Aggressive Community Treatment: A New Frontier in Mental Health Law* is an impressive compilation of information about coercive mental health treatment. The editors identify four similar themes that emerge in their contributors' writings that are instructive in the current exploration of involuntary interventions (Dennis & Monahan, 1996, pp. 8–9):

- The need perceived by mental service providers to sometimes resort to coercive tactics to sustain people with mental disorders in the community.
- The *angst and ambivalence* engendered in these providers when they see no viable alternatives to using coercion — since they recognize it has the potential for great abuse.
- The importance of the process by which interventions are coercively imposed.
- Coercion is used when other resources are unavailable and could be avoided if they became more available.

While many social work interventions can be complex with multidimensional ethical implications, interventions characterized as involuntary may prove to be especially problematic, as well as controversial, for social workers in mental health since involuntary treatment interventions impact one of social work's most treasured values — self-determination. This impact has led to social work and allied authors (Taylor & Bentley, 2005; Bentley & Taylor, 2002; Dewees, 2002; Kutchins & Kirk, 1997; Bentley, 1993) pointing out the potential conflict between some involuntary treatment interventions and social work's historical stance and current Code of Ethics, which allows for restriction of self-determination only when risk is "foreseeable and imminent" (NASW, 1997). Other social work writers strongly disagree with this perceived incompatibility between social work values and involuntary or beneficent treatment interventions (Murdach, 1996; Rosenson, 1993) and cite the consumers' *right to treatment* as an important area for social work support, not just the *right to refuse treatment* (Mizrahi, 1992). A third position points out that taking for and against positions in this debate distracts the mental health community from more important questions about the state of service delivery in the mental health arena (Saks, 2002).

Opinions aside, for many mental health practitioners, using coercive and involuntary treatments has become a familiar part of their social work responsibilities. These practitioners may regularly hospitalize consumers under involuntary orders or facilitate court orders for medication and outpatient treatment. At the very least, many practitioners are increasingly faced with negotiating difficult practice decisions with consumers who present for treatment under court mandate in ways that maximize their autonomy. Therefore, whether an individual practitioner believes involuntary treatment is just or unjust, knowledge of the types of treatment available, as well as the social work roles and values inherent in each, is important.

Accordingly, this chapter will not debate the merits of each type of treatment as such, but will deal with the "reality" of involuntary intervention at this time in our mental health landscape. Additionally, in the exploration of values inherent in the types of involuntary interventions, it should be kept in mind that while social work as a whole has a generally agreed upon set of values exemplified in our Code of Ethics (NASW, 1997), value conflicts exist primarily in the eye of the beholder in individual situations. Therefore, no two social workers will see a value-laden situation in the same way. For this reason, the exposition of values is meant to be an exploration only, not a defining statement.

TYPES OF INVOLUNTARY TREATMENT: PROTECTIVE HOLDS TO MANDATED OUTPATIENT

The types of involuntary treatment most in use in this country for people with serious mental illness are explored below. It should be noted that terminology may differ from state to state. Additionally, court orders for counseling in situations such as drunk driving and domestic violence are not included, as the focus here is on services for persons with serious mental illness. For most types of involuntary treatment, the value issues consist of tensions between autonomy or self-determination and paternalism. Taken another way, it is difficult, if not impossible, to maximize personal liberty while at the same time ensuring the greatest community safety. While an ideal society attempts to do both, the two concepts are in some degree mutually exclusive, which is why some citizens are detained, committed, and monitored if they pose a threat to their community. Mental health intervention is no different; value decisions in practice (on both individual client and larger mental health policy levels) often consist of a daunting balancing act between maintaining personal liberty and ensuring community safety. The traditional criteria for mandated treatment is called dangerousness criteria and have governed mental health interventions since the deinstitutionalization era (Torrey & Zdanowicz, 1999). This dangerousness standard is analogous to

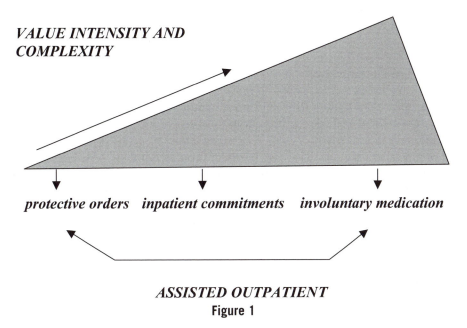

ASSISTED OUTPATIENT
Figure 1

maximizing personal liberty. Critics of the dangerousness criteria have called for a change to need for treatment criteria, already existing in some states (Torrey & Zdanowicz, 1999), which would be similar to ensuring the greatest community safety. So while most value issues in involuntary treatment can be boiled down to these two issues (liberty vs. community or self-determination vs. paternalism), this chapter attempts to explore the *intensity* of these value issues involved in each of the involuntary interventions (Figure 1).

Protective Holds

A protective hold is called by many names, which vary from state to state, such as temporary detention order, green warrants, 72-hour hold, and protective order. It is generally understood as a detention order that forces a person to be evaluated on an inpatient basis for a certain period, usually not exceeding three days. Usually persons are detained based on the judgment by a mental health professional (often social workers) that they are an imminent danger to themselves or others or substantially unable to care for themselves due to their mental illness. The detainee is held and evaluated for a period and then a civil commitment hearing takes place, in which the person may be released, committed, or allowed to voluntarily commit himself or herself.

Value Issues

As far as types of involuntary treatment go, protective holds may be one of the least controversial. This is, in part, due to the standard of "imminent danger" that most of these state provisions include. Indeed, social workers have a parallel standard embedded in the National Association of Social Workers (NASW) Code of Ethics that allows for the restriction of self-determination when danger is "imminent and foreseeable" (NASW, 1997). Additionally, while the period involved could seem very long to a person who believes he or she is being held unjustly, a time limit of 24 to 72 hours may seem, to the professionals involved, a small price to pay in guaranteeing continued safety of the client and community. The main social work values involved in protective holds, self-determination and the right of individuals and communities to be safe, therefore have a low level of intensity and complexity.

Social Worker Roles

Social workers could be involved in protective holds in several ways. A typical social worker role in protective holds would be as the *initiator* of the process. This may occur when a social worker perceives that a client is in imminent danger of harming himself or herself or others and the client will not willingly admit himself or herself into a secure psychiatric unit. Additionally, social workers may be the *facilitators* of protective orders in that as a member of a local crisis team, they may perform the actual mental health assessment that indicates the necessity for a protective order. They may also provide education to families who wish to initiate protective orders for a member who is showing signs of acute mental illness. An additional social worker role in the area of protective holds would be as psychiatric unit staff, who work with clients while they are under such a hold and facilitate their release and discharge plans, their commitment and treatment plan, or their commitment and transfer to another facility.

Inpatient Commitments

After an individual is detained and evaluated for the period allowed for by the protective order, he or she then has the right to a commitment hearing, which is a civil process involving a judge or special justice, a representative for the committing doctor or institution, legal representation for the client, and the client himself or herself, along with any family members. At the end of the hearing, which may take place on the unit or at a local courthouse, the client is either (1) released with or without a commitment to outpatient, (2) committed to the facility, (3) committed to another facility, or (4) allowed to voluntarily commit to the facility. There is generally a period attached to the commitment; for example, a commitment to an acute care psychiatric unit may last for 7 to 10 days or up to 30, whereas a commitment to a state institution may allow for a greater length of time. Generally, the treating psychiatrist can release a client at any time when he or she is under a commitment. The commitment also does not allow for involuntary medication in and of itself; involuntary medication can be granted with a separate proceeding.

Value Issues

While the social work value of self-determination is again implicated in commitment proceedings, it is to a higher intensity than in protective holds. This is due to the fact that commitments may last a longer period and may tend to "follow" a person, in that it becomes part of his or her history and may impact on his or her ability to own a gun in some states, for example. Additionally, clients are not generally allowed to choose the facility they wish to be committed to; the facility itself must be "willing" to treat them, a choice that may be influenced by the type or presence of health insurance. In other words, a client without insurance who needs additional inpatient days may be committed to a state psychiatric facility. Because clients are not allowed to leave the hospital until their psychiatrist releases them from the commitment, their ability to work, spend time with their family, and generally pursue their own happiness is restricted by the commitment. All of these factors may give the social workers involved in the process pause, especially as they may occur in the absence (unlike during the protective order process) of imminent and foreseeable risk. Instead, the client who is committed may enter the hospital as a danger to self or others but be committed at a time when he or she is *not imminently dangerous but still in need of treatment.* Social workers who are comfortable with requiring treatment with this criteria may find commitment consistent with their personal values and philosophy, while those who believe liberty should be restricted only during dangerousness may find the process dissonant with their own values (Taylor & Bentley, 2005). Therefore, inpatient commitment presents a moderate level of value intensity and complexity.

Social Worker Roles

Social worker roles in commitment are similar to those involved in protective orders. Hospital social workers may be responsible for contacting interested parties such as family members, independent evaluators, lawyers, and judges about the time and place of hearings. They may also act as witnesses in the proceedings, most generally as representatives of the psychiatrist or the hospital. This representation again has the potential for conflict for social workers, since their opinion regarding the need for commitment may differ from the psychiatrists'.

Involuntary Inpatient Medication

While persons committed to the hospital are not allowed to leave, they still have the right to refuse medication unless they become acutely dangerous to self or others (physically abusive to staff, actively trying to hurt themselves) or are placed under a court order for some type of treatment. The treatment most frequently is medication, but may also include electroconvulsive therapy (ECT). The order for involuntary medication is obtained in a similar way to a commitment, but may require more in-depth paperwork, completed by the treating psychiatrist detailing the type of treatment requested of the court. If the court does order treatment as a result of this proceeding, an individual client can be forced to take medication, often in an injectable, long-lasting form, such as an injection of a decanoate neuroleptic.

Values Issues

Because the order to treat is probably one of the most restrictive types of involuntary treatment, the value issues it raises are more intense and complex than in the case of protective orders and commitments. For example, not only is a person's freedom of movement curtailed when he or she is committed to a hospital, but in a medication order his or her actual *person* is subject to contact with an (at least initially) unwanted (possibly long-term hazardous) substance. For this reason, self-determination and issues of freedom may come into conflict with actual job responsibilities for social workers in these cases. Additionally, social workers involved in the order to treat process may feel differently about different clients. For example, a client who is floridly psychotic and refusing medications may feel less problematic for a social worker than a client who has bipolar disorder and is manic but refusing medications with a more "logical" argument.

Social Worker Roles

While social workers cannot order medication for the client faced with an order to treat, nor actually administer the medication or other treatment, they may still be in the position of advocating for the order on behalf of the hospital psychiatrist, being a witness in the proceeding and explaining the process to both the client and interested significant others. For the social worker who has qualms about requiring clients to take medications — many of which have significant side effects and may or may not be the long-acting variety — this may present conflict with the social worker's view of his or her role as an advocate for the client's *wishes*. For others, the role feels consistent with their view of their role as advocate for the client's *best interests*.

Mandated Outpatient Commitment

Outpatient commitment is generally thought to be a "legal strategy that utilizes court orders and other means to force individuals with psychiatric disabilities to participate in mandatory treatment" (Bazelon Center, 2004). In fact, a whole constellation of services that can be classified as involuntary exist (Monahan et al., 2001), including representative payees and housing tied to treatment compliance. Additionally, some may characterize assertive community treatment programs as a type of involuntary outpatient intervention, as they tend to target reluctant clients who are often in and out of psychiatric facilities. Programs, such as the one New York's Kendra's Law provides for, which are called anything from mandated outpatient to outpatient commitment to assisted outpatient, are being increasingly touted as a remedy for the problem of the treatment-reluctant mental health consumer. Florida recently became the 42nd state in the United States to authorize assisted outpatient treatment (Treatment Advocacy Center, 2004). As it is a fairly new implementation of involuntary treatment, mandated outpatient services will be discussed here in greater detail.

In mandated outpatient laws such as Kendra's Law, all of the types of involuntary treatment discussed so far may be included. For example, persons with mental illness must comply with a medication regime similar to an order to treat; if they do not, they may be detained by way of a protective order and then committed to a mental health facility (Moran, 2000). Generally, the affected client is found to be in *need* of treatment by the court based, as in Kendra's Law, on the following criteria (Bazelon Center, 2004):

- A prediction that an individual may become violent at an indefinite time in the future
- Supposed "lack of insight" on the part of the individual, which is often no more than disagreement with the treating professional
- The potential for deterioration in the individual's condition or mental status without treatment
- An assessment that the individual is "gravely disabled"

These *need of treatment criteria* are a departure from the standard for inpatient commitment based on *imminent danger to self and others* and have been quite alarming for those stakeholders who see them as a treatment-expanding addition to mental health intervention based on vague, shades-of-gray language that justifies liberty-limiting mental health treatment (Bazelon Center, 2004; Manisses Communications Group, 2001; Moran, 2000). On the other hand, for those who advocate for the *right to treatment* superceding the *right to refuse treatment* for individuals who need treatment, laws like Kendra's Law are a step in the right direction.

Values Issues

Mandated or assisted outpatient involves all of the value issues present in other interventions because it can include all of these interventions; however, the value issues can be even more intense and complex in this form of involuntary treatment. For example, curtailment of freedom while persons are in a mental hospital is one thing, but to continue to require the persons to comply with a treatment plan after they are on "their own time" may strike some social workers as more of *mental health "parole"* than outpatient treatment. Other social workers may see the client who is subject to outpatient commitment as benefiting from *increased self-determination*, since he or she is able to maintain in the community instead of in a hospital setting. For these reasons, the complexity and intensity of values issues in involuntary outpatient commitments very much depend on the individual social worker's perspective of whether or not community orders are less restrictive than inpatient hospitalization (Davis, 2002). Not surprisingly, the value issues involved in involuntary treatment are currently being hashed out in a lively debate in the social work and allied press (Bentley & Taylor, 2002; Torrey & Zdanowicz, 2002).

Social Worker Roles

Social workers in community agencies may be in the position with involuntary outpatient treatment to *monitor client adherence* to treatment regimens in their roles as case managers, members of street or mobile teams, or assertive community treatment workers. In the event that a client is not adhering to his or her treatment plan, as evidenced by failure to show up for medication, appointments, or drug screens, social workers may then be in the position to *enforce* outpatient commitment by initiating protective orders or referring the client to a higher authority. In laws like Kendra's Law, social workers may also *initiate* involuntary outpatient proceedings for clients who they feel are in need of this type of intervention. In another type of community-based involuntary treatment, the use of representative payees, social workers may link clients to payees and serve as liaisons between the two.

SOCIAL WORKERS AND INVOLUNTARY TREATMENT: THE FUTURE

The competing tensions between liberty or personal choice and community safety dictate the episodic waxing and waning of mental health treatment in this country. At the current time, there has been a call for expansion of alternatives for treatment-reluctant mental health consumers, which may be in reaction to several high-profile events in which a person with mental illness committed a crime (e.g., Kendra Webb's murder in New York, Andrea Yeats, etc.). Waning interventions, on the other hand, may occur in reaction to attempts at reforming interventions that do not meet the "least restrictive" requirement for mental health interventions. An example of this can be seen in the deinstitutionalization era. Faced as we are with an era of generally expanding community interventions for persons with mental illness, as social workers, with an interest in protecting self-determination if at all possible, we are motivated to choose alternatives that can be client choice expanding. In this way, social workers can carve out a new role for themselves with involuntary treatment interventions — that of *innovator*. Indeed, literature exists already on some of these alternatives or additions to traditional mandated treatment, including proxy decision making, also called advanced mental health directives or psychiatric living wills (Bazelon Center, 2004; Rosenson & Kasten, 1991).

Advanced mental health directives have been offered as an alternative to traditional involuntary treatment. Called "one of the more promising innovations to give patients greater voice in their psychiatric treatment" (Appelbaum, 2004), practice benefits of advanced directives include:

- Promote individual autonomy and empowerment in the recovery from mental illness
- Enhance communication between individuals and their families, friends, health care providers, and other professionals
- Protect individuals from being subjected to ineffective, unwanted, or possibly harmful treatments or actions

- Help in preventing crises and the resulting use of involuntary treatment or safety interventions, such as restraint or seclusion (National Mental Health Association, 2004)

CONCLUSION

As Dennis and Monahan (1996) point out, involuntary treatment has been with us in one form or another for centuries, and it shows no signs of going anywhere. It is therefore essential that social workers have a working knowledge of the types of involuntary treatments in order to inform practitioner and agency response. This knowledge and experience are especially important when considering policy issues that dictate future types of treatment that can reflect creative, choice-expanding alternatives to traditional involuntary treatment interventions.

Beyond simply having knowledge about involuntary treatment interventions, it is important for social workers to also be able to articulate and dialogue about the value issues that are stirred in situations where involuntary treatments are utilized. Being subjected long term to situations that may feel uncomfortable for social workers due to the mismatch between job duties and personal or professional values may lead social workers to experience "professional dissonance" or a negative feeling of conflict and ambivalence (Taylor & Bentley, 2005). As such negative feelings can accrue over time and possibly lead to burnout, it is imperative that social workers have an outlet in the workplace to discuss the individual issues that arise in involuntary treatment deliberations. Supervision and peer support have been affirmed by seasoned social workers as ways of dealing with professional dissonance (Taylor & Bentley, 2005). More research on social workers and involuntary treatment is needed, beyond the opinion pieces we have thus far relied on.

Finally, as involuntary treatment interventions are subjected to efficacy studies, more information about their utility will be available for social workers when deciding on an intervention. For this reason, more studies of the effectiveness of involuntary interventions need to be done, in particular, further studies of outpatient commitment, which until this point have been fairly inconclusive (Manisses Communications Group, 2001; Bazelon Center, 2004). Additionally, studies about involuntary treatment that specifically seek out the voices and opinions of clients who have been under this type of treatment are essential to developing a client-centered understanding of involuntary treatment for practitioners. While some studies have been done in this area, particularly on client feelings after involuntary medication (Wynn, 2004; Schwartz, Vingiano, & Perez, 1988), more studies on all forms of involuntary treatment, from the client perspective, are needed.

REFERENCES

Appelbaum, P.S. (2004). Psychiatric advanced directives and the treatment of committed patients. *Psychiatric Services*. Retrieved November 5, 2004, from http://www.namiscc.org/Advocacy/2004/Fall/PsychiatricAdvanceDirectives.htm

Bazelon Center. (2004). Position on Outpatient Commitment of the New York Association of Psychiatric Rehabilitation Services (NYAPRS). Retrieved on November 4, 2004, from http://www.bazelon.org/issues/commitment/positionstatement.htm

Bentley, K.J. (1993). The right of psychiatric patients to refuse medications: where should social workers stand? *Social Work*, *38*, 101–106.

Bentley, K.J. & Taylor, M.F. (2002). Assisted outpatient treatment/commitment: a step forward or backward for mental health systems and clients? In H.J. Karger & J. Midgeley (Eds.), *Controversial issues in social policy* (2nd ed., pp. 187–199). Boston: Allyn and Bacon.

Davis, S. (2002). Brief report: autonomy v. coercion: reconciling competing perspectives in community mental health. *Community Mental Health Journal*, *38*, 239–250.

Dennis, D.L. & Monahan, J. (Eds.). (1996). *Coercion and aggressive community treatment: a new frontier in mental health law*. New York: Plenum Press.

Dewees, M. (2002). Contested landscape: the role of critical dialogue for social workers in mental health practice. *The Journal of Progressive Human Services, 13*, 73–91.

Kutchins, H. & Kirk, S.A. (1997). *Making us crazy: DSM: The psychiatric bible and the creation of mental disorders*. New York: Free Press.

Manisses Communications Group, Inc. (2001). Study: court-ordered care alone doesn't yield better outcomes. *Mental Health Weekly, 11*, 3.

Mizrahi, T. (1992). The right to treatment and the treatment of mentally ill people. *Health and Social Work, 17*, 7–12.

Monahan, J., Bonnie, R.J., Appelbaum, P.S., Hyde, P.S., Steadman, H.J., & Swartz, M.S. (2001). Mandated community treatment: beyond outpatient commitment. *Developments in Mental Health Law, 21*, 1–18.

Moran, M. (2000). Coercion or caring? *American Medical News, 43*, 26–31.

Murdach, A.D. (1996). Beneficence re-examined: protective intervention in mental health. *Social Work, 41*, 26–31.

National Association of Social Workers (NASW). (1997). *Code of ethics*. Washington, DC: Author.

National Association of Social Workers (NASW). (2004). *General fact sheets: social work profession*. Retrieved on November 12, 2004, from http://www.naswdc.org/pressroom/features/general/profession.asp

National Mental Health Association. (2004). *NMHA policy position statement: psychiatric advance directives*. Retrieved on November 5, 2004, from http://www.nmha.org/position/advancedirectives.cfm

Rosenson, M.K. (1993). Social work and the right of psychiatric patients to refuse medication: a family advocate's response [Point and Viewpoint]. *Social Work, 38*, 107–112.

Rosenson, M.K. & Kasten, A.M. (1991). Another view of autonomy: arranging for consent in advance. *Schizophrenia Bulletin, 17*, 1–7.

Saks, E. (2002). *Forced treatment and the rights of the mentally ill*. Chicago: University of Chicago Press.

Schwartz, H.I., Vingiano, W., & Perez, C.G. (1988). Autonomy and the right to refuse treatment: patient's attitudes after involuntary medication. *Hospital and Community Psychiatry, 39*, 1049–1054.

Taylor, M.F. (2002). Professional dissonance among social workers: the collision between values and job tasks in mental health practice (doctoral dissertation, Virginia Commonwealth University). *Dissertation Abstracts International, 63*, 2000.

Taylor, M.F. & Bentley, K.J. (2005). Professional dissonance among social workers: the collision between values and job tasks in mental health practice. *Community Mental Health Journal, 41*, 469–480.

Torrey, E.F. & Zdanowicz, M. (1999). Hope for cities dealing with the mental illness crisis. *Nation's Cities Weekly, 22*, 2–3.

Torrey, E.F. & Zdanowicz, M. (2002). Assisted outpatient treatment/commitment: a step forward or backward for mental health systems and clients? In H.J. Karger & J. Midgeley (Eds.), *Controversial issues in social policy* (2nd ed., pp. 179–186). Boston: Allyn and Bacon.

Treatment Advocacy Center. (2004). Breaking News: New Law in Florida. Retrieved on November 5, 2004, from www.psychlaws.org

Wynn, R. (2004). Psychiatric inpatients' experiences with restraint. *Journal of Forensic Psychiatry and Psychology, 15*, 124–145.

8

NEUROPSYCHIATRIC PERSPECTIVES FOR COMMUNITY MENTAL HEALTH THEORY AND PRACTICE

WILLIAM H. WILSON

INTRODUCTION

This chapter explores the contribution of modern neuropsychiatry and psychopharmacology to community mental health theory and practice. Over the past 50 years there has been an explosion of scientific knowledge regarding the brain and the development of effective medical treatments for many symptoms of "mental illness." Together, these two factors transformed the basic understanding of the cause of mental illness and spurred the development of biologically-based psychiatric treatments. In 1950, there was little knowledge of the brain's role in mental illnesses such as schizophrenia and bipolar affective disorder. Psychological theories abounded, and little credence was given to the notion that these disorders could be based on problems with brain function. However, by the end of the decade, new medications reduced schizophrenic hallucinations, alleviated depression, and reduced mood swings. Each medication was chemically unique and treated only a particular set of mental symptoms. Clearly there was some biological basis to these disorders if medications could treat their symptoms.

The success of the early medications drove research into more effective medicines. Technological advances in brain imaging, molecular genetics, and cell biology have led to sophisticated, yet still partial, understanding of the neurological basis of major psychiatric disorders, and to the development of increasingly efficacious medications. "Mental illnesses," more accurately referred to as "psychiatric disorders" or "neuropsychiatric disorders," are now best conceptualized as long-standing disorders in brain function, caused by both genetic and environmental factors. Environmental factors are both physical and psycho/social. Biomedically- and socially-based treatments have been proven to improve brain function.

Current perspectives in biological psychiatry examine the way that a brain grows and adapts to its environment. Genetics clearly affects the way that this occurs; however, experience and interaction with the world have a marked impact on the brain's development.

There is no longer a sharp distinction between "nature" and "nurture," but rather a continuing give and take, between brain structure and function and the experience of being in the world. A dramatic example of the brain's ability to change occurs with Post Traumatic Stress Disorder (PTSD), which causes changes in brain structure and functioning.

> Neuroimaging studies have demonstrated significant neurobiologic changes in PTSD. There appear to be 3 areas of the brain that are different in patients with PTSD compared with those in control subjects: the hippocampus, the amygdala, and the medial frontal cortex. The amygdala appears to be hyperreactive to trauma-related stimuli. The hallmark symptoms of PTSD, including exaggerated startle response and flashbacks, may be related to a failure of higher brain regions (i.e., the hippocampus and the medial frontal cortex) to dampen the exaggerated symptoms of arousal and distress that are mediated through the amygdala in response to reminders of the traumatic event.

Nutt & Malizia, 2004

There is growing recognition of the influence of positive social experience in healthy brain development and in the treatment of neuropsychiatric disorders. This acceptance that brain change is affected by experience as well as by genetics cuts through the empty rhetoric that pits psychological theories and treatments against biological ones. A perspective of brain plasticity based on genetics and environment allows for a realistic, comprehensive, and hopeful view of neuropsychiatric disorders (Neugenboren, 1999).

As with all types of medical care, the success of neuropsychiatric treatment depends not only on science, but also on the social context in which care is delivered, and the values of the people giving and receiving that care. Thus, to understand the impact of neuropsychiatry upon the community, economics, ethnicity, gender, and consumer empowerment must be considered along with notions of brain structure and the molecular biology of the nervous system. When used in the context of adequate social support and culturally sensitive, person-centered services, neuropsychiatry provides powerful tools to allow individuals with mental illnesses to live more stable, fulfilling lives. In the absence of such values, neuropsychiatric explanations may be used to discredit the perspectives of people who receive care and to inappropriately divert funding of essential psychological care and social supports to the purchase of medication. Clearly, an understanding of neuropsychiatric disorders and pharmacotherapy is essential for any provider of community mental health care, and for administrators of community mental health services.

In this chapter, recipients of care for neuropsychiatric disorders will at times be referred to as *patients*. The word *patient*, however, describes a person only insofar as he or she is receiving a medical service. The word should not be used as a comprehensive descriptor of the person outside of that medical relationship. The patient in the medical relationship is also likely to be a "client" of other service providers, a "consumer" of various services, a son or daughter, a spouse, a student, or an employee. The chapter references include sources of reliable information for general readers as well as more advanced sources for readers who have a background in biology and medicine. Online references are included in addition to texts and journals that should be readily available through public and academic libraries.

WHAT IS A NEUROPSYCHIATRIC DISORDER?

A basic assumption of neuropsychiatry is that problems in brain structure and function give rise to disturbances of thought, emotion, and behavior. A corollary is that treatment will be most effective if it is directed toward this specific brain malfunction. Thus, a key activity of biological psychiatry has been to parse the large historical category of "madness" or "insanity" into discrete syndromes on the basis of symptoms, age of onset, course of the illness, and similar factors. In psychiatry, as in other branches of medicine, the description of a syndrome is followed by a scientific search for the cause of the disorder, the associated physiological abnormalities, and the means to ameliorate the symptoms and, less often, to cure the illness. A giant step in classification was taken at the beginning of the 20th century, when the German psychiatrist Emil Kraepelen distinguished the syndrome we now call *schizophrenia* from what we term *bipolar affective disorder*. More recent research has shown that these disorders do in fact differ in response to medications, genetics, and a variety of aspects of brain function.

When the cause of a "mental illness" has been adequately traced to a physical process in the brain, that illness comes to be considered "physical" rather than "mental," although the symptoms and duration of the illness are, of course, unchanged and psychiatric intervention may be necessary. Examples of this change in diagnosis from mental to physical illness include epilepsy, psychosis related to syphilis, and psychosis related to thyroid dysfunction. Research regarding the physical basis of major psychiatric disorders such as schizophrenia and bipolar disorder has convinced the medical community to regard these illnesses as physical. Nonetheless, insurance companies, the government, and the public continue to regard these illnesses as mental.

The "official" definitions of psychiatric syndromes are articulated, and periodically updated, by the American Psychiatric Association in its *Diagnostic and Statistical Manual* (DSM). The current version is the fourth edition, with text revision — the DSM-IV-TR (American Psychiatric Association, 2000). Classification in the DSM-IV-TR relies, for the most part, on descriptions of symptoms and natural history of the illness. The upcoming revision, DSM-V, is scheduled for publication in 2010 and is expected to place more emphasis on measurable biological factors, such as gene expression and findings of various types of brain imaging (Charney, Barlow, et al., 2002).

PRINCIPLES OF PSYCHOPHARMACOLOGY

The effects of psychiatric medication on thought, experience, and behavior result from the medication's ability to modulate the activity of nerve cells in the brain (Stahl, 2000). Nerve cells communicate with each other by releasing chemicals (neurotransmitters) into the specialized junctions between cells (synapses). The chemical message is received when the neurotransmitter attaches to a specific receptor on the next nerve cell, changing the shape of the receptor and thereby turning on a cascade of chemical processes within the cell. Alternatively, a neurotransmitter may cause another type of receptor to open or close a channel through which electrically charged particles can move in and out of the cell, altering the cell's likelihood of sending on an electrochemical message to other cells.

Many psychiatric medications either inhibit or boost the action of particular neurotransmitters. The brain disturbance in most psychiatric disorders is more than a simple overabundance or absence of a certain neurotransmitter. Nonetheless, manipulation of neurotransmitter effects has been helpful in many disorders by stimulating or depressing the overall activity of some parts of the brain. Most medications affect the monoamine neurotransmitters (dopamine, norepinephrine, and serotonin). These small molecules are found in bundles (tracts) of nerves that run from the brain stem (where the brain meets the spinal cord) to structures throughout the brain. These nerve bundles, or tracts, can be thought of as "volume controls" for the different parts of the brain. Release of neurotransmitter molecules increases or decreases the activity level of nerve cells in the areas they innervate. The therapeutic effects of some medications are immediately evident. More often, symptomatic improvement accrues gradually, over weeks or months, as the brain slowly adjusts to changes in neurotransmission.

The classes of psychiatric medications (antipsychotics, antidepressants, mood stabilizers, and the like) are named for the clinical action that is most pronounced or that was first studied. Many medications have broader clinical utility than their name implies. The mechanism of action and uses of each of the main groups of psychiatric medications are discussed below. Readers are encouraged to consult the references given in this section for a more thorough discussion of this subject.

SPECIFIC DISORDERS AND PHARMACOLOGICAL TREATMENTS

The DSM-IV-TR groups neuropsychiatric syndromes into psychotic disorders, mood disorders, anxiety disorders, personality disorders, and dementias, along with several other categories that have less relevance to community mental health. Any of these types of disorders may be complicated by concurrent substance abuse. This section reviews the features and treatments of the most prevalent disorders. More thorough descriptions of these and other disorders and their treatment are available on the Web Site of the National Alliance on Mental Illness (www.nami.org). Full discussion may be found in standard psychiatric textbooks (Hales & Yudofsky, 2002; Pliszka, 2003; Schatzberg & Nemeroff, 2004; Stahl, 2000, 2004). The descriptions that follow are drawn from these sources. The following sections describe the disorders that are most likely to be encountered in community mental health practice, emphasizing the interplay of brain function, behavior, and neuropsychiatric treatment.

Psychotic Disorders

Psychotic disorders are conditions in which the characteristic symptoms involve abnormal sensory experiences along with unrealistic and disorganized thought processes. By far the most common psychotic disorder is schizophrenia, a devastating illness found in approximately one percent of the population worldwide (Freedman, 2003). Individuals with schizophrenia usually have rather unremarkable childhoods, although in retrospect they may seem awkward or odd in comparison with unaffected siblings. Characteristic symptoms are auditory hallucinations (hearing voices that others do not), delusions, and disorganized thought and behavior, which usually emerge in late adolescence or early adulthood, following some months of decline in social role performance. If these symptoms are fully present for six or more months, the duration of the illness is likely to be lifelong.

No single neurological abnormality explains schizophrenia. Rather, there are diffuse problems in a number of brain areas that generate problems in the communication networks among brain regions that are responsible for normal sensory processing and cognition. There tends to be an overall decrease in the amount of brain tissue, and often nerve cells are not ordered properly within the cerebral cortex. The causes of these abnormalities are also multifactorial, sometimes indicating faulty fetal development as well as degenerative changes in adolescence. Schizophrenia has a clear genetic component. Several genes that are involved in the development and maintenance of neuronal function have been implicated. Having only one of the genes is unlikely to lead to illness. However, having several of these genes makes illness more likely by making the brain more vulnerable to damage by environmental factors such as maternal viral infection, birth complications, or perhaps physiological stressors later in life. The combination of genetic vulnerability and physiological stress leads to manifestation of the illness.

Treatment of schizophrenia is designed to relieve symptoms and restore normal social function. Antipsychotic medications are the mainstay of biological treatment, along with social support and comprehensive psychiatric rehabilitation. With proper treatment and social support, many people with schizophrenia are able to make a substantial recovery. Too often, however, few resources for treatment and social support are available, leading to repeated hospitalization and poor social functioning. The first generation of antipsychotic medications (typical antipsychotics) became available in the 1950s and are reasonably effective in decreasing hallucinations and delusions, but people tended to dislike the side effects. These medications interfere with motor system functioning, causing tremors, muscle stiffness (pseudo-parkinsonism), and muscle cramps (acute dystonia). If taken for months or years, as is usually necessary, there is a high likelihood of developing disfiguring and disabling muscle tics and writhing movements, known as tardive dyskinesia. Patients often complain of feeling mentally dull or uncreative. The newer generation of antipsychotic medications (atypical antipsychotics) are largely free of these side effects. They also appear to minimize apathy, social withdrawal, and cognitive deficits, such as problems with remembering, planning, and sequencing.

Some of the newer medications (particularly olanzapine and clozapine) are likely to cause weight gain that can lead to diabetes and problems with high levels of cholesterol and fat in the blood (American Diabetes Association, 2004). Together these factors increase the risk for heart disease and stroke, and require diet and exercise regimens along with medical care. Taking medications that do not cause these metabolic side effects can minimize the problem. If it is necessary to use the medications that cause these side effects, patients should be carefully monitored and receive treatment for them should they occur.

Antipsychotic medications reduce symptoms during acute episodes of psychosis. If the medications are continued, further symptomatic improvement may occur and there is much less likelihood of relapse. However, to have these continuing benefits, daily medication must be taken. The rate of relapse rises even with 10 missed doses in the course of a year (Weiden, Kozma, Grogg, & Locklear, 2004). Many people with schizophrenia do not take their medication as scheduled. There are myriad reasons for lack of adherence to treatment. Medication may be too expensive or difficult to obtain. The person may not understand why the medication is necessary. The person may think that he or she is being forced to take the medication without realizing that taking the medication can make his or her life easier. Community caregivers can encourage adherence by providing information regarding the medication and the importance of monitoring to the patient and his or her family in the context of a supportive relationship. Long-acting injectable medication is one option for individuals who have difficulty taking daily medication, and for patients who simply prefer to receive medication in this manner. Two of the typical antipsychotics are available as monthly injections. These medications share all of the drawbacks of the oral typical antipsychotics. One of the newer antipsychotics is available as an injection that is given every two weeks (long-acting risperidone for injection). This medication has the advantages of the newer medications and usually has fewer side effects than the oral form (Kane, 2003; Kane et al., 2003).

Case 1

During the autumn of his second year at college a young man gradually lost interest in friends and activities and stopped attending classes. He was hospitalized for five days in the spring after he stopped eating because he believed that "some people" were poisoning his food. He also believed that they had implanted a microchip in his jaw that broadcast his thoughts to them. Although he was unsure who these people were, he could hear several of them commenting on his behavior, even when no one was in the room. His parents were baffled, and expressed disappointment in their son's poor academic performance. He accepted treatment with antipsychotic medication, resumed eating and drinking, and gradually became less preoccupied with his delusions. His parents enrolled in a family education program on mental illness. He returned to school in the fall, taking a reduced course load. He received medications and supportive counseling from a local community mental health center. His parents allowed him to live in their home and supported his academic plans.

Mood Disorders

Depression and bipolar affective disorder are serious public health concerns and are the most frequently encountered mood disorders in community mental health practice. Periods of elation and depression are part and parcel of normal life. Clinical mood disorders are only diagnosed when problems with mood are so severe and so long lasting that they interfere with daily functioning. Serious depression affects approximately five percent of the population. Nearly twice as many women as men report suffering from depression. Biological and social factors help to explain this disparity. For women, the hormonal changes associated with puberty, pregnancy, childbirth, and menopause increase the risk for major depression (Brockington, 2004; Buist, 2001; Rasgon et al., 2002). The stress of being both caregiver and breadwinner, limited educational, economic, or professional opportunities, and the tendency to be more expressive of emotion and more willing to seek help have also been suggested as explanations why there are more reported bouts of depression in women.

Depression affects more than mood. Along with feelings of sadness, worthlessness, or irritability, a person with depression is likely to be lethargic, inattentive, and to have irregular patterns of eating and sleeping. The neurological underpinnings of depression seem to involve improper regulation of the neurotransmitters serotonin and norepinephrine. Most medications for depression stimulate the action of these neurotransmitters. As with schizophrenia, complex genetic factors are associated with the disorder. Major depressive episodes tend to recur; among individuals who have one depressive episode, three-fourths of them will have at least one more during their lifetime. In severe depressions, psychotic symptoms similar to those seen in schizophrenia may occur (hallucinations, delusions). These symptoms remit as depression resolves.

Bipolar affective disorder (formerly known as manic depression), although less common than major depression, is highly prevalent, affecting about 1.2% of the population. Manic episodes, the hallmark of bipolar disorder, are periods of days or weeks during which a person has marked elation or irritability, increased energy, and is unrealistically optimistic, perhaps even delusional. During such episodes a person may engage in destructive social activities; profligate spending and sexual adventurism are common. At times, manic episodes may occur without any depressions; however, most individuals tend to cycle between mania and depression, with some intervening intervals of fairly stable moods. The incidence of bipolar disorder is similar in women and men, although women tend to have more rapid cycling between depression and mania.

Particular psychotherapeutic interventions (e.g., interpersonal psychotherapy, cognitive therapy) are useful for depressed patients who retain sufficient function to engage in treatment. These may be used in conjunction with antidepressant or mood-stabilizing medications. Antidepressant medications tend to alleviate the physical aspects of depression and to normalize mood over a period of six to eight weeks. Continued use of antidepressants is protective against the recurrence of depressive episodes. The older medications (monoamine oxidase inhibitors [MAOIs], tricyclic antidepressants [TCAs]) are highly toxic in overdose, and thus are rarely prescribed. The newer antidepressants (selective serotonin reuptake inhibitors [SSRIs], serotonin/norepinephrine uptake inhibitors [SNRIs]) are far less dangerous in overdose and are now the preferred agents. All of these medications can have undesirable side effects, including mania and, in rare cases, intensifying depression. For these reasons, antidepressant medications need to be carefully monitored. The majority of the problems with the medications occur when practitioners underestimate potential problems and offer little follow-up care.

Bipolar disorder is treated with mood stabilizers, which are sometimes used in conjunction with antidepressant medications. Examples of mood stabilizers are lithium salts and medications such as divalproex that were initially developed to treat epilepsy. The medications used to treat schizophrenia are also effective in treating mania and in reducing its recurrence. All atypical antipsychotics are now either approved by the Food and Drug Administration (FDA) for this use or are currently under review by the FDA as antimanic agents. Medication treatment often reduces the length and severity of manic and depressive episodes. Continued treatment lengthens the intervals between episodes and reduces the severity of subsequent episodes.

Case 2

Ms. B is a 45-year-old single woman who lives quietly by herself in an apartment. She has a clerical job, two close women friends, and takes part in few activities outside of work. She was hospitalized five times between ages 32 and 38 for three depressive and two manic episodes. After all but the last episode, she discontinued her medications, saying that she did not need them. During one depressive episode she took an overdose of medications that resulted in four days of treatment in an intensive care unit. During a manic episode she hitchhiked to another city and lived for a month on the streets as a prostitute. She now takes medication faithfully, saying that she will "do anything" to ward off future episodes of depression and mania.

Severe depression does not always respond to medication and may be life threatening. A person suffering from depression may attempt or complete suicide, or become incapable of self-care. In any case, severe depression inflicts tremendous suffering. Electroconvulsive therapy (ECT) is the single most effective treatment for depression, at least in the short term. It is usually reserved for refractory cases because of lingering public distrust of the treatment, based on past problems with the way that the treatment was administered. At present, ECT is administered under general anesthesia in an operating room. A small electrical current is applied to the scalp, causing the brain to have a brief epileptic-type seizure. There is no seizure activity in the body because of the anesthetic. Following the treatment, an individual will have temporary confusion and memory disturbance. Between 6 and 10 treatments are usually given over the course of two to three weeks. The therapeutic effects are likely due to the high levels of neurotransmitters released during the seizure.

Two new treatments are likely to become available in the United States within the next few years. Transcranial magnetic stimulation (TMS), now in clinical use in Canada, involves the use of magnetic fields to stimulate brain regions. No seizure is induced and no anesthesia is required. Multiple treatments are necessary, on a schedule similar to ECT. Vagal nerve stimulators (VNS) are surgically implanted devices similar to cardiac pacemakers that deliver stimuli to the vagus nerve in the neck. These devices are currently used for the treatment of epilepsy and appear very promising for treatment of severe refractory depression as well.

Suicide is the 11th leading cause of death in the United States. Approximately 60% of people who commit suicide have been diagnosed with a mood disorder, while approximately 15% of people with serious depressions eventually kill themselves. Suicide is also common among people with schizophrenia, although the rates are less than with depression. Three times as many women attempt suicide, but four times as many men complete suicide. Firearms are involved in 55% of completed suicides. The use of alcohol and street drugs increases suicide risk. Studies have found low levels of the neurotransmitter serotonin in the brains of people who have committed suicide.

Anxiety Disorders

A degree of anxiety is an unavoidable part of life. Such disorders are only diagnosed when anxiety cripples the ability of an individual to function socially. Explanations of the biological basis of anxiety disorders focus on overactivity of regions such as the amygdala, which normally assess risks and activate the *fight-or-flight reaction*. The neurotransmitters serotonin and gamma-amino butyric acid (GABA) are involved in the mediation of anxiety.

Generalized anxiety disorder is a condition of virtually unremitting anxiety. In panic disorder, anxiety is sudden and intense. Individuals often feel that they are dying and may seek emergency medical treatment. Agoraphobia complicates panic disorder, as people learn to avoid having attacks in public by staying in the relative safety of their own homes. Outreach programs are essential in treating individuals who are often unwilling to venture outside to keep appointments.

Posttraumatic stress disorder (PTSD) is a recurrent anxiety disorder. First described in combat soldiers, and then in disaster victims, it has also been found in survivors of rape and domestic violence. Individuals with PTSD experience a variety of emotional and behavioral symptoms, including emotional withdrawal and decreased ability to be intimate, vivid emotional recollection of traumatic events triggered by sights or sounds that are reminiscent of those events, and nightmares. As noted above, there are clear structural and functional brain abnormalities in PTSD.

Obsessive-compulsive disorder (OCD), which occurs in more than two percent of the U.S. population, is marked by the seemingly unnecessary repetition of mental and physical activity in order for an individual to ward off anxiety. For example, a woman may wash her hands until the skin is raw. Yet if she does not wash her hands for even a few minutes, she begins to worry that there are germs on her hands. She may know that her hands are not covered with dangerous germs, yet she still feels compelled to wash them for this reason.

There are two main types of medications for anxiety disorders. The benzodiazepine medications quickly relieve anxiety. These Valium-like drugs are often useful in the short term, but tend to be considerably less useful when used for longer periods. Medications that were initially developed to treat depression (SSRIs and SNRIs) are now treatments of choice for anxiety disorders. These medications are often used in conjunction with cognitive behavioral psychotherapy.

Case 3

A 28-year-old man and his fiancée have been coming to a community mental health center for couples' counseling. He misses two consecutive appointments. His counselor telephones him, and he reports that he is trying not to leave the house because he was afraid that he would have another "spell." He had had three sudden attacks of chest pain and overwhelming anxiety that have resulted in trips to the emergency room, where evaluation determined that he was medically healthy. He agreed to come for psychiatric evaluation with his fiancée. He began treatment with an SSRI medication for panic disorder and within two weeks was much more confident and was no longer fearful of leaving the house. He had occasional brief feelings of mild panic, but was able to control these episodes with cognitive techniques he had learned from his counselor.

Personality Disorders

Beginning with the third edition of the *Diagnostic and Statistical Manual* (DSM-III) certain long-standing patterns of thought and behavior have been termed *personality disorders*. Initially these were assumed to be learned patterns of behavior, with less of a neurological component than other disorders. More recently this notion has been challenged. For example, schizotypal personality disorder appears to be a mild form of schizophrenia. Borderline personality disorder (BPD), which is characterized by features such as chronically unstable mood, volatile interpersonal relationships, extremely low tolerance for being alone, and repeated self-harm, now appears to be a catchall for disorders that may lead to similar presentations. Among the causes of BPD are posttraumatic states arising from childhood physical and sexual abuse, and variants of bipolar affective disorder. Medications are useful for some individuals with personality disorders. For example, antipsychotic medication might reduce mildly delusional thoughts in an individual with schizotypal personality disorder. Mood stabilizers, SSRIs, and atypical antipsychotics are at times useful in reducing impulsive actions and facilitating realistic thinking for people with borderline personality disorder (Soloff, 2000).

Case 4

A woman in college has a series of four boyfriends. Each was attracted by her gregarious personality, but was eventually put off by her demanding, clinging behavior. She was initially enamored of each boyfriend, but within weeks she invariably became disillusioned. When breaking up with one of the boyfriends the woman took an overdose of aspirin and was hospitalized overnight. During another breakup she found that cutting her skin with a razor blade relieved tension. She dropped out of school and began intermittently using heroin. Psychiatric assessment at a community mental health center led to a diagnosis of borderline personality disorder. After six months of dialectical behavior therapy (Robins & Chapman, 2004) and low-dose atypical antipsychotic treatment, she had stopped using heroin and was cutting herself less frequently. Her relationship with her current boyfriend was stormy at times, but had lasted longer than any previous relationship. She had also found a full-time job.

Dementias

Dementias are problems with cognition and behavior that are caused by the destruction of brain tissue, primarily in the elderly. The most familiar of these is dementia of the Alzheimer's type (Alzheimer's Association, 2004), which is caused by a gradual loss of brain tissue accompanied by deposition of abnormal materials (amyloid plaques and neurofibrillary tangles) within brain cells. The prevalence of Alzheimer's dementia increases with age. At age 65, 1 in 10 individuals is affected; nearly half of individuals above the age of 85 have the illness. The onset of symptoms is quite gradual, with a slow decline in memory, orientation, problem solving, and language skills. As the illness progresses, personality change and anxiety, depression, delusions, and hallucinations are common. At present there is no cure and the illness eventually leads to death.

The anticholinesterase medications (donepezil, rivastigmine, galantamine) slow but do not stop the expression of symptoms in mild to moderate dementia. Memantine, a medication that blocks a particular receptor for the neurotransmitter glutamate, is similarly useful in more advanced illness. While Alzheimer's dementia is usually thought of as a neurological, as opposed to a psychiatric, illness, the emotional and behavioral symptoms often lead to the requirement for institutional care.

Another form of dementia that is often seen in community mental health practice is the dementia that follows head injury (Brain Injury Association of America, 2004). Approximately 5.3 million Americans are disabled as the result of traumatic brain injury; 80,000 new cases of disability occur annually. Disability is likely to be lifelong. Vehicular accidents are the leading cause of such injuries. Both cognitive problems (memory, attention, difficulty shifting from one task to another, problem solving) and emotional problems (anxiety, depression, and impulsivity) are common. Medications ameliorate the emotional symptoms.

Case 5

A 27-year-old graduate student was struck by a car while riding his bicycle to class. He sustained a major closed-head injury and was in a coma for several days. Two years later he has no obvious signs of the accident and is back in school. However, he is failing all of his courses because he is unable to concentrate. His family notes that his mood is different. Formerly even-tempered, he is now often giggly or irritable, sometimes making overly ambitious or grandiose plans. He is argumentative with his professors. A mood-stabilizing medication helps to smooth his mood and allows him to interact more easily with his professors. He continues in a program of cognitive rehabilitation and supportive psychotherapy with a psychologist to maximize his cognitive abilities and adjust to the cognitive and emotional disability that has followed the accident.

Substance Abuse

Psychiatric disorders are often complicated by concurrent substance abuse (Anonymous, 2003; Drake & Mueser, 2000; Flaum & Schultz, 1996; Margolese, Malchy, Negrete, Tempier, & Gill, 2004). Epidemiological studies estimate that 50% or more of individuals with schizophrenia misuse or abuse alcohol or street drugs (Dixon, 1999). The interactions of street drugs and alcohol with the biology of neuropsychiatric disorders are complex. At times, psychiatric disorders follow as a direct consequence of substance abuse; for example, long-term psychosis similar to schizophrenia is caused by prolonged amphetamine abuse. At other times, individuals may use street drugs and alcohol as "self-medication" to relieve depression or to ease the suffering from psychiatric illness (Kessler, Nelson, & McGonagle, 1996; Regier et al., 1990). Nicotine may help people with schizophrenia to think more clearly. At other times, individuals may have two separate problems: substance abuse and neuropsychiatric illness. Programs that address only substance abuse or mental health are often ineffective with individuals who have coexisting problems. Rather, integrated "dual diagnosis" programs offer the best chance for successful outcomes. Such programs address both problems simultaneously from multiple perspectives:

> In addition to a comprehensive integration of services, successful programs include assessment, assertive case management, motivational interventions for patients who do not recognize the need for substance abuse treatment, behavioral interventions for those who are trying to attain or maintain abstinence, family interventions, housing, rehabilitation, and psychopharmacology. (Drake & Mueser, 2000)

Case 6

Mr. N is a 45-year-old man with a history of schizophrenia. He has a master's degree in computer science but has never worked. Three years ago he was discharged from a mental health social support program because his continued alcohol use (6 to 12 beers daily) impaired his ability to participate. He then enrolled in a 12-step alcohol treatment program. Although he had adhered to treatment with antipsychotic medications, he became increasingly delusional during the confrontational group sessions that were part of the treatment, dropped out, and continued to drink beer. He has now completed six months in a dual diagnosis program and has achieved three months of sobriety, with a decrease in delusions and hallucinations.

SOCIAL ISSUES: GENDER, ETHNICITY, AND ECONOMICS

To this point, neuropsychiatry has been discussed primarily in terms of biology and medical issues. However, neuropsychiatry, like all aspects of medicine, is a social activity, part of the social fabric, and thus all of the large social issues of the day are found within the practice of neuropsychiatry. This section discusses neuropsychiatry in the context of these issues.

Gender Issues

The biological differences between the sexes can be easily accommodated within the biomedical framework of neuropsychiatry. For example, the differences in hormonal fluctuations between men and women are measurable, as are the correlations of these fluctuations with various disorders. In pregnant women, medications need to be tailored to the needs of the fetus as well as the mother (Yonkers et al., 2004).

However, the social dimensions of gender add another dimension to neuropsychiatric practice. Definitions of neuropsychiatric disorder almost always include a statement to the effect that the disorder must be severe enough to impair social functioning. The definition of social functioning is itself a social construct, based on what may be questionable norms of expected behavior. Once one moves beyond discussion of the ability to perform basic self-care, the qualities of *functional* social behavior become increasingly murky. One observer may attribute nonnormative behavior to an individual's problems with brain function, impairing the person's ability to achieve his or her life goals. Another observer may attribute the same behavior to the individual's struggle against oppressive social norms. When the ability to function socially is equated with social conformity, neuropsychiatric interventions can easily be invoked to reinforce existing social norms rather than to foster individual growth and achievement.

In the 1950s, antianxiety medications were indiscriminately prescribed to women, supposedly to assist them in coping with their problems. A variety of antianxiety medications (then known as tranquilizers) were needlessly prescribed, often creating patterns of use, abuse, and addiction. This irresponsible use of neuropsychiatry was enthusiastically promoted by pharmaceutical industry advertising, and the drugs were prescribed by (mostly male) psychiatrists and family doctors who should have known better. Many women accepted this use of medication, which is quite understandable given the authoritative medical endorsement behind the medications. Rather than increasing women's autonomy, self-determination, and true functional ability, such use undermined women's efforts to reshape their roles in post–World War II American society. The situation was aptly described in "Mother's Little Helper," the popular Rolling Stones' song (Jagger & Richards, 1967):

> What a drag it is getting old.
> "Kids are different today," I hear ev'ry mother say.
> Mother needs something today to calm her down.
> And though she's not really ill, there's a little yellow pill.
> She goes running for the shelter of a mother's little helper
> And it helps her on her way, gets her through her busy day....

By now we should have moved beyond blatant gender stereotyping and misuse of psychopharmacology. The rhetoric (including direct advertising to women) and symbolism may have changed, but the overpromotion of psychotropic medication in a way that demeans and underestimates women continues. Fortunately, there is more public awareness of the phenomenon, and some degree of corrective action comes both from within the psychiatric community and from government regulators.

For example, in 2000 the Food and Drug Administration requested that pharmaceutical manufacturer Eli Lilly pull one of its television commercials for Sarafem (Stockbridge, 2000). Sarafem is a brand name form of fluoxetine, the antidepressant medication that is also marketed as Prozac and that is now available in a generic version. Sarafem, which had received FDA approval for the treatment of premenstrual dysphoric disorder, comes in pastel-colored capsules, apparently to appeal to women. In the television advertisement in question, a woman is shown struggling with a poorly functioning supermarket cart. The voiceover says, "Think it's PMS? It could be PMDD," and the answer to the woman's frustration is, of course, Sarafem. The FDA noted that the advertisement "trivialized the seriousness of PMDD." It would have been helpful, of course, for the agency to point out that the advertisement also trivialized women's lives and added to the confusion regarding the proper role of neuropsychiatric intervention (In, 2002).

Two case examples contrast the difference between inappropriate and appropriate use of medication for women with anxiety.

Case 7

A 35-year-old woman consults a doctor because she is unhappy in her work and marriage. She has no obvious symptoms of neuropsychiatric disorder. The doctor reassures her that she will be all right and that she should take antianxiety medications when she has difficulty coping. Over the next six months her use of medication increases. She frequently runs out of medication before she is scheduled to refill it and experiences increased anxiety as a withdrawal symptom. Her marriage and job remain unsatisfying.

Case 8

A 35-year-old woman has had past episodes of severe depression that are accompanied by auditory hallucinations telling her to kill herself. With consistent use of antidepressant and antipsychotic medication, her mood is considerably more stable and she has no hallucinations. She functions well as a mother. Her husband abruptly announces that he has found someone else, moves out of the house, and files for divorce. The woman begins having clearly defined outbreaks of panic, with uncontrollable shaking of her body and feelings that she is dying. Medical evaluation reveals no physical concerns. The woman fears that her husband will be given custody of their children unless she is able to control the episodes of anxiety. Under psychiatric supervision, she begins taking an antianxiety medication and increases the dosage of the antidepressant. The panic episodes become less severe and less frequent. She begins to rebuild her life, now a single parent.

The gender of the caregiver is often important in ensuring that the patient is comfortable in disclosing personal information and in planning treatment. In most cases patients should be allowed to choose the gender of their psychiatrist. For example, women who have been sexually or physically abused by a man may not be comfortable talking about these things with a male doctor, and are likely to form a more useful therapeutic relationship with a female doctor. Men may likewise have comfort issues in dealing with a physician or psychiatrist. The issue is not so much that people of differing genders cannot understand or be helpful to each other. The issue is that people who are in distress need to find caregivers with whom they are able to quickly form trusting relationships. Community mental health programs should assess and honor their clients' preferences regarding the gender of their caregivers, including their psychiatrists.

Race and Ethnicity

Race and ethnicity are important factors in neuropsychiatric care, according to a report from the U.S. Public Health Service (Department of Health and Human Services, U.S. Public Health Service, 2001) and a professional monograph (Ruiz, 2000). The incidence of major mental illnesses is similar across ethic and racial groups. No known differences in brain functions are attributable to race or ethnicity. Physicians need to be aware of differences in the frequency of particular genes that regulate breakdown and elimination of medications by the liver drug metabolism within particular populations. For example, with some Asian patients, a physician would be wise to begin some medications at lower doses than are recommended by the manufacturer, as many Asians may metabolize the drug more slowly than people of European extraction.

Issues of cultural competency are less easily managed than simple biological factors and are central to the provision of high-quality care (Strakowski, 2003). To make meaningful assessments and to form a working relationship with a patient, a clinician must be fully conversant with the patient's culture. Without an understanding of cultural norms, attitudes toward health and illness, ways of expressing concerns, and cultural and political history, it is impossible to evaluate mental and behavioral symptoms. Psychiatric clinics that serve multicultural populations need to be organized to ensure culturally competent care. For example, at the Intercultural Psychiatric Program at the Oregon Health & Science University (http://www.ohsu.edu/psychiatry/clinics/), which provides treatment to refugees and immigrants who speak 17 languages other than English, psychiatrists are either fluent in the language and a member of the patient's cultural group, or are paired with a bilingual mental health counselor from that ethnic group.

Members of racial and ethnic minorities have less access to psychiatric care (and to medical care in general), and the care they usually receive is of inferior quality than that available to the general population (Department of Health and Human Services, U.S. Public Health Service, 2001). Given the ubiquity of institutionalized racism, it is not surprising that it has been identified as a factor in neuropsychiatric care (Strakowski, Shelton, & Kolbrener, 1993).

In some settings, African Americans have had higher rates of being misdiagnosed with schizophrenia than White Americans and have been treated with inappropriately high doses of medication. There seem to have been a number of reasons, including the blatantly racist notion among White psychiatrists that Black patients did not merit as thorough an evaluation. Other factors have more to do with issues of cultural competence among White psychiatrists treating Black patients. For example, White psychiatrists mistook the wariness among poor Black patients for paranoid delusions rather than appreciating the cultural reasons that these patients were hesitant to disclose personal information to middle-class White doctors. In another instance, White doctors underdiagnosed PTSD due to a lack of understanding that Black soldiers had been involved in combat (Paul, 1999). Caregivers and system planners need to ensure that ethnic bias is not clouding neuropsychiatric diagnosis and treatment.

Economics

Psychiatric medications are discovered, manufactured, and sold through the system of global capitalism, rather than through nonprofit mechanisms. Governmental research agencies such as the National Institute for Mental Heath do not fund research into drug development. Noncorporate research organizations such as medical schools and universities are not able to fund the level of research required to develop medications. Thus, medication development is largely driven by the profit motive at the corporate level. This funding mechanism has effects not only on drug pricing, but on the type of drugs that are developed, and on treatment decisions driven by industry-supported professional education and advertising to both professionals and consumers (Moncrieff, 2003).

Because psychiatric illness tends to render many individuals unable to work, the burden of paying for psychiatric treatment and medications falls largely on governmental insurance programs, rather than on private insurance that people usually obtain through their employment. Newer, less toxic, more effective medications tend to be expensive. Whereas a year's treatment with a first-generation antipsychotic medication such as haloperidol may cost around $300, a year's treatment with a new-generation agent may cost up to $6,000.

The actual costs of treatment need to be figured more broadly. The latest generation of antipsychotics has been shown to decrease rehospitalization rates, and the savings associated with decreased hospitalization may offset the higher pharmacy costs. There are numerous other savings when a person's symptoms and functioning improve, such as less absenteeism from work when a family member has to care for the individual and lower costs for emergency rooms, police contacts, and mental health courts. Many of these savings are difficult to capture, or show up on budgets other than of the agency that purchases the medication. However, health system planners need to look at overall costs when making decisions regarding medication purchases (Knapp, 2000; Revicki, 1999). Public expenditures for psychiatric medications represent a very large proportion of the budgets of already financially strapped government health programs, and these expenditures have been growing at rates that outpace those of other health costs. In Florida, Medicaid spent about $440 million on mental health medications in 2003, representing 20% of the total medication expenditure (Sharp, 2004). Mental health medication costs for Florida Medicaid rose by 35% each year from 2000 through 2002, while the prices of other medication classes increased by only 11%.

A number of strategies directed at reducing drug costs through management of the individual patients' care have been largely unsuccessful, but frustrating to both patients and physicians (The Lewin Group, 2000). Some of these strategies require a patient fail treatment with a less expensive medication before getting the preferred medication, or add time-consuming preauthorization procedures that must be completed before a patient is able to receive insurance coverage for a particular medication. Efforts to reduce costs at the individual level continue (Sharp, 2004), but may have relatively little impact compared to more comprehensive (but politically unappealing) reform of the relationship between the government and the pharmaceutical industry.

STIGMA AND PERSON-CENTERED CARE

Society stigmatizes people who suffer from neuropsychiatric disorders. This stigma reflects fear, ignorance, and a desire to exclude anyone who is different. Insurance coverage for neuropsychiatric disorders is often less generous than for "physical illness." The media's portrayals of individuals with neuropsychiatric disorders, or of treatment, are often unrealistic and disparaging. A person known to have psychiatric illness may find it difficult to obtain housing or employment. Stigma has often been evident in the systems of care for individuals with psychiatric disorders. While large state hospitals were initially intended as humane refuges from the stress of living in society, they quickly became dumping grounds for persons that society would rather forget or ignore. As these hospitals emptied, the streets took their place. Society's neglect of the homeless has replaced its former neglect of institutionalized people.

From a medical point of view, psychiatric diagnoses appear free of stigma. An accurate diagnosis is highly valuable because it describes a problem in the most precise terms, and points to possible ways to improve functioning or relieve suffering. However, neuropsychiatric diagnoses easily take on the same function as stigmatizing social labels, both within and outside the health care system. In other words, the diagnosis becomes the overall descriptor of the person, and often a rationale for disregarding, denigrating, or discarding the person. For example, a person who is known to be a schizophrenic may find it hard to have his point of view taken seriously in any disagreement with a "normal" person. Within health care systems, individuals diagnosed with psychiatric disorders often receive substandard care, as their complaints of physical problems are taken to be more evidence of "mental illness," and efforts toward preventative care are not pursued as aggressively as with "normal" people. Medical and social professionals need to be aware of the distinction between diagnosis and labeling, and to avoid the pernicious effects of stigma.

Person-centered care may be used within care systems to address problems of stigma (Cohn, 2001; Talerico, O'Brien, & Swafford, 2003). This approach emphasizes person-centered language (e.g., saying "a person with schizophrenia," not "a schizophrenic") and constant attention to the subjective experience of people who are receiving care. Many caregivers are truly unaware of the experiences of people under their care. Staff may benefit from programs and training in which consumers and family members share accounts of their experiences of care for neuropsychiatric disorders.

A person-centered culture within a care system is unlikely to develop without the open and continued support from the program's administration. Such support cannot simply take the form of value statements. Rather, it needs to be modeled though efforts to ensure that staff members believe that they are being treated with dignity and respect. Attitudes and processes with the working organization tend to be conveyed to the recipients of care. The psychiatric inpatient service at the Oregon Health & Science University has adopted such a person-centered value system. Monthly interdisciplinary staff retreats incorporated presentations by consumers and by staff members whose culture was already more person centered. Over the course of the year, staff took pride in noting a marked decrease in the use of seclusion and restraint, with no increase in injuries.

Consumerism, Advocates, and Critics

People who use neuropsychiatric services and their family members currently play active roles as advocates and critics of neuropsychiatric research programs and service delivery systems (McLean, 2000). Mental health "consumerism" began in the United States in the 1970s as the "ex-patient" movement, which expressed radical political opposition to all of psychiatry, largely because of the substandard care that individuals had received in the large, underfunded state hospitals of the day. Around the same time, the National Alliance on Mental Illness (NAMI) got its start, as family members demanded better services and an end to blaming parents for the psychiatric disorders in their children. The current consumer movement has diversified and matured to champion a variety of positions. The term *psychiatric survivor* has replaced *ex-patient* among opponents of psychiatry. NAMI has evolved into an effective national advocacy group, lobbying for improved services and more research, in addition to providing education and support at the local and state levels.

Many consumers recognize the value of neuropsychiatric service and advocate for availability and quality of services, rather than for their abolition. Empowerment is a universal theme among all of the groups. Inclusion of consumers in the design, implementation, and monitoring of psychiatric research and service provision is increasing. Family and consumer perspectives are also essential elements in psychiatric training and should be integrated into medical school curricula and psychiatric residency training programs (as they are at the Oregon Health and Science University). Pharmaceutical companies have recognized the power of consumer groups and at times offer financial assistance to these organizations. This support allows consumer groups to flourish, but also opens the door to possible commercial bias in educational and advocacy activities.

Along with some people who have been justifiably unhappy with the care they have received for neuropsychiatric disorders, the academic antipsychiatry movement has challenged the validity of the scientific basis of neuropsychiatry and rejected psychiatric care altogether. The antipsychiatry movement lingers on the fringe of academia, as blanket arguments against the neuroscientific basis of psychiatric disorders are difficult to sustain. From a scientific perspective, such criticism of neuropsychiatry now seems trivial. Neuroscience has advanced to the point that it is simply not possible to deny the neurological basis of schizophrenia and other major psychiatric disorders, just as it is impossible to deny the physiological basis of arthritis or diabetes.

Given the limited recourses, the complexity of society, and the pervasiveness of stigma, providing services in a way that fosters personal dignity, encourages healthy autonomy, and nurtures the human spirit is a continual challenge. Professionals should look upon consumer groups as essential partners in the struggle to improve services. Consumers and professionals alike should avoid the easy but indefensible solution of simply turning away from neuropsychiatry due to the seemingly chronic shortcomings in service provision.

SUMMARY

Neuropsychiatry provides a useful perspective on what has been termed mental illness, and a powerful set of tools to improve mental and social functioning. While neuropsychiatry focuses on brain structure and function, current understanding of the brain emphasizes its interaction with the physical and social environment. Thus, dichotomous views of mental illness being caused by either nature or nurture and being treated by either psychosocial interventions or medications no longer fit with our understanding of the central nervous system. These *either/or* perspectives have been replaced with a *yes/and* point of view in which genetics and the brain continually adapt and respond to their social and physical environment. The scientific findings of neuropsychiatry must be used in the context of the person: the goal of treatment is not to fix a brain; it is to improve a particular person's life. As a large-scale social undertaking, neuropsychiatry is influenced by society and politics. For better or worse, neuropsychiatry is profoundly influenced by gender, culture, economic systems, and resource allocation. Neuropsychiatry offers a perspective and a set of tools. What we do with this perspective and these tools depends upon our values and our commitment to putting those values into practice.

REFERENCES

Alzheimer's Association. (2004). Home page. Retrieved August 10, 2004, from http://www.alz.org/overview.asp

American Diabetes Association, A.P.A., American Association of Clinical Endocrinologists, North American Association for the Study of Obesity. (2004). Consensus development conference on antipsychotic drugs and obesity and diabetes. *Diabetes Care, 27*, 596–601.

American Psychiatric Association. (2000). *Diagnostic and statistical manual of mental disorders* (4th ed., text revision). Washington, DC: Author.

Anonymous. (2003). Dual diagnosis. Part II. A look at old reliable and promising new approaches to the treatment of mental illness with substance abuse. *Harvard Mental Health Letter, 20*, 1–5.

Brain Injury Association of America. (2004). Home page. Retrieved August 10, 2004, from http://www.biausa.org/Pages/home.html

Brockington, I. (2004). Postpartum psychiatric disorders. *Lancet, 363*, 303–310.

Buist, A. (2001). Treating mental illness in lactating women. *Medscape Women's Health, 6*, 3.

Charney, D.S., Barlow, D.H. et al. (2002). Neuroscience research agenda to guide development of a pathophysiologically based classification system. In D.J. Kupfer, M.B. First, & D.A. Regier (Eds.), *A Research Agenda for DSM-V* (pp. 31–83). Washington, DC: American Psychiatric Association.

Cohn, F. (2001). Existential medicine: Martin Buber and physician-patient relationships. *Journal of Continuing Education in the Health Professions, 21*, 170–181.

Department of Health and Human Services, U.S. Public Health Service. (2001). *Mental health: culture, race, and ethnicity. A supplement to mental health: a report of the surgeon general.* Washington, DC: Author.

Dixon, L. (1999). Dual diagnosis of substance abuse in schizophrenia: prevalence and impact on outcomes. *Schizophrenia Research, 35* (Suppl.), S93–S100.

Drake, R.E. & Mueser, K.T. (2000). Psychosocial approaches to dual diagnosis. *Schizophrenia Bulletin, 26*, 105–118.

Flaum, M. & Schultz, S.K. (1996). When does amphetamine-induced psychosis become schizophrenia? *American Journal of Psychiatry, 153*, 812–815.

Freedman, R. (2003). Schizophrenia. *New England Journal of Medicine, 349*, 1738–1749.

Hales, R.E. & Yudofsky S.C. (Eds.). (2002). *The American psychiatric publishing textbook of clinical psychiatry.* Arlington, VA: American Psychiatric Publishing.

In, J. (2002). Marketing Mother's Little Helper. Women's ENews. Retrieved August 5, 2004, from http://www.womensenews.org/article.cfm/dyn/aid/949/context/archive

Jagger, M.P. & Richards, K. (1967). *Mother's little helper.* New York: ABKCO Music.

Kane, J.M. (2003). Strategies for improving compliance in treatment of schizophrenia by using a long-acting formulation of an antipsychotic: clinical studies. *Journal of Clinical Psychiatry, 64* (Suppl. 16), 34–40.

Kane, J.M., Eerdekens, M., Lindenmayer, J.P., Keith, S.J., Lesem, M., & Karcher, K. (2003). Long-acting injectable risperidone: efficacy and safety of the first long-acting atypical antipsychotic. *American Journal of Psychiatry, 160,* 1125–1132.

Kessler, R., Nelson, C. & McGonagle, K. (1996). The epidemiology of co-occurring addictive and mental disorders: implications for prevention and service utilization. *American Journal of Orthopsychiatry, 66,* 17–31.

Knapp, M. (2000). Schizophrenia costs and treatment cost-effectiveness. *Acta Psychiatrica Scandinavica, Supplementum, 102,* 15–18.

The Lewin Group. (2000). *Access and utilization of new antidepressant and antipsychotic medications.* Report to the Office of the Assistant Secretary for Planning and Evaluation and National Institute of Mental Health, U.S. Department of Health and Human Services. Retrieved August 10, 2004, from http://aspe.hhs.gov/health/reports/Psychmedaccess/

Margolese, H.C., Malchy, L., Negrete, J.C., Tempier, R., & Gill, K. (2004). Drug and alcohol use among patients with schizophrenia and related psychoses: levels and consequences. *Schizophrenia Research, 67,* 157–166.

McLean, A.H. (2000). From ex-patient alternatives to consumer options: consequences of consumerism for psychiatric consumers and the ex-patient movement. *International Journal of Health Services, 30,* 821–847.

Moncrieff, J. (2003). *Is psychiatry for sale? An examination of the influence of the pharmaceutical industry on academic and practical psychiatry* (Maudsley Discussion Paper 13). London: Kings College London.

Neugenboren, J. (1999). *Transforming madness.* Berkeley: University of California Press.

Paul, A.M. (1999). Painting Insanity Black. Retrieved August 10, 2004, from www.salon.com/books/it/1999/12/01/schizo/index.html

Pliszka, S.R. (2003). *Neuroscience for the mental health clinician.* New York: Guilford Press.

Rasgon, N.L., Altshuler, L.L., Fairbanks, L.A., Dunkin, J.J., Davtyan, C., Elman, S., & Rapkin, A.J. (2002). Estrogen replacement therapy in the treatment of major depressive disorder in peri-menopausal women. *Journal of Clinical Psychiatry, 63* (Suppl. 7), 45–48.

Regier, D.A., Farmer, M.E., Rae, D., Locke, B.Z., Keith, S.J., Judd, L.L., & Goodwin, F.K. (1990). Comorbidity of mental disorders with alcohol and other drug abuse. *Journal of American Medical Association, 19,* 2511–2518.

Revicki, D.A. (1999). Pharmacoeconomic studies of atypical antipsychotic drugs for the treatment of schizophrenia. *Schizophrenia Research, 35* (Suppl.), S101–S109.

Robins, C.J. & Chapman, A.L. (2004). Dialectical behavior therapy: current status, recent developments, and future directions. *Journal of Personality Disorders, 18,* 73–89.

Ruiz, P. (Ed.). (2000). *Ethnicity and psychopharmacology.* Arlington, VA: American Psychiatric Publishing.

Schatzberg, A.F. & Nemeroff, C.B. (Eds.). (2004). *The American Psychiatric Publishing textbook of psychopharmacology* (3rd ed.). Arlington VA: American Psychiatric Publishing.

Sharp, B. (2004). *Medicaid mental health drug recommendations: governor's FY 2004–05 budget recommendations.* Florida Agency for Health Care Administration. Retrieved from http://www.fdhc.state.fl.us/Medicaid/deputy_secretary/recent_presentations/mental_health_drugs_031104.pdf

Soloff, P.H. (2000). Psychopharmacology of borderline personality disorder. *Psychiatric Clinics of North America, 23,* 169–192.

Stahl, S.M. (2000). *Essential psychopharmacology: neuroscientific basis and practical applications* (2nd ed.). New York: Cambridge University Press.

III

Community Mental Health
with Underserved Populations

This section addresses oppression and discrimination in community mental health. At the heart of the discussion are concerns around making client services accessible and identifying components of culturally competent programming.

Jaimie Page and Joel Blau in "Public Mental Health Systems: Breaking the Impasse in the Treatment of Oppressed Groups" identify the common themes and experiences of oppressed groups and call upon the community mental health field to reexamine its approach to the treatment of oppressed groups. Their analysis includes comprehensive strategies to improve services. The chapter pays particular attention to issues of race, class, and gender.

The next four chapters highlight the needs of specific populations that have experienced discrimination and neglect in the mental health care system. The section examines issues related to selected groups and is not intended as exclusive. "Stigma, Sexual Orientation, and Mental Illness: A Community Mental Health Perspective," by Jessica Rosenberg, Samuel J. Rosenberg, Christian Huygen, and Eileen Klein, argues that the needs of lesbian, gay, bisexual, and transgendered persons with serious mental illness must be conceptualized in a framework of "dual stigma."

In "African Americans and Mental Health," Alma J. Carten provides a historical analysis of the legacy of the slave experience and the uniqueness of the black cultural experience. She identifies racist assumptions about the etiology and behaviors of blacks and documents patterns of discrimination in the mental health treatment of African Americans, concluding that mental health disparities will persist as long as societal inequities continue.

"Mental Health Issues of Chinese Americans: Help-Seeking Behaviors and Culturally Relevant Services," by Winnie W. Kung and Yi-Fen Tseng, discusses the ethnic-specific needs of Chinese Americans. Cultural belief systems and the components of a culturally responsive service delivery model are outlined.

The last chapter of this section, "Psychological Intervention with Hispanic Patients: A Review of Selected Culturally Syntonic Treatment Approaches," by Manny John González and Gregory Acevedo, examines causal reasons for the underutilization of mental health services by Hispanics and provides an excellent discussion of their treatment needs, reviewing some best practice treatment models.

9

PUBLIC MENTAL HEALTH SYSTEMS

Breaking the Impasse in the Treatment of Oppressed Groups

JAIMIE PAGE AND JOEL BLAU

In this chapter, we explore mental health treatment of oppressed groups. First, we will highlight the experiences of selected groups who have been historically oppressed. Then, after we examine the commonalities between these groups, we will recommend strategies to break the impasse in their treatment.

For the public mental health system, addressing the needs of untreated individuals who then become marginalized and destitute is a major challenge (Sharfstein, 2000). This challenge exists because of the intersection between oppression and public mental health: those with untreated mental illnesses may become, or continue to be, marginalized, impoverished, and isolated as a result of the psychosocial deterioration that follows lack of treatment. An equally important aspect of oppression and public mental health, though, relates to these individuals with untreated mental illness who are *already* marginalized and oppressed due to existing social, political, and economic structures. The two aspects are inextricably related. Powerlessness, isolation, deprivation, and mental illness and stress are directly associated with oppression (Serrano-Garcia & Bond, 1994). As Hanna, Talley, and Guindon (2000) note, oppression has profound implications for the delivery of mental health services. Yet it is a subject that is largely avoided in the public mental health sector.

Oppressive structures limit individuals' ability to access and receive treatment that is relevant, culturally appropriate, affordable, and addresses structural oppression. The discussion here focuses on how oppressive structures within society, such as classism, racism, and heterosexism, including those found within public mental health systems, create an impasse in the treatment of oppressed groups. Myths of group homogeneity often have detrimental effects on research, practice, and diversity, and individuals within the group. Nevertheless, if we are to successfully break the impasse in community mental health treatment of oppressed groups, it is helpful to explore the "common human threads" that link oppressed groups together (Serrano-Garcia & Bond, 1994).

PROBLEMS WITH THE PUBLIC MENTAL HEALTH SYSTEM

Many problems inherent with community mental health centers (CMHCs) affect oppressed groups in particular, and the broader groups of mental health consumers in general. They warrant some introductory comments. Historically, a primary list of these problems includes lack of funding, fragmentation, decentralization, poor administrative and service planning, poor programmatic oversight, lack of accountability, weak or nonexistent linkages between psychiatric hospitals and CMHCs, a preoccupation with medication and compliance, complex and sometimes contradictory legislative provisions, and neglect of those with serious mental illness (Grob, 1994; Torrey, 1997; Sharfstein, 2000). A broader list might even be expanded to encompass factors such as jurisdictional rivalries among levels of government, provider bias, community resistance, financial disincentives, insufficient community resources, inadequately trained staff, and skewed national priorities (Arce & Vergare, 1987).

Rosenheck (2000) contends that professional disengagement from the severely mentally ill and disinterest in providing practical assistance in housing, income, and activities were among the factors that led to the downfall of the community mental health movement. Community mental health centers attempted to correct their failure to serve the severely mentally ill with some success, but by the 1990s, the stagnant resources, weakened political support for marginalized populations, deteriorated community and environmental circumstances, and decline in civic activities had effectively undermined the movement (Rosenheck, 2000). The result has been community mental health centers lacking in service capacity, service technology, and accountability; high caseloads and staff burnout; inability to engage and treat people who do not or cannot access traditional treatment; and complex bureaucracies often consisting of new financial mergers and acquisitions that lack the mission and staffing needed to provide for those most in need of care (Arce & Vergare, 1987).

Of course, many of the problems with, and faced by, CMHCs stem from problems at the federal level that work to perpetuate the impasse in effective treatment of oppressed groups. Examination of the dynamics of social policy reveals deeply ingrained patterns reflecting the laggard role of the federal government in social policy in general, and community mental health in particular (Sharfstein, 2000). In addition, fragmentation, overemphasis on research and training without financial support to implement the findings, and market-driven policy responses such as privatization and managed care have also impeded the development of better mental health policies. Lastly, the new federalism, or devolution, has given more power and autonomy to states to develop local social service programs as state officials see fit, often resulting in further oppression or exclusion of vulnerable groups (Schneider & Netting, 1999). In summary, current conditions in the public mental health system create environments that are counterproductive in addressing oppression, and in fact, may play a role in promoting it.

OPPRESSED GROUPS: COMMON THEMES AND EXPERIENCES

Oppressed groups include those who are very poor or homeless; people of color, including immigrants; and lesbian, gay, bisexual, and transgendered (LGBT) persons. Of course, people with physical disabilities experience oppression, as do women, those formerly or currently involved in corrections systems, and others. But the individuals discussed here are already at risk of dual discrimination or oppression because of mental illness combined with group membership in one of these groups. Many are multiply oppressed, as in the case, for example, of an individual with a mental illness who is a person of color and gay. It is inaccurate, overstated (Hanna et al., 2000), and unfair to imply that all minority groups are oppressed or assume a role of victim, but it is accurate to say that members of these non-dominant groups continue to live in an environment of oppression (Hanna et al., 2000), and therefore require careful, pointed attention.

To begin with, mainstream mental health (and other) service settings present barriers to services for many oppressed individuals and groups. Mainstream settings are often in-flexible, provide Eurocentric approaches to care, including the lack of culturally appropriate assessment tools (U.S. Department of Health and Human Services, 1999), and reflect strong provider bias against the oppressed group(s) (Flynn Saulnier, 2002; Snowden, 2003). In addition to lacking integration with those systems and other providers, mainstream service providers often fail to recognize and accept agencies that serve oppressed groups, further marginalizing these agencies within the mental health system (McVey, 2001). Of course, the lack of economic and political power among oppressed groups can dampen professional interest, which can also lead to stigma by association on the part of the provider (Drury, 2003). Finally, the persistent neglect of oppressed groups in professional community mental health literature further impedes progress (Taylor Gibbs & Fuery, 1994; Silka & Tip, 1994; Rothblum, 1994a).

Public mental health systems consistently fail to address several experiences and outcomes that oppressed groups share. Members of oppressed groups often experience negative attitudes on the part of the larger society, stigma, professional bias and countertransference, and increased risk for some mental health issues. Nondominant groups often prefer non-traditional services, self-help, and mutual support systems. Other shared experiences include increased stress associated with an oppressed group status (Serrano-Garcia & Bond, 1994; Walters, Simoni, & Evans-Campbell, 2002); poverty; increased health disparities and substance use (Walters et al., 2002); lack of income, housing, and insurance; and a compromised political voice (Silka & Tip, 1994).

Serrano-Garcia and Bond (1994) observe that oppressed groups have all been neglected and marginalized. This marginalization is accompanied by the consequences of prejudice, discrimination, and oppression, such as ghettoization, labeling, denial of access to social resources (economic and political), and equitable social participation, as well as denial of their civil rights. Oppressed groups are also prone to economic exploitation. Recognizing the common themes between oppressed groups, we simultaneously need to identify experiences unique to the groups, as well as those unique to individuals. The study of oppression also requires the understanding that all "isms" (racism, classism, sexism, etc.) are social constructions that operate to reinforce existing power structures: there is no hierarchy among them (Schmitz, Stakeman, & Sisneros, 2001). As Schmitz et al. (2001) also note, "if you can oppress one group of people, you can oppress all and establish boundary mechanisms to keep oppressions intact" (p. 615). We turn now to some of those groups that have historically been oppressed.

VERY POOR AND HOMELESS

The association between poverty, welfare dependence, depression, anxiety, and substance abuse has been articulated (U.S. Surgeon General, 1999; Taylor, 2001). Homeless people with mental illness, especially those who are unable or deemed unwilling to access traditional services, are a group particularly prone to oppression. Homeless mentally ill people are among the powerless people in society (Cohen, 1989) and experience higher rates of victimization (Rosenheck & Lam, 1997), acute medical illness, trauma, and death (Martell et al., 1992). Yet, homeless people historically have been unable to access these mainstream services because traditional community mental health service approaches have not worked for this population (Belcher & Ephross, 1989; Berman-Rossi & Cohen, 1988; Kuhlman, 1994; Levy, 2000; Morse et al., 1996; Putnam, Cohen, & Sullivan, 1986; Rowe, 1999; Sheridan, Gowan, & Halpin, 1993; Susser, Goldfinger, & White, 1990).

The barriers to CMHCs for homeless people have been cited. A 2003 study demonstrated that 92% of nontraditional programs serving homeless people with serious mental illness experience difficulty when trying to transfer care to CMHCs (Page, 2004). The barriers echoed observations by others, including CMHC incapacity (Rosenheck & Dennis, 2001), inadequacy (Chafetz, 1990; Goldfinger, 1990), and lack of housing, income, and insurance (The National Health Care for the Homeless Clinician's Network, 2003–2004). CMHCs fail to provide the array of comprehensive services needed by homeless people, as well as critical pretreatment alternatives for those who are not ready for more traditional treatment services (Levy, 2000). Existing community mental health systems are frequently unable to provide the comprehensive services that the population requires, because those systems are designed to treat less impoverished and less impaired individuals (Goldfinger, 1990).

Drury (2003, p. 204) summarizes the ways providers created barriers to services for homeless clients by refusing to cross traditional boundaries of service delivery culture: "By maintaining exclusionary policies, separate philosophies of care, conflicting treatment modalities, and categorical funding criteria, [providers] reinforced barriers to service and widened the cultural divide between providers and PHMI [persons who are homeless and mentally ill]." Other barriers include the stigma associated with homelessness (Phelan, Link, & Moore, 1997), conflicting philosophy (Lovell & Cohn, 1998), the requirement that clients have "insight" (Rowe, Fisk, Frey, & Davidson, 2002), lack of programmatic and clinical flexibility (Sheridan et al., 1993), inappropriate expectations of homeless people (McQuistion et al., 1991), and lack of outreach services (Morse & Caslyn, 1996).

The consequences associated with the inability to transfer client care to community mental health centers are serious. The first is swelling caseloads for staff of programs for the homeless, rendering them unable to provide either a full range of services to existing clients (Francis, 2000) or further outreach services to untreated homeless people in need of help (Rosenheck & Dennis, 2001). Staff working in programs for homeless people try to cope with the fallout from the vast discrepancies between their programs and community mental health centers by bending rules, finding loopholes, and investing extra time and labor in clients, many of whom end up dropping out of care (Francis, 2000). In the end, untreated homeless people with serious mental illness are more likely to remain homeless and underserved (National Coalition for the Homeless–National Health Care for the Homeless Council Joint Policy Statement, 2001) and are more exposed to risks of violence (Rosenheck & Lam, 1997), acute medical illness, trauma, and death (Martell et al., 1992).

PEOPLE OF COLOR

The effects of racism are found throughout society, including within public mental health systems. Williams, Neighbors, and Jackson (2003) have observed the relationship between racialized social structures, health, and mental health. Perceptions of discrimination, they report, are linked to long-term health and mental health consequences. Here again, oppression causes mental health problems, while it simultaneously prevents treatment. Institutionalized populations, for example, are disproportionately represented by minority groups, including civil commitments, jails, and prisons (Snowden, 2003). In addition, the use of emergency and inpatient hospitalization for mental health problems is more frequent for people of color than for Caucasians (Chun-Chung Chow, Jaffee, & Snowden, 2003). People of color are less likely to seek help than Caucasians and experience more mistrust — for a variety of reasons, including historical trauma and reluctance or fear of governmental intervention, especially among immigrants (U.S. Surgeon General, 1999). Other issues common among people of color include issues around the stigma of mental health, lack of insurance, and clinician bias.

Clinician bias is reflected, for example, in the overdiagnosis, misdiagnosis, and increased rates of involuntary treatment among people of color (U.S. Surgeon General, 1999). As Snowden (2003) notes, bias occurs at many levels — in particular, individual clinicians' beliefs and actions, including their hostility, naïvete, and general intolerance, as well as their tendency to label clients as unreceptive to treatment. Since observations about specific racial groups have been noted, a few will be highlighted here regarding African Americans, Asians, and indigenous people.

The prevalence of disparities in the use of mental health services between African Americans and Caucasians in the United States is well established (Theriot, Segal, & Cowsert, 2003). Poverty, disinclination to seek help, and lack of services have been noted as factors that have resulted in African Americans' delay in seeking mental health services (U.S. Department of Health and Human Services, 1999). Studies indicate that African Americans prefer self-help agencies over traditional mental health services (Theriot et al., 2003). For African American women, the effects of racism and sexism can have an interactive effect that compounds oppression (Taylor Gibbs & Fuery, 1994).

Asians are less likely to seek mental health services than Caucasians, African Americans, and Hispanics/Latinos. Reasons cited include the effects of stigma, shame, and language difficulties (Sue et al., 1994), especially among immigrants from Southeast Asia who have experienced trauma and hardship related to the immigration process (Silka & Tip, 1994). Asian cultures emphasize community, hierarchical order, focus on elders, mutual assistance, and folk healing. They avoid confrontation and the psychologizing of problems. When traditional providers ignore these preferences, it results in misunderstandings and further barriers (Silka & Tip, 1994). Likewise, Chinese Americans have also experienced language-based and racial/ethnic discrimination, seek informal help from existing support networks, lack insurance, and avoid formal mental health services (Spencer & Chen, 2004). It is hardly surprising then that as Spencer and Chen (2004) note, Asian Americans and Pacific Islanders are three times less likely than Caucasians to use available mental health services.

Indigenous cultures include Pacific Islanders, Native Americans, and Alaska Natives. Native Americans are overrepresented in psych inpatient care compared to whites (Snowden & Cheung, 1990). Many Native Americans and Alaska Natives who experience the effects of historical trauma emphasize the protective functions of family and community, spirituality, traditional healing practice, oral tradition, and group identification (Thurman, Allen, & Deters, 2004; Walters et al., 2002). After more than 500 years of missionary activities, and the loss of land and sacred sites, indigenous cultures have also experienced the degradation of their religious and cultural practices (Walters et al., 2002). Among these groups, depression, alcohol use, suicide, cultural and identity loss, cultural isolation, and vocational stresses are significant problems (McBride, 2003).

Gutierrez, Yeakly, and Ortega (2000), in their comprehensive review of Latino issues in social work, found that Latinos are at risk for poverty, health, and mental health problems, as well as an array of social problems, like lower education, unemployment, and overinvolvement in the criminal justice system. Like other people of color, Latinos under-utilize mental health services. They identify a list of values that are characteristic of Latino populations: allocentrism (commitment to groups rather than the individual), harmony and avoidance of conflict, familism (attachment to family), a preference for closeness in interpersonal space, flexible time orientation, and traditional male/female gender role expectations. The lack of attention on mental health issues of Latinos is striking. In their review of professional literature on Latinos, Gutierrez et al. (2000) found that only 4% of the articles written between 1975 and 1998 focused on mental health issues. This finding is even more striking given that Latinos are the largest ethnic minority group in the United States (Gutierrez et al., 2000).

LESBIAN, GAY, BISEXUAL, AND TRANSGENDERED PERSONS (LGBT)

Despite the removal of homosexuality as a diagnostic category from the *Diagnostic and Statistical Manual of Mental Disorders* in 1973, public and professional attitudes toward LGBT remain negative (Rothblum, 1994b). They are often barred from public institutions (Bradford et al., 1994), receive little research attention, and are subjected to provider bias (Flynn Saulnier, 2002; Rothblum, 1994b). The risk for some mental health issues like depression, isolation, anger, and depression, and barriers to treatment are also higher (Greene, 1994; Rothblum, 1994b). A large survey completed by 1,925 lesbians showed that 18% had attempted suicide, 70% had been physically abused, 32% had been raped or sexually attacked, and 19% had been involved in incestuous relationships (Bradford et al., 1994).* Lack of income and insurance was reported as barriers to receiving care. Garnets and D'Augelli (1994) found that three problems in the contemporary lesbian and gay communities serve as a source of powerlessness and stressors: (1) stresses related to coming out, (2) heterosexism, and (3) difficulties identifying with a community.

MULTIPLE LAYERS OF OPPRESSION

Many individuals experience oppression from multiple sources, with an array of complex issues at work affecting their experience of oppression. Gay Latinos are one example of a group that is dually or multiply oppressed. Diaz, Ayala, Bein, and Henne Marin (2001) found that gay and bisexual Latino men experience a high rate of psychological distress related to social discrimination and resulting poverty and unemployment, which compromises their mental health. For gay/bisexual Latinos with serious mental illnesses like schizophrenia, the psychological distress is even more pronounced, as the effects of stigma against serious mental illnesses are more visible. There are further implications for multiply oppressed LGBT. In many ethnic minority families and communities, a lesbian or gay orientation is marked by denial, because orientation is categorized as belonging to the dominant, but not the racial-ethnic culture, and violates one's ethnicity. Further, there is often a sense of conflicting loyalties between the two communities, and the potential for loss of support should one disclose his or her orientation, in an already small ethnic group (Greene, 1994).

---

* The authors note that the sample is demographically different than women in the general population (younger, more educated) and that there was no control group.

STRATEGIES TO BREAK THE IMPASSE

Given the rise in the numbers of people with minority group status, especially racial and ethnic minority groups (U.S. Surgeon General, 1999), and the continuation of oppression in the United States, the community mental health field is called to revisit its approach, or lack thereof, to the treatment of oppressed groups. Simultaneous examination of the common themes between oppressed groups, differences between groups, as well as individual differences point to specific strategies that can help break the impasse in their mental health treatment. These strategies include (1) increasing civic participation, (2) advocating for housing and health/mental health insurance, (3) improving access and appropriateness of services, (4) providing opportunities for sensitivity training and multicultural education, (5) decreasing stigma, (6) improving research, (7) advocating for the prioritization of funding for organizations that serve oppressed groups, and (8) increasing practitioner understanding about the types and dynamics of oppression.

The first strategy is to increase the power of oppressed groups through the promotion of *increased civic engagement*, particularly during periods of economic decline. Rosenheck (2000) draws the direct connection between civic involvement and community mental health care. He notes an increase in the prevalence of mental illness in recent years, which corresponds to the decline in civic culture in America, and the observation that with a decline in social capital in the United States, it may be difficult to establish and maintain effective community-based service systems. Snowden (2003) showed that coerced treatment increased with economic decline, which was related to greater insecurity, frustrations, and intolerance. Social justice advocacy efforts by mental health professionals are important aspects of counseling (Arredondo & Toporek, 2004) and necessary ingredients of good community mental health care (Cohen et al., 2003; Melton, 2003; Safarjan, 2002). In fact, consciousness raising and political action are often necessary in order to achieve social justice for oppressed groups (Nelson et al., 1998).

Counseling approaches in serving oppressed populations must focus not on adjustment to oppression, but *liberation* from oppression (Hanna et al., 2000). As such, greater advocacy efforts must take place to ensure accessible, affordable housing, universal health care, and sufficient income.

Access to CMHC services can be improved with *better accessibility and appropriateness of services*. In order to improve access, CMHCs must increase their clinical and programmatic flexibility, cultural competence, availability of technologies in multiple languages, and incorporate nontraditional approaches to care and healing. Understanding of the histories, beliefs, and practices of diverse groups should be reflected in program technology such as intake and assessment forms and practices and treatment planning (Gutierrez et al., 2000). Practitioners must also be culturally literate in more than one area, as in the case of LGBT people of color (Greene, 1994).

Practices should be realistic and take into account the exigencies of life, including life on the streets and shelters for homeless people. Diaz et al. (2001) stress the importance of addressing social isolation and issues of self-worth in order to nurture the high resiliency, family acceptance, community involvement, and social activism that significantly alleviate the negative consequences of social discrimination on mental health. Finally, CMHCs should work to strengthen existing social supports within communities and continue to emphasize mutual assistance and self-help efforts.

Community mental health systems should provide better opportunities for *sensitivity training and multicultural education*. The cultural value system in traditional mental health settings is often incompatible with the cultural value systems of many culturally diverse and oppressed populations (Richardson & Molinaro, 1996). As such, CMHCs, universities, and residency/internship programs should provide opportunities for sensitivity training and education, and hold staff and students accountable for demonstrating that sensitivity and cultural competency in their client interventions (Arredondo & Toporek, 2004; Harley et al., 2002). Rather than being considered peripheral, the inclusion of oppression in educational settings should be mainstreamed into curriculum and discussions. Further, there should be more recruitment of individuals who may be representative of oppressed groups (Taylor Gibbs & Fuery, 1994).

Graduate programs should provide multicultural education that focuses on providing knowledge and skills necessary to help end oppression and promote social justice (Wallace, 2000). Specific areas that need attention are multicultural issues, linguistic diversity, immigrant issues, sexual orientation issues, and disability studies (Arredondo & Toporek, 2004; Wallace, 2000). Harley et al. (2002) specifically encourage the incorporation of issues of race, class, and gender into the counseling curriculum. These strategies may pose a difficult challenge, however, since the basic structure and culture of universities is dominated by Western culture, entrenched in systems of control (Wallace, 2000) and hierarchy, and dominated by white, heterosexual men in power.

Mental health organizations should better prepare staff on how to incorporate oppressed groups in service technologies or, more accurately, how to incorporate the technology so it better fits oppressed groups and individuals. For example, organizations can better serve lesbians by demonstrating understanding about the negative consequences of "coming out" — in particular, by enforcing discrimination policies and letting lesbians know that they are welcome (Flynn Saulnier, 2002). Latinos will be better served when the organization understands cultural values issues in counseling, like *personalissmo* (developing a personal relationship before starting a professional relationship), and culturally specific ways that Latinos express distress or *ataque de nervios* (Gutierrez et al., 2000). Harley et al. (2002) encourage counselors to postpone making clinical decisions about oppressed clients until sufficient trust and rapport have been established with them.

Professional organizations can play an important role as well. The multicultural counseling competencies ("competencies") were developed by the Association of Multicultural Counseling and Development (AMCD). Criticisms of the competencies have included the perception that the competencies are not grounded in research, the attention by counselors to racial issues that may be, in essence, racist, and a questionable emphasis by counselors in directing mental health consumers to be more sociopolitically active (Weinrach & Thomas, 2002). Some of these criticisms are clarified and further discussed by Arredondo and Toporek (2004). The respectful and forthright discussions in the literature about these and other aspects of oppression are encouraging and should be continued. Finally, educational and service programs should be held accountable for effecting demonstration of sensitivity and multicultural competence at all levels — faculty, students, and staff (Arredondo & Toporek, 2004).

Programs that effectively serve oppressed groups, such as nontraditional programs for the homeless and those that serve immigrants, should work to decrease stigma associated with mental illness and poverty, and improve acceptance of their clients and their agencies (McVey, 2001). Advocacy groups can help in these efforts as well. Values-based partnerships between providers, stakeholders, and oppressed groups should also be formed. These partnerships focus efforts on achieving key values like power sharing, social justice, and diversity. They can be beneficial as long as they acknowledge the power imbalance between professionals and the oppressed groups with whom they work, and recognize that they exist for the oppressed group's benefit (Nelson, Prilleltensky, & MacGillivary, 2001).

Improved research related to oppression and its relationship to the quantity and quality of mental health treatment is also needed. Several experts have cited the dearth of attention, content, and appropriateness of research related to oppressed groups (Arredondo & Toporek, 2004; Van Voorhis & Wagner, 2002). But conventional research is often irrelevant, because it is based on Eurocentric values, methodologies, and concepts that compromise the validity of the findings (Walters et al., 2002). Research should focus instead on help-seeking behaviors, coping strategies, and strengths, and should use instruments that draw on the subject's expertise. Chun-Chung Chow et al. (2003) stress the importance of studying specific stressors, patterns of symptomatology, coping strategies, and help-seeking behaviors of black women, for example, in addition to isolating the effects of race, gender, and socioeconomic status. Arredondo and Toporek (2004) emphasize the need for further research that specifically examines the cultural experiences of multicultural clients in the counseling process, as well as the ethical issues and practices that arise. Harley et al. (2002) call for more research that assesses the effectiveness and impact of approaches implemented that address issues of race, class, and gender. And there is great need for culturally specific research methodologies. For example, Gutierrez et al. (2000) emphasize the need for valid sampling procedures with Latinos and culturally appropriate instruments, including valid methods for translating these instruments.

Mental health research will be more relevant and appropriate in its quest to explore issues around oppression when it includes consumers in the process and rectifies power imbalances between consumers and professionals. Research will also be stronger in the fight against oppression when social justice is interwoven into the research process, as in the case when consumers research the services they use and are able to access research resources (Ochocka, Janzen, & Nelson, 2002). Gutierrez et al. (2000) highlight the potentially negative effects of research on the Latino community. For example, research has been used to reinforce stereotypes of Latinos and has led to barriers in their receiving resources (Gutierrez et al., 2000).

A major criticism of research is the failure to implement research findings into practice. There is rarely a change in policy or any increased funding for services following the dissemination of research findings, and efforts to integrate findings have been inadequate (U.S. GAO, 2000). There has been some progress in this area, as in the case of the federal government providing funding for such implementation, but much is needed to support the implementation of technologies, information, and practices that will help in the delivery of services to oppressed populations. Further, *funding for organizations that serve oppressed groups should be prioritized*, and the federal government should be pressed to disseminate widely research findings that provide guidelines for successful treatment interventions.

Public mental health financing efforts should also address the problems created by the increase in market-driven approaches to mental health care, such as privatization, business mergers, and Medicaid managed care, which have been linked to significant decreases in mental health referrals and barriers to services (U.S. GAO, 2000; Johnsen et al., 1998). The infusion of funding alone, however, may not be enough to motivate organizations to improve the delivery of mental health services, given that research has shown that organizations do not always behave in predictable ways when given substantial incentives to do things differently (Ridgely, Mulkern, Giard, & Shern, 2002). Efforts to end oppression, then, must take place at multiple levels simultaneously.

One such level focuses on *increasing practitioner understanding about the types and dynamics of oppression.* According to Harley et al. (2002), consumers affected by oppression, in often intersecting positions of race, class, and gender, may view traditional approaches to mental health services and interventions as counterproductive to their well-being. Mental health providers, then, are called to examine the existence of and effects of oppression in their own systems of care: "the patterns of cultural supremacy and positionalities must be disrupted in counseling practices and pedagogy" (p. 235).

Practitioners must also understand the types of oppression: primary (blatant forms of oppression through force or deprivation), secondary (when one benefits from the oppression of others), tertiary (when a member seeks acceptance by the dominant group by abandoning his or her own group), and mixed (when one is both oppressed and an oppressor) (Hanna et al., 2000). Hanna et al. (2000) also point out the role of oppressors that frequently go unnoticed by those oppressors. For example, those who are in power are often much less perceptive about the dynamics of oppression than those who are oppressed, even in counseling relationships. Second, many are complicit in diminishing perceptions of those who are oppressed in order to escape their own feelings of guilt. Third, propaganda messages are used by those in power when they start to become aware of the perceptive powers of those who are oppressed. Propaganda messages are those given by the larger, dominant society that diminish the value of the oppressed. When internalized, these messages can easily become the source of mental health and other problems. Mental health counselors, then, are called to recognize and validate the perceptive skills of their clients, helping them disidentify with propaganda messages and address the emotions that accompany their internalization. Hanna et al. (2000) go a step further and challenge counselors to address oppression in their clients who are oppressors, and to build empathy and awareness in those clients. These interventions and approaches, however, will require a level of sophistication and self-awareness on the part of practitioners that most mental health systems are ill-equipped to address in a comprehensive and effective manner.

In summary, there are unique aspects and experiences within oppressed groups, and individuals within those groups. While recognizing the uniqueness of individuals, it is critical that the community mental health field understand the commonalities between those groups, and begin to incorporate that understanding into new strategies that can help address and end oppression. Highlights of those commonalities are that oppressed groups are underrepresented in mental health treatment and overrepresented in institutions. They experience various forms and manifestations of stress, historical loss, discrimination, and isolation, and may experience poverty and other serious social problems. Mental health issues may be experienced, described, and approached in ways that are incongruent with traditional approaches to care. Traditional Western approaches to mental health care and research are frequently irrelevant, inappropriate, and entrenched in values associated with the very system that seeks to oppress them. The mental health field should do more to help turn the tide of oppression, beginning with a better understanding of both the overt and subtle facets of oppression and by eradicating it through sufficient housing, health care, and income. Aggressive, appropriate attention to oppression in education, research, and professional publications will also help break the impasse in service delivery, as will promoting service technologies that respect, incorporate, and build upon existing cultures and worldviews.

REFERENCES

Arce, A.A. & Vergare, M.J. (1987). Homelessness, the chronic mentally ill and community mental health centers. *Community Mental Health Journal, 23*, 242–249.

Arredondo, P. & Toporek, R. (2004). Multicultural counseling competencies — ethical practice. *Journal of Mental Health Counseling, 26(1)*, 44–55.

Belcher, J.R. & Ephross P.H. (1989). Toward an effective practice model for the homeless mentally ill. *Social Casework, 70(7)*, 421–427.

Berman-Rossi,T. & Cohen, M. (1988). Group development and shared decision making: work with homeless mentally ill women. *Social Work with Groups, 11(4)*, 63–78.

Bradford, J., Caitlin, R., & Rothblum, E.D. (1994). National Lesbian Health Care Survey: implications for mental health care. *Journal of Consulting and Clinical Psychology, 62*, 228–242.

Chafetz, L. (1990). Withdrawal from the homeless mentally ill. *Community Mental Health Journal, 26(5)*, 449–461.

Chun-Chung Chow, J., Jaffee, K., & Snowden, L. (2003). Racial/ethnic disparities in the use of mental health services in poverty areas. *American Journal of Public Health, 93(5)*, 792–797.

Chung, H., Teresi, J., Guarnaccia, P., Meyers, B.S., Holmes, D., Bobrowitz, T., Eimicke, J.P., & Ferran, E. (2003). Depressive symptoms and psychiatric distress in low income Asian and Latino primary care patients: prevalence and recognition. *Community Mental Health Journal, 39(1)*, 33–46.

Cohen, M.B. (1989). Social work practice with homeless mentally ill people: engaging the client. *Social Work, 34(6)*, 505–509.

Cohen, C.I., Feiner, J.S., Huffine, C., Moffic, H.S., & Thompson, K.S. (2003). The future of community psychiatry. *Community Mental Health Journal, 39(5)*, 459–471.

Diaz, R.M., Ayala, G., Bein, E., Henne, J., & Marin, B.V. (2001). The impact of homophobia, poverty, and racism on the mental health of gay and bisexual Latino men: findings from 3 U.S. cities. *American Journal of Public Health, 91(6)*, 927–932.

Drury, L.J. (2003). Community care for people who are homeless and mentally ill. *Journal of Health Care for the Poor and Underserved, 14(2)*, 194–207.

Flynn Saulnier, C. (2002). Deciding who to see: lesbians discuss their preferences in health and mental health care providers. *Social Work, 47(4)*, 355–365.

Francis, L.E. (2000). Conflicting bureaucracies, conflicted work: dilemmas in case management for homeless people with mental illness. *Journal of Sociology and Social Welfare, 27*, 97–112.

Garnets, L.D. & D'Augelli, A.R. (1994). Empowering lesbian and gay communities: a call for collaboration with community psychology. *American Journal of Community Psychology, 22*, 447–471.

Goldfinger, S.M. (1990). Homelessness and schizophrenia: a psychosocial approach. In M.I. Herz, S.J. Keith, & J.P. Docherty (Eds.), *Handbook of Schizophrenia*, Vol. 4, *Psychosocial Treatment of Schizophrenia*. Amsterdam: Elsevier Science Publishers, pp. 355–385.

Greene, B. (1994). Ethnic-minority lesbians and gay men: mental health and treatment issues. *Journal of Consulting and Clinical Psychology, 62*, 243–251.

Grob, G.N. (1994). *The Mad Among Us: A History of Care of America's Mentally Ill*. Cambridge, MA: Harvard University Press.

Gutierrez, L., Yeakly, A., & Ortega, R. (2000). Educating students for social work with Latinos: issues for the new millennium. *Journal of Social Work Education, 36*, 541–557.

Hanna, F.J., Talley, W.B., & Guindon, M.H. (2000). The power of perception: toward a model of cultural oppression and liberation. *Journal of Counseling and Development, 78*, 430–441.

Harley, D.A., Jolivette, K., McCormick, K., & Tice, K. (2002). Race, class, and gender: a constellation of positionalities with implications for counseling. *Journal of Multicultural Counseling and Development, 30*, 216–238.

Johnsen, M.C., Morrissey, J.P., Landow, W.J., Starrett, B.E., Calloway, M.O., & Ullman, M. (1998). The impact of managed care on service systems for persons who are homeless and mentally ill. *Research in Community and Mental Health, 9*, 115–137.

Kuhlman, T. (1994). *Psychology on the streets: mental health practice with homeless persons*. New York: John Wiley & Sons.

Levy, J.S. (2000). Homeless outreach: on the road to pretreatment alternatives. *Families in Society: The Journal of Contemporary Human Services, 81*, 360–368.

Lovell, A. & Cohn, S. (1998). The elaboration of "choice" in a program for homeless persons labeled psychiatrically disabled. *Human Organization, 57(1)*, 8–20.

Martell, J., Seitz, R., Harada, J., Kobayashi, J., Sasaki, V., & Wong, C. (1992). Hospitalization in an urban homeless population: the Honolulu Urban Homeless Project. *Annals of Internal Medicine, 116*, 299–303.

McBride, B. (2003). Aspects of community healing: experiences of the Sault Sainte Marie Tribe of Chippewa Indians. *American Indian and Alaska Native Mental Health Research: The Journal of the National Center, 11*, 67–84.

McQuiston, H., D'Ercole, & Kopelson, E. (1991). Urban street outreach: using clinical principles to steer the system. In Cohen, N. (Ed.), *Psychiatric Outreach to the Mentally Ill*, San Fransisco, CA: Jossey-Bass, 17–27.

McVey, C.C. (2001). Coordinating effective health and mental health continuity of care. *Corrections Today, 63*, 58–62.

Melton, G.B. (2003). Mental health and social justice: a vision for the 21st century. *American Journal of Orthopsychiatry, 73(3)*, 245–247.

Morse, G. & Caslyn, R.J. (1996). Mentally disturbed homeless people in St. Louis: needy, willing, but underserved. *International Journal of Mental Illness, 14 (4)*, 74–94.

Morse, G., Calsyn, R., Miller, J., Rosenberg, P., West, L., & Guilliland, J. (1996). Outreach to homeless mentally ill people: conceptual and clinical considerations. *Community Mental Health Journal, 32*, 261–274.

National Coalition for the Homeless (2001). *McKinney Report*. Washington, D.C.

National Health Care for the Homeless (2003–2004). 2003–2004 Policy Statement. Retrieved on April 21, 2004, from www.nhchc.org/advocacy/PolicyPapers/index.htm

Nelson, G., Prilleltensky, I., & MacGillivary, H. (2001). Building value-based partnerships: toward solidarity with oppressed groups. *American Journal of Community Psychology, 29*, 649–677.

Ochocka, J., Janzen, R., & Nelson, G. (2002). Sharing power and knowledge: professional and mental health consumer/survivor researchers working together in a participatory action research project. *Psychiatric Rehabilitation Journal, 25*, 379–387.

Page, J. (2004). Programs That Serve Homeless People with Serious Mental Illness: A Nationwide Exploration of Non-Traditional Treatment Approaches, Success, and Barriers to Transferring Care to Community Mental Health Systems. Unpublished Doctoral Dissertation. Stony Brook University, School of Social Work.

Phelan, J., Link, B.G., & Moore, R.E. (1997). The impact of the label "homeless" on attitudes toward poor persons. *Social Psychology Quarterly, 60(4)*, 323–337.

Putnam, J.R., Cohen, N.C., & Sullivan, A.M. (1986). Innovative outreach services for the homeless mentally ill. *International Journal of Mental Health, 14*, 112–124.

Richardson, T.Q. & Molinaro, K.L. (1996). White counselor self-awareness: a prerequisite for developing multicultural competence. *Journal of Counseling and Development, 74*, 238–242.

Ridgely, M.S., Mulkern, V., Giard, J., & Shern, D. (2002). State mental health policy: critical elements of public-sector managed behavioral health programs for severe mental illness in five states. *Psychiatric Services, 53(4)*, 397–399.

Rosenheck, R. (2000). The delivery of mental health services in the 21st century: bringing the community back in. *Community Mental Health Journal, 36*, 107–123.

Rosenheck, R. & Dennis, D. (2001). Time-limited assertive community treatment for homeless persons with serious mental illness. *Archives of General Psychiatry, 58*, 1073–1080.

Rosenheck, R. & Lam, J. (1997). Client and site characteristics as barriers to service use by homeless persons with serious mental illness. *Psychiatric Services, 48*, 387–390.

Rothblum, E.D. (1994a). Introduction to the special section: mental health of lesbians and gay men. *Journal of Consulting and Clinical Psychology, 62*, 211–212.

Rothblum, E.D. (1994b). I only read about myself on bathroom walls: the need for research on the mental health of lesbians and gay men. *Journal of Consulting and Clinical Psychology, 62*, 213–220.

Rowe, Michael (1999). *Crossing the border: encounters between homeless people and outreach workers.* Berkeley: University of California Press.

Rowe, M., Fisk, D., Frey, J., & Davidson, L. (2002). Engaging persons with substance use disorders: lessons from homeless outreach. *Administration and Policy in Mental Health, 29(3)*, 263–273.

Safarjan, B. (2002). A primer for advancing psychology in the public sector. *American Psychologist, 57(11)*, 947–955.

Schneider, R.L. & Netting, F.E. (1999). Influencing social policy in a time of devolution: upholding social work's great tradition. *Social Work, 44*, 349–357.

Schmitz, C.L., Stakeman, C., & Sisneros, J. (2001). Educating professionals for practice in a multicultural society: understanding oppression and valuing diversity. *Families in Society: The Journal of Contemporary Human Services, 82*, 612–622.

Serrano-Garcia, I. & Bond, M.A. (1994). Empowering the silent ranks: introduction. *American Journal of Community Psychology, 22*, 433–446.

Sharfstein, S. (2000). Whatever happened to community mental health? *Psychiatric Services, 51*, 616–620.

Sheridan, M., Gowan, N., & Halpin, S. (1993). Developing a practice model for the homeless mentally ill. *Families in Society: The Journal of Contemporary Human Services, 74*, 410–421.

Silka, L. & Tip, J. (1994). Empowering the silent ranks: the Southeast Asian experience. *American Journal of Community Psychology, 22*, 497–530.

Snowden, L. (2003). Bias in mental health assessment and intervention: theory and evidence. *American Journal of Public Health, 93*, 239–243.

Snowden, L. & Cheung, F.K. (1990). Use of inpatient mental health services by members of ethnic minority groups. *American Psychologist, 45*, 347–355.

Spencer, M.S. & Chen, J. (2004). Effect of discrimination on mental health service utilization among Chinese Americans. *American Journal of Public Health, 94*, 809–814.

Sue, S., Nakamura, C.Y., & Chung, R.C. (1994). Mental health research on Asian Americans. *Journal of Community Psychology, 22(2)*, 61–67.

Susser, E., Goldfinger, S., & White, A. (1990). Some clinical approaches to the homeless mentally ill. *Community Mental Health Journal, 26*, 463–490.

Taylor, L.C. (2001). Work attitudes, employment barriers, and mental health symptoms in a sample of rural welfare recipients. *American Journal of Community Psychology, 29(30)*, 443–463.

Taylor Gibbs, J. & Fuery, D. (1994). Mental health and well-being of black women: toward strategies of empowerment. *American Journal of Community Psychology, 22*, 559–583.

Theriot, M.T., Segal, S.P., & Cowsert, M.J. (2003). African-Americans and comprehensive service use. *Community Mental Health Journal, 39*, 225–237.

Therman, P.J., Allen, J., & Deters, P. (2004). The circles of care evaluation: doing participatory evaluation with American Indian and Alaskan Native communities. *The Journal of the National Center, 11(2)*, 139–155.

Torrey, E.F. (1997). *Out of the shadows: confronting America's mental illness crisis.* New York: John Wiley & Sons.

U.S. Department of Health and Human Services (1999). *Mental Health: A Report to the Surgeon General.* Rockville, MD: U.S. Department of Health and Human Services, Substance Abuse and Mental Health Services Administration, Center for Mental Health Services, National Institutes of Health, National Institute of Mental Health.

United States General Accounting Office Report to Congressional Requester (2000). *Homelessness: Barriers to Using Mainstream Programs.* GAO/RCED-00-184.

Van Voorhis, R. & Wagner, M. (2002). Among the missing: content on lesbian and gay people in social work journals. *Social Work, 47*, 345–355.

Wallace, B.C. (2000). A call for change in multicultural training at graduate schools of education: educating to end oppression and for social justice. *Teachers College Record, 102*, 1086–1111.

Walters, K.L., Simoni, J.M., & Evans-Campbell, T. (2002). Substance use among American Indians and Alaska natives: incorporating culture in an "indigenist" stress-coping paradigm. *Public Health Reports, 117*, 104–118.

Weinrach, S.G. & Thomas, K.R. (2002). A critical analysis of the multicultural counseling competencies: implications for the practice of mental health counseling. *Journal of Mental Health Counseling, 24*, 20–35.

Williams, D.R., Neighbors, H.W., & Jackson, J.S. (2003). Racial/ethnic discrimination and health: findings from community studies. *American Journal of Public Health*, 93, 200–208.

10

STIGMA, SEXUAL ORIENTATION, AND MENTAL ILLNESS
A Community Mental Health Perspective*

JESSICA ROSENBERG, SAMUEL J. ROSENBERG,
CHRISTIAN HUYGEN, AND EILEEN KLEIN

Marginalized communities present some of the greatest challenges and opportunities in the field of community mental health. The challenges can seem daunting, but the rewards — vastly increased quality of life, social support, and treatment compliance, as well as significant reductions in the use of emergency services such as hospitalization — are potentially enormous. The present chapter examines an innovative response to the needs of lesbian, gay, bisexual, and transgender (LGBT) consumers. We hope to demonstrate that such a response can be effective and feasible, that it can be informed by recent work on stigma and how it operates, and that such a response can have a significant impact on consumers' lives.

In building effective community mental health responses to the specific needs of marginalized populations, we must begin by considering those needs. The treatment needs of LGBT individuals who suffer from serious mental illness are generally overlooked (Rosenberg, Rosenberg, Huygen, & Klein, 2005). Research suggests that the mental health needs of this population differ from those of the heterosexual seriously mentally ill, and that mainstream mental health care systems may not fully address their concerns (Cochran, 2001).

The LBGT seriously mentally ill individual, if untreated, is at increased risk for a host of co-occurring disorders and related problems, including substance abuse, HIV/AIDS, and involvement in the criminal justice system (Cochran, Sullivan, & Mays, 2001; Fergusson, Horwood, & Beautrais, 1999; Sandfort, de Graaf, Bijl, & Schnabel, 2001). Fergusson et al. (1999) found that by age 21, LGBT individuals were at increased risk for major depression, conduct disorders, substance abuse and dependence, suicidal ideation, and suicide attempts. The pattern holds at midlife as well. Cochran et al. (2001) found evidence that lesbian, gay, and bisexual respondents to the National Survey of Midlife Development in the United States showed increased risk for psychiatric disorders as compared with heterosexual women and men.

---

* This chapter is based on the article "No Need to Hide: Out of the Closet and Mentally Ill," published in *Best Practices in Mental Health: An International Journal*, 1, 72–85, 2005, and is used with permission of Lyceum Books, Inc.

Similarly, Hellman, Sudderth, and Avery (2002) found higher rates of bipolar and depressive disorders in LGBT males than in control males; however, that study found no significant differences between LGBT and control females.

LGBT individuals with serious mental illness live with a double burden of stigma. Society discriminates against their sexual and gender identity, as well as their mental health status. This means that in mental health settings such as inpatient units and outpatient treatment settings, they often attempt to hide their sexual or gender identity; conversely, when interacting with members of the LGBT community they are often reluctant to disclose their mental health status. This often means that they lack any safe context in which they can articulate and manifest the full range of challenges and obstacles that affect their lives. The fact that the field of mental health has in the past conflated these two stigmas by defining homosexuality itself as a kind of mental illness is a particularly corrosive aspect of the situation in which LGBT consumers often find themselves.

This chapter will present an overview of the dynamics of the dual stigma of being an LGBT person living with a major mental illness. The chapter will discuss an innovative community mental health program, the Rainbow Heights Club, that was developed to address the unique social needs of this population and help them to participate maximally in the community.

STIGMA

As noted above, LGBT individuals with serious mental illness are subject to dual stigma, which stems from societal discrimination toward same-sex preference and bias against mental illness.

In the classic perspective elaborated by Goffman (1963), stigma is conceptualized as an "attribute that is deeply discrediting" and that reduces the bearer "from a whole and usual person to a tainted, discounted one" (p. 3). Persons who are stigmatized possess characteristics that position them outside of the expectations established by socially accepted norms. Stigma represents a relational attribute, a "mark", associated with a person that links him or her to undesirable stereotypical characteristics (Link & Phelan, 2001). Stigma is not merely a label, but rather, directs social attention to something "in the person" that inherently makes the person tainted. As such, the victims of stigma are blamed for "being" socially unacceptable. Whereas individuals diagnosed with cancer are referred to as "having cancer," individuals diagnosed with schizophrenia are seen as "being schizophrenic." Research shows that stigma is a central process that has serious consequences in shaping the pursuit of activities related to life chances: occupation, education, health, and general well-being. In the case of LGBT persons with severe mental illness, this becomes compounded by the duality of the stigmatization process and the spillover into all areas of social and subjective experience.

The process of stigmatization unfolds when five critical components converge: (1) labeling, (2) stereotyping, (3) separating "us" from "them," (4) status loss and discrimination, and (5) an imbalance of power (Link & Phelan, 2001).

LABELING

LGBT sexual and gender identity is labeled as different from the heterosexual norm. Similarly, the condition of mental illness is marked as a difference from the presumed norm of mental health.

LINKING HUMAN DIFFERENCE WITH NEGATIVE ATTRIBUTE

Once LBGT persons who are seriously mentally ill have been socially labeled as "different," the second step in the stigmatization process is to assign these differences a negative attribute. As such, gays and lesbians are perceived to be different in negative ways, as amoral or deviant. In addition, their mental illness leads to further social exclusion due to societal attitudes toward mentally ill persons, including the belief that the mentally ill are dangerous and bizarre.

THEM AND US

LGBT persons are denied access to basics such as housing and employment. The mentally ill experience a similar situation when confronted with the NIMBY (not in my backyard) phenomenon when residential programs seek to develop housing or there is a rehabilitation program featuring supported employment. There is a denial of access, and in extreme cases, when a stigmatized group becomes dehumanized, they can become victims of fatal violence.

STATUS LOSS AND DISCRIMINATION

Once the process of stigma construction evolves to the point where negative associations are group specific, members of such groups experience downward mobility and status loss, and due to their negative stereotype, become the subject of discrimination. Low social status engenders low self-esteem. For those who are chronically mentally ill, a process of self-designation evolves where clients refer to themselves as having become a schizophrenic, rather than having schizophrenia (Estroff, 1981). Their illness defines who they are and evolves into a loss of social roles and identity. Identification with the LGBT sexual minority population further complicates this loss of social acceptance. The comparatively higher incidence of substance abuse and suicide among LGBT adolescents attests to the deleterious effects of stigma (Fergusson et al., 1999).

STIGMA: AN IMBALANCE OF POWER

The ability to construct a complex system such as stigma is dependent on an imbalance of power: those who actively participate in stigmatizing others must have the power to proceed unchecked, and victims of stigma must lack sufficient power and recourses to counter and oppose status loss, marginalization, and a reduction in life chances. In effect, the process of social stigmatization rests on social, economic, and political power over the populations designated for stigma. Despite the demographic incidence of homosexuality (estimated 4 to 10% of the population, often higher in large metropolitan areas), LGBT people remain a socially marginalized population that does not readily self-identify, particularly when in positions of power, such as elected officials, corporate executives, and professionals. Similarly, the mentally ill are equally underrepresented in positions of social and political power. Whereas they are overwhelmingly dependent on social programs for their subsistence, they have not become a political voting block capable of influencing the political process.

The dual stigmatization of LGBT consumers is visible in many aspects of popular culture. In numerous popular movies such as *Silence of the Lambs*, the sadistic, psychotic serial killer is often homosexual; and routinely, in movies as well as in life, the parents of people who disclose a same-sex sexual orientation instantly ask themselves and one another "what they did wrong." Combined with the misguided insistence of certain political groups that homosexuality is a "lifestyle choice" rather than an inalienable inherent aspect of a human being, this can give rise to the sense, on the part of an LGBT person living with mental illness, that he or she is somehow to blame for his or her condition, and that they do not deserve competent or culturally sensitive treatment.

Thus, in the field of mental health, stigma constitutes a psychosocial stressor that warrants the attention of mental health practitioners and planners as a public health matter. In this light, the development and implementation of the Rainbow Heights Club exemplifies a community mental health response to a targeted population. The challenge was to create a program that would confront the manifold stresses created by stigma and provide an affirmative atmosphere for psychological, social, emotional, and physical well-being. The staff developed and, through grant funding, implemented their idea to create the Rainbow Heights Club, a supportive, sensitive place to affirm one's identity as an LGBT consumer of mental health services.

PROGRAM DESCRIPTION

Rainbow Heights Club is a psychosocial and advocacy program that serves LGBT people ages 18 and up who have a past or present Axis I diagnosis. The emphasis is on creating a safe space within which people can disclose both their sexual and psychiatric issues, find social support and acceptance, feel like a welcome member of a community, and find that they can offer support and acceptance to others. The Rainbow Heights Club opened its doors in September 2002, with a membership of 15 and a daily census of 4 or 5 people. The daily program was unstructured, with one formal group planned daily, no support groups, and relied on the milieu provision of support to members. As of May 2005, the club has over 250 members, with about 100 more joining every year; daily attendance is between 25 and 30. The club's growth was facilitated through extensive consumer input and outreach.

Ongoing consumer input is an indispensable part of the work at the Rainbow Heights Club. To solicit consumer input and — even more importantly — to promptly act on it are paramount in empowering consumers and in valuing what they have to say. Community meetings, support groups, and discussion and activity groups were added to the schedule at members' request. Members requested that the club have a computer room, and currently there is a place for members to have Internet access and use literacy software, typing skills programs, and word processing, all of which are avidly pursued by club members.

At the club, all staff and members respect the right of all members to express their sexual and gender identity however they see fit. This is a particularly important point for transgender club members, because many of them would not be able to pass a psychiatric evaluation and be approved for gender reassignment surgery; others would not choose to do so; and most would find it very difficult to afford a full physical transition. For both personal and external reasons, therefore, the range of choices people at Rainbow Heights Club make about how they will enact their sexual or gender identity is very broad. Some transgender club members have had gender reassignment surgery; some have used hormones; some have changed the way they dress, speak, or carry themselves; and for some, their gender identity is a matter of personal inner experience and conviction.

The following are suggested guidelines toward effective and culturally competent treatment with LGBT mental health consumers.

Use Inclusive Language

In many clinics and inpatient units, male patients are routinely asked, "Are you married, or do you have a girlfriend?" Many LGBT consumers will interpret this as a signal that the care provider is unwilling to hear about relationships that fall outside a heterosexual paradigm, and some of them will be silenced. Using more inclusive language, such as "Are you in a relationship right now? What kind of people do you tend to have relationships with?" is a simple change that may have far-reaching results.

Be Aware of Subtle Signals You May Be Sending

Nearly all LGBT people at some point in their lives have lost or disrupted relationships with friends, family members, or religious communities over disclosure of their sexual or gender identity. As a result, many of them are hypervigilant toward possible clues as to whether a given person may or may not be accepting and supportive of them. The use of routine language such as that in the previous example can unintentionally telegraph a heterosexist point of view. Conversely, hanging even a small pro-LGBT flyer in your waiting room, or posting information about LGBT resources in your community, may make LGBT consumers feel that their disclosures are welcome.

Welcome and Normalize Consumer Disclosures

A tentative disclosure of LGBT identity or experience can be welcomed with a simple "I'm glad you told me that." This can be followed with the kind of comment that would follow upon any consumer's mentioning of a relationship or experience: "What's he like?" or "Where did you meet her?" Showing an LGBT consumer that you are willing to put yourself in his or her shoes can have a tremendous effect on the working alliance and undo some of the estrangement from the mental health establishment that many LGBT consumers experience.

Utilize Knowledge about Consumer Sexuality in Discharge Planning

At Rainbow Heights Club, a number of consumers have a long history of decompensations and hospitalizations, whereas others have long-standing, supportive, monogamous relationships. If you are working with consumers, the person's romantic partner as well as their friends are all part of your treatment team. You need to be hearing about them, and if possible you should be talking with them. Partners, loved ones, friends, and family can provide crucial information, invaluable support for treatment compliance, and ongoing monitoring of the consumer's mental status.

Avoid Pathologizing

Many care providers pathologize any aspect of a consumer's expression of his or her sexual or gender identity, interpreting it as further evidence of the person's illness. However, LGBT consumers' efforts to express their sexuality and find connections with others are often the locus of a great deal of creativity, resilience, courage, and even playfulness. Conversely, it is not helpful to assume that any expression of a consumer's sexuality or gender identity is to be celebrated. Any such activity should be pragmatically evaluated in terms of its effect on the consumer's physical and emotional health, self-esteem, and relationships.

For each club member, the benefits of participation in the club are different. Some enjoy the possibility of having friends who are also LGBT consumers. Others take advantage of the chance to develop a budding repertoire of social skills in a safe and supportive environment. Still others focus on the chance to express themselves artistically or in writing. Along the way, they are all learning to be more comfortable telling their stories, and they are all learning how universal many aspects of their stories can be.

The two following vignettes vividly illustrate the many and varied ways that the Rainbow Heights Club members have benefited from this program:

Laura

Laura, a member of Rainbow Heights Club, is a Latina lesbian who wears a short crew cut and roomy, comfortable men's work clothes. On her first day at a new mental health clinic, she was sitting in the waiting room when a staff member walked through the room and said to the receptionist, "Mira esa puta (look at that dyke)." The man turned out to be her therapist. When staff asked her whether she had told the man she had understood perfectly well what he had said, she replied, "No! I had a lot of stuff I had to get off my chest." She added that she avoided talking about her sexuality or her relationship in her treatment. This story demonstrates the lengths to which LGBT people with mental illness feel they must go in order to get some vestige of assistance from a system they believe fundamentally does not care about them. Laura's story also shows that many LGBT people with mental illness remain in the closet, even with their therapists, and that they often do not believe that they deserve, or have the right to demand, competent and respectful treatment.

Steven

Steven is a 60-year-old Caucasian male with a history of numerous psychiatric diagnoses, treatment with an extensive array of medications, and numerous hospitalizations over the past 30 years. Although he rarely participates in structured support or activity groups at the club, he makes extensive use of opportunities for informal socializing with other club members in a safe environment. He is currently stable, entirely free of medications, and has not been hospitalized since he started attending the club two years ago. He is a valued member of the Rainbow Heights community: he is a source of playful humor as well as thoughtful advice. Moreover, several months ago he sought and found a part-time job that lets him attend the club, and he has been proudly and successfully employed ever since. He credits the support and encouragement of club members with enabling him to make these changes in his life.

CONCLUSION

Perhaps the most striking fact about Rainbow Heights is that only 10 of Rainbow Heights Club's 250 members have been hospitalized in the nearly two years that the club has been open. Considering that all Rainbow Heights members are diagnosed as severely mentally ill and that the majority of them have a history of repeated hospitalization, it is clear that the support provided by the club is making a significant difference in keeping this population stable and in the community. This outcome demonstrates the importance of providing culturally sensitive and specific psychosocial support and advocacy services, within a peer-based environment. We feel strongly that mental health consumers who are members of a number of marginalized, oppressed communities can benefit from the establishment of similar agencies addressing their particular needs. At Rainbow Heights, the consumer's view of the problem is accepted. This attitude of respect and affirmation for the consumer's point of view is critical to maintaining a seriously and persistently mentally ill person in the community.

REFERENCES

Cochran, S.D. (2001). Emerging issues in research on lesbians' and gay men's mental health: does sexual orientation really matter? *American Psychologist, 56*, 931–947.

Cochran, S.D., Sullivan, J.G., & Mays, V.M. (2001). Prevalence of Psychiatric Disorders, Psychological Distress, and Treatment Utilization among Lesbian, Gay, and Bisexual Individuals in a Sample of the U.S. Population (unpublished manuscript). Available from Susan D. Cochran, Department of Epidemiology, School of Public Health, University of California, Los Angeles, Box 951772, Los Angeles, CA 90095-1772.

Estroff, S. (1981). *Making it crazy: an ethnography of psychiatric clients in an American community.* Berkeley: University of California Press.

Fergusson, D.M., Horwood, L.J., & Beautrais, A.L. (1999). Is sexual orientation related to mental health problems and suicidality in young people? *Archives of General Psychiatry, 56*, 876–880.

Goffman, E. (1963). *Stigma: notes on the management of spoiled identity.* Englewood Cliffs, NJ: Prentice Hall.

Hellman, R.E., Sudderth, L., and Avery, A.M. (2002). Major mental illness in a sexual minority psychiatric sample. *Journal of the Gay and Lesbian Medical Association, 6*, 97–106.

Link, B. & Phelan, J. (2001). *On stigma and its public health applications.* Paper presented at Stigma and Global Health: An International Conference, Bethesda, Maryland.

Rosenberg, S., Rosenberg, J., Huygen, C., & Klein, E. (2005). No need to hide: out of the closet and mentally ill. *Best Practices in Mental Health: An International Journal, 1*, 72–85.

Sandfort, T.G.M., de Graaf, R., Bijl, R.V., and Schnabel, P. (2001). Same-sex sexual behavior and psychiatric disorders: findings from the Netherlands Mental Health Survey and Incidence Study (NEMESIS). *Archives of General Psychiatry, 58*, 85–91.

11

AFRICAN AMERICANS AND MENTAL HEALTH

ALMA J. CARTEN

Mental illness is one of the most perplexing and debilitating social problems affecting American society today. The human and fiscal costs of mental illness are enormous when considering the suffering endured by families with a mentally ill member, the disruptive effects of mental disorders on community life, and the large share of public resources consumed for rehabilitative treatment and loss of productivity in the workplace (Mechanic, 1989; Fellin, 1996).

Race is an equally perplexing aspect of American culture that has played a central role in shaping the economic, political, and social landscape of American society since the colonial period. The consequences of social, economic injustice, and power imbalance experienced by African Americans and other racial and ethnic minorities in the United States are reflected in deep racial disparities in mental health outcomes and have become cause for national concern (USDHHS, 1999, 2001).

The supplement to the Surgeon General's Report on Mental Health (USDHHS, 2001a) examines mental health services for African Americans, American Indians and Alaska Natives, Asian Americans and Pacific Islanders, and Hispanic Americans. Drawing on international and national research findings, the report documents dramatic disparities for these minority groups in mental health services and their underlying knowledge base. Racial and ethnic minorities are found to have less access to mental health services, are less likely to receive care, and when they did receive care, it was more likely to be of poor quality. The report concludes "racial and ethnic minorities bear a greater burden from unmet mental health needs and thus suffer a greater loss to their overall health and productivity" (USDHHS, 2001a, p. 3).

African Americans occupy a unique place in American culture and national life. The history of African Americans since being brought to this country as slaves has been marked by discrimination, exclusion, and violence perpetrated against them by the dominant culture. Black Americans continue to be influenced by a legacy of slavery, and suffer the consequences of cumulative and interactive effects of social and economic injustices that account for their persistent overrepresentation among underserved at-risk populations who live under environmental conditions that increase risk for mental illness. Moreover, irrespective of their educational, economic, political, or social standing, few African Americans will escape the effects of racism and devaluation of their personal and group identity that may contribute to poor mental health outcomes.

This chapter examines the experiences of Americans of African descent in the mental health system. As is the case with other ethnic and racial groups, there is much within group diversity among African Americans. This heterogeneity has increased significantly with the arrival of new black immigrants from the Caribbean, South America, and Africa (Francis, 2000), whose mental health needs are influenced by stressors associated with the refugee and immigration experiences that for some are exacerbated by the exposure to personal violence and trauma (Balgopal, 2000; Potocky-Tripodi, 2002). Although the discussion may be applicable to other blacks, it focuses on American-born blacks who self-identify as African American and trace their ancestry back to slavery. The discussion has the following purposes:

1. To examine the historical context of the development of mental health services and residual influences from the past on contemporary problems of access, availability, and quality of care for African Americans.

2. To review the current status of African Americans and the complexity of factors influencing etiology and prevalence, and help-seeking and service utilization behaviors of African Americans.

3. Describe culturally competent practices that may contribute to improved mental health outcomes for African Americans.

HISTORICAL CONTEXT OF MENTAL HEALTH SERVICES FOR AFRICAN AMERICANS

The Legacy of the Slave Experience

There is an extensive literature examining slavery as an American institution. What is missing from this literature is an exploration of the implications of the mental anguish and psychological trauma experienced by blacks under the slave system. Contemporary research and theory development offer a new lens for understanding the psychological impact of forced dislocation, violence, and acts of terrorism required to maintain the slave system. Slaves suffered the cumulative effects of being uprooted from their homelands, the horrors of the middle passage, and inhumane treatment during the period of transition to the new country. The institutionalization of slavery in American society and the ending of the slave trade added new layers of mental anguish by forcing slaves to breed new generations knowing that their children would be destined to live out their lives under the same intolerable conditions.

The persistent and unrelenting assaults on the mental integrity and the suppression of the human spirit combined with terrorist practices of mass behavior control necessary to enforce group submissiveness were not without consequence on the individual and group psychic of blacks. Perhaps the most debilitating were those practices designed to destroy any semblance of family life, resulting in the callous disregard of kinship bonds and family attachments essential to the psychological well-being of children and adults. Slaves existed in a perpetual state of fear and uncertainty under a system where there was the ever-present threat that a parent, child, sibling, or mate could be raped, tortured, maimed, killed, or sold away at the will of the slave owner.

Historical accounts of the experience of blacks in America mirrored and reinforced the assumptions about the inferiority of blacks that dominated intellectual and popular thought of the developing country. To justify a practice diametrically opposed to Judeo-Christian moral imperatives and democratic values on which the new republic was founded, slavery was portrayed as a benevolent practice that was in the best interests of blacks. The New Deal's Works Progress Administration's Federal Writer's Project, *Slave Narratives: A Folk History of Slavery in the United States*, contains more than 2,300 first-person accounts from former slaves of their experiences in slavery. These personal oral histories illustrate that slavery was anything but a benevolent system, contradict the stereotype of the contented slave, and expose the full horrors and severity of the system. The narratives were compiled between 1936 and 1938 in 17 states, illuminating that in recent U.S. history many American blacks were the direct descendents of former slaves and living at a time of legalized separation of the races, and when President Franklin Roosevelt declined to lend his support to an antilynching bill, although the murder of blacks by White lynching mobs was common in both the North and South (Trattner, 1994). For them, slavery was anything but folklore from a distant past, but highly personalized family histories that would likely be passed down over the generations and a mirror of current experiences in a white racist society.

SCIENTIFIC RACISM

Historically, epidemiological studies on the prevalence and need for mental health services in blacks reflected prevailing ideology of the period that served to provide a rationale and justification for slavery and discrimination against blacks after emancipation. For example, during the colonial period blacks were reported as having low susceptibility for mental illness, paralleling assumptions of emerging scientific theories that blacks were not of sufficient level of mental development to exhibit mental health problems. These studies would later report differences in prevalence as to geographic location, with higher rates of mental illness in free blacks living in the North. It was asserted that the primitive psychological development of blacks made them especially well-suited for a life of servitude and rendered them content with their situation. The independence of freedom, on the other hand, led to symptoms of derangement and lunacy. Normal blacks were described as happy, faithful, and content with their lot in life. Those who were mentally afflicted were described as having no regard for property rights, irresponsible in work, and contributed to disturbances. For example, drapetomania, literally translated as "flight from home madness," was the formal diagnosis given to runaway slaves. Dysaethesia Aethiopica, caused by "insensibility of nerves" and "hebetude of mind," was the psychological diagnosis assigned to blacks who were noncompliant and disruptive (Thomas & Sillen, 1979).

Racist assumptions about etiology and the behavior of blacks and discrimination were predominating themes in shaping the underlying theoretical base for mental health services and the quality of care provided the black mentally ill beginning in the colonial period. Racist ideology and discriminatory practices continued into Reconstruction and the years of Jim Crow laws and became entrenched as formal systems of care developed for the mentally ill in the early 19th century.

Early Forms of Care for the Black Mentally Ill

Enslaved blacks suffering from mental disorders were the responsibility of their owners. A literature review of the development of mental health services for blacks conducted by Jackson (2005) found that South Carolina Colonial Assembly made provisions for the public maintenance of lunatic slaves whose masters were unable to care for them. And between 1880 and 1919 separate asylums were developed for blacks in Southern and border states, with some continuing in operation as separate facilities well into the 20th century.

Reporting in the literature on the care of the black mentally ill is sparse. It is likely that their care followed patterns of outdoor relief for the white mentally ill and they were looked after informally by relatives or other slaves in the tightly knit care systems characterizing life in the slave community. Free blacks found refuge in public facilities as the poorhouse, jails, and workhouses. The Freedman Bureau was established by the federal government in 1865 to provide comprehensive services to former slaves. After the discontinuation of the bureau in 1872, in large measure, blacks continued to rely on family and self-help efforts like fraternal orders, women's clubs, and faith-based organizations for the meeting of unmet social needs. Mentally ill Blacks would also be cared for in segregated facilities, with the trend toward institutional-based care for the mentally ill beginning in the early decades of the 1800s (Trattner, 1998; Jackson, 2005).

Between 1843 and 1853 the efforts of Dorthea Dix, the first reformer to advocate for the mentally ill, resulted in the founding of hospitals for the mentally ill throughout the South and the North. The Tennessee Hospital for the Insane was the first of these state hospitals to make provisions for the Black mentally ill, and in 1867 separate quarters were constructed to house the black mentally ill. Most states followed suit, creating separate facilities for the black mentally ill that were fewer in numbers and of poorer quality (Trattner, 1998).

Continuing Influences

Mental health theories are premised in a medical model based in American and Western culture. The body of knowledge informing policy, practice, and research in the field of mental health has been informed by a Eurocentric perspective that mirrors and reflects social and scientific thought that reinforced racist theories that continued well into the 20th century. G. Stanley Hall, founder of the American Psychological Association, in his widely read book on adolescence published in 1904 described Africans, Indians, and Chinese as members of adolescent races, offering a biological explanation for their incomplete development and racial inferiority (Thomas & Sillen, 1979). As late as 1950 some articles in the medical journals continued to assert that blacks were too mentally uncomplicated and intellectually limited to be susceptible to mental illness or suicide (Thomas & Sillen, 1979).

The need to legitimate slavery and discrimination was a powerful contributing factor in the spread of modern racism. Consequently, stereotypes, myths, and misconceptions about African Americans permeate all aspects of institutional and organizational life in the United States. The residuals of scientific racism are present in contemporary mental health services and influence access and availability of mental health services for African Americans and slowed the development of a knowledge base necessary for informing culturally competent practice with African Americans. One example is the erroneous view that African Americans are poor candidates for the psychotherapies or other forms of insight therapy because of Eurocentric assumptions about limitations in verbal and communication skills, preference for environmental versus personal change, present orientation, and focus on concrete outcomes as opposed to abstract goals with future orientation (Casimir & Morrison, 1993).

DEFINING CONCEPTS OF MENTAL HEALTH, RACE, ETHNICITY, AND CULTURE

Mental Health and Mental Illness

Mental health and mental illness may be seen as existing along a continuum of severity ranging from neurotic, or idiosyncratic behaviors and personality traits that have little if any consequence on the individual's ability to carry out major life roles relative to family, work, and intimate relationships, to those behaviors and thought processes that are totally incapacitating and render the individual incapable of distinguishing the boundaries between real-life events and those of their inner world. *Healthy People 2010* (USDHHS, 2000) defines mental health as a state of successful functioning resulting in productive activities, fulfilling relationships, and the ability to adapt to change and cope with adversity. Because of the dynamic interplay between the individual and the environment, mental health is also viewed as a fluid versus constant state as the individual confronts the highs and lows of life transitions and crises of varying degrees of severity over the life cycle.

Race, Ethnicity, and Culture

Race, ethnicity, and culture are ambiguous concepts that are often used interchangeably but have distinctive, if interrelated, meanings. Race is generally thought of by most people as a biological category, although the scientific basis for classifying humans based on physical attributes of skin color, facial features, or hair texture has long been disputed. An official statement of the American Anthropological Association asserted that although race is not considered a valid biological classification, race has significant social meaning and has been used to assign some groups to perpetual low status, while assigning others privilege, power, and wealth (Pinderhughes, 1988; Longres, 2000). Ethnicity may overlap with race and generally refers to collective groupings of people who share a common heritage that may include history, language, national origin, ancestry, or culture. An overriding feature of ethnicity is the sense of shared experiences and belonging among individuals who identify with a specific ethnic group. Culture refers to the shared values, beliefs, customs, and artifacts of a society, usually learned and transmitted from generation to generation, an embracing all of its material and symbolic products. The dominant culture for most of American history has been a reflection of Western beliefs, systems, values, and norms of Judeo-Christian white Americans. These dominant norms are embedded and mirrored in all aspects of institutional and organizational life, including mental health organizations, and have played a central role in restraining the development of a theoretical base for understanding mental health problems in ethically diverse populations.

Uniqueness of the Black Cultural Experience

The dual perspective integrates assumptions about the historical and social construction of concepts of race, ethnicity, and culture to set forth a useful framework for understanding unique aspects of the black cultural experience and impact of power imbalances on interpersonal and social functioning (Chestang, 1973; Norton, 1978; Pinderhughes, 1988; Longres, 2000). The dual perspective calls attention to the unique experience of African American culture that requires the black individual to simultaneously function in two worlds, and the need to develop adaptive coping responses that allow for the successful functioning in both of these worlds. This perspective posits that while all individuals must function in two spheres: the immediate or nurturing environment, comprised of family, friends, and supportive institutions, and the sustaining system, or institutions of the wider society within which the individual must interact in order to meet basic survival needs of employment, health care, and education. For blacks, as a member of a minority group, the sustaining system is a world in which the attitudes and institutions are designed to inhibit, prohibit, and block goal achievement, and where their aspirations to lead self-fulfilled and productive lives are consistently frustrated (Chestang, 1973; Norton, 1978; Pinderhughes, 1986).

Because of these realities of the cultural experience of blacks, it is now recognized that behaviors previously interpreted by dominant culture norms as pathological may in fact be indicators of adaptive strengths and coping behaviors that make it possible to survive and achieve under oppressive conditions of the larger environment.

PROTECTIVE AND RISK FACTORS

Mental health professionals no longer ignore the effects of racism in its many forms in creating psychological and environmental stresses that increase risk for mental health problems in African Americans. Kesseler et al. (1999) examined the prevalence of two forms of discrimination in blacks and whites. Major discrimination, which included events like police harassment or being fired from a job, were reported with a lifetime prevalence of 50% for African Americans compared to 31% for whites. This form of discrimination was associated with psychological and major depression for both blacks and whites. Day-to-day perceived discrimination, which is associated with generalized anxiety and distress, was reported by 25% of African Americans as occurring often, while only 3% of Whites reported perceived discrimination as occurring often in their lives.

Several social scientists offer insights for understanding etiology, risk and protective factors, and help-seeking behaviors of blacks in light of the effects of racial discrimination and oppressive conditions of the environment. Spirituality, self-help, and the reliance on family and informal helpers are attributes characteristic of the black experience (Chatters, Taylor, & Neighbors, 1989; Neighbors & Jackson, 1984; Rogler et al., 1989; Taylor, Chatters, & Celious, 2003). The ability to preserve in the face of adversity and transcend oppressive conditions of the larger environment is identified as an enduring characteristic of blacks and the black community. Billingsly (1968) and Hill (1971) were among the first scholars to identify protective factors characteristic of blacks that contributed to the development of coping and adaptive behaviors, promoting an ability to persevere and achieve in the face of adversity. These included religious beliefs, family role adaptability, extended family ties, and sense of racial pride. Anchored in general systems theory and the strengths perspective, the pioneering work of these scholars contributed to the development of resilience theories now widely accepted as providing a more accurate framework for understanding the behaviors of many vulnerable and oppressed groups (Gramercy, 1971; Longres, 2000).

On the other hand, some scholars assert that some blacks are not able to ward off these assaults on personal and group integrity, and succumb to the traumatizing effects of present-day racism, and hypothesize associative relationships between the lingering effects of unresolved trauma associated with the slave experience and prevalence of mental disorders in Blacks. A 1998 report of the Centers for Disease Control Prevention detailed the growth in the rate of suicide among black males while highlighting the failures of current efforts to effectively explain or stem the rise in suicide among this population. Poussaint and Alexander (2000) offer an explanation for this phenomenon by drawing an analogy between the anguish of the slave experience as expressed in the Negro spiritual "Lay My Burdens Down" and the reactions of some blacks today to the traumatic effects of racism. Thus, death, as for the slave, is seen as the only possible escape from a life of hopelessness and despair.

CURRENT STATUS

According to the U.S. Census approximately 12% of the American population, 33.9 million people, identify themselves as African American. Recent years have seen a reverse migration of blacks returning to the South, with more than 53% of African Americans now living in Southern states. African Americans represent significant within-group diversity relative to education, income, and socioeconomic status. Despite a history marked by oppression, Jim Crowism, legal segregation, and institutional racism, African Americans have made enormous advances when measured against the relatively short period since the enactment of antidiscrimination legislation in the 1960s. Over the last decades, the circumstances of African Americans have improved dramatically on almost all well-being indicators. There has been a strong and steady growth in the black middle class, and the number of blacks completing high school and enrolling in college is increasing. Despite these gains, when considered in aggregate, African Americans are relatively poorer and experience more hardships than other ethnic and racial groups. In 1999, approximately 22% of African American families lived in poverty, compared to 13% for all Americans (U.S. Census, 2001a). A notable development in the African American community is the polarization around income. At the same time of a growth in the middle class, recent years have seen the development of what has been referred to as an underclass living under extreme conditions of entrenched multigenerational poverty (Wilson, 1987).

The interrelationship between mental health and physical health needs, and connection between mind and body have been given increased validation in recent years (USDHHS, 1999). Disparities in mental health outcomes for African Americans mirror disparities in physical health when compared to other racial and ethnic groups. These disparities cover a range of physical problems that include higher mortality rates until the age of 85 years, higher rates of infant mortality, diabetes, asthma, circulatory and heart disease, prostrate cancer among males and breast cancer among women, even though black women are more likely to have a mammogram than White women, higher rates of HIV/AIDS, and other chronic conditions (USDHHS, 2001a; Robert, Wood, & Johnson, 1991; Center for Health Economics Research, 1993).

PREVALENCE AND NEED FOR SERVICE

Need for service refers to the prevalence of mental disorders within certain groups and is a critical factor for determining whether certain groups are underutilizing or overutilizing mental health services. The manner in which individuals respond to mental health distress or the recognition of a mental health problem is referred to as their help-seeking behaviors. These behaviors and patterns of service utilization are the process by which individuals engage in seeking and receiving services from mental health providers (Fellin, 1996). Whether low utilization rates are a reflection of low prevalence rates within a certain group can be difficult to determine.

Epidemiological studies are critical for understanding the frequency and distribution of mental disorders in certain segments of the population. This information is essential for the accuracy of diagnosis and development of effective treatment interventions necessary for closing the gap in mental health outcomes for African Americans. However, determining whether the rate of mental illness in African Americans differs from that of whites and isolating the factors that account for these differences is not a simple matter.

Because blacks are disproportionately represented among the poor, and because there is a high correlation between poverty and minority group status, it is difficult to tease out and distinguish the effects of poverty from race and culture in an examination of etiology. While blacks have higher psychiatric admissions, research shows disproportionate high rates of admission by race to all type of facilities, with blacks being admitted at a higher rate than any other ethnic and racial group (Snowden & Cheung, 1990; Scheffler & Miller, 1989; Manderscheid, 1987). The early findings of Grier and Cobbs (1968) emphasizing the failure of health professionals to distinguish between aspects of paranoia associated with the African American history of racism and discrimination from psychopathology continue to be apparent in contemporary research findings. Several investigators have found that African Americans are assigned more severe psychiatric diagnoses and overdiagnosed for schizophrenia and underdiagnosed for affective disorders (Snowden & Cheung, 1990; Trierweiler et al., 2000; Fellin, 1989; Jones & Gray, 1986; Neighbors, Jackson, Campbell, & Williams, 1989).

The misdiagnosis of African Americans may be attributed to several factors. These include bias of the psychological testing, the interview situation, predisposition of the clinician, and institutional racism. It is also suggested that a major reason for the errors made in diagnosis are diagnosticians who are unfamiliar with mental illness as it manifested in populations of color (Fellin, 1989; Jones & Gray, 1986; Neighbors et al., 1989).

The *Diagnostic and Statistical Manual of Mental Health Disorders* (DSM-IV) published by the American Psychiatric Association is the most widely used classification of mental disorders nationally and internationally, and is giving increasing attention to the role of culture in the diagnosis and assessment of mental illness. Since 1994 the manual has included a listing of cultural-bound syndromes, which are clusters symptoms that appear more commonly in some cultures than others. For example, eating disorders of anorexia and bulimia are common mental health problems in American and Western cultures. Isolated sleep paralysis, defined as an inability to move and experienced while the individual is awakening or falling asleep, is reported as a cultural-bound syndrome common in African Americans. Although somatization, the reporting of physical symptoms for which there is no medical finding, is not confined to African Americans, somatic symptoms are reported more frequently by African Americans than whites (USDHHS, 2001a). Falling out, characterized by dizziness and sudden collapse, is identified in the DSM-IV, "Outline of Culture-Bound Syndromes," as common in African Americans (APA, 1994, p. 846).

There are acknowledged limitations of the effectiveness of the DSM-IV for capturing behaviors idiosyncratic to specific cultures and the nuances of language in the individual's reporting of symptoms and the clinician's interpretation of these. For example, *falling out*, which is included in the outline of culture-bound syndromes, is a term frequently used by blacks to denote a disagreement or an argument between individuals. The term *bad nerves* for some blacks may be used to describe a range of emotions and feelings or as a code word for mental illness (Wagner & Garner, 1994). A new edition of the manual is scheduled for publication in 2012. The revisions will give greater attention to the role of race, ethnicity, and culture in the diagnosis and treatment of mental illness.

Despite difficulties of isolating the effects of race and discrimination on individual behavior, and findings of national epidemiologic studies of psychiatric disorders in the United States (Kessler et al., 1996) that the rates of mental illness among African Americans are similar to those of whites when controlling for differences in income, education, and marital status, it is also known that poverty and its attendant problems and racism create stresses that contribute to high prevalence rates of mental disorders in African Americans (USDHHS, 2001a). African Americans are also more likely to live in low-income communities troubled by high rates of unemployment, crimes against property and person, substance abuse, and deaths from violence, and are disproportionately represented among special populations that are high risk for mental health problems. For example, the National Vietnam Readjustment Study found that rates of posttraumatic stress disorder are 21% for Black veterans and 14% for white veterans despite whites comprising 85% of the total veteran population. The prevalence of cognitive impairments associated with dementia and Alzheimer's are higher for older Black Americans than for the white elderly (USDHHS, 2001a). Blacks are overrepresented in special populations like the homeless, incarcerated, individuals impacted by HIV/AIDS, the chemically addicted, and children in foster care, where the rates of mental disorders are higher than for the general population (USDHHS, 2001a).

BARRIERS, ACCESS, AND SERVICE UTILIZATION

Race, culture, ethnicity, and belief systems associated with these influence the individual's attitudes about mental illness, the manner in which symptoms are expressed, as well as help-seeking behaviors and use of mental health services.

African Americans have a long tradition of self-help, reflecting values of their African heritage of collectivism and kinship bonds, as well as from necessity, since up until World War II blacks were excluded from participation in public and private social welfare programs, or relegated to segregated programs of lower quality. This tradition of self-help is also reflected in help-seeking behaviors in coping with problems of mental, health. For example, African Americans are more likely to look to family, friends, church, and informal helpers as ministers before turning to formal mental health systems (Jones & Gray, 1986; Neighbors, 1985). Values and belief systems that influence the interpretation the individual gives to symptoms of mental distress also influence help-seeking behaviors. Mental illness carries a high degree of stigma for some African Americans. Stigmatization combined with a mistrust of mental health providers can contribute to low utilization and retention rates. Lack of health care has been identified as a barrier to mental health care for African Americans because health insurance is an employer-provided benefit and African Americans have high unemployment rates or are employed in menial jobs that do not offer this benefit (USDHHS, 2001a). However, several authors have found that when the need for services is controlled, despite availability of health insurance, and whether seen by public or private providers, African Americans are less likely to use mental services than other groups, which make it necessary to look beyond socioeconomic reasons for explaining the low utilization rates (Neighbors, 1985; Gary, 1987; George, 1987; Rogler et al., 1989; Padgett et al., 1995).

The problems experienced by African Americans in mental health are recorded by a number of authors (Fellin, 1996; Snowden, 2001; Neighbors, 1985; Gary, 1987; Swanson & Ward, 1996; Davis & Ford, 2004). The 1994 congressional briefings, as cited in Fellin (1996), recognized historical and cultural factors unique to how African Americans experience mental health services and have implications for service utilization, including "a history of discrimination; ongoing economic stresses, informal networks of supports, including church and extended families, continuing problems of access to health care; symptom expression that is often different from that in the general population and under-representation of minorities among treatment professionals and researchers" (p. 142).

Swanson and Ward (1995) present a conceptual framework for the differentiation of barriers to access to mental health services into four categories: sociocultural, systemic, economic, and individual. Sociocultural barriers include fear and mistrust of formal systems based on the historical mistreatment and devaluation experienced in these systems; stigmatization associated with mental health services, found more commonly in African Americans and contributing to a feeling of embarrassment and shame and an unwillingness to discuss problems with professionals (USDHHS, 2001a; Snowden, 2001); and belief systems anchored in spirituality that when unacknowledged by the clinician contribute to low treatment retention rates. Systemic barriers to effective treatment are identified as culturally inappropriate measurement instruments that affect the accuracy of the assessment and subsequent treatment plan formulation, and clinical bias occurring when African Americans are evaluated using norms and standards of the dominant culture, or because of cultural incompetence, bias, and stereotypical assumptions of the individual clinician. Economic barriers are most frequently based on socioeconomic status, with African Americans being overrepresented among low-income groups, with less access to health insurance and a greater reliance on public mental health systems, where they face difficulties obtaining high-quality care from well-trained clinicians. In addition, individuals of low socioeconomic status often live in rural areas or improvised inner city neighborhoods where few mental health providers are located (Davis & Ford, 2004; USDHHS, 2001a). Individual barriers are related to the interpretive meanings given to feelings of mental distress as well as values and belief systems about mental illness that influence whether the feelings of distress are recognized to be symptoms of mental illness, and confusion about whether symptoms are of sufficient severity and duration to warrant seeking formal mental health services.

Culturally Competent Services

Since the 1960s and the civil rights movement, ethnocentric assumptions of the concept of the melting pot (Glazer & Moynihan, 1963), which has informed race relationships in the United States, have given way to the new concepts of pluralism and multiculturalism. This view values the diversity of lifestyles and contributions of many ethnic and racial groups to the richness of American life, and pays special attention to ethnic and racial minorities who suffer from the effects of long-term oppression, discrimination, and powerlessness (Pinderhughes, 1988; Longres, 1995). In the field of mental health, the Community Mental Health Centers Act of 1963 reflected shifting paradigms in the conceptualization of diagnosis and treatment of mental illness to an emphasis on the person in environment formulation and the assumption that the etiology of mental illness is directly related to the social environment. Longres (2000) articulates "the critical perspective" that focuses on injustices rooted in institutional arrangements and encourages social service workers to plan and evaluate social welfare services and programs from the standpoint of marginalized groups.

Culturally competent services are grounded in the assumption that service utilization rates are improved and treatment outcomes enhanced when services and treatment are congruent with the cultural beliefs of the ethnic minority group. Culturally competent practice is defined as a set of attitudes, beliefs, knowledge, and skills that the clinician must possess in order to work effectively with clients who are of a difference culture than the clinician (USDHHS, 2001a; Lum, 1999; Pinderhughes, 1989; Longres, 1995). Culturally competency moves beyond earlier concepts of ethnic or cultural sensitivity to a concern for practice effectiveness. Thus, the culturally competent clinician must include program evaluation and practice evaluation as an integral part of practice with clients (Potocky-Tripodi, 2002).

The DSM-IV gives special attention to the central role of the clinician who is trained in the Western medical model, and not without his or her own personal bias about the behaviors of ethnic and racial minorities. The clinician must interpret and give meaning to the client's presentation of symptoms. She is also responsible for assessment, treatment planning, and making the final judgment about whether the patient's symptoms and the presentation of these meet the criteria for a specific diagnosis: "A clinician who is unfamiliar with the nuances of an individual's cultural frame of reference may incorrectly judge as psychopathology those normal variations in behaviors, beliefs or experiences that are particular to an individual's culture" (APA, 1994).

The outline for "Cultural Formulation" in the DSM-IV calls the attention of the clinician to five specific areas: (1) identify the patient's cultural identity, (2) explore possible cultural explanations of the illness and expressions of symptoms, (3) examine the cultural elements of the patient-clinician relationship, (4) consider the cultural factors related to the psychosocial environment and level of functioning, and (5) synthesize information from the overall cultural assessment in the determination of a course of care.

Solomon (1983) offered the following case example to illustrate the salience of culture and client belief systems in the therapeutic relationship:

> Mr. W. is a sixty-nine-year-old African American retired construction worker who has lived alone since the death of his wife three years ago. His two adult children are married, live in the city and visit frequently. However, their relationship has been deteriorating since the death of Mrs. W. Mr. W. has also exhibited moderate depression since her death. He has been treated by his physician for a variety of mild, somatic complaints for which no organic basis can be found. Of late, Mr. W. has become more argumentative with his children, accusing them of planning to put him in an institution so that they can have his property. They have responded by avoiding him which is increasing his isolation.
>
> Since the death of his wife, Mr. W.'s church attendance has been irregular. His minister visited him at home in an effort to get him re-involved with the church. Mr. W. shared his feelings of growing mistrust about his children with the minister, accusing them again of conspiring against him. The minister suggested he see a counselor in a special counseling program sponsored by the church. At his first meeting with the social worker, Mr. W. tearfully shared his feelings about his children and fears of being placed in an institution. He also revealed this was the first time he had cried since his wife's death. When he returned for the second visit he told the worker he had "prayed a lot" and had a dream in which God came to him and said: "Keep the faith, I will see that your problems are solved." He interpreted this as a sign that he should only trust in God and ended treatment with the worker. The worker, who was familiar with the role religion plays in the lives of older Blacks, replied: "God works in mysterious ways, have you considered that I may be the instrument he will use to help you solve your problems?" Mr. W. was silent for a moment, and responded that perhaps he should continue in therapy with her.

Many older black Americans suffer from depression, often expressed as somatic symptoms, that is often undiagnosed and treated by health care professionals and unrecognized by family members or caretakers (USDHHS, 2001). Acknowledged disparities in access and availability to preventive mental health services make it highly unlikely that older blacks will recognize symptoms of mental distress, or have opportunities to grieve and mourn normative losses occurring over the life circle within a therapeutic relationship. The cumulative effects of these losses and consequences of the failure to receive treatment may come together and begin to unfold in grief reactions to the loss of the older person's life partner. Similarly, early signs of dementia may also go unrecognized by family members who are uninformed about the aging process, and therefore these may not be reported to primary care physicians. For Mr. W.'s children, the paranoia about their motivation may be viewed and interpreted as rationale behavior and not the early signs of dementia, since their father, as is the case with most African Americans, has more than likely been preoccupied with material resources and finances for much of his life.

Client belief systems play a central role in the therapeutic process (Carone & Barone, 2001). This case illustrates the significance of religion and spirituality in the lives of African Americans, how these influence attitudes about mental health services, and the tendency of African Americans to seek help from informal helpers with the initial onset of symptoms of mental distress (USDHHS, 2001a). The presence of mental health services in his church facilitated access and availability to services by making it possible for Mr. W. to be seen in his community by a professionally trained social worker. In this case, there is cause for optimism about outcome, since the clinician illustrates cultural competency in her recognition of the meaning of religion in the lives of many older black Americans. Her culturally competent response facilitated engagement and encouraged Mr. W. to commit to a continuation of the treatment relationship.

SUMMARY AND CONCLUSIONS

The historic failures of the mental health system to respond to the mental health needs of African Americans are well documented in the research and practice literature (USDHHS, 2001). African Americans in need of mental health services face a number of barriers to quality care. These barriers are categorized as sociocultural, systemic, economic, and individual (Swanson & Ward, 1995), and influence help-seeking behaviors, services utilization and retention, and contribute to the dramatic racial disparities in mental health outcomes (USDHHS, 2001a). However, more research is needed for a better understanding of the causes of these disparities to tease out the differing effects of socioeconomic factors, including lack of health insurance, attitudes and behaviors of African Americans about mental health, or culturally incompetent practices in clinical decision making, assessment, and treatment.

The commitment of the federal government in making mental health services more effective for African Americans and other racial and ethnic minorities is reflected in several funded initiatives of the National Institute of Mental Health. These include the funding of several centers nationally to conduct research on minority populations. Grant awards are given to the Council on Social Work Education to support the minority fellowship program to increase the number of doctoral minority students majoring in mental health research, and prepare minority social work professionals for leadership in mental health research and in the delivery of mental health services. The Office of Minority Health was created to encourage health policies that eliminate health disparities for ethnic and racial minorities, and oversees goal achievements of *Healthy People 2010* (USDHHS, 2000), a special initiative, also seek to reduce health disparities. The supplement to the surgeon general's report on mental health (USDHHS, 2001a, pp. 4–5) takes a closer looks at the mental health needs of minorities and endeavors to (1) understand better the nature and extent of mental health disparities, (2) present the evidence on the need for mental health services and the provision of services to meet those needs, and (3) document promising directions toward the elimination of mental health disparities and the promotion of mental health.

Despite these efforts, African American professionals continue to be underrepresented in the field of mental health at all levels. This underrepresentation of African Americans in the mental health field not only has implications for clinical decision making, access, and availability of culturally relevant services for individuals, families, and communities, but also results in an absence of an African American voice in mental health policy and program decision making in a largely white-controlled system.

It is not likely that the mental health outcomes for African Americans, the quality of services provided them, or the gap in mental health disparities will be closed in the absence of fundamental changes that address societal inequities and bring blacks into the economic, social, and political mainstream in American society. Given the magnitude of the issues, mental health professionals face daunting challenges in the near future to ensure that all Americans have access to the full range of quality mental health services needed to lead self-fulfilled and productive lives.

REFERENCES

American Psychiatric Association (APA). (1994). *Diagnostic and statistical manual of mental disorders* (4th ed.). Washington, DC: Author.

Balgopal, P.R. (Ed.). (2000). *Social work practice with immigrants and refugees.* New York: Columbia University Press.

Billingsley, A. (1968). *Black families in white America.* Englewood Cliffs, NJ: Prentice Hall.

Brown, C. & Palenchar, D. (2004). Treatment of depression in African American primary care patients. *African American Research Perspectives, 10,* 55–65.

Carone, D.A. & Barone, D.F. (2001). A social cognitive perspective on religious beliefs: their functions and impact on coping and psychotherapy. *Clinical Psychology Review, 21,* 989–1003.

Casimir, G.J. & Morrison, B.J. (1993). Rethinking work with multicultural populations. *Community Mental Health Journal, 29.*

Chatters, L.M., Taylor, R.J., & Neighbors, H.W. (1989). Size of the informal network mobilized in response to serious personal problems. *Journal of Marriage and the Family, 51,* 667–676.

Chestang, L. (1973). Character Development in a Hostile Environment (Occasional Paper 3). University of Chicago, School of Social Service Administration.

Chestang, L. (1980). *Competencies and knowledge in clinical social work: a dual perspective. Toward a new definition of clinical social work* (pp. 1–12). Washingon, DC: National Association of Social Workers.

Davis, S. & Ford, M. (2004). A conceptual model of barriers to mental health services among African Americans. *American Research Perspectives, 10,* 44–55.

Fellin, R. (1989). Perspectives on depression among blacks. *Health and Social Work, 14.*

Fellin, R. (1996). *Mental health and mental illness: policies, programs and services.* Itasca, IL: F.E. Peacock Publishers.

Francis, A. (2000). Social work practice with African-descent immigrants. In P.R. Bagopal (Ed.), *Social work practice with immigrants and refugees.* New York: Columbia University Press.

Gary, L.E. (1987). Attitudes of black adults toward community mental health centers. *Hospital and Community Psychiatry, 38,* 10.

George, L.K. (1987). Psychological and social determinants of help-seeking. In *Perspectives on depressive disorders: a review of recent research.* Washington, DC: Department of Health and Human Services.

Glazer, N. & Moynihan, P. (1963). *Beyond the melting pot.* Cambridge, MA: Harvard University Press.

Gramezy, N. (1971). Vulnerability research and the issue of primary prevention. *American Journal of Orthopsychiatry, 41*, 101–116.

Grier, W.H. & Cobbs, P.M. (1968). *Black rage.* New York: Basic Books.

Hill, R.B. (1971). *The strengths of black families.* New York: National Urban League.

Hu, T., Snowden, L.R., Jerrell, J.M., & Nguyen, T.D. (1991). Ethnic populations in public mental health: service choices and level of use. *American Journal of Public Health, 18*, 1429–1434.

Jackson, V. (2005). *In our own voices: African American stories of oppression, survival and recovery in the mental health system* (pp. 1–36, 4–8).

Jones, B.E. & Gray, B.A. (1986). Problems in diagnosing schizophrenia and affective disorders among blacks. *Hospitals and Community Psychiatry, 37*.

Kessler, R.C., Berglund, P.A., Zhao, S., Leaf, P.J., Kouzis, A.C., Bruce, M.L., Freidman, R.L., Grosser, R.C., Kennedy, C., Narrow, W.E., Kuehnel, T.G., Laska, E.M., Manderscheid, R.W., Rosenheck, R.A., Santoni, T.W., & Schneier, M. (1996). The 12-month prevalence and correlates of serious mental illness (SMI). In R.W. Manderscheid & M.A. Sonnenschein (Eds.), *Mental health, United States.* Rockville, MD: Center for Mental Health Services.

Kessler, R.C., Price, R.H., & Wortman, C.B. (1985). Social factors in psychopathology: stress, social support, and coping processing. *Annual Review of Psychology, 36*, 531–572.

Longres, J. (2000). *Human behavior in the social environment* (3rd ed.). Itasca, IL: F.E. Peacock.

Lum, D. (1999). *Culturally competent practice: a framework for growth and action.* Pacific Grove, CA: Brooks/Cole Publishing Company.

Mechanic, D. (1989). *Mental health and social policy* (3rd ed.). Englewood Cliffs, NJ: Prentice Hall.

Neighbors, H.W. (1985). Seeking professional help for personal problems: black Americans use of health and mental health service. *Community Mental Health Journal, 21*.

Neighbors, H.W., Bashshur, R., Price, R., Selilg, S., Donabedian, A., & Shannon, G. (1992). Ethnic minority mental health service delivery: a review of the literature. *Research in Community and Mental Health, 7*.

Neighbors, H.W. & Jackson, J.S. (1984). The use of informal and formal help: Four patterns of illness behavior in the black community. *American Journal of Community Psychology, 12* (6), 629–644.

Neighbors, H.W., Jackson, J.S., Campbell, L., & Williams, D. (1989).The influence of racial factors on psychiatric diagnosis: a review and suggestions for research. *Community Mental Health Journal, 25*.

Norton, D. (1978). *The dual perspective.* New York: Council on Social Work Education.

Padgett, D.K., Patrick, C., Burns, B.J., & Schlesinger, H.J. (1995). Ethnicity and the use of outpatient mental health services in a national insured population. *American Journal of Public Health, 84*.

Pinderhughes, E. (1988). Significance of culture and race in the human behavior curriculum. In C. Jacobs & D. Bowles (Eds.), *Ethnicity and race: critical concepts for social work.* Silver Spring, MD: National Association of Social Workers.

Poussaint, A.F. & Alexander, A. (2000). *Lay my burden down: unraveling suicide and the mental health crisis among African Americans.* Boston: Beacon Press.

Potocky-Tripodi, M. (2002). *Best practices for social work with refugees and immigrants.* New York: Columbia University Press.

Rogler, L.H. (1993). Culture in psychiatric diagnosis: an issue of scientific accuracy. *Psychiatry, 56*.

Rogler, L.H. & Cortes, D.E. (1993). Help-seeking pathways: a unifying concept in mental health care. *American Journal of Psychiatry, 150*.

Rogler, L.H., Malgady, R.G., & Rodriguez, O. (1989). *Hispanics and mental health: a framework for research.* Malabar, FL: Krieger.

Snowden, L.R. (2001). Barriers to effective mental health services for African Americans. *Mental Health Services Research, 3*, 181–187.

Snowden, L.R. & Cheung, F.K. (1990). Use of inpatient mental health services by members of ethnic minority groups. *American Psychologist, 45*.

Snowden, L.R. & Liberman, M.A. (1994). African American participation in self help groups. In T.J. Powell (Ed.), *Understanding the self help organization.* Thousand Oaks, CA: Sage Publications.

Solomon, B.B. (1983). Value issues in working with minority clients. In Rosenblatt, A. & Waldfogel, D. (Eds.) *Handbook of clinical social work* (pp. 866–867). San Francisco: Jossey-Bass Publishers.

Swanson, M.G. & Ward, A.J. (1995). Recruiting minorities into clinical trials: toward a participant friendly system. *Journal of the National Cancer Institute, 87*, 1747–1759.

Taylor, R.J. & Chatters, L.M.N. (1991). Religious life. In J.S. Jackson (Ed.), *Life in black America.* Newbury Park, CA: Sage.

Thomas, A. & Sillen, S. (1979). *Racism and psychiatry.* NJ: The Citadel Press.

Trattner, W.I. (1999). *From poor law to welfare state: a history of social welfare in America* (6th ed.). New York: The Free Press.

Trierweiler, S.J., Neighbors, H.W., Munday, C., Thompson, S.E., Binion, V.J., & Gomez, J.P. (2000). Clinician attributions associated with diagnosis of schizophrenia in African American and non-African patients. *Journal of Consulting and Clinical Psychology, 68*, 171–175.

U.S. Census Bureau. (2001a). *Profiles of general demographic characteristics: 200 census of population and housing, United States.* Author.

U.S. Census Bureau. (2001b). *The black population in the United States.* Author.

U.S. Department of Health and Human Services. (1999). *Mental health: a report to the surgeon general.* Rockville, MD: Author.

U.S. Department of Health and Human Services. (2000). *Healthy people 2010.* Rockville, MD: Author.

U.S. Department of Health and Human Services. (2001a). *Mental health: culture, race and ethnicity, a supplement to mental health: a report to the surgeon general.* Rockville, MD: Author.

U.S. Department of Health and Human Services. (2001b). *Healthy people 2001.* Rockville, MD: Author.

U.S. Department of Health and Human Services. (2001c). *Youth violence: a report to the Surgeon General.* Rockville, MD: Author.

U.S. Department of Health and Human Services, Office of Minority Health. (2003). About OMH. Retrieved December 19, 2003, from http://www.omhrc.gov/OMH

Wilson, J. (1987). *The truly disadvantaged: the inner city, the underclass and public policy.* Chicago: The University of Chicago Press.

12

MENTAL HEALTH ISSUES OF CHINESE AMERICANS

Help-Seeking Behaviors and Culturally Relevant Services

WINNIE W. KUNG AND YI-FEN TSENG

The growth of the Chinese American population in the United States has been phenomenal in the past two decades. With an increase of 102.6% from 1980 to 1990, and another 75% from 1990 to 2000 (Chinese American Data Center, 2005), the population had reached over 2.8 million in 2000. Chinese is the largest subgroup within the Asian American Pacific Islander population in the United States and constitutes about 23% of this racial group (U.S. Citizenship and Immigration Services, 2002). It was estimated that by 2030 the Asian American population will be 22 million, constituting 6.2% of the total U.S. population (U.S. Census Bureau, 2005). The growth of the Chinese American population is also expected to be in a steady pace. Despite the vast diversities within the Asian American group, much of the core Chinese culture, such as Confucianism and Buddhism, is shared by many other Asian groups, such as Koreans, Japanese, and Southeast Asians. Thus, understanding on the Chinese population could shed light on the experiences of some other Asian groups.

In 1990 more than 63% of all Chinese Americans were immigrants, and the majority of the remaining percent were children of immigrants (U.S. General Accounting Office, 1990). The recency of their migration and the stronger tie to Chinese culture may have placed greater adaptation pressure on them to a Western society, resulting in concomitant mental health strains. Thus, their service need and experience in utilizing mental health services warrant some attention. Based on a review of recent literature and our personal and professional experiences, this chapter examines help-seeking behaviors of less acculturated Chinese Americans and the provision of culturally relevant mental health services to them. Specifically, the following aspects will be addressed: (1) the underutilization of mental health services and factors affecting help seeking, (2) culturally responsive mental health service delivery models, and (3) culturally sensitive clinical approaches in working with this group.

HELP-SEEKING BEHAVIORS OF CHINESE AMERICANS

Underutilization of Mental Health Services

Earlier literature on help-seeking behaviors on mental health-related issues provided a general picture of the Asian American population as a whole, while information on ethnic breakdown for Chinese Americans was not obtainable. However, the consistent pattern of underutilization of mental health services by Asian Americans gives some hints on how the Chinese Americans might have fared. As noted by Zhang, Snowden, and Sue's (1998) study on inpatient, outpatient, residential treatment, residential support, and partial care services in California, Asians were often underrepresented in mainstream mental health services compared to other ethnic groups relative to their population size. In another study of national data, Asians were three times less likely to use available services than the Caucasian population (Matsuoka, Breaux, & Ryujin, 1997). While this phenomenon may reinforce "the model minority" myth, the lower demands of services may, in actuality, simply reflect a situation of unmet needs rather than actual fewer psychological disturbances (Lee, Lei, & Sue, 2001; Lin & Cheung, 1999; Kung, 2003). This latter view is suggested by the fact that when Asian Americans come for mental health services, their problems appear more severe and chronic, often requiring more intensive care and longer hospitalization, thus suggesting a delay in treatment due to a reluctance to seek help (Akutsu, Snowden, & Organista, 1996). Moreover, many Asians tend to be noncompliant with recommended treatment, resulting in higher attrition rate, shorter stay in outpatient treatment, and poorer outcome (Tsui & Schultz, 1985; Zane, Enomoto, & Chun, 1994). The undocumented status and recency of migration are an added disadvantage to mental patients, as indicated by a recent study of Fuzhounese from South China, the latest wave of Chinese immigrants to the United States (Law, Hutton, & Chan, 2003). These patients have higher hospitalization and rehospitalization rates, and lower treatment compliance, than documented Fuzhounese and non-Fuzhounese Chinese patients.

Chinese tend to use mental health services as the last resort, only after having sought help from friends and family, general medical practitioners, and trying alternative treatments (Kleinman, 1988; U.S. Department of Health and Human Services [DHHS], 2001). A recent study based on the Chinese American Psychiatric Epidemiological Study (CAPES) confirmed such reluctance to use mental health services (Kung, 2003). Among the 253 respondents who have at least one lifetime diagnosable mental disorder, only 15% ever sought help from mental health professionals, which is much lower than the 48% reported in the National Comorbidity Survey on the general American population (Kessler et al., 1994).

Throughout the rest of the chapter, we shall draw several relevant findings from the CAPES, so we shall briefly describe this study here. The CAPES is the largest psychiatric epidemiological study of a specific ethnic group using a community representative sample of Chinese Americans between the ages of 18 and 65. This two-wave study was conducted in 1993 to 1994 in Los Angeles County, with 1,747 respondents in the first wave and 1,503 in the subsequent wave. Most of the respondents are immigrants (95%) from Taiwan (29%), Mainland China (23%), Hong Kong (14%), and many are from Southeast Asian countries (Takeuchi, Chun, Gong, & Shen, 2002).

Factors Affecting Help Seeking

Seeking help for mental discomforts often involves rational decision making regarding the costs and presumed benefits associated with available options (Pescosolido & Boyer, 1999). Although seeking help may release individuals from distress, many are reluctant to do so because of the perceived social cost of what is believed to be an open acknowledgment of their inadequacy in managing their personal lives (Nadler, 1987). Culture also affects one's perception of mental problems and the decision to seek help (Kleinman, 1988; Lau & Takeuchi, 2001; Takeuchi et al., 2002). In the CAPES, as many as two-thirds of Chinese Americans migrated to the United States as adults, and for this group the impact of Chinese culture is high when they contemplate seeking help for mental distress (Spencer & Chen, 2004).

In the following, we shall discuss how sociodemographics and culture-related factors affect Chinese Americans in their help seeking for emotional problems.

Sociodemographic Characteristics

Chinese women, not unlike others in their gender group, are socialized to be more open to acknowledge their need for help (Tata & Leong, 1994). However, what is intriguing for this population is the magnitude of the contrast between the genders. According to the CAPES data, when a diagnosable psychiatric disorder is involved, women are 158 times more likely to use mental health services than men; they are also more likely to seek help from informal and alternative sources (Kung, 2003). Interestingly, men with high self-esteem are eight times more willing to use mental health help compared to women of comparable self-regard.

Socioeconomic status has been identified as another key determinant of service utilization. Chinese Americans with low economic resources tend to have a greater need for psychological intervention, presumably because financial stress can cause and exacerbate psychiatric symptoms (Law et al., 2003; Takeuchi et al., 2002). However, individuals with low income are less likely to be medically insured. The CAPES indicated that individuals without medical insurance are 3.5 times less likely to obtain treatment from mental health services than those with medical insurance (Kung, 2003), but are more likely to use informal help (Spencer & Chen, 2004). Other practical concerns over time and money involved in treatment, language proficiency, and knowledge of how to obtain service also form barriers to immigrants from utilizing mental health services (Kung, 2004).

Culture-Related Factors

Cultural Beliefs about the Nature of Mental Distress and Its Coping

According to Chinese culture and traditional Chinese medicine, the mind and the body are an integrated entity (Tseng, 2004). In addition, Chinese tend to somatize emotional problems and emphasize the physical expression of one's distressed state (Kleinman, 1988; Zhang et al., 1998). This leads many Chinese Americans to turn to physicians, herbalists, and acupuncturists for help instead of mental health professionals (Kung, 2001; Yeung & Kung, 2004). The attribution of mental illness to biological pathology also raises concerns over a "genetic taint," which would place intense stigma upon the entire family, and hence the denial and avoidance of mental health services (Kung, 2001; Pearson, 1993; Yeung & Kung, 2004).

Confucian, Buddhist, and Taoist philosophies partly attribute mental disturbances to the transience of human developmental phases (Weisz, McCaarty, Eastman, Chaiyasit, & Suwanlert, 1997). Thus, Chinese may regard emotional distress as part of normal life to be tolerated (Chan & Parker, 2004). The use of passive coping strategies, such as avoidance, withdrawal, minimizing the problem, resignation to and acceptance of fate, have been widely identified as characteristic of Asian coping styles, which reinforce the tendency to deny the need for help (Bjorck, Cuthbertson, Thurman, & Lee, 2001; Scotton, 1998). Even when mental distress is acknowledged, avoidance of morbid thoughts is seen as a positive attempt to regain mental health (Sue, Wagner, Ja, Marguillis, & Lew, 1976; Root, 1985).

Moreover, the use of talk therapy, in which individuals openly discuss their personal problems and examine their thoughts and feelings, is alien to the Chinese cultural value of self-effacement and reticence in verbalizing intense emotions (Lau & Takeuchi, 2001; Leong & Lau, 2001). This further reduces psychotherapy as a viable option for treating mental distress.

Interestingly, the CAPES data did not yield significant linkage between traditional cultural beliefs about mental health treatment and actual service use (Kung, 2004). The author attributed this nonsignificant finding to the crude measurement of cultural barriers used in the study. More sophisticated empirical studies of cultural impact are definitely warranted.

Acculturation

The extent to which Chinese Americans retain their original culture and the level of acculturation to American values and systems affect their help seeking. More acculturated individuals have more positive attitudes toward seeking professional mental health help (Tata & Leong, 1994; Ying & Miller, 1992). The CAPES data showed that such positive effect extends to actual help seeking from all sources for the whole community sample (Kung, 2003). However, for the subsample of respondents with at least one lifetime mental disorder, acculturation becomes a negative impact on mental health service use. It was suggested that more acculturated Chinese Americans have social circles that offer more superficial relationships resulting in less self-disclosure of personal distress. Since social network is an important source of referral for mental health services, the reduced social support is associated with less service use (Kung, 2003).

Personality Traits

Internalized cultural values may affect an individual's personality traits and in turn exert an impact on the use of external help. The CAPES found that individuals with hardy personalities who see life changes and difficulties as challenges and who tend to employ more active coping and stay involved with others and social institutions are more likely to use mental health and medical services to deal with mental distress (Kung, 2003). Given the seeming dissonance between Chinese culture and mental health service use, it requires someone with hardy personality to break through the cultural barriers to seek help from a potentially stigmatizing source.

To summarize, from both a theoretical basis and empirical findings, Chinese Americans are more likely to seek mental health help if they are female, of higher socioeconomic status, have less tendency to emphasize somatic complaints, take more active roles in facing life challenges, and are more willing to break cultural barriers.

CULTURALLY RESPONSIVE SERVICE DELIVERY MODELS

Given the cultural constraints on the expression of mental health issues among Asian Americans, the prevalence and severity of mental disorders, and the low service use and ineffectiveness of mental health treatment with this population, concerns have been raised over the adequacy of the approach of mainstream service to meet their needs (U.S. DHHS, 2001; Zane, Sue, Castro, & George, 1982). In the past few decades, attempts have been made to address the service gap. What follows is a delineation of various approaches to deliver culturally responsive services to Chinese Americans with some specific examples.

Improving Accessibility and Availability

Given the striking disparities in mental health service use among Asian Americans and Pacific Islanders compared to other ethnic minorities, the surgeon general's report recommended that access to treatment be improved (U.S. DHHS, 2001). Due to the tendency to somatize mental distress, the lack of awareness of its onset, and the stigma attached to mental illness, primary care physicians are often the first help source Chinese Americans approach when faced with mental distress (Chen, Kramer, & Chen, 2003; Yeung et al., 2004a). This tendency suggests three possible strategies in adapting service delivery: (1) to enhance the capacity of primary care physicians to provide mental health services, (2) to integrate primary care and mental health services in one setting (Chen et al., 2003; Lu, 2002), and (3) to strengthen referral for service.

The Primary Care and Mental Health Services Bridge Program in New York City was a pioneering project launched in 1997 to provide a linkage between primary care and mental health services through co-location and collaboration (Chen et al., 2003). The project involved two programs. The first program involved the training of primary care physicians to detect, treat, and manage patients with mental disorders. Primary care physicians were trained to use culturally syntonic words to explain how mental health problems are linked to the biological systems. In addition, bilingual-certified psychiatric social workers were co-located in the primary care centers to smooth the interagency referral process. The bilingual clinicians also took care to incorporate patients' beliefs of culturally relevant alternative treatments, such as acupuncture and relaxation therapy, into their treatment plan. The second program of the Bridge project involved community education to increase awareness of mental health, reduce stigma, and promote mental health services in the community. Radio programs and community forums, including testimony from mental health service consumers, were employed to reach out to the ethnic community. This intervention led to a 7.2 times increase in the number of patients identified with mental illness from 1997 to 2002. In addition, there was an increase in the patients' overall satisfaction rating with mental health treatment, and increased referral rates for off-site treatment (Chen et al., 2003). The Bridge project was replicated in Boston in 2000 (Yeung et al., 2004b) with similar positive outcomes. There was an increase of 60% referrals from primary care physicians to mental health service within one year.

Other organizational changes in existing services could also be made to improve the availability of mental health services to Chinese Americans. These include longer opening hours, shorter treatment regimens, and more affordable charges (Kung, 2003; Spencer & Chen, 2004). Moreover, increased funding for services to new or uninsured immigrants with mental illness who lack medical insurance is imperative to enhance service access (Law et al., 2003; Spencer & Chen, 2004).

Developing Ethnic-Specific Service Programs

Much discussion on the barriers to mental health service use among Asian Americans reflected the failure of the mainstream system to respond to culturally specific needs. Studies have indicated a positive effect on continuance of treatment and outcome when there is a match between clients and therapists in ethnicity and language (Fujino, Okazaki, & Young, 1994; Gamst, Dana, Der-Karabetian, & Kramer, 2000). Over the past three decades, in response to the growing Chinese immigrant population, efforts have been made to go beyond ethnic and language matching by establishing mental health programs in Chinese communities in major cities throughout the country (Chow, 1999). Not only do these programs provide bilingual services, but these ethnic-specific agency settings offer cultural ambiance — from physical decorations to posters and announcements in Chinese — and receptionists speak the native language, making them more welcoming and cozy to many monolingual and less acculturated clients (Sue, 1998) and leading to higher return rates and longer stays in treatment (Takeuchi, Sue, & Yeh, 1995). Three major characteristics are noted in these ethnic-specific programs. First, they provide horizontal linkage to other health or social service programs for clients at different rehabilitation phases with diverse needs, facilitating many immigrants who are unfamiliar with community resources (Chow, 1999; Zane et al., 1982). Second, vertical integration within the agency is available to provide comprehensive services, such as child care, processing of immigration documents, and even getting driver's licenses, so as to help immigrants adjust to a new environment (Chow, 1999; Zane et al., 1982). Third, clinicians recognize the value of traditional Chinese medicine and alternative approaches to Western mental health treatment, thereby expressing their respect for clients' cultural beliefs. These modifications enhance clients' satisfaction and lengthened their stay in treatment (Chen et al., 2003).

An example of such an ethnic-specific program is the Chinese American Planning Council in New York City (Chow, 1999). This program adopts a multiservice community model providing counseling and mental health treatment, health care, drug abuse treatment, protective services, vocational rehabilitation, housing referral, child and elderly care, and legal and employment services. Also provided are case management and advocacy for children, youth, seniors, families, and immigrants. The program was named DECENT, which denotes developmental, educational, comprehensive, empowerment, networking, and teamwork principles. Residents in the community can meet their many needs at one agency (Chow, 1999), thereby reducing the likelihood of being identified as mentally ill and stigmatized when receiving mental health services from the agency.

Promoting Community Education

Community education to improve knowledge about the preservation of mental health and the nature of mental illness among Chinese Americans helps to reduce stress and the stigma attached to mental illness. Such community education programs can be provided through community centers, public media, Medicaid application booths, and English as a second language classes to increase the population's knowledge of access and tendency to use mental health services at an early stage of the illness (Kung, 2001; Spencer & Chen, 2004).

It is clear at this point that culturally responsive service delivery models such as the Bridge and the DECENT programs, which aptly addressed the cultural-specific needs of the Chinese American population, bore encouraging results.

CULTURALLY SENSITIVE CLINICAL PRACTICE WITH CHINESE AMERICANS

Not only are Asian Americans reluctant to seek mental health service, but when they do, the results are often less than satisfactory, with high attrition rate, poor treatment outcome, and low satisfaction with therapists (Wu, 1994; Leong, Wagner, & Kim, 1995; Zane et al., 1994). Because of the different cultural backgrounds and immigration experiences Chinese American clients bring, Western psychotherapy or counseling approaches need to be adapted to be useful. Culturally sensitive treatment not only enhances its effectiveness, but also increases treatment compliance and reduces attrition (Tseng, 2004; Leong et al., 1995). The following discussion focuses on the clinician-client relationship, appropriate counseling or psychotherapy approaches, and involvement of family members in treatment.

Clinician-Client Relationship: Expectations of Clinician's Role and Characteristics

With a Confucian background that emphasizes hierarchy in relationships, less acculturated Chinese Americans tend to see mental health professionals as authority figures (Kleinman, 1988; Pearson, 1993; Scotton, 1998) who, with their knowledge and expertise, would "heal" them or "cure" their mental illness (Chien & Banerjee, 2002; Tseng, 2004). In a culture in which gift giving is seen as a way of expressing care and cementing relationships, clients often expect to receive a certain "gift" or direct benefit from the therapist, which could be in the form of alleviation of problem, hope and normalization, and a trusting relationship (Sue & Zane, 1987). In fact, therapists' sharing of strategies or advice in handling certain situations is positively related to clients' perceived quality of the treatment session (Kim et al., 2003).

As an expression of competence, clinicians are expected by Chinese Americans to take an active, directive, and instructional role in the helping process (Sue & Zane, 1987; Tseng, 2004). Many Chinese would feel disappointed, confused, and frustrated when placed in an open-ended, nondirective relationship with clinicians in which the clients are asked to come up with solutions themselves. The expectation of a quick, directive response from the clinician is exacerbated by the urgency of need when clients show up for treatment after a long delay (Kung, 2001).

Being an expert does not mean being cold and distant. Clinicians' professional distant stance is distrusted by Chinese American clients, who often prefer a warm, supportive, directive, and parent-like benevolent helper (Tung, 1991; Wu, 1994). A confrontational approach is also not desirable. Before the authority figure, some Asian patients may appear receptive to certain treatment recommendations, including medication, but do not follow through. They often adjust their treatment in search of what works for them. Sometimes this involves combining the treatment with other traditional alternative approaches (Lo & Fung, 2003; Ying, 1997). This phenomenon of adjusting treatment recommendations on their own may be reduced if clinicians are seen as informed, sensitive, and open to clients' concerns (Kung, 2001; Scotton, 1998). Hence, an authoritative instead of authoritarian (Tung, 1991), directive instead of nondirective, sensitive and supportive instead of confrontational clinicians' style of relating is more acceptable to Chinese clients.

Counseling Approaches

Due to the fact that talk therapy is exotic and culturally unfamiliar to many Chinese American clients, some initial orientation is helpful (Tseng, 2004; Chien & Banerjee, 2002). Clinicians will be able to engage them better if clear and mutually agreed upon treatment goals are stated early in treatment and clients are informed throughout the process how the activities in which they are engaged are relevant to attaining the treatment goals (Kung, 2001).

Since seeking mental health services is often the last resort after unsuccessful attempts of self- and informal help, many Chinese clients expect immediate and tangible help leading to symptom relief (Sue & Zane, 1987; Tung, 1991). Clinicians are well advised to employ problem-solving rather than insight-oriented treatment approaches (Dana, 1998; Ho, 1990; Berg & Miller, 1992). The problem-solving approach increases the perception of the relevance of therapeutic activities, hence strengthening the working alliance between therapists and clients (Bordin, 1979), and builds clients' self-esteem and future competence (Dana, 1998), thereby combating the demoralized feelings of the reluctant help seekers.

The action-oriented focus of problem-solving therapy on thinking and doing rather than feeling also fits Chinese clients (Chien & Banerjee, 2002; Ying, 1997). In Chinese culture, emotions, especially negative affects, are often suppressed, for fear that they may get out of control and bring shame by disrupting harmony within oneself, with nature, and with one's community (Wu, 1994). Given the cultural practice of withholding emotions, the use of catharsis in the treatment process, such as the use of empty-chair techniques, would need a lot of prior explaining to be acceptable to clients. Since mental health professionals are often perceived as teachers (Kleinman, 1988; Pearson, 1993), Chinese clients would respond well to a psychoeducational approach, e.g., imparting knowledge on the cause and course of mental illnesses (Kung, 2001).

Since reaching out to seek mental health help involves the admission of some kind of failure to deal with personal issues (Nadler, 1987), and given the immense stigma attached to mental disturbance among Chinese Americans, it would be helpful to give them a positive and face-saving framework to view the use of such services. As discussed earlier, hardy Chinese who perceive life difficulties as challenges tend to take a more active stance to find a solution, including seeking external help; therapists can reframe the use of mental health services as a positive step toward meeting life challenges and enhancing self-efficacy (Kung, 2003).

The use of passive coping strategies such as avoidance and resignation to fate has been widely identified as characteristic of Asian coping styles (Bjorcket et al., 2001; Jung, 1995). In fact, patient forbearance of life's suffering is highly valued in Chinese culture (Scotton, 1998). Many Chinese clients adopt the notions of predestination, karma, and multiple lives to explain and externalize their difficulties and suffering (Hung, Kung, & Chan, 2003). Therapists should recognize both the positive and negative impact of such coping: while such fatalistic attitudes may lead to passivity and diminish clients' impetus for change, they may also offer peace and healing, since with karma justice will prevail in the end, whether it is in this life or the next. Therapists can use such notions of predestination and multiple lives as a metaphysical framework to comfort and induce hope in clients while encouraging them to do all they can to live well in this life, and leave karma to ultimately bring forth justice (Hung et al., 2003).

As discussed earlier, being immigrants in this country requires a lot of adaptation and getting acquainted with the systems. Chinese clients may have many other human service needs besides mental health care (Takeuchi, Mokuau, & Chun, 1992). Clinicians should be ready to perform case management functions or ensure that such service is provided to link clients to needed community resources.

Involving Family and Other Social Support in Treatment

Rooted in a sociocentric and family-oriented culture based on Confucian values, Chinese clients' well-being has to be considered in the context of their relation with their family (Kung, Hung, & Chan, 2004; Tseng, 2004). One of the treatment implications is in the formulation of therapeutic goals. Instead of aiming individual self-actualization and independence, interpersonal harmony and social connectedness, especially with family members, should be given high priority (Lefley, 1998; Kung, 2001).

The definition of family in Chinese culture goes beyond the nuclear family; thus, emotional investment in families of origin is expected (Chien & Banerjee, 2002). Hence, the standard by which therapists gauge clients' level of differentiation and enmeshment among family members should be adjusted. In the literature on family intervention for patients suffering from schizophrenia, treatment goals include having patients attain independent living and reducing patient-family exchanges when the family has high expressed emotions (Anderson, Reiss, & Hogarty, 1986). These goals need to be modified for Chinese families. Relatives should be coached to maintain low-key communication with patients, and the latter should be encouraged to perform appropriate roles and functions in the family (Kung, 2001).

To help clients improve their familial relationships, it is beneficial to involve family members in the treatment process. As therapists try to promote communication among family members, they should be aware that some relatively indirect and nonverbal modes of expression are well accepted within the culture, e.g., preparing some favorite food for a relative as an expression of affection, leaving a note to indicate concern in a respectful way, or communicating through a third party (Chien & Banerjee, 2002). In contrast, direct confrontations have to be handled with care (Lo & Fung, 2003). To help resolve conflicts or attain some agreement within the family, therapists may consider first seeing different parties separately to negotiate the terms of compromise before bringing them together for a final discussion and contract (Berg & Jaya, 1993). This procedure is not unlike the cultural practice of using respected elders as mediators to resolve familial conflicts.

SUMMARY AND CONCLUSION

In this chapter we discussed the mental health service needs of Chinese Americans — the largest subgroup of the fast-growing Asian American population, composed largely of immigrants. To unravel the factors influencing the group's striking pattern of underutilization of mental health services, we examined the sociodemographic and culture-related factors. Being male, especially with low self-esteem, having low socioeconomic status and no medical insurance, and lacking knowledge of access and language proficiency often become barriers to seeking mental health treatment. In addition, many Chinese cultural beliefs about the nature of mental disorder and customary coping strategies turn this group away from professional help. Fortunately, individuals with higher acculturation and an outlook of life that sees changes and difficulties as challenges are more open to receiving needed help.

Given the specific needs of this ethnic group, attempts have been made to develop culturally responsive service delivery models. These have offered some promising results. The Bridge program with its integration of primary care and mental health services and sensitivity to cultural hindrances and preferences in the treatment process reflected an appropriate cultural adaptation. The horizontal and vertical integration of services provided by ethnic-specific multiservice centers also aptly addressed the multiple needs of an immigrant population hampered by language barriers and limited knowledge of access to services. With the continual increase of this population and the recent influx of undocumented Fuzhounese immigrants with complex needs, expansion of ethnic-specific services is called for.

As more Chinese Americans are willing to use mental health services, clinicians have to be prepared to provide clinical services that are culturally sensitive. We suggested a supportive, directive clinician-client relationship, problem-solving and psychoeducational approaches, and treatment goals that encompass not only the well-being of the individuals, but also harmonious familial relationships. As we reviewed the clinical literature, it became apparent that much was based on clinicians' past experiences and practice wisdom (e.g., Tung, 1991; Wu, 1994) or inferences based on some qualitative studies (e.g., Hung et al., 2004). Few empirical studies that examined the therapeutic processes and effectiveness of certain treatment models were available. Thus, systematic research through rigorous process and outcome studies is needed to develop intervention approaches that can really be tailored for the specific needs of Chinese Americans.

REFERENCES

Akutsu, P.D., Snowden, L.R., & Organista, K.C. (1996). Referral patterns in ethnic-specific and mainstream programs for ethnic minorities and whites. *Journal of Counseling Psychology, 43*, 56–64.

Anderson, C.M., Reiss, D.I., & Hogarty, G.E. (1986). *Schizophrenia and the family: a practitioner's guide to psychoeducation and management*. New York: The Guilford Press.

Berg, I.K. & Jaya, A. (1993). Different and same: family therapy with Asian-American families. *Journal of Marital and Family Therapy, 19*, 31–38.

Berg, I.K. & Miller, S.D. (1992). Working with Asian American clients: one person at a time. *Families in Society, 73*, 356–363.

Bjorck, J.P., Cuthbertson, W., Thurman, J.W., & Lee, Y.S. (2001). Ethnicity, coping, and distress among Korean Americans, Filipino Americans, and Caucasian Americans. *The Journal of Social Psychology, 141*, 421–442.

Bordin, E.S. (1979). The generalizability of the psychoanalytic concept of the working alliance. *Psychotherapy: Theory, Research & Practice 16*, 252–260.

Chan, B. & Parker, G. (2004). Some recommendations to assess depression in Chinese people in Australia. *Australian and New Zealand Journal of Psychiatry, 38*, 141–147.

Chen, H., Kramer, E.J., & Chen, T. (2003). The Bridge program: a model for reaching Asian Americans. *Psychiatric Services, 54*, 1411–1412.

Chien, W.W. & Banerjee, L. (2002). *Caught between cultures: the young Asian American in therapy*. In E. Davis-Russell (Ed.), *California School of Professional Psychology handbook of multicultural education, research, intervention, and training* (pp. 210–220). San Francisco: Jossey-Bass.

Chinese American Data Center. (2005). Rate of Change in Chinese American Population, 1850–2000. Retrieved on February 17, 2005, from http://members.aol.com/chineseusa/00tre.htm

Chow, J. (1999). Multiservice centers in Chinese American immigrant communities: practice principles and challenges. *Social Work, 44*, 70–81.

Dana, R.H. (1998). Asians and Asian Americans. In R.H. Dana (Ed.), *Understanding cultural identity in intervention and assessment* (pp. 141–173). Thousand Oaks, CA: Sage.

Fujino, D.C., Okazaki, S., & Young, K. (1994). Asian-American women in the mental health system: an examination of ethnic and gender match between therapist and client. *Journal of Community Psychology, 22*, 164–176.

Gamst, G., Dana, R.H., Der-Karabetian, A., & Kramer, T. (2000). Ethnic match and client ethnicity effects on global assessment and visitation. *Journal of Community Psychology, 28*, 547–564.

Ho, M.K. (1990). *Intermarried couples in therapy*. Springfield, IL: Charles E. Thomas.

Hung, S.L., Kung, W.W., & Chan, C.L. (2003). Women coping with divorce in the unique sociocultural context of Hong Kong. *Journal of Family Social Work, 7*, 1–22.

Jung, J. (1995). Ethnic group and gender differences in the relationship between personality and coping. *Anxiety, Stress, and Coping, 8*, 113–126.

Kim, B.S.K., Hill, C.E., Gelso, C.J., Goates, M.K., Asay, P.A., & Harbin, J.M. (2003). Counselor self-disclosure, East Asian American client adherence to Asian cultural values, and counseling process. *Journal of Counseling Psychology, 50*, 324–332.

Kessler, R.C., McGonagle, K.A., Zhao, S., Nelson, C.B., Hughes, M., Eshleman, S., Wittchen, H.-U., & Kandler, K.S. (1994). Lifetime and 12-month prevalence of DSM-III-R psychiatric disorders in the United States: results from the National Comorbidity Survey. *Archives of General Psychiatry, 51*, 8–19.

Kleinman, A. (1988). *Rethinking psychiatry: from cultural category to personal experience*. New York: Macmillan/The Free Press.

Kung, W.W. (2001). Consideration of cultural factors in working with Chinese American families with a mentally ill patient. *Families in Society: The Journal of Contemporary Human Services, 82*, 97–107.

Kung, W.W. (2003). Chinese Americans' help seeking for emotional distress. *Social Service Review*, *77*, 110–134.

Kung, W.W. (2004). Cultural and practical barriers to seeking mental health treatment for Chinese Americans. *Journal of Community Psychology*, *32*, 27–43.

Kung, W.W., Hung, S.L., & Chan, C.L. (2004). How the socio-cultural context shapes women's divorce experience in Hong Kong. *Journal of Comparative Family Studies*, *35*, 33–50.

Lau, A. & Takeuchi, D. (2001). Cultural factors in help-seeking for child behavior problems: value orientation, affective responding, and severity appraisals among Chinese-American parents. *Journal of Community Psychology*, *29*, 675–692.

Law, S., Hutton, M., & Chan, D. (2003). Clinical, social, and service use characteristics of Fuzhounese undocumented immigrant patients. *Psychiatric Services*, *54*, 1034–1037.

Lee, J., Lei, A., & Sue, S. (2001). The current state of mental health research on Asian Americans. *Journal of Human Behavior in the Social Environment*, *3*, 159–178.

Lefley, H.P. (1998). The family experience in cultural context: implications for further research and practice. In H.P. Lefley (Ed.), *Families coping with mental illness: the cultural context* (pp. 97–106). San Francisco: Jossey-Bass Publishers.

Leong, F.T. & Lau, A.S. (2001). Barriers to providing effective mental health services to Asian Americans. *Mental Heatlh Services Research*, *3(4)*, 201–214.

Leong, F.T., Wagner, N.S., & Kim, H.H. (1995). Group counseling expectations among Asian American students: the role of culture specific factors. *Journal of Counseling Psychology*, *42*, 217–222.

Lin, K.M. & Cheung, F. (1999). Mental health issues for Asian Americans. *Psychiatric Services*, *50*, 774–780.

Lo, H.-T. & Fung, K.P. (2003). Culturally competent psychotherapy. *Canadian Journal of Psychiatry*, *48*, 161–170.

Lu, F. (2002). The poor mental health care of Asian Americans. *Western Journal of Medicine*, *176*, 224.

Matsuoka, J.K., Breaux, C., & Ryujin, D.H. (1997). National utilization of mental health services by Asian Americans/Pacific Islanders. *Journal of Community Psychology*, *25*, 141–145.

Nadler, A. (1987). Determinants of help seeking behaviors: the effects of helper's similarity, task centrality and recipient's self esteem. *European Journal of Social Psychology*, *17*, 57–67.

Pearson, V. (1993). Families in China: an undervalued resource for mental health? *Journal of Family Therapy*, *15*, 163–185.

Pescosolido, B.A. & Boyer, C.A. (1999). How do people come to use mental health services? Current knowledge and changing perspectives. In A. Horwitz & T. Scheid (Eds.), *A handbook for the study of mental health: social context, theories, and systems* (pp. 392–411). New York: Cambridge University Press.

Root, M. (1985). Guidelines for facilitating therapy with Asian American clients. *Psychotherapy*, *22*, 349–356.

Scotton, B.W. (1998). Treating Buddhist patients. In H.G. Koenig (Ed.), *Handbook of religion and mental health* (pp. 263–270). San Diego: Academic Press.

Spencer, M.S. & Chen, J. (2004). Effect of discrimination on mental health service utilization among Chinese Americans. *American Journal of Public Health*, *94*, 809–814.

Sue, S. (1998). In search of cultural competence in psychotherapy and counseling. *American Psychologist*, *53*, 440–448.

Sue, S., Wagner, N., Ja, D., Marguillis, C., & Lew, W. (1976). Conceptions of mental illness among Asian and Caucasian-American students. *Psychological Reports*, *38*, 703–708.

Sue, S. & Zane, N. (1987). The role of culture and cultural techniques in psychotherapy. *American Psychologist*, *42*, 37–45.

Takeuchi, D.T., Chun, C.A., Gong, F., & Shen, H. (2002). Cultural expressions of distress. *Health: An Interdisciplinary Journal for the Social Study of Health, Illness and Medicine*, *6*, 221–235.

Takeuchi, D.T., Mokuau, N., & Chun, C.A. (1992). Mental health services for Asian Americans and Pacific Islanders. *Journal of Mental Health Administration*, *19*, 237–245.

Takeuchi, D.T., Sue, S., & Yeh, M. (1995). Return rates and outcomes from ethnicity-specific mental health programs in Los Angeles. *American Journal of Public Health*, *85*, 638–643.

Tata, S.P. & Leong, F.T.L. (1994). Individualism-collectivism, social-network orientation, and acculturation as predictors of attitudes toward seeking professional psychological help among Chinese Americans. *Journal of Counseling Psychology, 41*, 280–287.

Tseng, W. (2004). Culture and psychotherapy: Asian perspectives. *Journal of Mental Health, 13*, 151–161.

Tsui, P. & Schultz, G.L. (1985). Failure of rapport: why psychotherapeutic engagement fails in the treatment of Asian clients. *American Journal of Orthopsychiatry, 55*, 561–569.

Tung, M. (1991). Insight-oriented psychotherapy and the Chinese patient. *American Journal of Orthopsychiatry, 61*, 186–194.

U.S. Census Bureau. (2005). U.S. Interim Projections by Age, Sex, Race, and Hispanic Origin. Retrieved on January 4, 2005, from http://www.census.gov/ipc/www/usinterimproj/

U.S. Citizenship and Immigration Services. (2002). *2002 yearbook of immigration statistics.* Retrieved on September 12, 2004, from http://uscis.gov/graphics/shared/aboutus/statistics/Immigs.htm

U.S. General Accounting Office (1990), Asian Americans: a status report. Retrieved on September 12, 2004, from http://161.203.16.4/d24t8/141300.pdf

U.S. Department of Health and Human Services. (2001). Asian health care for Asian Americans and Pacific Islanders. In *Mental health: culture, race, and ethnicity — a supplement to mental health: a report of the surgeon general.* Rockville, MD: Author.

Weisz, J.R., McCaarty, C.A., Eastman, K.L., Chaiyasit, W., & Suwanlert, S. (1997). Developmental psychopathology and culture. Ten lessons from Thailand. In S. Luthar, J. Burack, D. Cicchetti, & J. Weisz (Eds.), *Developmental psychopathology: perspective on adjustment, risk and disorder* (pp. 568–592). New York: Cambridge University Press.

Wu, J. (1994). On therapy with Asian patients. *Contemporary Psychoanalysis, 30*, 152–168.

Yeung, A.S., Chan, R., Mischoulon, D., Sonawalla, S., Wong, E., Nierenberg, A.A., & Fava, M. (2004b). Prevalence of major depressive disorder among Chinese-Americans in primary care. *General Hospital Psychiatry 26*, 24–30.

Yeung, A. & Kung, W.W. (2004). How culture impacts on the treatment of mental illnesses among Asian Americans. *Psychiatric Times, 21*, 34–36.

Yeung, A., Kung, W.W., Chung, H., Rubenstein, G., Roffi, P., Mischoulon, D., & Fava, M. (2004a). Integrating psychiatry and primary care improves acceptability to mental health services among Chinese Americans. *General Hospital Psychiatry, 26*, 256–261.

Ying, Y. (1997). Psychotherapy for East Asian Americans with major depression. In E. Lee (Ed.), *Working with Asian Americans: a guide for clinicians.* New York: The Guilford Press.

Ying, Y. & Miller, L.S. (1992). Help seeking behavior and attitude of Chinese Americans regarding psychological problems. *American Journal of Community Psychology, 20*, 549–556.

Zane, N., Enomoto, K., & Chun, C.A. (1994). Treatment outcomes of Asian- and white-American clients in outpatient therapy. *Journal of Community Psychology, 22*, 177–191.

Zane, N., Sue, S., Castro, F.G., & George, W. (1982). Service system models for ethnic minorities. In L.R. Snowden (Ed.), *Reaching the underserved: mental health needs of neglected populations.* Beverly Hills: Sage Publications.

Zhang, A.Y., Snowden, L.R., & Sue, S. (1998). Differences between Asian and White Americans' help seeking and utilization patterns in the Los Angeles area. *Journal of Community Psychology, 26*, 317–326.

13

PSYCHOLOGICAL INTERVENTION WITH HISPANIC PATIENTS

A Review of Selected Culturally Syntonic Treatment Approaches

MANNY JOHN GONZÁLEZ AND GREGORY ACEVEDO

The underutilization of mental health services by Hispanics has been well documented in the literature (Applewhite, Wong, & Daley, 1991; Fabrega, 1990; Mezzich, Ruiz, & Muñoz, 1999; Rogler, Cortes, & Malgady, 1991; Rogler, Malgady, & Rodriguez, 1989; Woodward, Dwinell, & Arons, 1992). Hispanics encounter numerous obstacles that prevent them from successfully navigating through the mental health system. These obstacles include language barriers, lack of health insurance, lack of affordable mental health services, limited access to bilingual and bicultural service providers, and lack of information on accessing mental health services. This reality is further compounded by the fact that research appears to suggest an increased rate of mental health disorders among Hispanics (Kessler, McGonagle, Zhao, & Nelson, 1994; Malgady & Constantino, 1998). Kessler et al. (1994) and Malgady and Rogler (1993) have noted that Hispanics, in comparison to other ethnic groups and non-Hispanic Whites, present with higher levels of prevalence rates in the area of major depression, other mood disorders (including dysthymia and bipolar depression), and cognitive impairments. Hispanics represent a growing population in disproportionate need of mental health services.

In deference to self-ascription, the terms *Hispanic* and *Latino* will be used interchangeably in this chapter. Persons of Hispanic heritage may ascribe themselves as Hispanic or Latino. Since the Census 2000, the U.S. Census Bureau now recognizes both terms to describe this population.

Hispanics are one of the fastest growing ethnic groups in the United States. The Latino population in the United States increased by more than 50% between 1990 and 2000 to 32.8 million, representing 12.0% of the total population (U.S. Census Bureau, 2001a). The overall youthfulness, birthrate, and levels of immigration have contributed to the growth of the Hispanic population. In addition, the diversity of national origin groups among Latinos has increased. Hispanics can be of any race and from over 20 national origins, with emerging communities of Dominicans, Colombians, El Salvadorans, Nicaraguans, and Peruvians, for example, adding to the larger and more established communities of Mexicans, Puerto Ricans, and Cubans.

In 2000, 39.1% of Latinos were foreign born (U.S. Census Bureau, 2001b). The number and proportion of Hispanic immigrants has grown rapidly since 1960. In 2000, 14.5 million Hispanics comprised almost one-half of the 28.4 million U.S. foreign-born population (U.S. Census Bureau, 2002). Mexicans are by far the largest Latino immigrant group, accounting for more than half the Hispanic immigrant population, and they are the largest foreign-born group in the nation, nearly six times larger than the next highest group of foreign-born in the United States, Chinese immigrants (U.S. Census Bureau, 2002).

Hispanic immigration to the United States has reach unprecedented levels and has dispersed across the nation, including states, regions, cities, and towns that previously had virtually no Latino residents. Hispanics are concentrated in a number of metropolitan areas. The largest Latino immigrant groups, Mexicans, Cubans, Dominicans, and Colombians, as well as island-born Puerto Ricans, are located in four metropolitan areas: New York, Los Angeles, Miami-Dade, and Chicago. Each area has a significant Latino population with a diversity of Hispanic national origin groups. These areas are traditional destinations for the largest and most long-standing Latino groups — Mexicans, Puerto Ricans, and Cubans — and are the chosen destinations of emerging Latino groups, such as Dominicans, Colombians, Salvadorans, and Guatemalans (Suro and Singer, 2002). Mexicans live largely in Los Angeles and several cities in the state of Texas. Caribbean-born Latinos tend to live in New York or Miami. Central Americans are concentrated in Los Angeles and South Americans in New York (U.S. Census Bureau, 2002). In recent decades, Puerto Ricans and Mexicans have experienced a widespread geographic dispersion. Puerto Rican and Mexican migration and residence have dispersed from the original hubs of migration and most long-standing communities in the United States.

Hispanics are one of the poorest ethnic groups in the United States. Latinos have high rates of poverty among full-time workers and poverty among working husbands in intact families with children, and may suffer from the effects of economic downturns more than non-Latinos and benefit less from periods of economic growth (Suro, 1998). Low levels of educational attainment compound Hispanic socioeconomic vulnerability.

When compared to other racial and ethnic groups, Latinos present a profile that sometimes appears counterintuitive and is not sufficiently explained by existing wisdom or scholarship. One of the most striking examples is in the area of health (Brown & Yu, 2002; Hayes-Bautista, 2002). As birth outcomes demonstrate, "in spite of high risk factors, Latina birth outcomes more closely resemble those of the non-Hispanic White and Asian/Pacific Islanders populations, which had higher income, more education, and better access to first-trimester care. None of this would be expected from the standard norms and models" (Hayes-Bautista, 2002, p. 221). When applied to Latino populations, established theoretical models that explain patterns and variations of illness and disease yield "results that are confusing, seemingly paradoxical, and of little use in creating policies and programs aimed at the Latino population" (Hayes-Bautista, 2002, p. 216), thus the growing need for Latino-based metrics and models.

In light of these demographic shifts, and the differences between and within the various Hispanic national origin groups, including linguistic diversity and immigration status, the development of models for mental health practice within Latino communities takes on increased significance. The mental health issues associated with the migration experience are reason enough to justify the relevance and need for treatment models or approaches of community mental health attuned to Hispanics. It appears evident that as the rate of

Hispanics increases in the United States, so will the need for competent bicultural and bilingual mental health services.

This chapter draws attention to the key common cultural characteristics of the Hispanic population and their relevance for the delivery of effective mental health services. Emphasis is given to selected culturally syntonic treatment approaches or models that may be used by mental health practitioners in treating the psychosocial needs of Hispanic patients in diverse clinical settings. Wherever possible, selected mental health approaches that are empirically supported for their effectiveness in the treatment of Hispanic patients have been included in the chapter.

COMMON CULTURAL CHARACTERISTICS OF HISPANICS

The psychological treatment of Hispanic patients must be predicated on an understanding of how specific cultural values or characteristics directly affect how mental health practitioners provide effective psychotherapeutic culturally syntonic services. Sandoval and De la Roza (1986) as well as other Hispanic scholars (Castex, 1994; Garcia & Zea, 1997; Gil, 1980; González & González-Ramos, 2005; Santiago-Rivera, Arredondo, & Gallardo-Cooper, 2002) have identified and described the salient cultural values or characteristics that should inform the treatment strategies employed in the amelioration of psychological distress among Hispanics. The values or characteristics are *simpatía, personalismo, familismo, respeto,* and *confianza.* Mental health practitioners must be mindful of the fact that irrespective of differences within or among Latino ethnic groups (e.g., Cubans, Mexicans, Puerto Ricans), Hispanics do share similarities based on these traditional core values. Hispanics' level of acculturation, socioeconomic class, and family and gender roles, however, will affect both their adherence to traditional cultural values or characteristics and utilization of mental health services. Examples of traditional Hispanic cultural values/characteristics and how they may impact provision of mental health care are described below:

- *Simpatía* relates to what many call *buena gente* (the plural form of a nice person). Hispanics are drawn to individuals who are easygoing, friendly, and fun to be with. *Simpatía* is a value placed on politeness and pleasantness. Avoidance of hostile confrontation is a vital component of this specific ethnocultural value. In mental health settings, *simpatía* includes the view that clinicians will be noticeably polite and pleasant. The Hispanic patient may view a relatively neutral attitude on the part of the service practitioner as negative.
- *Personalismo* as a cultural trait or value is reflected in the tendency of Hispanic patients to relate to their service providers personally rather than in an institutional or impersonal manner. Hispanic patients expect to develop a warm personal relationship with their provider of care (e.g., psychologist, psychiatric social worker, mental health nurse practitioner), characterized by interactions that occur proximally. Hispanic patients may expect appropriate physical contact, such as a handshake or a hand on the shoulder in some circumstances. Hispanic patients who strongly adhere to the value of *personalismo* are most concerned about the relationship between themselves and the provider of care and less concerned about the institutional auspice responsible for the delivery of a specific type of social or clinical service. Psychotherapeutic engagement efforts must first be aimed at developing a culturally relevant patient-therapist relationship before attempting to implement any type of therapeutic change-oriented service.

- *Familismo* is a collective loyalty to the nuclear and extended family that outranks the individual. The extended family within the Hispanic culture includes members that are biologically related to each other, as well as members that join the family system via *compadrazco* (godparentage). Biological parents select *compadres* (godparents) before the baptism or christening ceremony of a child. Historically, this practice is directly linked to Catholicism. Godparents assume a vital resource role in the Hispanic family, particularly during times of crisis, when instrumental and emotional support may be needed. Because of this cultural value, Hispanics are often willing to sacrifice their individual needs or wants for the welfare of the group (i.e., the family). This cultural value or characteristic is manifested in a shared sense of responsibility by Hispanics to care for children, provide financial and emotional support, and participate in decision-making efforts that involve one or more members of the nuclear or extended family. It is important to note that this cultural value (*familismo*) remains strong even among highly acculturated families (Santiago-Rivera et al., 2002). Mental health intervention must be aimed at enlisting family support in the preventive care and treatment of Hispanic patients. This practice will help to ensure compliance with mental health care recommendations, which in turn can result in successful psychosocial care outcomes.

- *Respeto* (respect) dictates appropriate deferential behavior toward others based on age, gender, social position, economic status, and authority. Within the Hispanic community, older adults expect respect from youngsters, women from men, men from women, adults from children, teachers from students, employers from employees, and so on. Helping agents — such as psychiatrists and psychotherapists of diverse professional disciplines — by virtue of their skills, education, and training are afforded a high level of respect as authority figures. Hispanic patients often look forward to what helping professionals may say and will value their direction and services. Helping agents must keep in mind, however, that respect within the Hispanic culture implies a mutual and reciprocal deference. Hispanic patients expect for providers of professional care to treat them with returned respect, and premature termination from mental health treatment may occur if they perceive that respect is not being shown.

- *Confianza* (trust) refers to the intimacy and familiarity in a relationship. The term in Spanish implies informality and ease of interpersonal comfort. Hispanics tend to be highly attuned to others' nonverbal messages. For example, non-Spanish-speaking mental health practitioners should be particularly sensitive to this tendency when establishing outreach or treatment relationships with patients who primarily only speak Spanish. Over time — and with the use of a qualified translator — by respecting the patient's culture and showing personal interest, providers of mental health services can expect to win the trust of Hispanic patients. Clinicians who are able to develop a bond of trust (*confianza*) with Hispanic patients may eventually notice a level of improvement in the patient's psychological status, and a willingness of the patient to comply with mental health care recommendations and risk reduction advice.

The essence of the most common traditional Hispanic values or characteristics may be summarized in the following points: (1) unity and interdependence among members of the nuclear and extended family; (2) expectation for the family (nuclear and extended) to care for the young and the elderly; (3) flexible sense of time — many Hispanic patients adhere to a present-time orientation; (4) physical closeness and touching within an appropriate context may be expected during conversation or an interpersonal exchange; and (5) respect for tradition and traditional family and social roles (Taylor, 1989).

GENDER ROLE ISSUES AND UTILIZATION OF MENTAL HEALTH SERVICES

Demarcated gender roles are an important component of the Hispanic relational matrix. Traditional gender roles within the Hispanic family structure have intrinsically been linked to the concepts of *marianismo* and *machismo*. *Marianismo*, the term associated with Hispanic female socialization, implies that girls must grow up to be women and mothers who are pure, long suffering, nurturing, pious, virtuous, and humble, yet spiritually stronger than men (Garcia & Zea, 1997). The concept of *marianismo* is religiously associated with the Virgin Mary, and therefore, it is directly tied to the Roman Catholic faith. Although *marianismo* has contributed to a view of Hispanic women as docile, self-sacrificing, and submissive, it is clear that from a family systems viewpoint that women (particularly mothers) are the silent power in the family structure.

The gender role socialization of Hispanic males has centered on the construct of *machismo*. *Machismo* has been defined in the social science literature as the cult of virility, arrogance, and sexual aggressiveness in male-to-female relationships (Santiago-Rivera, 2002). From a Hispanic perspective, however, Sandoval and De la Roza (1986) have noted that *machismo* refers to a man's responsibility to provide for, protect, and defend his family. Loyalty and sense of responsibility to family, friends, and community make a Hispanic male a good man. Hispanic males are to be honorable and responsible men. Within the Hispanic family structure, men (especially fathers and husbands) command and expect respect from others. If mental health initiatives are to succeed, psychotherapists must be skilled at proffering this expected respect to Hispanic adult male patients. It is important to note that the process of acculturation may determine the degree to which both Hispanic males and females adhere to the concepts and cultural definitions of *machismo* and *marianismo*. Thus, adherence to these traditional roles may be more visible among recent Hispanic immigrants than among third- and fourth-generation Hispanics. Although Hispanic women are usually the silent power of the family, mental health practitioners that may wish to implement family-based clinical services must first strategically attempt to therapeutically engage male family members. Sandoval and De la Roza (1986, p. 174) have noted well the impact that *machismo* may have on the delivery of mental health services:

> Machismo is one of the Hispanic cultural traits which greatly affect therapeutic intervention, especially family therapy. Machismo might be the reason why the Hispanic male seeks help at a more advanced stage of deterioration than is typically the case with females. Apparently the Hispanic male needs to be in greater pain in order to seek mental health assistance. Machismo [may] negatively influence the therapeutic process. There is resistance by the male to get involved in couples or family therapy, since males [may] generally perceive this involvement as having a deteriorating effect on their integrity and authority.

RELIGION AND SPIRITUALITY

The literature on cross-cultural mental health services (e.g., Falicov, 1998; Flores & Carey, 2000; Ghali-Badillo, 1977; González & González-Ramos, 2005; Ramirez, 1998; Santiago-Rivera et al., 2002; Sue & Sue, 1999) has identified Hispanics as an ethnic minority group that may adhere to an array of religious or spiritual beliefs. From a mental health perspective, religion and spirituality may impact on how individuals view and relate to their psychological world and social environment. Comas-Diaz (1989), for example, has observed that for Hispanics, religion not only affects their conception of mental illness and treatment, but also influences their health-seeking behaviors. In some instances, when a religious value is placed on suffering and martyrdom (self-denial), certain Hispanics may opt not to seek mental health treatment (Acosta, Yamamoto, & Evans, 1982).

Historically, Hispanics have self-identified as Roman Catholics. However, conversion to Protestant sects/denominations is not an uncommon phenomenon within the Latino community. Currently, many Hispanics identify as Pentecostal, Seventh-Day Adventist, or Evangelical. In addition to adhering to institutionally organized religious belief systems, some Hispanic may profess faith in ancestral spiritual practices such as *santería*, *espíritismo*, or *curanderismo*.

Hispanics have used religion and spirituality as a survival mechanism within the context of an often hostile social environment. For example, for many immigrants, religion has served as a buffer against the toxic emotional effects of entrance into the United States. Urrabazo (2000) has noted the curative potential of faith and religion in therapeutically assisting undocumented Hispanic immigrants who have been robbed, raped, and beaten while crossing the border into the United States. Religion appears to emotionally sustain Hispanics who on a continuous basis are subjected to the realities of racism, discrimination, and social injustice. During times of psychological crisis or environmental distress, the religious belief systems of Hispanics may be used as a complementary adjunct to conventional psychotherapy. Mental health practitioners should become knowledgeable about their patients' belief systems, and they should be prepared to use this knowledge in developing culturally syntonic treatment plans. Providers of mental health care should recognize that for active (or practicing) religious Hispanics, the minister or priest — as well as the *santero*, *espíritista*, or *curandero* — is a highly influential person in their lives and, when appropriate, should be included as a member of any mental health treatment initiative. Mental health professionals, therefore, must be skilled at collaboratively working with the clergy or traditional folk healers in order to effectively address the psychosocial care needs of Hispanics. Clinicians must also be cognizant of the fact that for many Hispanics, the church provides an opportunity for mutual aid and social support. Urrabazo (2000) has documented that the growth of storefront churches in urban Latino communities provides evidence for understanding the desire of many Hispanics to belong to a "healing community" where self-validation, guidance, and social support may be found.

Because of the importance of religion and spirituality among individuals from Latin American and Caribbean descent, it is important to note that Hispanics do not dichotomize physical and emotional health or illness. Thus, the Hispanic culture tends to view health and psychological well-being from a more integrated or synergistic point of view. This view is expressed within a continuum that includes body, mind, and *espíritu* (spirit). Therefore, many Hispanic folk concepts of disease etiology appear to be related to the ill effects of experiencing intensely negative emotional states, such as fright, anger, or envy (The National Alliance for Hispanic Health, 2001). Treatments for these cultural maladies, therefore, are based on a variety of sociospiritual rituals, including purification, social integration, and — at times — penance (Kaiser Permanente Foundation, 2000). Hispanics may often consult *curanderos* (Mexican folk healers), *espíritistas* (spiritualists who are primarily Puerto Rican folk healers), or *santeros* (Cuban or Puerto Rican folk healers) in an attempt to seek symptom relief for physical or emotional complaints.

Nervios: An Example of a Cultural-Bond Physical and Emotional Syndrome

Nervios (nerves) refers to restlessness, insomnia, loss of appetite, headache, and nonspecific aches and pains (Kaiser Permanente Foundation, 2000; The National Alliance for Hispanic Health, 2001). *Nervios* is often linked to experiencing chronic, negative life circumstances, particularly in the domain of interpersonal relationships. Thus, this culture-bond syndrome may often be noticed in individuals who are experiencing maladaptive patterns of interpersonal relationships and communication as well as high levels of social stress. Closely linked to *nervios* are *ataque de nervios* (nerve attacks), which is a seizure-like conversion syndrome characterized by mutism, hyperventilation, hyperkinesis, and uncommunicativeness (Guarnaccia, De la Cancela, & Carillo, 1989; Lewis-Fernandez & Kleinman, 1994). *Ataque de nervios* may resemble a panic attack, but providers of mental health care should not confuse one with the other.

Folk healers (e.g., *curanderos*, *santeros*, or *espíritistas*) that are sought for the treatment of the above-described culture-bond condition will often perform special religious/spiritual rituals using a variety of methods, such as massage with special ointments, prayers, candles, herbal teas, baths, and invocations to specific Catholic saints or spirits. Adherence to the practice of folk healing is based on the fact that many Hispanics accept the possibility that illness and disease are linked to the supernatural world; therefore, spirits and witchcraft may cause or significantly contribute to psychological and physical distress. Illness and disease may also be linked to external environmental or internal (individual) factors, such as bad air, excess cold and heat, germs, dust, fear, envy, and shame. Mental health efforts that are aimed at improving the psychological status of Latinos in the United States must be based on an understanding that many Hispanics will probably conform to both a medical-biological model of help-seeking behavior and a spiritual model of symptom relief.

CULTURALLY SYNTONIC TREATMENT APPROACHES

Within the behavioral sciences, psychotherapy outcome research is now at a stage where the efficacy and effectiveness of specific psychosocial treatments have been demonstrated in the amelioration of mental health symptoms and psychological disorders found among adults, adolescents, and, to some extent, children (Hibbs & Jensen, 1996; Kazdin & Weisz, 2003; Seligman, 1996). Bernal, Bonilla, Padilla, and Perez-Prado (1998) and Miranda (1996), however, have empirically found that ethnic and language minorities are often excluded from treatment outcome research studies. These findings are of significant importance for Hispanics, who represent one of the largest minority groups in the United States. Rossello and Bernal (1999) have noted that "to the extent that minorities are systematically excluded from treatment research, we run the risk of constructing an ethnocentric psychological science: Most treatment-outcome research can only be generalized to White, middle-class, English speaking women who are seeking therapy" (p. 734). In spite of the exclusion of ethnic minority samples in the field of psychotherapy research, a number of culturally syntonic treatment approaches have been developed and tested for use with Hispanic patients in clinical settings. The following selected therapy approaches may be used by mental health practitioners in treating an array of psychosocial problems often observed among Hispanic adults, adolescents, and children.

Bicultural Effectiveness Training

Developed by Szapocznik and colleagues (1984, 1986), bicultural effectiveness training is a 12-session psychoeducational model that focuses on specific family interventions aimed at targeting intergenerational and intercultural conflict. Empirically tested with Hispanic families experiencing conflict with their adolescent children, bicultural effectiveness training is specifically designed to decrease acculturation-related stresses by two-generation Latino immigrant families. This psychoeducational treatment approach is predicated on a structural family theoretical framework (Minuchin, 1974) in which the individual is viewed as embedded in two contexts: the culture and the family. The basic premise of bicultural effectiveness training is that Hispanic families face special problems of adjustment due to their exposure and reaction to the acculturation process (Szapocznik, Rio, Perez-Vidal, Kurtines, & Santisteban, 1986).

Four primary constructs derived from family systems theory (Minuchin, 1974; Szapocznik et al., 1986, 1997) inform bicultural effectiveness training: (1) detour, (2) identified patient role, (3) reframing, and (4) boundaries. According to family systems theory, family problems are not confronted directly but are detoured through a third party, referred to as the identified patient or the party on which the systemic problem is projected. In implementing bicultural effectiveness training as a culturally syntonic treatment approach, the therapist diagnostically assesses the problem as defined by the family within the context of the presenting complaint or constellation of symptoms. The process of therapeutic change begins by the detouring of the problem away from the family or identified patient. This is accomplished through the reframing of the presenting problem as a cultural problem. As a result of redefining the problem in this manner, psychological distress in the family system is minimized, thus allowing the family to become more open to change. Reframing, according to Szapocznik and colleagues (1997), heightens awareness about things that are common among family members, deemphasizes intergenerational boundaries around the family, and promotes positive interaction patterns between parents and their children. An important therapeutic goal of bicultural effectiveness training is to increase acceptance of different values by family members. The successful implementation of this therapeutic goal is important for Hispanic families because they often experience intercultural conflict when the extrafamilial world introduces different and new stressors through some family members that are not shared or acceptable to other members within the same family system. This dynamic exacerbates interpersonal stress within families by creating rigid boundaries between its members and impeding necessary healthy transactions (Stanton, 1979).

Santiago-Rivera et al. (2002) have identified the following benefits of bicultural effectiveness training in providing mental health treatment to Hispanic patients:

1. The treatment approach takes the pathology out of intercultural conflict through the structured use of psychoeducational interventions.
2. The treatment model is clear, well developed, and may be easily implemented through the application of basic educational exercises that patients follow to increase cultural understanding and decrease intergenerational/intercultural familial conflict.
3. The "here and now" emphasis of the treatment approach is consonant with the present-time value orientation of many Hispanic patients.
4. The therapy model is effective in the treatment of adolescent problems where a delicate balance between autonomy and family connectedness is necessary.

The efficiency of bicultural effectiveness training in providing psychosocial care to Latino families is important given that psychiatric epidemiological studies of children and adolescents appear to suggest that Hispanic youth experience a significant number of mental health problems and, in most cases, more problems than Caucasian youth (U.S. Department of Health and Human Services [USDHHS], 2001). Glover, Pumariega, Holzer, Wise, and Rodriguez (1999), for example, found that Hispanic youth of Mexican descent in the Southwest reported more anxiety-related problem behaviors than white students. Lequerica and Hermosa (1995) also found that 13% of Hispanic children screened for emotional-behavioral problems in pediatric outpatient settings scored in the clinical range on the Childhood Behavior Checklist (CBCL). Similarly, other studies (e.g., Achenbach, Bird, Canino, & Phares, 1990; Chavez, Oetting, & Swain, 1994; Vazsonyi & Flannery, 1997) appear to indicate a greater frequency of delinquency behaviors among Hispanic youth in middle schools than among Caucasian youth.

In addition to anxiety and behavioral problems, depression is a serious mental health predicament affecting the psychosocial functioning and adjustment of Hispanic youth. Studies of depressive symptoms and disorders have revealed more psychosocial distress among Hispanic youth than Caucasian adolescents (USDHHS, 2001). This finding may be related to the fact that about 40% of African American and Hispanic youth live in poverty, often in chaotic urban settings that disrupt family life and add considerable stress to their already fragile psychological condition (Allen-Mears & Fraser, 2004). Nationally, for example, Roberts, Chen, and Solovitz (1995) and Roberts and Sobhan (1992) have empirically noted that Hispanic children and adolescents of immigrant descent report more depressive symptomatology than do Caucasian youth. In a later study that relied on a self-report measure of major depression, Roberts, Roberts, and Chen (1997) found that Hispanic youth of Mexican descent attending middle school were found to have a significantly higher rate of depression than Caucasian youth at 12% versus 6%, respectively. These findings held constant even when the level of psychosocial impairment and sociodemographic variables were taken into account.

Social/Environmental Change Agent Role Model

Given the fact that many Hispanic patients (primarily new immigrants and refugees) often lack instrumental support from their U.S.-based extended families, many attempt to negotiate complex environmental conditions (e.g., employment, housing, medical care, learning English as a second language) with minimal appropriate guidance. Predicated on this notion, Atkinson et al. (1993b) developed a dimensional psychosocial intervention approach (social/environmental change agent role model) for the mental health treatment of ethnic-racial minority patients that recognizes the impact of the social environment in promoting or handicapping psychological growth and development. Within this treatment model, the mental health clinician treating Hispanic patients can function as an agent for change or as a consultant or advisor to an identified individual patient acting to strengthen the patient's support systems. Because the successful mental health treatment of Hispanics may also require case advocacy and home visits, both environmental manipulation and home-based treatment services are quite consonant with the tenets of this therapeutic approach.

Atkinson et al. (1993a) recommend that the following three factors be diagnostically assessed when treating an ethnic minority patient: (1) the patient's level of acculturation, (2) the perceived cause and development of the presenting problem (internally caused vs. externally or environmentally caused), and (3) the specific goals to be attained in the treatment process. In implementing this treatment model with Hispanic patients, however, mental health care providers must be prepared to extend their professional role beyond that of psychotherapist to that of advocate, mediator, educator, and broker.

Ego-Supportive Therapy

Given the fact that the mental health problems of Hispanic patients are often exacerbated by socioeconomic stressors, racism, and political oppression, an ego-supportive treatment approach may also be effective in meeting the psychosocial needs of this population. According to Goldstein (1995, p. 168):

> Ego-supportive intervention focuses on the client's current behavior and on his conscious thought processes and feelings, although some selected exploration of the past may occur.... A here-and-now and reality-oriented focus identifies current stresses on the client; restores, maintains, and enhances the client's conflict-free areas of functioning, adaptive defenses, coping strategies, and problem-solving capacities; and mobilizes environmental support and resources.

Within the parameters of this treatment approach, empowerment of patients and work with their social environment are promoted. In addition, the following practice principles, relevant to the experience of Hispanics in the United States, are endorsed: appreciating the impact of the sociopolitical context on the functioning of patients; balancing a focus on ethnic/cultural group membership and individualization of the patient; enhancing patient strengths; building self-confidence, self-esteem, and personal power; educating patients about options to problem resolution and maximizing choice; linking patients to needed resources; connecting patients to mutual aid groups and peer supports; and encouraging collective and political action (Goldstein, 1995, pp. 231–238).

CONCLUSION

Providing psychological intervention to Hispanic patients is both a challenging and rewarding professional endeavor. It requires clinical skill, empathy, and an awareness of how cultural values, gender roles, and religion or spirituality impact the effective delivery of mental health services. Because Hispanics represent one of the largest ethnic minority groups in the United States, mental health clinicians should be familiar with selected culturally syntonic treatment approaches that may be effective in ameliorating psychosocial distress within this population. This chapter has identified selected therapeutic models that appear to be efficient in addressing the mental health needs of Latino patients. While empirical validation of all the selected treatment approaches noted in this chapter has not been documented in the behavioral science literature, it is important to underscore that psychotherapy outcome research with Hispanics is progressively occurring within the mental health field. Practitioners, therefore, must acquire a level of expertise in implementing culturally syntonic treatment models that are supported by either research evidence or tacit knowledge. In providing culturally syntonic treatment, mental health professionals should view themselves as catalysts who are assisting the Hispanic community in reaching its psychological and social potential.

REFERENCES

Achenbach, T.M., Bird, H.R., Canino, G., & Phares, V. (1990). Epidemiological comparisons of Puerto Rican and U.S. mainland children: parent, teacher, and self-reports. *Journal of the American Academy of Child and Adolescent Psychiatry, 29*, 84–93.

Acosta, F.X., Yamamoto, J., & Evans, L.A. (1982). *Effective psychotherapy for low-income and minority patients.* New York: Plenum Press.

Allen-Meares, P. & Fraser, M.W. (2004). *Intervention with children and adolescents: an interdisciplinary perspective.* New York: Allyn and Bacon.

Applewhite, S.R., Wong, P., & Daley, J.M. (1991). Service approaches and issues in Hispanic agencies. *Administration and Policy in Mental Health, 9*, 27–37.

Atkinson, D., Morten, G., & Sue, D.M. (1993a). *Counseling American minorities* (4th ed.). Madison, WI: Brown and Benchmark.

Atkinson, D., Thompson, C.E., & Grant, S.K. (1993b). A dimensional model for counseling racial/ethnic minorities. *The Counseling Psychologist, 21*, 257–277.

Bernal, G., Bonilla, J., Padilla, L., & Perez-Prado, E. (1998). Factors associated to outcome in psychotherapy: an effectiveness study in Puerto Rico. *Journal of Consulting and Clinical Psychology, 54*, 329–342.

Brown, E.R. & Yu, H. (2002). Latino access to employment-based health insurance. In M.M. Suárez-Orozco & M.M. Páez (Eds.), *Latinos remaking America* (pp. 236–253). Berkeley, CA: David Rockefeller Center for Latin American Studies, Harvard University/University of California Press.

Castex, G.M. (1994). Providing services to Hispanic/Latino populations: Profiles in diversity. *Social Work, 39*, 288–296.

Chavez, E.L., Oetting, E.R., & Swain, R.C. (1994). Dropout and delinquency: Mexican-American and Caucasian non-Hispanic youth. *Journal of Clinical Child Psychology, 23*, 47–55.

Comas-Diaz, L. (1989). Culturally relevant issues and treatment implications for Hispanics. In D.R. Koslow and E.P. Salett (Eds.), *Crossing cultures in mental health* (pp. 31–48). Washington, DC: SIETAR International.

Fabrega, H. (1990). Hispanic mental health research: a case for cultural psychiatry. *Hispanic Journal of Behavioral Sciences, 12*, 339–365.

Flores, M.T. & Carey, G. (Eds.). (2000). *Family therapy with Hispanics: toward appreciating diversity.* Boston, MA: Allyn and Bacon.

Ghali & Badillo, S. (1977). Cultural sensitivity and the Puerto Rican client. *Social Casework, 58*, 459–468.

Gil, R.M. (1980). *Cultural attitudes toward mental illness among Puerto Rican migrant women and their relationship to the utilization of outpatient mental health services* (unpublished doctoral dissertation). New York: Adelphi University.

Glover, S.H., Pumariega, A.J., Holzer, C.E., Wise, B.K., & Rodriguez, M. (1999). Anxiety symptomatology in Mexican-American adolescents. *Journal of Family Studies, 8*, 47–57.

Goldstein, E. (1995). *Ego psychology and social work practice* (2nd ed.). New York: Free Press.

González, M.J. (1997). Clinical practice with Latinos: the case of Mrs. Rosa. In *Proceedings of the two-day cross cultural training conference: clinical practice with families and children in a multicultural society.* New York: Hunter College School of Social Work and the New York City Department of Mental Health, Mental Retardation and Alcoholism Services.

González, M.J. & González-Ramos, G. (Eds.). (2005). *Mental health care for new Hispanic immigrants: innovations in contemporary clinical practice.* New York: Haworth.

Guarnaccia, P.J., De la Cancela, V., & Carrillo, E. (1989). The multiple meanings of ataque de nervios in the Latino community. *Medical Anthropology, 11*, 47–62.

Hayes-Bautista, D.E. (2002). The Latino health research agenda for the twenty-first century. In M.M. Suárez-Orozco & M.M. Páez (Eds.), *Latinos Remaking America* (pp. 215–235). Berkeley, CA: David Rockefeller Center for Latin American Studies, Harvard University/University of California Press.

Hibbs, E.D. & Jensen, P. (Eds.). (1996). *Psychosocial treatments for child and adolescent disorders.* Washington DC: American Psychological Association.

Kaiser Permanente Foundation. (2000). *A provider's handbook on culturally competent care: Latino population*. Oakland, CA: Author.

Kazdin, A.E. & Weisz, J.R. (Eds.). (2003). *Evidenced-based psychotherapies for children and adolescents*. New York: Guildford.

Kessler, R.C., McGonagle, K.A., Zhao, S., & Nelson, C.B. (1994). Lifetime and 12-month prevalence of DSM-III-R psychiatric disorders in the United States: results from the National Comorbidity Study. *Archives of General Psychiatry, 51*, 8–19.

Lequerica, M. & Hermosa, B. (1995). Maternal reports of behavior problems in preschool Hispanic children: an exploratory study in preventive pediatrics. *Journal of the National Medical Association, 87*, 861–868.

Lewis-Fernandez, R. & Kleinman, A. (1994). Culture, personality and psychopathology. *Journal of Abnormal Psychology, 103*, 67–71.

Malgady, R.G. & Costantino, G. (1998). Symptom severity in bilingual Hispanics as a function of clinician ethnicity and language of interview. *Psychological Assessment, 10*, 120–127.

Malgady, R.G. & Rogler, L.H. (1993). Mental health status among Puerto Ricans, Mexican Americans, and non-Hispanic Whites: the case of the misbegotten hypothesis. *American Journal of Community Psychology, 21*, 383–388.

Mezzich, J.E., Ruiz, P., & Munoz, R.A. (1999). Mental health care for Hispanic Americans: a current perspective. *Cultural Diversity and Ethnic Minority Psychology, 5*, 91–102.

Minuchin, S. (1974). *Families and family therapy*. Cambridge, MA: Harvard University Press.

Miranda, G. (1996). Introduction to the special section on recruiting and retaining minorities in psychotherapy research. *Journal of Consulting and Clinical Psychology, 64*, 848–850.

The National Alliance for Hispanic Health (2001). *A primer for cultural proficiency: towards quality health services for Hispanics*. Washington, DC: Estrella Press.

Ramirez, M. (1998). *Multicutural/multiracial psychology: mestizo perspectives in personality and mental health*. Northvale, NJ: Jason Aronson.

Roberts, R.E., Chen, Y.W., & Solovitz, B.L. (1995). Symptoms of DSM-III-R major depression among Anglo, African, and Mexican American adolescents. *Journal of Affective Disorders, 36*, 1–9.

Roberts, R.E., Roberts, C.R., & Chen, R. (1997). Ethnic differences in levels of depression among adolescents. *American Journal of Community Psychology, 25*, 95–110.

Roberts, R.E. & Sobhan, M. (1992). Symptoms of depression in adolescence: a comparison of Anglo, African, and Hispanic Americans. *Journal of Youth and Adolescence, 216*, 639–651.

Rogler, L.H., Cortes, D.E., & Malgady, R.G. (1991). Acculturation and mental health status among Hispanics: convergence and new directions for research. *American Psychologist, 46*, 585–597.

Rogler, L.H., Malgady, R.G., & Rodriguez, O. (1989). *Hispanics and mental health: a framework for research*. Malabar, FL: Krieger.

Rosello, J. & Bernal, G. (1999). The efficacy of cognitive-behavioral and interpersonal treatments for depression in Puerto Rican adolescents. *Journal of Consulting and Clinical Psychology, 65*, 734–745.

Sandoval, M.C. & De la Roza, M. (1986). A cultural perspective for serving the Hispanic client. In H.P. Lefley & P.B. Pedersen (Eds.), *Cross-cultural training for mental health professionals* (pp. 151–181). Springfield, IL: Charles C. Thomas.

Santiago-Rivera, A.L., Arredondo, P., & Cooper-Gallardo, M. (2002). *Counseling Latinos and la familia: a practical guide*. Thousand Oaks, CA: Sage.

Seligman, M.E.P. (1996). The effectiveness of psychotherapy: the consumer reports study. *American Psychologist, 50*, 965–974.

Stanton, M.D. (1979). Drugs and the family. *Marriage and Family Review, 2*, 1–10.

Sue, D.W. & Sue, D. (1999). *Counseling the culturally different: theory and practice*. New York: John Wiley.

Suro, R. (1998). *Strangers among us: Latino lives in a changing America*. New York: Vintage.

Suro, R. & Singer, A. (2002). *Latino growth in metropolitan America: changing patterns, new locations*. Washington, DC: Brookings Institution.

Szapocznik, J., Rio, A., Perez-Vidal, A., Kurtines, W., & Santisteban, D. (1986). Family effectiveness training (FET) for Hispanic families. In H.P. Lefley & P.B. Pedersen (Eds.), *Cross-cultural training for mental health professionals* (pp. 245–261). Springfield, IL: Charles C. Thomas.

Szapocznik, J., Santisteban, D., Kurtines, W., Perez-Vidal, A., & Hervis, O. (1984). Bicultural effectiveness training: a treatment intervention for enhancing intercultural adjustment in Cuban American families. *Hispanic Journal of Behavioral Sciences, 6,* 317–344.

Szapocznik, J., Kurtines, W., & Santisteban, D.A. (1997). The evolution of structural ecosystemic theory for working with Latino families. In J. Garcia & M.C. Zea (Eds.), *Psychological interventions and research with Latino populations* (pp. 166–190). Boston: Allyn and Bacon.

Taylor, O. (1989). The effects of cultural assumptions on cross-cultural communication. In D.R. Koslow & E.P. Salett (Eds.), *Crossing cultures in mental health* (pp. 18–30). Washington, DC: SIETAR International.

U.S. Census Bureau. (2001a, March). *Census 2000 population characteristics: the Hispanic population in the United States.* Washington, DC: U.S. Government Printing Office.

U.S. Census Bureau. (2001b, May). *Census 2000 brief: the Hispanic population.* Washington, DC: U.S. Government Printing Office.

U.S. Census Bureau. (2002, February). *Census 2000 brief: current population survey: coming to America: a profile of the nation's foreign born (2000 update).* Washington, DC: U.S. Government Printing Office.

U.S. Department of Health and Human Services. (2001). *Mental health: culture, race, and ethnicity — a supplement to mental health: a report of the surgeon general.* Rockville, MD: Author.

Urrabazo, R. (2000). Therapeutic sensitivity to the Latino spiritual soul. In M.T. Flores & G. Carey (Eds.), *Family therapy with Hispanics: toward appreciating diversity* (pp. 205–227). Boston, MA: Allyn and Bacon.

Vazsonyi, A.T. & Flannery, D.J. (1997). Early adolescent delinquent behaviors: associations with family and school domains. *Journal of Early Adolescence, 17,* 271–293.

Woodward, A.M., Dwinell, A.D., & Arons, B.S. (1992). Barriers to mental health care for Hispanic-Americans: a literature review and discussion. *Journal of Mental Health Administration, 19,* 224–236.

IV

Mental Illness and the Homeless

The chapters in this section address one of the most serious problems experienced by persons with severe mental illness — homelessness. James W. Callicutt, in "Homeless Shelters: An Uneasy Component of the *De Facto* Mental Health System," underscores the link between mental illness and homelessness, contextualizes homeless shelters as a part of a fragmented mental health care system, and argues that homeless shelters function as a component of the *de facto* mental health system. His discussion examines three homeless shelters in north-central Texas and provides a typology of homeless shelters, paying particular attention to the ways in which these shelters provide mental health services.

"The Practice Effectiveness of Case Management Services for Homeless Persons with Alcohol, Drug, or Mental Health Problems," by Philip Thomas, is an excellent discussion of case management models for treating homeless persons with drug, alcohol, or mental illness. Based on a review of the literature, Thomas identifies best practice case management models for working with this population.

Both Callicutt and Thomas address the lack of a clear definition of homelessness and present frameworks within which to examine the complex dimensions of contemporary homelessness.

The last chapter of this section, "We'll Meet You on Your Bench: Developing a Therapeutic Alliance with the Homeless Mentally Ill Patient," by Jenny Ross and Jennifer Reicher Gholston, provides a moving account of an outreach project that provides crisis intervention and psychiatric assistance to the mentally ill "treatment resistant" homeless in New York City. This chapter vividly depicts these individuals, the majority of whom are diagnosed as schizophrenic and have been living on the streets for years. Substantiating the link between mental illness, substance abuse, and homelessness, the authors note that over one-third of their clients are substance abusers.

Taken together, these three chapters provide valuable perspectives on the complex interplay between mental illness and homelessness, drawing clear connections between policy and practice.

14

HOMELESS SHELTERS:
*An Uneasy Component of the De Facto Mental Health System**

JAMES W. CALLICUTT

When President John F. Kennedy signed into law the Mental Retardation Facilities and Community Mental Health Centers Construction Act of 1963, the nation dramatically embarked on its *de jure* mental health policy of deinstitutionalization. This policy was based on the subsequently unrealized expectation that the necessary resources and services for the mentally ill to be appropriately maintained within the community would be provided (Accordino, Porter, & Morse, 2001).

To fast forward, in the final report of the President's New Freedom Commission on Mental Health (2003), the commission declared, "the mental health system is in disarray … lead[ing] to unnecessary and costly disability, homelessness, school failure and incarceration" (p. 3, quoted from the commission's interim report). Underscoring a link between mental illness and homelessness, Torrey (1988, 1997) vividly depicted the harsh penalty of homelessness all too often faced by mentally ill people. In examining the plight of homeless persons (men, women, children, and families), there is no escape from recognizing the somber function of homeless shelters. Rochefort (1997) described the significance of shelters in housing the homeless, particularly in New York City. Clearly, the operation of homeless shelters is big business.

HOMELESSNESS AND MENTAL HEALTH

This chapter concentrates on the role of the homeless shelter as a component of the *de facto* mental health system and asserts that there is a link between mental illness and homelessness as reflected by the disproportionate number of seriously mentally ill persons in the homeless population. Nevertheless, the National Coalition for the Homeless (2002) cites two trends as "largely responsible for the rise in homelessness over the past 20–25 years: a growing shortage of affordable rental housing and a simultaneous increase in poverty" (p. 1).

---

* Information for the agency descriptions is taken from published material such as Websites, annual reports, and brochures. Additionally, I thank the leadership of the shelters for their time and information given in personal interviews.

Homelessness is simply defined by Barker (1999) as "the condition of being without a home" (p. 218). Notwithstanding the definitional and methodological problems regarding efforts to count the homeless as discussed by the National Coalition for the Homeless (2002), an Urban Institute study (2000) in one estimate stated that in a given year about 3.6 million people, including 1.36 million children, are likely to experience homelessness. Furthermore, among the homeless people in cities surveyed by the U.S. Conference of Mayors (2003), approximately 23% are considered mentally ill. In contrast, Rossi (1989) indicated that 17 combined homeless studies reported a 34.3 average percentage with chronic mental illness. Also, as reported by the U.S. Task Force on Homelessness and Severe Mental Illness (1992), among the estimated 4 million people with severe mental illness in the United States, 5% are homeless. Still, institutionalization is generally not indicated even when these persons have multiple needs, although short-term inpatient psychiatric care may be appropriate at times (U.S. Force on Homelessness and Severe Mental Illness, 1992).

Given the realities of a disjointed and fragmented mental health system, we still acknowledge the existence of a *de facto* mental health system (Callicutt, 1997; Regier, Goldberg, & Taube, 1978). Barker (1999) defines *de facto*: "In actual fact, regardless of legal or normative standards" (p. 119). In this sense, we recognize that the *de facto* mental health system has components that include jails, prisons, and homeless shelters.

In this chapter, discussion focuses on three homeless shelters governed by volunteer boards of directors in north-central Texas. I provide descriptions of their programs and examine the relationship of a child development center to one of them. Then I locate these three shelters in a typology of homeless shelters based on the characteristics of each shelter, with particular attention to their respective provision of mental health services.

Each shelter takes a different approach to serving mentally ill residents. Approaches vary and include providing shelter services without special attention to mental health needs per se, referring adult residents with mental health needs to specialized mental health services in the community, referring all preschool children to an exemplary child development center where mental health assessments are routinely conducted and therapeutic services provided when indicated, providing a safe haven devoted exclusively to serving mentally ill men and women, and using telepsychiatry with residents who have major mental health issues.

THREE SHELTERS IN NORTH-CENTRAL TEXAS

North-central Texas, a 16-county metropolitan region centered around and including the cities of Dallas, Arlington, and Fort Worth, has a population of 5.1 million encompassing approximately 12,800 square miles (North Central Texas Council of Governments, 2004). The three homeless shelters described in subsequent sections are chosen to reflect differing philosophies and characteristics illustrating widely divergent practices. Thus, they are not intended to be representative of shelters in the region or of the cities in which they are located. To the contrary, they are purposively selected in order to illustrate service models to be examined in formulating a typology of shelters.

Arlington Life Shelter

Near the center of downtown Arlington, the Arlington Life Shelter provides services to homeless individuals and families in a facility with the capacity to serve 87 residents.

Mission Statement

Shepherding homeless men, women, and children toward a lifestyle of self-sufficiency.

Admission Criteria

For entry to the shelter, individuals must present a picture identification; have no convictions of assault, domestic violence, sexual offense, crimes against children, or weapons charges; and have no chronic serious mental illness. However, persons with mental health problems, including some persons with serious mental illnesses, are accepted for admission if deemed appropriate candidates for eventual employment.

Funding

Funding for the Arlington Life Shelter comes from organizations (27%), in-kind food service (26%), government (22%), individuals (19%), and special events (6%). Only 9% of the agency's expenses go for administration and fund-raising, whereas resident services receive 79% and facilities 12%. The income for 2003 was $1,180,039.

Programs and Services

Basic Life Needs

Shelter services include the provision of shelter, meals, and encouragement for homeless men, women, and children through a structured nine-week program geared toward returning the homeless to self-sufficiency. (During periods of extreme heat and cold, emergency shelter is provided.)

Employment Placement and Coaching

Arlington Life Shelter is unique in the region as the only shelter with a work requirement. The nine-week program provides coaching, technical, and practical services to match residents with jobs with higher pay and opportunities for benefits and advancement.

Social Work Services

Assist in identifying and removing or overcoming barriers to self-sufficiency. Attention is given to acquiring financial management skills and maintaining employment. Mandatory drug treatment is provided at the shelter for residents with substance abuse issues.

Children's Services

Comprehensive services are provided to infants, children, and teens to assist them in developing skills and resiliency for living in their unpredictable world.

Education Services

Adults complete 36 hours of classes in topics that include financial management, parenting, and computer skills. Children receive two hours of computer instruction and tutoring daily. School-age children attend local public schools.

Mental Health Services

The shelter initiated a telepsychiatry program in 2001. "Telepsychiatry links residents diagnosed with schizophrenia, bipolar disorder, severe depression or schizo-affective disorder to a psychiatrist in Fort Worth via secure computer linkages. Residents are able to begin medication within eight hours of their appointment" (Arlington Life Shelter, 2004, pp. 1–2). Arlington Life Shelter reports that 80% of the telemedicine participants are stabilized and placed in employment within six weeks of entry into the agency program. The shelter is among the first in the nation to use this technology. In addition, it has expanded this program to include residents at two other Arlington agencies, the Salvation Army and women's shelter.

"Telepsychiatry is the use of electronic communication and information technologies to provide or support clinical psychiatric care at a distance" (American Psychiatric Association [APA], 1998, p. 2). Telepsychiatry may be delivered at a broad range of sites, including hospitals, emergency rooms, schools, nursing homes, prisons, offices, clinics, and, in this instance, a shelter for the homeless (APA, 1998). Applications include prehospital assessment, posthospital follow-up care, consultation, and medication management. "Live interactive 2-way audio video communication-videoconferencing … has become synonymous with telemedicine involving patient care, distant education, and administration" (APA, 1998, p. 2). This is the modality used effectively at the Arlington Life Shelter.

Staffing

Social work is the predominant professional discipline among the staff. The executive director is a licensed master social worker (MSSW degree). She has four staff with BSW degrees. They are the director of program services, the transitional housing case manager, the employment case manager, and the community relations coordinator. There are 11 other paid staff members, plus 6 or 7 resident assistants, 3 graduate social work interns, and a chaplain intern.

Service Statistics

During 2003, Arlington Life Shelter served 1,178 residents. African Americans comprised 41%; Hispanics, 8%; Native Americans, 3%; Asians, 1%; and whites, 47%. Resident-reported disabilities included drug/alcohol abuse, 23%; physical disability, 7%; dual diagnosis (mental health and substance abuse), 6%; serious mental illness, 5%; and other disability, 9%, for a total of 50%. Children made up 23% of the residents; men, 50%; and women, 27%. As to age, 49% were 31 to 50, 24% were 18 to 30, 20% were birth to 17, and 7% were 51 or older.

The Arlington Life Shelter has broad community support, including critical relationships with elected officials and other community leaders whose service as volunteers go far beyond window dressing.

Family Gateway

Family Gateway is a multifaceted agency with two facilities in Dallas providing housing services for the homeless. One of these, the Annette G. Strauss Family Gateway Center in the downtown area, has 30 bedrooms and serves single- or two-parent families with children. The second is Gateway Apartments in near northeast Dallas. Here, 25 two- and three-bedroom apartments are available to single- or two-parent families with children who are former residents of Family Gateway Center and meet other eligibility criteria (Family Gateway, 2003b).

Mission Statement

Family Gateway, in cooperation with the religious community, private sector, and governmental entities, provides comprehensive services to children whose families are in crisis: counseling, temporary housing, job search and placement assistance, transitional living apartments, and community transition services. The program offers training and counseling that are intended to restore dignity, stability, and self-sufficiency to the family unit. All programs and environments are designed to create an atmosphere of emotional, social, and economic empowerment (Family Gateway, 2003c).

Admission Criteria

Eligibility criteria for the Gateway Center include being a single- or two-parent family with children, residents of Dallas County, a U.S. citizen, not fleeing an abusive situation, and motivated to enter, benefit from, and complete a 10-week program. Proof of homelessness also must be established. Further eligibility criteria for acceptance into the Gateway Apartments include being former residents of Family Gateway Center, a willingness to abide by apartment rules, and the motivation to participate in a long-term rehabilitation program designed to achieve employment and housing in the community (Family Gateway, 2003c).

Programs and Services

As mentioned previously, the Annette G. Strauss Family Gateway Center and the Gateway Apartments provide residential services to homeless families. Gateway to Jobs, the locus for screening, assessment, job search, and placement assistance, provides teaching and coaching to participants with an emphasis on meeting performance requirements in the workplace. Potential employers are served through this quality-controlled "one-stop shopping" point. The third program focus is through Community Transition Services, which extends support services to former resident families, primarily through referrals. Regularly scheduled home visits and telephone contacts are incorporated in the services of the program. A resale shop (Family Treasures) was opened in 1998 to house the Customer Service Training Program. A subsequent section on service statistics further identifies an array of services delivered by Family Gateway.

Staffing

Family Gateway has 29 full- and part-time staff members. The executive director holds a master's degree in rehabilitation. Other staff members include a licensed master social worker (LMSW), a grant writer with a bachelor's degree in journalism, an accountant with a BS degree, a BSW volunteer coordinator, clerical staff, and two intake specialists with associate of arts degrees. A cook prepares lunch and dinner at Family Gateway Center. Volunteers play an important role also, donating approximately 800 hours of service per month.

Service Statistics

In 2003 there were 313 children (155 families) served at the Annette G. Strauss Family Gateway Center. There were 118 children (53 families) served at Gateway Apartments, 251 children (113 families) served in Community Transition Services, and 145 parents served in Gateway to Jobs/Customer Service Training. "One year after program completion, 67% of the children are in families maintaining employment or continuing job training, and 75% of the children are in families living in housing in the community" (Family Gateway, 2003c).

As to family status, single female parents headed 78%. Among the adults, 57% were 30 years old or younger and 66% were high school graduates. Regarding ethnicity, 75% were African American, 12% were Caucasian, 10% were Hispanic, and 3% were other. Almost half (48%) of the children were preschoolers. Most of the families (86%) had been homeless three months or less (Family Gateway, 2003c).

Approximately 25% of the adults were referred for mental health services, and all of the preschool children were referred to Vogel Alcove, the exemplary child development center described later in this chapter. There, developmental screening and referral to outside sources for medical, psychological, or educational service is made as needed. In addition, psychotherapy, including marital and family therapy for parents, is provided by master's-level social workers when indicated (Vogel Alcove, 2003b).

Fund Raising

With a total revenue of $1,579,500 for 1993, the agency receives funds from 19 sources (Family Gateway, 2003a). Among the largest funding sources are foundations ($350,000), government grants ($300,000), the Korshak Lunch fund-raising event ($250,000), and corporations ($175,000). In addition, $40,000 is contributed by individuals, $73,000 from congregations, $30,000 from service organizations, $85,000 from Family Treasures sales, and $4,000 from Family Treasures recycling. Other diverse sources provided the balance of the revenue for 2003.

Presbyterian Night Shelter

During the frigid winter of 1983, a homeless man crawled into an abandoned van in Fort Worth seeking shelter from a wind chill factor of minus six degrees. He froze to death. As area shelters were overflowing at the time, representatives from three Fort Worth Presbyterian churches came together, formed a nonprofit corporation to start a free night shelter for homeless persons, and the Presbyterian Night Shelter opened on December 10, 1984, with three persons receiving shelter that first night. However, it was soon filled to capacity and in 1987 moved to its current location and is now the largest shelter in Tarrant County, Texas. (Fort Worth, Arlington, and the mid-cities are in Tarrant County.) It has provided over 2 million nights of stay and served over 4 million meals. It occupies the unique position of being the "first and only free emergency homeless shelter in the area without length-of-stay restrictions" (Presbyterian Night Shelter, n.d.).

Mission Statement

"The mission of the Presbyterian Night Shelter is to provide for the needs of the homeless while respecting their dignity. We are a shelter of last resort; a sanctuary without cost to anyone in need" (Presbyterian Night Shelter, 2003, p. 1).

The guiding philosophy is to operate a campus of facilities that serves with respect high-risk homeless persons, including the mentally ill, families with children, the elderly, infirm, veterans, and adult male and female individuals (Suggs, 2003).

Admission Criteria

Clinging resolutely to the philosophy of the founding direct and current chairman emeritus, the Reverend Dr. Robert W. Bohl, the Presbyterian Night Shelter does not require an ID for admission. The basic criterion for admission to the shelter is to be in need of shelter. Persons seeking admission are searched for the possession of drugs, alcohol, and weapons, in the interest of safety and security. In addition, shelter residents are tested for tuberculosis by the local health department. The operating principle for admission is to keep the process simple and fundamentally barrier-free. Intake is nightly from 5:00 to 7:00 P.M.

Funding/ Income

Total income for the Presbyterian Night Shelter for 2003 was $2,009,223. It was received from 10 sources, the largest being from federal grants (23%), followed by individual contributions (20%), other revenue (16%), First Presbyterian Church (8%), United Way designated gifts (8%), veterans per diem (8%), program receipts (6%), faith community (4%), organizations/businesses (4%), and foundations (3%) (Presbyterian Night Shelter, 2003).

Programs and Services

Shelter Services

The night shelter per se provides safe shelter, a hot evening meal and cold breakfast, access to a shower, and laundry facilities. Families with children, the elderly, infirm, mentally ill, and veterans may remain in the shelter around the clock. A full-time social worker is available to help with resource connections, including telephone access, a message board, mail services, and documents (e.g., birth certificates, IDs) needed to obtain employment. A work therapy program employs 35 homeless people to handle various day-to-day operations, including switchboard, intake, and kitchen and clean-up duties (Presbyterian Night Shelter, n.d.). Mats, cots, or beds are provided in separate sleeping areas for men and women — no private rooms.

Safe Haven

Safe Haven houses 20 severely mentally ill people at no charge. A nonthreatening residential environment is provided with the goal of establishing a trusting relationship to facilitate the client's acceptance of available mental health services. This Safe Haven is named to memorialize a master's degree social worker who was homeless, had been a client of the Presbyterian Night Shelter, and had family resources, but nonetheless was murdered on the streets of Fort Worth.

A provision for the creation of safe havens was included in the 1992 amendments to the Stewart B. McKinney Homeless Assistance Act (U.S. Department of Housing and Urban Development, 2001). The McKinney Act stated: "A Safe Haven is a form of supportive housing that serves hard-to-reach homeless persons with severe mental illness who are on the street and have been unable or unwilling to participate in supportive services" (U.S. Department of Housing and Urban Development, 2001, p. 3).

Characteristics of Safe Haven facilities include (U.S. Department of Housing and Urban Development, 2001, p. 3):

- Twenty-four-hour residence for eligible persons who may reside for an unspecified duration
- Private or semiprivate accommodations
- Overnight occupancy limited to 25 persons
- Low demand services and referrals
- Supportive services to eligible persons who are not residents on a drop-in basis

Financial support for the operation of the Presbyterian Night Shelter's Safe Haven comes mainly from the U.S. Department of Housing and Urban Development.

Veterans

A transitional program provides separate private dormitories located within the night shelter for 20 male and 4 female homeless veterans. This transitional housing program is operated in cooperation with the Dallas VA Medical Center. Case management covers occupational therapy and job training and placement. Referrals to intake are made through the VA.

Women with Children

A two-story 20,000-square-foot facility, the Lowdon-Schutts Building, for homeless women with children opened in December 2000. It can accommodate up to 100 persons. Like the night shelter, it has no length-of-stay restrictions, and services are provided free. In addition to affording emergency shelter, there are 13 private rooms for transitional housing. It has the distinction of being the only shelter in the area that accepts families with children over 12 years of age with the approval of the director. Intake is available from 10:00 A.M. to 5:00 P.M., Monday through Friday — appointments made via telephone call.

Staffing

Three program directors report to the executive director, who holds a master's degree in urban affairs and has been with the agency for 13 years. There are 12 professional staff program managers, 40 part-time hourly employees, and 18 that are homeless and in the work program. They receive stipends and training. The part-time staff perform security monitoring and similar duties.

Service Statistics

In 2003, 182,726 homeless men, women, and children received safe shelter. The highest number served in one night was 900. More than 1,000 meals per day were served (431,610) (Presbyterian Night Shelter, 2003). These persons were served through the various program components. Since December 1984, the Presbyterian Night Shelter has served more than 4 million meals and has provided shelter to more than 2 million people.

VOGEL ALCOVE

In order to provide a broader context regarding shelter services in the Dallas area, this section gives a brief sketch of the Vogel Alcove, an acclaimed child development center that began operation in March 1987 (then named the Alcove Childcare Center for the Homeless), serving 11 children from homeless families living at the Downtown Family Shelter (now Family Gateway) (Vogel Alcove, n.d.).

The Alcove Childcare Center was established as the top priority of the Dallas Jewish Coalition for the Homeless, comprised of 21 Jewish organizations. The coalition, a private, nonprofit, nonreligious organization, engaged in extensive research that saw child care emerge as a major gap in the service delivery network, and ultimately the project focus for the organization.

After being renamed the Vogel Alcove following the death of Thelma (a co-founder of the Alcove) and Philip Vogel in a plane crash at Dallas–Fort Worth airport in 1988, the Alcove has moved twice to larger quarters. It now has a daily capacity of 113, serving children ages six weeks to six years (Vogel Alcove, 2003a). It receives referrals from 22 different affiliated agencies, including homeless shelters, domestic violence shelters, and transitional housing programs. "The Vogel Alcove remains the primary provider of exemplary child care, developmental and social services in the Greater Dallas area" (Vogel Alcove, n.d.). Since March 1987 the Vogel Alcove has provided nurturing, safe care for more than 8,500 homeless children using existing local resources to provide nutrition, physical, and mental health services (Vogel Alcove, 2003a).

The Vogel Alcove's executive director holds a master's degree in social work, as do other members of the social work staff. It is accredited by the National Academy of Early Childhood Programs and has received numerous awards. Further, it was featured as a model program for homeless children in a 1994 newsletter of the Bazelon Center for Mental Health Law in Washington, D.C.

The budget for the fiscal year 2002–2003 was $2,197,491. A budgeted staff of 43 full-time plus four contract professionals provided services to homeless children in the greater Dallas area. Almost 85% of the budget went to programs and services. The governing body of this nonprofit agency is the board of directors, consisting of 44 community volunteers plus the executive director. Also, there is a 42-member volunteer advisory board (Landix, 2004).

AN ELEMENTAL TYPOLOGY OF HOMELESS SHELTERS

Through the previous descriptions I have given details regarding three homeless shelters in north-central Texas and a thumbnail sketch of a child development center for homeless children shelter residents in Dallas. In the subsequent sections I lay out a limited typology of homeless shelters based on the characteristics of the three shelters. Attention is especially given to how the three shelters respond to the mental health needs of their clientele.

Johnson (1990) studied homeless shelter services in St. Louis and articulated a typology of homeless shelter organizations. The three types presented by Johnson (1990) are (1) Level I, basic services of food and shelter; (2) Level II, stabilization services, which includes transportation, laundry, showers, mental health services, medical care, and other services; and (3) Level III, personal growth services, which includes case management, peer counseling, day care, housing placement, work experience, and other services.

In reviewing the mental health service relationship to the three shelters previously discussed, I further adapt the typology explicated by Johnson (1990) and formulate three types:

Type A: The giant-umbrella model
Type B: The job one model
Type C: The family-first model

Type A: The Giant-Umbrella Model

The Presbyterian Night Shelter exemplifies this model by:

1. Accepting mentally ill homeless for food and shelter (Johnson's Type I) with virtually zero barriers for acceptance (a first tier of service inclusiveness).
2. Operating a women and children's facility for unrestricted stays while offering case management and referrals for mental health issues among other services (a second tier of specialized services).
3. Operating a safe haven with long-term occupancy for 10 mentally ill men and 10 mentally ill women. Residents are encouraged to link with formal community agencies for services, but this is not required (a third tier of specialized services).

Numbers 2 and 3 are stabilization services (Johnson, 1990). (Note: Work experience and opportunities mentioned in the description of programs and services of the Presbyterian Night Shelter may be considered Johnson's Level III personal growth services [Johnson, 1990]).

Type B: The Job One Model

As the only shelter in the Dallas–Fort Worth metroplex with a work requirement, the Arlington Life Shelter illustrates this model with the following features:

1. Admission criteria are used to screen candidates for shelter residence. Only those with a potential for successful, gainful employment are accepted.
2. Those accepted are provided a bundle of services aimed at preparing the client for employment.
3. Specialized services (on site) are provided to clients with mental health problems. In particular, telepsychiatry links the client to a psychiatrist of the countywide mental health center. The client is at the Arlington Life Shelter and the psychiatrist is at another location. Medication may be prescribed and provided. Thus, persons who are mentally ill receive mental health services needed to move them forward toward employment. (These services conform to Level III in Johnson's typology [Johnson, 1990]).

Type C: The Family-First Model

Family Gateway is organized and operated around the premise that homeless families (single- or two-parent families with children) are the priority population for the agency.

1. The Annette Strauss Center provides safe shelter and other services for the priority population for up to 10 weeks.
2. The Gateway Apartments offer safe housing for eligible families who have been served through the Annette Strauss Center. Families may stay up to a year. The emphasis here is on transitional services. Objectives include strengthening fragile families via counseling, job training, placement, and subsequent stable housing in the community.
3. An estimated 25% of the clients are assessed and referred for mental health services.
4. Children (to age 6) are referred to an exemplary child development center, the Vogel Alcove, and emotional and mental health issues are addressed. Play therapy is provided for children when appropriate. Here again, Family Gateway's services fit the description of Level III in Johnson's typology (Johnson, 1990).

In the preceding discussion, the three homeless shelters described in this chapter are characterized as Type A, the giant-umbrella model; Type B, the job one model; and Type C, the family-first model. Each model involves giving basic food and shelter services, and each of the three models provides transitional services and personal growth services. Differences are observed with regard to admission criteria and priority populations. Each shelter performs a unique and valuable service in north-central Texas.

SUMMARY

This chapter has described three distinct homeless shelters in north-central Texas, with attention given to the provision of services to the mentally ill. Each of the shelters serves the mentally ill in different ways, including no-barrier acceptance for emergency services, operation of a safe haven for homeless male and female mentally ill persons, using the technology of telepsychiatry on site at the shelter, assessment and making referrals to mental health community agencies, and using the sophisticated services of a model child development agency in Dallas.

From the descriptions of the three shelters, an elemental typology of shelters was extracted in which the three respective shelters serve as exemplars of divergent program design, focus, and service to homeless people, with special attention given to meeting mental health needs.

The Center for Mental Health Services reported a total of 4,546 mental health organizations operating in 2000. This number came from the Survey of Mental Health Organizations and General Hospital Mental Health Services (Manderscheid & Henderson, 2004). Clearly absent in the statistics compiled via this survey are the organizations identified as components of the *de facto* mental health system in the beginning of this chapter, that is, jails, prisons, and homeless shelters.

In the brief reviews of the three homeless shelters presented in this chapter, it is clear that mentally ill persons receive life-sustaining and life-enhancing services from each of them. Also, as alluded to previously, homelessness is considered to be largely the product of the lack of affordable rental housing and poverty. Furthermore, vulnerability factors impacting homelessness include mental illness and addictive disorders, often co-occurring. Comprehensive strategies to combat homelessness must include the provision of low-income housing, jobs providing livable wages, transportation, health services, and educational services. In addition, persons with severe mental illness or addictive disorders or both should receive specialized services tailored to their respective needs.

Still, as recently as April, 14, 2005, the Dallas City Council (2005) voted to build a Homeless Assistance Center on a site in the southern end of downtown Dallas. This suggests, in part, that the use of shelters for the homeless is increasing and that shelters will continue to be "an uneasy component of the *de facto* mental health system."

REFERENCES

Accordino, M.P., Porter, D.F., & Morse, T. (2001). Deinstitutionalization of persons with severe mental illness: context and consequences. *Journal of Rehabilitation, 67,* 16–21.

American Psychiatric Association. (1998). Resource document on telepsychiatry by video conferencing. Retrieved April 19, 2005, from www.psych.org/psych_Pract/tp_paper.cfm

Arlington Life Shelter. (2004). Mental health services. Retrieved December 9, 2004, from www.arlingtonlifeshelter.org

Barker, R.S. (1999). *The social work dictionary.* Washington, DC: National Association of Social Workers.

Callicutt, J.W. (1997). Overview of the field of mental health. In T.R. Watkins & J.W. Callicutt (Eds.), *Mental health policy and practice today* (pp. 3–16). Thousand Oaks, CA: Sage.

Dallas City Council. (2005, April 14). [Other council action]. *The Dallas Morning News,* p. B5.

Family Gateway. (2003a). *Consolidated budget.* Dallas, TX: Author.

Family Gateway. (2003b). [Leaflet]. Dallas, TX: Author.

Family Gateway. (2003c, February). Fact sheet (leaflet). Dallas, TX: Author.

Johnson, A.K. (1990). Homeless shelter services in St. Louis (university microfilm AAT9114685). *Dissertation Abstracts International, 51.*

Landix, B. (2004, Winter). From the executive director. *Vogel Alcove News,* 3; 12.

Manderscheid, R.W. & Henderson, M.J. (Eds.). (2004). *Mental health, United States, 2002* (Center for Mental Health Services DHHS Publication SMA 3938). Rockville, MD: Substance Abuse & Mental Health Services Administration.

National Coalition for the Homeless. (2002, September). How Many People Experience Homelessness? (NCH fact sheet 2). Washington, DC: Author.

New Freedom Commission on Mental Health. (2003). *Achieving the promise: transforming mental health care in America. Final report* (DHHS Publication SMA-03-3832). Rockville, MD: Author.

North Central Texas Council of Governments. (September 2004). DFWinfo.com

Presbyterian Night Shelter. (2003). *Annual report.* Fort Worth, TX: Author.

Presbyterian Night Shelter. (n.d.). *History and service.* Fort Worth, TX: Author.

Regier, D.A., Goldberg, J.D., & Taube, C.A. (1978). The *de facto* U.S. mental health services system: a public health perspective. *Archives of General Psychiatry, 35,* 685–693.

Rochefort, D.A. (1997). *From poorhouses to homelessness: policy analysis and mental health care* (2nd ed.). Westport, CT: Auburn House.

Rossi, P.H. (1989). *Down and out in America: the origins of homelessness.* Chicago: University of Chicago Press.

Suggs, J.M. (2003, Summer). A message from the executive director. *Nightlight,* 1.

Torrey, E.F. (1988). *Nowhere to go: the tragic odyssey of the homeless mentally ill.* New York: Harper & Row.

Torrey, E.F. (1997). *Out of the shadows: confronting America's mental illness crisis.* New York: Harper & Row.

U.S. Conference of Mayors. (2003, December). *Sodexis hunger and homelessness survey 2003.* Washington, DC: Author.

U.S. Department of Housing and Urban Development. (2001). *In from the cold: safe havens for homeless people.* Retrieved April 19, 2005, from www.hud.gov/offices/cpd/homeless/library/havens/index.cfm

Urban Institute. (2000, February). *A new look at homelessness in America.* Washington, DC: Author.

Vogel Alcove. (2003a). Fact sheet (leaflet). Dallas, TX: Author.

Vogel Alcove. (2003b). Description of Program Activities. Retrieved January 27, 2005, from http://www.vogelalcove.org/services.html

Vogel Alcove. (n.d.). History (leaflet). Dallas, TX: Author.

15

THE PRACTICE EFFECTIVENESS OF CASE MANAGEMENT SERVICES FOR HOMELESS PERSONS WITH ALCOHOL, DRUG, OR MENTAL HEALTH PROBLEMS

PHILIP THOMAS

A consistent finding of the ongoing research of homeless populations reveals that those with alcohol, drug, or mental health problems (ADM) remain the most vulnerable and overrepresented group (Rosenheck, Bassuk, & Salomon, 1999; Stein & Santos, 1998). While mainstream resources play important roles in the care of the homeless, they are not sufficient in themselves to help the homeless, particularly those with ADM problems. Outreach and case management (CM) are often identified as two needed adaptations to the normal service delivery system (McMurray-Avila, Gelberg, & Breakey, 1999; Stephens & Dennis, 1991). As a result, this chapter reviews the evidence about the effectiveness of the diverse CM models and approaches for the homeless who experience ADM problems. Based upon the evidence of effectiveness, best practice models for CM services will be identified in hopes of enabling other social work practitioners and researchers to become aware of the empirically supported knowledge relative to work with the homeless.

HOMELESSNESS

Definitions of homelessness are essential to research and service programs as they dictate both the size and characteristics of the population. Historically, homelessness has not been clearly or operationally defined, which has fueled arguments over its incidence and prevalence. There is no consensus as to the most appropriate definition. Some believe the more narrow definition of "literally homeless" is best, as its specificity guides policy and resources to those who have the greatest need and permits replication of studies (Peroff, 1987). On the other hand, shelter- and street-specific definitions of homelessness are not able to capture other dimensions of contemporary homelessness (Argeriou, 1995). In such cases, definitions are not sensitive enough for the differentiation of subgroups (i.e., marginal and recent). It is estimated that about 80% of homeless persons exit homelessness within two to three weeks (Culhane, Chang-Moo, & Wachter, 1996). For the most part, the definition of homelessness included in the Stewart B. McKinney Homeless Assistance Act of 1987 represents an operational compromise between the broad and narrow definitions, as it conceptualizes homelessness on a continuum. This definition of homelessness, as established by Public Law (Pub. L.) 100-77, follows:

> An individual who lacks a fixed, regular, and adequate nighttime residence, or an individual who has a primary nighttime residence that is: (a) a supervised publicly or privately operated shelter designed to provide temporary living accommodations (including welfare hotels, congregate shelters, and transitional housing for the mentally ill); (b) a public or private place that provides a temporary residence for individuals intended to be institutionalized; or (c) a public or private place not designed for, or ordinarily used as, regular sleeping accommodations for human beings. (Veterans Health Services and Research Administration, Backhus, 1999, p. 2)

PREVALENCE ESTIMATES

In December 1999, the Federal Interagency Council on the Homeless released descriptive data from the National Survey of Homeless Assistance Providers and Clients (NSHAPC) representing the most reliable estimates of the size of homeless populations to date (Burt, Aron, Lee, & Valente, 2001; Shukla, 1999). Conservative estimates (October/November 1996 NSHAPC projection) reveal that 2.3 million adults and children, or nearly 1% of the U.S. population, are likely to experience an episode of homelessness at least once during a year. This probability increases to 6.3% if one considers only people living in poverty (Burt et al., 2001). However, corresponding projections based on the NSHAPC count in February 1996 reveal that 3.5 million adults and children are likely to experience homelessness each year (Burt et al., 2001). Among the homeless, disabilities associated with ADM problems are common, accounting for approximately 50% of those in emergency shelter (Culhane et al., 1996). According to Burt et al. (2001, pp. 102–105):

> The proportion of clients who had one or more ADM problems was high (66 percent) for the past month (that is, 34 percent did not report any problems), and reached 86 percent for their lifetimes. As the time increases, the proportion of clients reporting only one problem decreases, and the proportion reporting combinations increases. For lifetime problems, 47 percent reported mental health problems accompanied by alcohol problems, drug problems, or both.

Clearly people with ADM problems are overrepresented among the homeless (five to six times that of the general population), as only 4% of the U.S. population has ADM problems (Rosenheck et al., 1999).

CAUSAL ANALYSIS

The reasons why people become homeless are as complex as the individuals experiencing homelessness. Many of the factors leading to homelessness are highly correlated with one another and most do not have an independent impact on the risk of homelessness (Rosenheck, 1996). Adding to the complexity, there is no clear direction of causation, as homelessness is both a cause and effect of other serious problems, such as poverty, mental illness, and poor physical health. However, for the sake of simplicity, most researchers agree that there are interrelated functional and structural causal perspectives (Burt et al., 2001; Koegel, Burnam, & Baumohl, 1996; Rosenheck, 1996).

Structural Explanations

Structural explanations of homelessness often focus on inequitable distribution of societal resources causing at-risk individuals to be systematically underserved (Koegel et al., 1996). Examples include poverty, racial discrimination, prejudice, reduced public support, deinstitutionalization, and fragmentation of society's social safety net programs (Koegel et al., 1996; Rosenheck et al., 1999). Two of the more frequently cited structural causes of homelessness are that incomes and industrial jobs have declined since 1973. In addition, there has been an 18% decline in the real value of the minimum wage, leaving many without a livable income (Rosenheck, 1996). The combination of these two factors puts a greater burden on those with the least education and transferable skills.

The U.S. Department of Housing and Urban Development estimates that 5 million households in the United States have incomes below 50% of the local median. These individuals pay more than half of their income for rent on housing that is substandard. Moreover, there has been a 5% decline in the number of low-cost housing units, with federal rental assistance programs not being able to fill the gap due to long waits for Section 8 vouchers (U.S. Department of Housing and Urban Development, 2001). The equation is simple: too few low-cost housing units for too many low-income people during a climate of declining public support for the poor results in increased prevalence of homelessness (Koegel et al., 1996).

Functional Explanations

On the other hand, functional explanations tend to find the locus of homelessness within the individuals themselves (mental illness, substance abuse, poor adjustment). By focusing on these functional causes and effects of homelessness, proponents of the functional argument believe policies have a greater chance of providing individuals with the needed treatment and rehabilitation that will enable them to take advantage of housing that they otherwise could not secure or maintain (Koegel et al., 1996).

Given the complex web of causation discussed above, it follows that homelessness is both a cause and effect of structural and functional factors. If homelessness is thought of as a game of musical chairs, the structural factors are the ones responsible for the removal of chairs (e.g., low-cost housing), while functional factors determine who loses their seats (Koegel et al., 1996; Rosenheck, 1996). Those affected most profoundly are often the most vulnerable due to their ADM problems (Stein & Santos, 1998).

CASE MANAGEMENT

The origins of case management (CM) as a means of linking clients to needed services in the community started in the late 19th century and derive primarily from social work traditions (Rapp & Chamberlain, 1985). Traditionally, CM has been provided to the seriously mentally ill to replace and coordinate the many services provided in state hospitals. Over time, CM has become a more refined intervention used differentially among diverse populations, such as children, the elderly, and public welfare recipients (Sullivan, Wolk, & Hartmann, 1992). Since the 1980s, CM has proved to be the cornerstone for serving homeless populations (Lam & Rosenheck, 1999) and has derived its prominence due to increasing concern with service effectiveness (Rapp, 1998a) and managed care (Solomon & Draine, 1995).

Definitional Issues

Despite its importance as a service component in the area of mental health and homelessness, the diversity of CM tasks and approaches has reinforced the lack of consensus regarding its definition. Although there is little consensus on a definition of CM or a single approach, a few common themes and core components have emerged: (1) outreach and engagement, (2) assessment, (3) development of a case plan, (4) procurement of services, (5) monitoring and advocacy, and (6) tracking and evaluation (Mueser & Bond, 2000; Sullivan et al., 1992). These components have contributed to a broad definition of CM: a pragmatic and collaborative approach to offering practical assistance (i.e., housing, finances, medications, access to services) and enhancing the social functioning of persons with mental illness through assessment, counseling, teaching, modeling, and advocacy (Mueser & Bond, 2000; Sullivan et al., 1992).

Practice Approaches

Without consensus on a definition of CM, the development of a wide variety of CM approaches and models is not surprising. The terms *models* and *approaches* are at times used interchangeably. However, *models* can be defined as a complex set of interventions designed to achieve specific goals, whereas the term *approach* often refers to a treatment philosophy that is not formally specified in all details (Morse, 1999).

Solomon (1992) identifies four types of models: assertive community treatment, strengths CM, rehabilitation, and generalist CM. Other researches have distinguished six types: brokered, clinical, strengths, rehabilitation, assertive community treatment, and intensive CM (Mueser, Bond, Drake, & Resnick, 1998).

Rather than models or approaches, others have defined dimensions along which CM programs might differ. These include type of staff, emphasis on outreach, client:staff ratios, shared versus individual caseloads, time and duration of availability (24 hours, lifetime, time limited), medication delivery, type of care (direct care vs. brokerage of services), target population, locus of contact (setting), and inclusion of payee services (Marshall & Lockwood, 1998; Ziguras & Stuart, 2000).

Also gaining popularity are *hybrid* and *tiered* approaches (stage-wise CM), where different levels of service intensity are matched with different levels of client need (Mueser & Bond, 2000). Bedell, Cohen, and Sullivan (2000) reviewed eight published literature reviews of CM and determined that three categories of CM approaches existed: full service (attempt to directly provide all clinical and support services needed), hybrid (some services provided directly and some brokered), and brokered (provide very little direct service). Let us take a closer look at these approaches.

Full Service

Assertive Community Treatment (ACT)

ACT was originally established as an effective community-based intervention for the nonhomeless severely mentally ill. Proponents of ACT eschew the notion that it is a type of CM (Morse, 1999). Nevertheless, it shares many elements of other CM models and will be considered here for the purposes of this chapter. Elements of the original model (Stein & Santos, 1998) include a multidisciplinary staff team approach, often directed by a psychiatrist; a low client-to-staff ratio (10 to 1), shared caseloads; 24-hour availability, time-unlimited services; and locus of contact in the community. Goals often focus on help with symptom management, relapse prevention, enhancing supportive social and family systems, meeting basic needs, enhancing quality of life and social functioning, preventing hospitalization, and assistance with locating and maintaining work. Research is now looking toward its implementation with various subpopulations of persons with severe mental illness, such as the homeless (Dixon, Krauss, & Kernan, 1995; Morse, Calsyn, & Allen, 1992). Other examples of full-service approaches include training in community living, assertive outreach, and the Bridge program (Test, 1992; Bond, McGrew, & Fekete, 1995).

Hybrid Approaches

Continuous Treatment Teams (CTT)

CTT is often considered a variation of ACT (Morse et al., 1992). It refers to a multidisciplinary team approach to serving the seriously mentally ill. Program components include a multidisciplinary team of mental health workers, including a psychiatrist; outreach; ongoing responsibility for providing and coordinating treatment whether or not in the hospital (i.e., one-year duration); shared and relatively small caseload size (15:1); and a locus of care in the client's natural setting.

> Although presented as distinct from ACT, a review of the literature suggests some ambiguity surrounding specific ways in which the CTT model departs from the ACT model, and some make little or no distinction between ACT and CTT. (Johnsen et al., 1999, p. 330)

Intensive Case Management (ICM)

ICM gets its name from the conceptualization of being more intense than usual brokered CM. ICM is a CM approach, as it has emerged from the field in absence of an extensive theoretical or research base (Morse, 1999). Caseload ratios are often 10:1 or 15:1. It has many of the same admission criteria and goals as ACT, but is less clearly defined and often operationalized differently across programs. It typically does not use a shared-client team approach.

The Strengths Model

The strengths model is yet another hybrid model of CM used to address the needs of the seriously mentally ill. As the name of the model suggests, it is based on the humanistic and pragmatic principle of focusing on individuals' strengths rather than pathology (Rapp, 1998b). The case manager's role blends functions of therapist and broker toward the dual purpose of identifying, securing, and sustaining resources that are both internal and external to the client (Rapp, 1998b; Rapp & Chamberlin, 1985). The model's components are (1) focus on the person in environment; (2) use of paraprofessionals or consumers; (3) strengths assessment; (4) heavy emphasis on outreach, engagement, and relationship; (5) resource acquisition; and (6) emphasis on self-determination (i.e., high degree of responsibility given to the client) (Rapp, 1998b). Client-to-staff ratios are often 20:1, and clients have 24-hour access to staff. Time of services to clients is indefinite, and case managers have individual caseloads, which are shared for purposes of backup. However, the strengths model does utilize a group supervision/team approach for case planning and review (Rapp, 1998b). While often used with a broad nonhomeless population of persons with severe mental illness, it has been implemented in the ACCESS demonstration project for the homeless (Johnsen et al., 1999; Morse, 1998).

Clinical Case Management (CCM)

CCM is an aggressive approach to assisting the mentally ill that stresses the importance of formal clinical training and services (individual and group therapy). Case managers take a longitudinal perspective of the course of an illness, and they strive for the maintenance of the client's physical and social environment, with the goals of enhancing the client's basic survival, personal growth, community participation, and recovery. The typical client-to-staff ratio of CCM is 1:15. However, case size should be flexible, based on the type and intensity of clinical services provided (Kanter, 1989).

Critical Time Intervention (CTI)

Early research has indicated some promise for the CM approach known as CTI. This approach is designed to prevent first episodes of homelessness as well as recurrent homelessness by augmenting the continuity of care for individuals being discharged from institutions to community living (Susser et al., 1997). CTI is time limited and focuses on the time of overlap before and after discharge. A primary element of CTI is that postdischarge services are delivered by staff that have established a relationship with the client while hospitalized. CTI is similar to ACT in that its focus is on *in vivo* support. However, more emphasis is placed on the critical transitional time of discharge to the community. Once the client is situated in the community, the primary responsibility of care is transferred to existing supports in the community. CTI staff do not have to be professionals, but they are supervised by a psychiatrist or mental health professional (Herman et al., 2000).

Brokered Approaches

Brokered Case Management (BCM)

BCM includes the traditional CM functions of assessment, planning, referral, and monitoring. However, the case manager provides little to no direct service or outreach to the client and has no responsibility for ensuring that the brokered services are completed. Brokered case managers are often bachelor-level professionals based in an office from where they coordinate caseloads of 30 or more. Other brokered approaches of CM are specialist, generalist, and supportive (Bedell et al., 2000). While common, these approaches are not recommended for homeless populations (Morse et al., 1997).

METHODS

Electronic database searches were conducted yielding over 200 articles in English-language journals representative of various sociological, epidemiological, substantive, theoretical, and experimental studies. The initial search produced results that included outreach and a range of housing alternatives often referred to as supportive housing. While CM may be a component of supportive housing and outreach, it is not necessarily the defining component. Thus, for this review, supportive housing and outreach are not considered a CM approach, but rather a form of specialized housing or service that exists along a continuum.

To distinguish the quality and validity of the evidence-based findings, a simple distinction among experimental (pretest-posttest control group design, posttest-only control group design, Solomon four-group design), quasi-experimental (nonequivalent control group design, time series designs), and preexperimental (case study, one group pretest-posttest design, static group comparison, posttest-only design with nonequivalent groups) studies is used (Rubin & Babbie, 1997). "All other research variables being constant, the most valid conclusions about the effectiveness of CM services must be derived from experimental studies using random assignment" (Morse, 1999, p. 9). Preexperimental and quasi-experimental designs are beneficial when it is impossible to achieve random assignment, as they include comparison groups without random assignment, timeline and pre- and post-analysis, and retrospective case reviews (Morse, 1999; Rubin & Babbie, 1997).

FINDINGS

Experimental ACT Studies

ACT is one of the best researched CM models, with over 25 randomized controlled trials evaluating its effectiveness. However, as of 1992, only one (Morse, 1999) of the studies specifically addressed its application to homeless persons. At the time of this review, approximately 11 experimental studies of ACT services for homeless clients with ADM problems have been published, along with a number of quasi-experimental and nonexperimental studies.

Lehman et al. (1999) and Lehman, Dixon, Kernan, DeForge, and Postrado (1997) tested the efficacy of a modified ACT model for homeless persons with severe and persistent mental illness. Clients are referred to a "miniteam" consisting of a case manager, psychiatrist, and consumer advocate. However, the entire team works together in decision making and is knowledgeable about most of the clients. In addition, the modified ACT model assumes a time-limited rather than time-unlimited framework for service delivery. Finally, a family outreach worker and consumer advocate was added to provide services to a subgroup of families and clients. However, many other original ACT components remain, such as 24-hour coverage and low client-to-staff ratios (9 to 1).

Through stratified random assignment, half the participants received ACT services and the other half received services as usual (community mental health centers). Preliminary findings showed that the ACT clients spent more days stably housed and used fewer crisis-oriented services and more outpatient visits than did the comparison group. ACT clients also had greater symptom reduction and greater improvements in life satisfaction and health. No differences were found in areas of employment and interpersonal relations. Overall, the authors concluded that it is possible to modify the ACT model for homeless subgroups.

Herinckx, Kinney, Clarke, and Paulson (1997) randomly assigned homeless persons with severe mental illness to one of two ACT teams or a usual-care (UC) control condition. Results showed that the ACT teams retained 68% of their clients versus 43% in UC. UC clients were more than twice as likely to drop out due to dissatisfaction with treatment as ACT clients were. For each additional night homeless during the six-month period prior to enrollment in the study, there was a 14% increase in the probability of dropout. The authors concluded that ACT has a greater ability to engage and retain formerly homeless clients in mental health care than does care as usual.

Korr and Joseph (1995) studied a group of clients in a state hospital who were randomly assigned to ACT or routine services. At six-month follow up, 36 ACT clients were housed compared to 15 receiving routine services. None of the ACT clients had returned to the streets or to shelters. The authors concluded that ACT was an effective means to house the mentally ill homeless.

Morse et al. (1997) conducted an experimental study comparing three types of CM (ACT vs. ACT + community workers vs. brokered CM) for the mentally ill who were homeless or at risk of homelessness and in acute crisis. Clients were primarily recruited from emergency rooms and inpatient units. The ACT-only treatment group conformed to the standard ACT treatment principles described above, with the exception of a few modifications to meet the special needs of the homeless: (1) assertive outreach to shelters and specialized training in engaging the homeless; (2) team did not have a psychiatric nurse; (3) psychiatrist was available for only two hours a week; and (4) medication services were obtained primarily through linkages with private or clinic-based psychiatrists. The ACT + community worker treatment group was the same as the ACT-only group. However, clients were also assigned a paraprofessional who assisted with activities of daily living (ADLs) and leisure, primarily in the later stages of treatment. The brokered CM treatment group followed standard CM principles, described in the CM models section above.

Results indicated that clients in the two ACT groups were more satisfied with their treatment and had fewer symptoms in the areas of thought disorder and unusual activity. Clients in the ACT-only group averaged more days stably housed than clients in both the ACT + community worker and brokered CM. No significant treatment group differences were found between the treatment groups on income, anxiety/depression, hostility/suspicion, self-esteem, and substance abuse variables. The authors concluded that ACT is a more effective intervention for mentally ill persons at risk of homelessness or homeless than brokered CM. In a very similar study, Morse et al. (1992) conducted an experimental study that randomly assigned clients to ACT versus a community mental health clinic versus a drop-in center. Once again, ACT proved to be the most effective service for the same population (Morse et al., 1992).

In another publication of the above-mentioned study, Wolff et al. (1997) reported on the cost-effectiveness of three approaches to CM for the homeless or at risk of homeless mentally ill described above. They found that there was no statistically significant difference between the treatment conditions in terms of total costs. However, the ACT conditions spent less money on inpatient services than did brokered CM, but more on CM services and meeting basic needs (food stamps, housing, SSI). The authors concluded that overall, ACT achieves better outcomes at no greater cost than brokered CM.

Shern et al. (2000) tested a psychiatric rehabilitation approach of services for the homeless and severely mentally ill. Participants were randomly assigned to the experimental Choices program or offered information on "standard treatment." The Choices program was described as being similar in structure to the ACT program described above, with the addition of respite housing and a low-demand drop-in center. Results indicated that members of the Choices experimental program were more likely to attend a day program, more often met their basic needs, spent less time on the streets, and spent more time stably housed than those in the control group. The experimental group also reported greater life satisfaction and had fewer psychiatric symptoms than the control group. The authors concluded that with a comprehensive service model based on psychiatric rehabilitation principles, it is possible to engage homeless persons and improve their use of human services, housing conditions, quality of life, and mental health status.

Calsyn, Morse, Klinkenberg, Trusty, and Allen (1998) studied the impact of assertive community treatment on the social relationships of people who are homeless and mentally ill. Using two randomized experiments, they compared the effectiveness of ACT versus outpatient therapy, drop-in centers, and brokered CM. Clients receiving ACT services reported having more professionals as part of their support network. However, they did not report significant differences among treatment conditions on most of the other social relationship dimensions.

Experimental ICM

Braucht et al. (1995) studied a group of homeless individuals with substance abuse problems. Half of the clients randomly received comprehensive substance abuse services, while the other half received intensive CM in addition to the substance abuse services. Clients improved on average regarding their substance abuse housing, mental health, employment, and quality of life status. CM marginally increased client contact with counselors and was found to have little to no effect on outcomes.

Cox et al. (1998) studied homeless substance abusers to test the effectiveness of intensive CM in improving finances, residential stability, and reducing alcohol use. Subjects were randomly assigned to ICM or a control group and given follow-up measures at six-month intervals for a period of two years. Results showed significant group differences for those receiving ICM in all three outcome areas. The authors concluded that ICM had a beneficial effect for alcohol abusers.

Hurlburt, Hough, and Wood (1996) were interested in studying the effects of substance abuse on housing stability of homeless mentally ill persons receiving supported housing. Using a two-factor longitudinal design, clients were randomly assigned to four experimental conditions. Half the clients were given Section 8 vouchers, enabling access to independent housing. All clients received traditional CM, but half were provided ICM. Results revealed that clients were more likely to end up in independent housing if given the opportunity to obtain a Section 8 voucher. No differences emerged across the two different levels of CM. Housing stability was significantly mediated by several factors, primarily the use of drugs or alcohol. The authors concluded that supported housing can be very effective in helping the homeless achieve stable housing regardless of the associated CM model (ICM vs. traditional).

Stahler, Shipley, Bartelt, DuCette, and Shandler (1995) studied alternative treatments for homeless substance-abusing men. The treatments included (1) integrated comprehensive residential services, (2) on-site shelter-based ICM with referrals to a community network of services, and (3) usual-care shelter services with CM. Results indicated that all three treatment groups were associated with significant improvement, as evidenced by reduced substance use, increased employment, and increased stable housing. However, no differential improvements were found among the treatment groups.

Toro et al. (1997) randomly assigned homeless clients to ICM or a control group. Results indicated that regardless of the intervention, clients reduced the nights spent homeless as well as adverse physical health symptoms and stressful live events. However, clients receiving ICM had better quality of housing, fewer stressful life events, and less psychopathology than the control group.

Willenbring (1997) studied the (cost) effectiveness of three intensities of CM (intensive = caseload of 12, intermediate = caseload of 45, or episodic care only) with homeless substance abusers. Participants were recruited from a public detoxification center and randomly assigned to the treatment conditions. Results indicated that both CM treatments were associated with significant reductions in costs and use of detox and emergency services compared with episodic care. However, the two CM interventions did not differ. The authors concluded that there was no real advantage to a caseload of 12 over a caseload of 45. Overall, CM is a cost-effective treatment for homeless substance abusers.

Sosin, Bruny, and Reidy (1995) studied graduates from a short-term inpatient substance abuse program who were homeless and randomly assigned to one of three treatment conditions: (1) CM only, (2) CM + supported housing, or (3) normal aftercare in the community (control). The two treatment groups use a "progressive independence" approach, which targets obtaining basic needs and improving clinical status. Results showed that participants in both treatment groups had lower levels of substance abuse and higher levels of housing stability than the control group. Retention and residential stability were increased due to targeting immediate tangible resources (income maintenance and housing), and substance abuse was reduced with the assistance of supportive services and behavioral training in relapse prevention.

Lapham, Hall, and Skipper (1995) studied project H&ART, a randomized intervention trial for homeless substance abusers. CM plus peer-supervised housing was compared to peer-supervised housing only and to a housed and nonhoused control group. Results revealed graduation rates of about 25% for all three housed groups. The authors concluded that client personal motivation factors of recovery were more salient in determining outcomes than were program-related factors.

Experimental CTI

Susser et al. (1997) studied the effectiveness of a CM approach known as critical time intervention (CTI) in preventing recurrent homelessness. Ninety-six men with psychotic disorders who were discharged from a homeless shelter were randomly assigned to receive either CTI or usual services (mental health and rehabilitation referrals) only after their housing placement had been selected (ranging from board and care homes to single room occupancy). The men in the CTI intervention received nine months of CTI plus usual services (US), and then usual services only for the remaining nine months. Results showed that CTI was associated with a significant and lasting reduction in postdischarge homelessness (CTI had a mean of 30 nights vs. US with a mean of 91). In addition, CTI was associated with a significant decrease in negative symptoms at the six-month follow-up. There was no significant effect on positive or general psychopathology symptoms.

Experimental Brokered CM

Marshall, Lockwood, and Gath (1995) conducted a randomized controlled trial to evaluate a social services CM approach (brokered) for the chronically mentally ill who were homeless or at risk of being homeless. Forty clients each were randomly assigned to social services CM and to services as usual (care provided them before the study but not receiving another CM service). Results after seven months revealed no clinically or statistically significant differences between the treatment and control groups. At 14 months' follow-up, the CM group showed lower levels of deviant behavior than the control group. The authors concluded that social service CM (brokered) did not improve the quality of life or the social behavior of chronically mentally ill homeless and commented that it was unfortunate that social services case management had been widely implemented in the United Kingdom.

Quasi-Experimental

ACCESS (Access to Community Care and Effective Services and Supports)

ACCESS was a five-year demonstration program to provide outreach and CM services to the homeless mentally ill. The 18 program sites were not replications of ACT, but had many similar features, including multidisciplinary team organization, assertive outreach, high intensity of service, small caseloads, expanded hours of operation, and close collaboration with social support networks. A few specific differences from the ACT model were employed in some cases to fit homeless populations better. These included time-limited services and structural separation of outreach functions. Each site engaged and served a cohort of 100 clients (Chinman, Rosenheck, & Lam, 2000a).

An important component and principle of ACT is the time-unlimited services. Rosenheck and Dennis (2001) evaluated postdischarge changes in health status and service use associated with a time-limited modification of ACT for homeless persons with severe mental illness. Mental health, substance abuse, and housing outcomes did not differ significantly between the two groups. Those who received time-limited services worked more days and reported less outpatient service use than those who continued with ACT. The authors suggest that some homeless clients with ADM problems can benefit from time-limited ACT services, allowing a better distribution of ACT resources for the homeless (Rosenheck & Dennis, 2001).

Chinman et al. (2000a) studied a number of CM-related variables, such as the extent of the therapeutic alliance, client-case manager racial matching, and client-related characteristics that predict formation of a relationship with the client. There was no significant association between the quality of the therapeutic alliance and outcomes at 12 months. However, clients who significantly reduced the number of days homeless at 12 months had formed an alliance with their case manager by 3 months. The authors concluded that the therapeutic alliance between a client and the case manager in the context of a modified ACT model or ICM was significantly related with homelessness and modestly related with general life satisfaction. Assertive clinical outreach is seen as a way to overcome the barriers to developing a therapeutic relationship with this difficult-to-treat population. Providing a variety of pathways as a means of obtaining treatment should be explored in addition to being assigned a case manager (Chinman, Rosenheck, & Lam, 1999).

Another ACCESS study compared the clinical outcomes of services provided by consumer versus nonconsumer case managers. All clients improved significantly in both conditions. However, there were no significant Time × Case Manager Type interactions, suggesting that consumers could be a valuable asset for CM teams serving the homeless mentally ill (Chinman, Rosenheck, Lam, & Davidson, 2000b).

Lam and Rosenheck (1999) further examined CM data to determine if there were any differences in sociodemographic characteristics, service needs, and outcomes between those clients contacted through street outreach versus those contacted in shelters and other social service agencies. In general, those contacted on the streets tended to be male, older, spent more nights literally homeless, took longer to engage, and had psychotic disorders. Overall, they expressed less interest in treatment and were not as likely to agree to CM. However, those who did enroll in CM showed as much improvement as those who were engaged through shelters and agencies. This suggests that street outreach is an important and justified component of CM for the homeless ADM clients.

CONCLUSION

The benefits of CM services for persons who are homeless and suffering from ADM problems seem promising. Both the experimental and quasi-experimental evidence suggests that ACT, CTI, and ICM reduce the number of days homeless compared to the brokered CM or other standard approaches. In addition, some studies have shown an increase in service utilization, better engagement and retention, reduced symptoms, greater satisfaction with services, improved income, and increased quality of life (Blankertz, Cnaan, White, Fox, & Messinger, 1990; Morse, 1998). However, ACT remains the best researched CM model even when modified for homeless populations. As a result, it seems that the research strongly supports ACT and its modifications for the homeless as an evidenced-based practice and best practice among the current literature for homeless persons with ADM problems.

REFERENCES

Argeriou, M. (1995). Dimensions of homelessness. *Public Health Reports, 110,* 734–741.

Backhus, S.P. (1999). *Homeless veterans: VA expands partnerships, but homeless program effectiveness is unclear.* Washington, DC: Federal Document Clearinghouse.

Bedell, J.R., Cohen, N.L., & Sullivan, A. (2000). Case management: the current best practices and the next generation of innovation. *Community Mental Health Journal, 36,* 179–194.

Blankertz, L.E., Cnaan, R.A., White, K., Fox, J., & Messinger, K. (1990). Outreach efforts with dually diagnosed homeless persons. *Families in Society, 71,* 387–396.

Bond, G.R., McGrew, J.H., & Fekete, D.M. (1995). Assertive outreach for frequent users of psychiatric hospitals: a meta-analysis. *Journal of Mental Health Administration, 22,* 4–16.

Braucht, G.N., Reichardt, C.S., Geissler, L.J., Bormann, C.A., Kwiatkowski, C.F., & Kirby, M.W. (1995). Effective services for homeless substance abusers. *Journal of Addictive Diseases, 14,* 87–109.

Burt, M., Aron, L.Y., Lee, E., & Valente, J. (2001). *Helping America's homeless: emergency shelter or affordable housing?* Washington, DC: The Urban Institute Press.

Calsyn, R.J., Morse, G.A., Klinkenberg, W.D., Trusty, M.L., & Allen, G. (1998). The impact of assertive community treatment on the social relationships of people who are homeless and mentally ill. *Community Mental Health Journal, 34,* 579–593.

Chinman, M.J., Rosenheck, R., & Lam, J.A. (1999). The development of relationships between people who are homeless and have a mental disability and their case managers. *Psychiatric Rehabilitation Journal, 23,* 47–56.

Chinman, M.J., Rosenheck, R., & Lam, J.A. (2000a). The CM relationship and outcomes of homeless persons with serious mental illness. *Psychiatric Services, 51,* 1142–1147.

Chinman, M.J., Rosenheck, R., Lam, J.A., & Davidson, L. (2000b). Comparing consumer and non-consumer provided case management services for homeless persons with serious mental illness. *Journal of Nervous and Mental Disorders, 188,* 446–453.

Cox, G.B., Walker, R.D., Freng, S.A., Short, B.A., Meijer, L., & Gilchrist, L. (1998). Outcomes of a controlled trial of the effectiveness of intensive case management for chronic public inebriates. *Journal of Studies on Alcohol, 59,* 523–532.

Culhane, D., Chang-Moo, L., & Wachter, S. (1996). Where the homeless come from: a study of the prior address distribution of families admitted to public shelters in New York City and Philadelphia. *Housing Policy Debate, 7,* 327–365.

Dixon, L.B., Krauss, N., & Kernan, E. (1995). Modifying the PACT model to serve homeless persons with severe mental illness. *Psychiatric Services, 46,* 684–688.

Herinckx, H.A., Kinney, R.F., Clarke, G.N., & Paulson, R.I. (1997). Assertive community treatment versus usual care in engaging and retaining clients with severe mental illness. *Psychiatric Services, 48,* 1297–1306.

Herman, D., Opler, L., Felix, A., Valencia, J.D., Wyatt, R.J., & Susser, E. (2000). A critical time intervention with mentally ill homeless men: impact on psychiatric symptoms. *The Journal of Nervous and Mental Disease, 188,* 135–140.

Hurlburt, M.S., Hough, R.L., & Wood, P.A. (1996). Effects of substance abuse on housing stability of homeless mentally ill persons in supported housing. *Psychiatric Services, 47,* 731–736.

Johnsen, M., Samberg, L., Calsyn, R., Blasinsky, M., Landow, W., & Goldman, H. (1999). Case management models for persons who are homeless and mentally ill: the ACCESS demonstration project. *Community Mental Health Journal, 35,* 325–346.

Kanter, J. (1989). Clinical case management: definition, principles, components. *Hospital and Community Psychiatry, 40,* 361–368.

Koegel, P., Burnham, M.A., & Baumohl, J. (1996). The causes of homelessness. In J. Baumohl (Ed.), *Homelessness in America* (pp. 24–33). Phoenix, Arizona: The Oryx Press.

Korr, W.S. & Joseph, A. (1995). Housing the homeless mentally ill: Findings from Chicago. *Journal of Social Service Research, 21*(1), 53-68.

Lam, J.A. & Rosenheck, R. (1999). Street outreach for homeless persons with serious mental illness. *Medical Care, 37,* 894–907.

Lapham, S.C., Hall, M., & Skipper, B.J. (1995). Homelessness and substance use among alcohol abusers following participation in project H&ART. *Journal of Addictive Diseases, 14,* 41–55.

Lehman, A.F., Dixon, L., Hoch, J.S., Deforge, B., Kernan, E., & Frank, R. (1999). Cost-effectiveness of assertive community treatment for homeless persons with severe mental illness. *British Journal of Psychiatry, 174*, 346–352.

Lehman, A.F., Dixon, L., Kernan, E., DeForge, B.R., & Postrado, L.T. (1997). A randomized trial of assertive community treatment for homeless persons with severe mental illness. *Archives of General Psychiatry, 54*, 1038–1043.

Marshall, M. & Lockwood, A. (1998). *Assertive community treatment for people with severe mental disorders* (a Cochrane review). Oxford: update software (for the Cochrane Library).

Marshall, M., Lockwood, A., & Gath, D. (1995). Social services case management did not improve behaviour or quality of life in persons with long-term mental disorders. *Evidence-Based Medicine, 1*, 30–39.

McMurray-Avila, M., Gelberg, L., & Breakey, W.R. (1999). Balancing act: clinical practices that respond to the needs of homeless people. In L.B. Fosburg & D.L. Dennis (Eds.), *Practical lessons: The 1998 National Symposium on Homelessness Research* (pp. 8/1–8/42). Washington, DC: U.S. Department of Housing and Urban Development, U.S. Department of Health and Human Services.

Morse, G. (1999). A review of case management for people who are homeless: implications for practice, policy and research. In L.B. Fosburg & D.L. Dennis (Eds.), *Practical lessons: The 1998 National Symposium on Homelessness Research* (pp. 7/1–7/34). Washington, DC: U.S. Department of Housing and Urban Development, U.S. Department of Health and Human Services.

Morse, G.A., Calsyn, R.J., & Allen, G. (1992). Experimental comparison of the effects of three treatment programs for homeless mentally ill people. *Hospital and Community Psychiatry, 43*, 1005–1010.

Morse, G.A., Calsyn, R.J., Klinkenberg, W.D., Trusty, M.L., Gerber, F., Smith, R., Tempelhoff, B., & Ahmad, L. (1997). An experimental comparison of three types of case management for homeless mentally ill persons. *Psychiatric Services, 48*, 497–503.

Mueser, K.T. & Bond, G.R. (2000). Psychosocial treatment approaches for schizophrenia. *Current Opinion in Psychiatry, 13*, 27–35.

Mueser, K.T., Bond G.R., Drake, R.E., & Resnick, S.G. (1998). Models of community care for severe mental illness: a review of research on case management. *Schizophrenia Bulletin 24*, 37–74.

Peroff, K. (1987). Who are the homeless and how many are there? In R.D. Bingham, R.E. Green, & S.B. White (Eds.), *The homeless in contemporary society* (pp. 33–45). Newbury Park, CA: Sage Publications.

Rapp, C. (1998a). The active ingredients of effective case management: a research synthesis. *Community Mental Health Journal, 34*, 363–380.

Rapp, C. (1998b). *The strengths model: case management with people suffering from severe and persistent mental illness.* New York: Oxford University Press.

Rapp, C. & Chamberlain, R. (1985). CM services to the chronically mentally ill. *Social Work, 30*, 417–422.

Rosenheck, R.A. (1996, September 10). *Research on homelessness among veterans: causes and treatment outcomes.* Symposium conducted at the VA National Conference on Services for Homeless Veterans, Dallas, TX.

Rosenheck, R., Bassuk, E., & Salomon, A. (1999). Special populations of homeless Americans. In L.B. Fosburg & D.L. Dennis (Eds.), *Practical lessons: the 1998 national symposium on homelessness research.* Washington, DC: U.S. Department of Housing and Urban Development and the U.S. Department of Health and Human Services.

Rosenheck, R. & Dennis, D. (2001). Time-limited assertive community treatment for homeless persons with severe mental illness. *Archives of General Psychiatry, 58*, 1073–1080.

Rubin, A. & Babbie, E. (1997). *Research methods for social work* (3rd ed.). Pacific Grove: Brooks/Cole Publishing Company.

Shern, D.L., Tsemberis, S., Anthony, W., Lovell, A.M., Richmond, L., Felton, C.J., Winarski, J., & Cohen, M. (2000). Serving street-dwelling individuals with psychiatric disabilities: outcomes of a psychiatric rehabilitation clinical trial. *American Journal of Public Health, 90*, 1873–1878.

Shukla, R. (Interviewer). (1999). An Interview with Martha Burt (Web page). From URL http://www.urban.org/husing/homeless/burt_interview.html

Solomon, P. (1992). The efficacy of case management services for severely mentally disabled clients. *Community Mental Health Journal, 28,* 163–180.

Solomon, P. & Draine, J. (1995). The efficacy of a consumer case management team: two year outcomes of a randomized trial. *Journal of Mental Health Administration, 22,* 135–146.

Sosin, M.R., Bruni, M., & Reidy, M. (1995). Paths and impacts in the progressive independence model: a homelessness and substance abuse intervention in Chicago. *Journal of Addictive Diseases, 12,* 1–20.

Stahler, G.J., Shipley, T.F., Bartelt, D., DuCette, J.P., & Shandler, I.W. (1995). Evaluating alternative treatments for homeless substance-abusing men: outcomes and predictors of success. *Journal of Addictive Disease, 14,* 151–167.

Stein, L.I. & Santos, A.B. (1998). *Assertive community treatment of persons with severe mental illness.* New York: W. W. Norton.

Stephens, D. & Dennis, E. (1991). The diversity of case management needs for the care of homeless persons. *Public Health Reports, 106,* 15–20.

Susser, E., Valencia, E., Conover, S., Felix, A., Tsai, W., & Wyat, R.J. (1997). Preventing recurrent homelessness among mentally ill men: a critical time intervention after discharge from a shelter. *American Journal of Public Health, 87,* 256–262.

Sullivan, W.P., Wolk, J.L., & Hartmann, D.J. (1992). CM in alcohol and drug treatment: improving client outcomes. *Families in Society: The Journal of Contemporary Human Services, 73,* 195–203.

Test, M.A. (1992). Training in community living. In R.P. Liberman (Ed.), *Handbook of psychiatric rehabilitation* (pp. 153–170). New York: Macmillan Publishing Company.

Toro, P.A., Passero Rabideau, J.M., Bellavia, C.W., Daeschler, C.V., Wall, D.D., Thomas, D.M., & Smith, S.J. (1997). Evaluating an intervention for homeless persons: results of a field experiment. *Journal of Consulting and Clinical Psychology, 65,* 476–484.

U.S. Department of Housing and Urban Development. (2001). *A report on worst case housing needs in 1999.* Washington, DC: Economic Policy Institute.

Willenbring, M.L. (1997, May 22). *Case management for homeless public inebriates* (conference abstract). From the 150th Annual Meeting of the American Psychiatric Association, San Diego.

Wolff, N., Helminiak, T.W., Morse, G.A., Calsyn, R.J., Klinkenberg, W.D., & Trusty, M.L. (1997). Cost-effectiveness evaluation of three approaches to case management for homeless mentally ill clients. *American Journal of Psychiatry, 154,* 341–348.

Ziguras, S.J. & Stuart, G.W. (2000). A meta-analysis of the effectiveness of mental health case management over 20 years. *Psychiatric Services, 51,* 1410–1421.

16

WE'LL MEET YOU ON YOUR BENCH
Developing a Therapeutic Alliance with the Homeless Mentally Ill Patient

JENNY ROSS AND JENNIFER REICHER GHOLSTON

The beginnings of Project HELP (Homeless Emergency Liaison Project) were controversial. An alarming number of mentally ill were living on the streets of New York and were in danger of dying in the winter of 1982, and their mental illness kept them from coming in from the cold. Their numbers had reached epidemic proportions, largely as a result of the poor planning of deinstitutionalization, lack of adequate funding for much needed community support, and, of course, the lack of affordable housing. Mayor Koch's critically strategic response was to establish Project HELP to address the growing number of severely mentally ill patients living on the streets of New York who were seriously at risk — potentially harmful/dangerous to themselves or others.

Project HELP's mission was to identify the mentally ill homeless individuals "who resisted support and treatment" on the streets and assess their functional capacity; we were authorized under the Mental Hygiene Law to order an involuntary transport when necessary to a municipal hospital ER for further evaluation (Marcos, Cohen, Nardacci, & Brittain, 1990). We were to provide psychiatric evaluation and crisis intervention to the homeless mentally ill, initially anywhere in Manhattan south of 59th Street (now throughout the five boroughs of New York City). The project was designed to serve as a focal point in an unprecedented coordination of a network of city services, which included the New York City Department of Mental Health, Mental Retardation and Alcoholism Services, the Health and Hospitals Corporation, HRA, Gouverneur Hospital, and the NYPD.

While politicians and the city have changed since the early 1980s, we like to think that Project HELP has been a vital program in the midst of these many changes in the city and in homeless services since we were first established. While we were a premiere team with the mission to assess and hospitalize those homeless in need of more serious intervention, we have endured and adapted to the changing services and political environment around us. We bring to the table an extensive working knowledge and history of the chronically homeless mentally ill population, across the five boroughs, and 22 years. We have been part of the creation of a network of homeless services, have hosted citywide training for outreach workers, and have tracked and documented many years of many clients' lives and treatment. We have served as a consultant to many new programs in New York City as well as abroad (Denmark, Amsterdam, etc.), to the Department of Homeless Services and the Department of Health and Mental Hygiene. We also work with our fellow service providers to homeless clients, ensuring sound assessments of clients referred to us (as there are limited psychiatric services throughout the homeless programs).

We work creatively, clinically, and psychiatrically with our patients. We are of the opinion that we have amassed a good deal of working knowledge of the problems faced in overcoming homelessness and best practices. This chapter details some of this work by our staff.

There have been dramatic policy changes during the past 22 years since Project HELP's inception. The New York City Mental Hygiene Law and policy have shifted from a broad civil liberties commitment to New York City's "Quality of Life" campaign and court-mandated treatment. These changes reflect serious change in public attitude toward the homeless street activity and perceived dangerousness, as well as the political attitude about quality of life issues. Many outreach services, drop-in centers, and reception centers were funded over the years, and now DHS is once again reexamining these services in its new 10-year plan to overcome homelessness, now a nationwide effort.

However, New York has always been a destination and has struggled with the effects of daily living with the street homeless mentally ill. The reasons for homelessness are multifold — a result of fragmented services, restrictive hospital policies that result in a hasty discharge, lack of housing, and a highly expensive shelter system that exists without the necessary comprehensive social services component. For homeless individuals, the condition of becoming homeless is the culmination of their personal history and experience, their intrapsychic experience of mental illness and other disabilities, and many childhood risk factors, such as incidence of violence and trauma in childhood, neglect, abuse, abandonment, and trauma, (Caton, 1990; Felix, 2004), all of which need to be considered in working with the homeless mentally ill patient.

CLINICAL EXPERTISE

Our patients are homeless (2 to 28 years), generally with a diagnosis of schizophrenia (60%), bipolar illness (15%), or given a rule-out diagnosis of psychotic disorder NOS (20%), and 1% have major depression. Over one-third have an additional substance abuse problem (36%). Fifty-nine percent are males and 41% are females. Sixty-five percent are African American, 23% are Caucasian, and 11% are Hispanic. Two-thirds of our patients are 30 to 60 years old. Twenty percent are over 60 years old and 12% are under 30 years old. In looking at our patients, whom we hospitalize, we found that 43% were dangerous to self, 53% were dangerous to others, and 3% were dangerous to both self and others; another 1% were voluntary transports.

Our patients are unmedicated, isolated, with some degree of medical illness, known to other outreach teams, without social supports, unable to access services (e.g., soup kitchen), and suffering from chronic and severe mental illness that affects the total functioning on behalf of the individual to care for his or her own well-being. They often live for long periods of time on the street, with multiple daily interventions by more than one outreach team, without any cognitive or emotional change. They may communicate briefly with a worker or may not even make eye contact, again over long periods. We are often their only consistent contact with another adult. Because of their extreme isolation, they do not interact with others, they do not weave together a street family, and they do not generally panhandle. There are services available for them, such as DHS outreach teams and drop-in centers, to address their specific issues and provide private shelter with low demand, but not all avail themselves of these services. Outreach teams in the city provide case management to these patients within catchment areas, monitoring their mental health and fluctuations, providing lunches and other concrete services.

Project HELP's professional staff (social workers, psychiatrists, psychiatric nurses) have chased, followed, visited, and worked clinically with the New York homeless mentally ill population over the past 22 years. Our involvement is unique. Because we work in the five boroughs, 365 days a year (day and evening shifts), and are able to provide linkages across programs and catchment areas, we are able to follow clients through many services over long periods. We see clients, often in crisis, and are able to intervene through our long-established therapeutic alliance with some very long term homeless mentally ill clients. Although we have been frustrated by the system of homeless services, which remains fragmented, and the lack of affordable housing, we have found that working from a clinical perspective has allowed us to make significant changes in many individual lives.

Back in the early 1990s, Project HELP initiated a research project to determine what the long-term influence of voluntary versus involuntary hospitalization had on the ultimate progress of a patient toward recovery. We found that there was not a difference. Project HELP initiated the project because of the negative press and reaction to involuntary hospitalization, which we came to represent, before and after the Billy Boggs case, a.k.a. Joyce Brown (Cournos, 1989). Even after the establishment of the many outreach teams that canvas the city's homeless population by catchment area, Project HELP was the authorized mental health program to assess and commit a patient who was deemed "dangerous to self or others." This is a broad and subjective standard in some cases, since we must determine imminent danger based on a full mental status evaluation, on the spot, in the street, under a street lamp, sometimes with little case history, but with our highly developed antennae over many years of this kind of work, we must determine whether someone is resourceful enough, compensated enough to take care of himself or herself, and has the right to remain on the street without shelter. The police can remove someone during a cold weather alert to a shelter or hospital. They are somewhat more limited in their definition of dangerousness, which means active dangerousness (holding a knife, etc.). Project HELP's definition is whether there is "imminent danger in the foreseeable future," based on the Mental Hygiene Law.

What was found as a result of this study was that those patients who bonded with someone in the system had a more successful outcome of the treatment.

Project HELP keeps charts on all clients and has found that clients will often disappear and reappear several months, even years, later in a new location. Many clients will not give a name or may change their name depending on who they are speaking with, which is often a clinical indication of mental confusion or identity confusion. Making eye contact with a client can be a significant moment in which connection is made for the first time and a working relationship can begin to foster, making changes. Many clients are avoidant or paranoid and will not reveal any information about themselves, including their name. They will pick themselves up and start to walk away or return to an internal conversation/preoccupation. The street life creates a mental condition that reinforces their mental illness. For example, we often find clients with a diagnosis of paranoid schizophrenia sitting in an area with much noise, such as the entrance of a tunnel or bridge or in a city atrium near a false waterfall. Their internalized muttering cannot be heard above the racket of the environment.

There are two questions we ask: Why do these patients want to stay on the street? How can we work with them? These refractory homeless have been on the streets for years and years. It is not that hard to get someone who does not want to be homeless off the street. But we have worked with individuals who wanted to stay out there. Paranoia is a very common symptom, coupled with a history of trauma and abuse as children, and as adults in the streets. There is a deep lack of trust in many cases. Paranoia is certainly a major component of the mental disorders of homeless clients. There is a tremendous amount of internal chaos, and the client is not able to organize or comprehend the facets of daily living. There is a continuing irritation of mental disturbance. Personality disorders are also prevalent and coexistent with mental illness that are obstructive to any progress in treatment. But there are always windows of opportunity, if the client is able to develop trust.

These are the most difficult clients to engage, the core population who remain on the streets for many years and do not meet the criteria for involuntary hospitalization. They are resourceful enough to survive cold winters with many layers or to use their well-formed paranoid systems and "antennae" to know when a worker is coming to evaluate them, and so they then pick up and move in an almost restless fashion. These were the clients in the WTC who walked endlessly so that no security person could move or detain them. These clients speak incessantly in circles, seemingly responding to the workers' questions, agreeing to seek out housing and be willing to be transported to a drop-in center, but when the moment arrives for an escort, they do not show up or disappear before the intended appointment. For this reason, it is also not a simple task to house this patient. There are divergent views of engagement in the field of homelessness, from those of MTA Connections, who favor a nonintrusive stance, to those of the NYPD Homeless Outreach Unit, who give clients a choice to move or be taken to the hospital or central booking. We believe that engagement and alliance building are key to any changes in their situation.

ENGAGEMENT TOOLS

Our initial goal is to assess a person's needs and, most importantly, as part of our mission, a patient's level of dangerousness. In order to do this, we must observe a person's actions, as well as his or her surroundings and belongings. Does he have rotten food? How are her clothes hanging? Is he profoundly dirty? Are her bags blocking anything, or are the bags tightly packed and meant for quick moving?

Observation is the true beginning of engagement. As a team we must assess the situation from afar and decide on the best tactic of approach for engagement. We use both verbal and nonverbal approaches to gain permission from the patient to approach. Often we use the most nonthreatening tool — we present a lunch to the patient and proceed from there. If the patient is willing to accept the food, we might begin with simple pleasantries and discuss benign matters such as the weather (which also gives us an indication of the patient's reality and decision-making processes). We may ask: How are you doing? Have you eaten today? The sandwich is also an assessment tool. Does the patient refuse it? Does she throw it back at us? Does he have a verbal response? What motivates the patient's response?

We are always aware that we are entering the patient's "space" and are respectful of his or her personal space, immediately developing a therapeutic alliance. We gauge with our own sense of self, with our body sense and our intuition based on years of experience as clinicians as to how close to come when approaching someone. We are also asking in this exchange for the patient's permission to approach. We disclose our identity as an outreach team and we give the patient a reason as to why we are there. "We do outreach in the park and just wanted to make sure you're okay." We might choose to differentiate ourselves from the police or other outreach agencies with whom they may have had a negative interaction. We test their tolerance with an exchange of a few words. We might determine to watch a client from afar, again using our own sensing about his or her internal state and tolerance for interpersonal contact. This also gives us the opportunity to see how the community relates to the patient. Do people stop and give the person money, food, or clothing? Sometimes overly involved citizens will engage us on behalf of the patient or even offer lodging. We develop skills of verbal and nonverbal triage. The patient's surrounding environment often gives clues about his or her mental and emotional state. For example, patients often use packaging, large furniture boxes, sofas, and postal carts, from the totally exposed to the infinitely complex. These structures also may reflect levels of social adaptation, survival skills, and creativity and resourcefulness, in addition to delusional systems and psychosis. Humans survive because they adapt and work with their environment.

We do not press issues with clients immediately. We try to meet them where they are at and begin to develop a trusting alliance with them based on their timeline. It may take days, weeks, even years in some instances, to gain the trust of a patient living on the street. One patient, R, homeless for over 20 years, was interviewed by Channel 2 news, and when asked how Project HELP had helped her, she said, "They would know if I wasn't here."

We work in teams, and often the patient will respond more readily to one staff member than another, and we use the knowledge of the transference and have the favored worker begin the relationship and slowly involve the other team members through association. We will also play "good cop, bad cop," heightening the positive transference to one team member while allowing the other team member to provide for the patient's negative transferential feelings. We may align ourselves with the patient, asking such questions as "How are the people in the neighborhood treating you?" We attempt to stop ourselves from becoming the object of their paranoia, by also asking "Is anyone bothering you?"

We are assessing the patient at the same time that we are developing a therapeutic alliance. Rapidly, and with not a lot of information, we look at the here-and-now presentation and how the patient tends to relate (looking at extremes of behavior, explosiveness, and poor impulse control). Can he or she relate without looseness of association? We see the person in the situation. Does he or she need to be monitored closely (daily)? If a person is not a danger to self or others, we let him tell us his "story." We take an interest in how he sees his situation rather than assuming what he may need or what is best for him.

Observation plays a pivotal part in engagement and assessment. Besides observing behaviors, we must also be aware of smells. For example, a person may have a medical condition, such as cellulites, and the infection smell will confirm this before the patient might be willing to disclose this medical concern. Many times patients might be so disassociated from their selves and bodies that they are not even aware that they suffer from a condition until we bring it to their attention. Other medical issues for Project HELP patients are hypertension (9%), hypercholesterolemia (8%), AIDS/HIV+ (4%), leg infections (16%), respiratory illness (7%), lice or scabies (5%), diabetes (7%), and osteoarthritis (3%).

If immediate hospitalization is not required, Project HELP staff will continue to engage the client. Trust and understanding of the dynamics of the patient are developed slowly over time and allow for us to develop a service plan with them. Sometimes the plan may be as large as obtaining housing or as small as getting the patient to accept lunch or agree to think about visiting a drop-in center.

Overall, initial engagement is made up of observation and close monitoring of patient and community responses, which allow a therapeutic alliance to unfold, along with increasing trust.

THE THERAPEUTIC BOND AND COUNTERTRANSFERENCE

Engaging a client is the first step in the process of making an attachment, forging a bond, which can, over a very long period, encourage trust in another human being. This also applies to a homeless person who is suffering from an untreated Axis I diagnosis of major mental illness. It is a curious process, happening on the street, in public view, with no social supports and only a bagged lunch to offer in return for a social exchange. We respect the need for boundaries and take a firm and nurturing approach to directly engage clients on their terms, developing a rapport, and establishing a therapeutic alliance. We are often called to respond to a crisis, and although Project HELP has traditionally been an agent of change through the intervention of hospitalization, the client we meet is at a crossroads, decompensating, agitated by circumstances, symbolic or real, the subtle triggers from within or without, and we often find ourselves taking advantage of the immediate connection in the midst of the crisis situation. Our challenge, in assessment, is simply to engage in the process of the patient's internal world gone awry. These clients do not reach out to staff, even when they are more stabilized. These clients are frightened of the help offered, and as a result, can be very hostile and combative in reaction to the help offered. On the other hand, the attention can be well received, met with eye contact, and yet remain outside of the psychotic process, which is usually internally generated and impervious to attempts at intervention.

As with any of us, there are authority issues (Who are you?) as well as other various aspects of the transference. Generally, homeless mentally ill patients are isolated from others in their own community and not medicated for long periods, and are mostly not responded to well by the public (who are also afraid of the lurking shadow/figure cast by these patients). Our patients often live in their own feces, guided by their delusions and other unacknowledged needs. Many are hoarders and stuff their shirts with newspapers, cans, or other debris. There is a consensus that most of the homeless mentally ill are paranoid schizophrenic, but this misses many of the important individual details of the homeless patients and their emotional and physical environs, which many times symbolize their own personal history. Outreach and engagement are about observation, and this is what distinguishes the clinical work done on the streets. There are so many clues that detail a full assessment, and these provide the goals of treatment as well.

The therapeutic alliance that is forged with patients on the street is fraught with insurmountable challenges. On a basic level, they need shelter and other concrete services to better their situation, but most times they are not able to take advantage of such services offered them, which is when frustration quickly sets in. In fact, this is echoed by the media and policy makers when there is a discussion of the possible solutions to the enduring homeless condition that exists on the streets of New York and other large cities — how to solve the problem, which does not diminish despite the many services funded and provided.

The great challenge, from our point of view, is that the homeless are not attached, and in order to be able to accept any services, they *need* to be able to make an attachment despite the inconsistency of their situation. It is the issue of bonding on a very basic level. On the street, this requires creativity and resilience on the part of the worker and a deeper understanding of the process of therapeutic alliance and partnership in the growth/change process. Creativity fosters a vital link between worker and client. You start with where the client is at.

You must stay with him or her through the ruptures of treatment, which are many. One client dug through his cart filled with many objects and gave me a transitional object, a white veil for "my marriage" (although I was not getting married), saying, "I think that you will need this." It is the work of the therapist/outreach worker not just to forge this alliance and maintain a holding environment for the person's chaotic and primal mental processes, but to understand, interpret, and accept it. This is done without the aid of medication and requires attention to the underlying communication about patients' internal preoccupations and delusions. It takes time and timing of interventions and responses to develop trust. Unfortunately, the quest to end homelessness puts the cart before the horse. Or perhaps it ignores the significance of a therapeutic approach to a client who is disenfranchised, seen as a dangerous social ill, rather than as a human being with the same core needs.

The homeless mentally ill patient pushes a therapist to consider a real relationship that can foster trust and change. The conditions of street life and survival touch everyone in the city who witnesses these patients on a daily basis. To most, this relationship remains two-dimensional, but to the worker with a therapeutic view, the homeless mentally ill client becomes a patient whom you meet on a bench. We met T, a client of Project HELP, who had been homeless for about 20 years. Several times a week when we would see him, we invited ourselves to sit with him on a park bench and just encouraged him to tell us about his life experiences, and we associated back to him what we heard, thereby invoking a self-object mirroring transference (Kohut, 1984). After several weeks of this, he turned to us and said, "You can't do therapy on a bench." T was arrested one day for a quality of life infraction (public urination) and sent for a psychiatric assessment at Manhattan Psychiatric Center. It turned out that he had a sister in South Carolina and his parents had died, leaving them both a rather large house. He was stabilized on medication and relocated to South Carolina. Soon after he arrived there he contacted us for assistance because his new mental health provider would not give him his medication until he had proof of his having been a veteran and thus entitled to benefits. He eventually returned to NYC (after much conflict with his sister), and a teacher who had befriended him called us to tell us he was back.

At Project HELP we have remained open to what clients present, and how they present. We find ourselves coming to know many street people through the many years and through our many attempts to make change possible for them. We find them consistently in "their" spot, and we are faced each time with their hostility or guardedness, the results of the conditions of their mental illness and chronic homeless condition. They do not want services, they do not even want housing — maybe a lunch, but with no strings attached. What we have found is that when clients do not want what we have to offer, we need to diversify and try to meet their needs. In order to be successful, we need to have a clinical understanding of the dynamics that keep them on the street and a therapeutic understanding of their dilemma in order to make change possible. Often enough, this approach is missing, though well-intended outreach workers strive to "move" the client and get them to accept services, or frequently program staff want them to acknowledge their need for concrete services, such as a drop-in center or reception center, and substance abuse services in addition to psychiatric services, and they attempt to market these to the clients without a deeper understanding of the issues of homelessness and mental illness as it is experienced on the streets by them.

Getting clients off the streets (or out of the terminals, off the subway platforms, etc.) has been the challenge and is now the hot topic of discussion by the city. The problem still persists to this very day (since Koch's concerns about the clients dying on the street). It should be acknowledged that there are factors that predict homelessness — mental illness, poverty, substance abuse/drugs, disability, etc. These are the conditions that predicate a vulnerability to becoming homeless and potentially chronically homeless. Outreach teams engage, drop-in centers are weigh stations, and the ultimate solution is housing. However, a greater understanding of the therapeutic process and its tenets prove more valuable to the success of all of these services. Although, for example, drop-in centers are an excellent model of low-threshold, low-demand services for hard-core resistant clients and can work relatively well with this population, the eventual success or outcome for clients is dependent on their relational capacity to be cared for and to in turn feel as if they matter to another and be able to take care of themselves. This is most likely to happen in the context of a therapeutic relationship with a clinician. It is essential to making the changes that will lead to living inside, despite the delusions and psychotic process of mental illness that contributes to the deteriorating human connection on the streets. On the streets, the patient lives with the contents of his psychosis 24/7. Each visit has to count for a lot in order to make a difference. It should constitute a therapy session, one in which there is an exchange of some import, which can shift the internal matrix ever so slightly as to have the patient make eye contact, which he has not done before.

Some time ago, our base hospital had a determined new worker in the cafeteria, which supplies our bag lunches that we use as engagement tools to the homeless. He decided to order a new type of TV dinner, which warmed itself when the container was cracked at a certain spot. One of our clients who was always withdrawn lit up when he realized that he could warm up this dinner. It was the beginning of a change in our relationship with him. He was able to recognize us as the bringers of this dinner, and for him to be recognized by the bringing of this dinner. At this very moment, we became a "good enough mother" (Winnicott, 1960). On a very primal level he was able to feed himself something warm and (hopefully) nourishing. A number of our homeless patients have negatively commented on the food given to them by other outreach workers, yet are unaware of their capacity/ability to secure this food for themselves (e.g., at soup kitchens, in drop-in centers, which would require a desire expressed or fulfilled with another).

Each homeless mentally ill individual is a patient with a history of trauma, and each contact potentially fosters an emotionally healing experience. The psychological environment heals the patient and is a continuous connection over the days or years of contact. The hard-core resistant client does not trust the relationship to the helper and has not been given a reason to trust by a system that is not generally user-friendly. "Resistance" in psychoanalytic circles has been reinterpreted, focusing increasingly on obstacles in the therapeutic relationship that need to be resolved before growth can occur. It is the bond between therapist and patient that moves the patient, despite the system. This client requires constant support in order to form an attachment, and workers come and go; hospitalizations, complete with police enforcement, retraumatize the patient and provide no relief or safety.

One patient who relented after a number of years to come in our van when he was not feeling well was transported to the local drop-in center. He was interviewed by a psychiatrist for 20 minutes who spoke his native language (Romanian) because a social worker at the drop-in center was very motivated to help him and secured this connection with a sense of accomplishment. On Friday afternoon of that week, the patient poured lighter fluid all over himself in the middle of the day room and set himself on fire. He died several days later. It brought home how quickly we thought the patient was being helped by our services, was able to make a change, and how wrong we were. We all require slow change, which begins from shifting from within. The therapist, in turn, must provide both attention and understanding to the moment-to-moment self-experience (such as in therapy) and underlying emotional issues and complexes.

We also need to understand our own countertransference when helping these clients. There is often tremendous psychic pain and trauma that binds these clients, literally, to their spots. They are mostly disowned by their families, disenfranchised, and have turned away from social and emotional supports. Their delusions and psychosis are held in check by the battle for survival in the cold weather, muffled by the sound of tunnel or street traffic. Their mental illness becomes a shield and their delusions concretized internal beliefs. How is the street worker to understand and begin to get inside/experience their world of being homeless and mentally ill? There is a good deal of commitment and dedication on the part of these workers, which is ego-syntonic but often misses their deeper emotional reactions to the paranoia and extreme isolation.

Project HELP has been daring. One of our clients, L, was first referred to us by the 34th Street heliport personnel. L had set up a small encampment of his own, stretching tarps over metal posts and hiding behind a large postal cart. He peered out at us the first time we met him, and he had a terrible rash on his face. We offered lunch, which he accepted, but he refused any further contact over a number of weeks. As with many patients, there was a deep lack of trust, and therefore engagement and alliance building were key. There was a dilemma in that we could have made the case to take him to the hospital since he had this horrible rash on his face, but then he might not have ever talked to us again. So we had a dermatologist come and treat him on the streets. We really never thought that he would then agree to come in, but bringing him the specialist and the medications impressed him and improved his trust with the "outside world." Also, we were gentle with him when he finally agreed to come to the shelter. He would only take a small dose of medication because his voices were his "friends" and he did not want to lose them. We found a great residence to take him, and they did not mind his being so peculiar. He used to leave food out for the rats as he had bonded with them while homeless. Project HELP staff have sought to form a therapeutic relationship with these entrenched, refractory homeless in that we are providing a corrective emotional experience. We are the bridge to the outside world and are showing over the years that it is not such a bad place. These patients require a different kind of approach over a long period. L was able to live in a residence after having been homeless for 28 years.

There are many of these stories, working with the very resistant, isolated client. Some of these patients end up being hospitalized, either voluntarily or involuntarily. But many are resourceful and do not meet the criteria of dangerousness. Our stories then speak to the linkage we often provide between programs whose collaborative services can be used to serve the forging of a therapeutic alliance. Our focus remains on the therapeutic bond, and we remain at the center of this bond, reinforcing a therapeutic process with the patients, one in which we listen closely to what they are telling us and respond, encouraging trust, whether they want our help or not. A patient on the street will not talk with you unless he or she trusts you. Trust is established by the mutual agreement to make a connection. Eye contact is often the first step. There is, and should be, an emphasis on eliciting the patient's response, thereby inviting the patient to participate in his or her own change process.

SPECIALIZED INTENSIVE WORK

Project HELP has housed several clients directly from the street into an apartment through Pathways to Housing, a unique supportive apartment program with a strong case management component. We worked with their staff on the streets to engage certain patients — long-term chronically homeless and mentally ill for many years (10+ years). These were clients who did not meet the criteria of dangerousness, had been seen by local outreach teams, and generally refused any social services offered. These clients were considered hard-core homeless with a diagnosis of paranoid schizophrenia. They were all resourceful, took care of themselves and their belongings, but also seemed to feel that they were special, somehow more interesting conversationalists, or at least had interests of their own. We engaged all of these clients slowly and with great interest in their lifestyle choices.

In these cases, it takes tremendous perseverance and fortitude on the part of the staff to stay focused on developing and maintaining the therapeutic alliance, with attention paid to the ensuing ruptures and disappointments, supporting ego-syntonic elements and strengths, working creatively with defenses, maintaining respect and boundaries, and making apologies when ruptures occur. These clients need a close therapeutic alliance that can hear and repair the ruptures, as in any good therapy session. Clients need to be able to begin to see us as truly being partners in the preservation of their well-being, and we need to listen for these threads of ways in which they have not been cared for and are not able to care for themselves.

Our clients are New York savvy; they know what therapy is and can respond to interventions that reflect insight into their underlying issues of dependency, trauma, childhood abuse, and also their deep unmet needs, against which they are armored. What they do not need is for us to market our services or tell them what they need or to therapize them. They, like all of us, need to feel understood on a deeper level and experience a reparenting, emotionally corrective experience with another caring human being. They demand that we be real and immediate in our responses, or we will lose their attention and willingness to go along with us in our efforts to help them make changes and choices for a better life and heal their wounds through our therapeutic relationship with them.

Paranoia and paranoid thinking deserve mention, since they are so prevalent in this population. There are many symptoms of paranoia — for example, a belief that one is the object of poisoning (one client walked out of an apartment because she believed that poison was being gassed in), fear and expectation of attack, a fear of being betrayed, etc. However, these are all related to the human capacity for connection, and while paranoia is difficult to work with, especially when there are fixed delusions, generally these clients do have other strengths (e.g., resourcefulness, an intellectual ability) around which they can be engaged. It is important not to feed into the paranoia, maintain professional boundaries, and be as honest as possible (even paranoid people have something to be paranoid about).

Mr. T was a patient who was delusional and paranoid, although we did not observe any threatening or dangerous actions. He believed that he was a special forces agent and that his homemade structure was on a piece of land that was his designated post, property given to him by the government. He explained to us in detail that he had been living on this land for two years investigating a case against the "devil." Mr. T also informed us of his special powers, e.g., telepathy. We did not focus on his paranoia but rather inquired about the safety of his home, and he then stretched out his arm to help us walk across a wooden plank adjoining two rooms and gave us a detailed tour of his structure. He explained that he uses his SSI money to purchase cinder blocks and other building materials from Home Depot, which he has delivered to the site. This was a lengthy engagement, taking about two hours in total. Two weeks later we were called to stand by as HPD crashed into and destroyed Mr. T's home with bulldozers. We were present and interactive throughout the entire ordeal. Through the therapeutic alliance already established with Mr. T, we were able to avoid a hospitalization and transported him to a private shelter for mentally ill adults.

There are many untreated conditions, medical and psychiatric, in this population. There are a multitude of other factors to consider as well — undocumented immigrants, language barriers, cultural issues, deaf/mutes, etc. We love them all — like the patient who stood at the entrance to the Holland Tunnel. We asked him why he had chosen that spot, and he replied that he was going to Holland and is that not where the Holland Tunnel goes?

REFERENCES

Caton, C.L.M. (1990). *Homelessness in America*. New York: Oxford University Press.

Cournos, F. (1989, July). Involuntary medication and the case of Joyce Brown. *Hospital and Community Psychiatry, 40*, 736–740.

Felix, A.D. (2004). Life without walls: violence and trauma among the homeless. In B. Sklarew, S.W. Twemlow, & S.M. Wilkinson (Eds.), *Analysts in the trenches: streets, schools, war zones* (pp. 23–43). Hillsdale, NJ: The Analytic Press.

Kohut, H. (1984). *How does analysis cure?* Chicago: University of Chicago Press.

Marcos, L.R., Cohen, N.L., Nardacci, D., & Brittain, J. (1990). Psychiatry takes to the streets: the New York City initiative for the homeless mentally ill. *American Journal of Psychiatry, 147*, 1557–1562.

Winnicott, D.W. (1960). The theory of the parent-infant relationship. In M. Khan (Ed.), *The maturational processes and the facilitating environment* (pp. 37–55). New York: International Universities Press.

V

Community Mental Health: Organizational and Policy Issues

The chapters in this section examine the complex interplay between services, policy, funding, and organizational structure. Steven P. Segal, in "Social Work in a Managed Care Environment," presents an excellent overview and analysis of managed care and its impact on the social work profession, paying particular attention to the problems of providing managed mental health care to seriously mentally ill individuals. Providing a balanced view that highlights the positive as well as negative consequences of managed care, he asserts that "social work is in the right place at the right time" to maximize inherent opportunities offered by managed care.

In "Networks and Organizational Identity: On the Front Lines of Behavioral Health," Debra Anderson and Gary Marshall shift the unit of analysis to the individual in organizational networks. In this chapter, the focus is on how behavioral networks impact on the employees within the context of the work environment. As Segal aptly notes in the previous chapter, managed care employs a set of change- and control-oriented techniques to implement organizational change. Anderson and Marshall build on this concept and explore the implications of such changes on the individual's experience in the workplace and their capacity to work cooperatively together.

The next chapter in this section, "The Uncertain Future of Public Mental Health Systems: A West Virginia Case Study," by Elizabeth Randall and Mary Aldred-Crouch, documents the erosion of financial support for public mental health services. Their work, based in West Virginia, is a thoughtful analysis applicable to many states throughout the nation. The authors conclude that "there can be little doubt that this financial undermining has had a direct, negative effect on the quality and appropriateness of those services that remain in place." These authors suggest that the very future of comprehensive, community-based mental health services is in question.

The final selection of this text, "Mental Health Leadership in a Turbulent World," by W. Patrick Sullivan, examines the multiple challenges confronting community mental health service delivery. He portrays today's mental health leaders as confronting revolutionary changes from forces largely outside of their control. Survival in this turbulent world, asserts Sullivan, requires a sophisticated skill set and a commitment to core values.

The four selections in this section all highlight the significant challenges facing community mental health. Many strategies are presented designed to help make sense of this changing landscape and to persevere so that the promise of community mental health is kept for all of those who depend upon it.

17

SOCIAL WORK IN A MANAGED CARE ENVIRONMENT

STEVEN P. SEGAL

Managed care has created a new service environment that, to a large extent, eliminates distinctions that have sustained social work ideology and the profession throughout its history. A managed care approach shifts the emphasis of need assessment from that of the individual to that of the group. It eliminates the distinctions between agency-based and non-agency-based practice, between private and public practice, and many of the distinctions between not-for-profit and for-profit practice. This chapter considers why such distinctions that have served as the core of the social work profession are disappearing and discusses the new set of opportunities, challenges, and problems that have emerged with this approach.

Prior to 1990, managed care strategies were largely confined to health maintenance organizations (HMOs) serving a middle-class population through employee coverage plans. Competition for new health and mental health patients in the early 1990s, however, led managed care organizations (MCOs), seeking new markets, to become rapidly involved with the provision of services to the poor covered by Medicaid. From less than 10%, or 2.7 million of 28.3 million Medicaid beneficiaries in 1991, MCOs have captured 48%, or 15.4 million, of the 32.1 million beneficiaries in 1997 (*Washington Post*, 1998; Kilborn, 1998). Managed care strategies have become a major factor in the organizational plans of health and mental health agencies serving social work's traditional target population. Such strategies are spreading throughout the human services. In addition to the health and mental health areas, managed care strategies have already been implemented in corrections, child welfare, homeless services, and other sectors of social work activity (Barry, 1998; Shichor, 1995; Bickman, Summerfelt, & Noser, 1997).

Managed care refers to a variety of techniques packaged as unique strategies aimed at marshaling appropriate clinical and financial resources to ensure needed care (Winegar, 1996).

A given managed care strategy is uniquely constructed to fit an individual organizational recipe for reducing operating costs, expanding service options, increasing flexibility of asset utilization (i.e., of how employees, funding, and resources are used), and sharing risks associated with the helping endeavor (i.e., financial risks). The problem is always how to achieve these objectives.

A managed care strategy can also be conceived of as a combination of change- and control-oriented techniques that will lead to the aforementioned objectives. Though no unitary model of managed care exists, the managed care revolution is likely to effect changes in service ideology, organization, financing, government, and the relationship of providers to consumers and their families. Managed care strategies involve alterations of all these factors in different program packages. In fact, current wisdom indicates that when you have seen one managed care organization, you have seen one managed care organization.

MANAGED CARE STRATEGY: A COMBINATION OF CHANGE- AND CONTROL-ORIENTED TECHNIQUES

A managed care strategy employs a defined set of financial, access and utilization, and service control techniques to implement organizational change. In order to discuss the possible implications of changes brought on by the advent of a trend for organizations to adopt managed care strategies, it is first necessary to understand what the change-oriented techniques are and how they are used in managed care organizations (MCOs).

Financial Control Techniques

Financial control techniques include prepayment for a complete service package to a provider, and financial risk transfer to a client via deductibles or copayments. Prepayment for a service package as opposed to fee for service or item/intervention by intervention billing usually involves a capitation or case rate methodology. Though computed on a per capita basis, both of these methodologies involve paying for serving a population group rather than an individual. A capitation strategy asks the organization to provide a specified service package to a target population and pays a prearranged fee for each member of the population, regardless of whether or not they use the service. Since it is hard to estimate what the cost of care will be for an entire population, prepayment methods often employ a case rate methodology, whereby the organization receives a fixed fee for each patient based on the average cost of utilization for people in their severity or disorder category experienced by the organization in previous years.

Since, in the past, care was usually paid for on a fee-for-service basis and often covered all costs for the patient, the insurer assumed all the financial risks of underestimating the cost of care. Providers had the incentive to provide all the care they believed necessary, without regard to cost. If providers erred, it was usually on the side of overprovision of services. By paying the provider in advance for taking on the responsibility, the insurer transfers this financial risk. Providers' incentive is now to prescribe care conservatively. Clients, who in the past paid nothing for their care, shared no financial risk. The combination of lack of financial risk by both client and provider led to a situation thought by some to involve "moral hazard," i.e., the acquiescence in service utilization that often had little direction and might be considered by some as overprovision. Copayments and deductibles, which have now become commonplace, transfer some of the financial risk and responsibility for seeking care and following the treatment regimen to clients. Such sharing of responsibility for seeking care is meant to encourage a preventive health orientation among clients and discourage them from seeking unneeded care.

Unfortunately, need is a relative term. Working-class people, with marginal incomes, often find copayments to be too onerous and are discouraged to pay even modest amounts for preventive care. Such individuals are often weighing current tangible needs (e.g., a teddy bear for a child or, perhaps, a better meal) against some future risk that might be discovered in a prenatal care visit.

Another financial control technique involves the use of provider networks, in contrast to in-house staff. The role of the MCO shifts in this strategy from service provider to contractor for services, insurer, and quality overseer. Instead of employing a staff to offer services, the MCO employs a group of providers, at prenegotiated fees or at a case rate. Such providers may be private practitioners in their own offices or may be part of an organization that joins provider networks. Providers in such networks are invariably credentialed and have a documented claim to expertise in the treatment of the target condition. They are, however, responsible for their own overhead.

Access and Utilization Control Techniques

Access and utilization control techniques include: establishing a single point of entry for the service system, delineating specified levels of care, and implementing utilization management and review. Establishing a single point of entry for the system allows for the control of duplication of service provision by patient/clients shopping around. It also seeks to facilitate continuity of care.

This technique does not require a fixed geographic point of intake; it could include several physical offices with networked computer connections. Most important is the centralization of intake, so that all cases in the system are known and no duplicate services are offered. Continuity is achieved by having an information system that is case based (as opposed to intervention based) and can be accessed by all service providers.

Delineating specified levels of care enables an organization to target groups with different service needs. It helps delineate that portion of the service population that are chronic and in need of long-term care, and better determine the costs of interventions with this population. Particularly important are high service users, who may account for as much as 50% of the budget expenditures and whose care might be organized more efficiently and effectively.

Utilization review involves the review of practitioner treatment decisions by a person who usually has the power to authorize or deny expenditures. Such reviews can be prospective, concurrent, or retrospective (Tischler, 1990). Reviewers can be skilled supervisors or less skilled individuals operating from management service protocols. From a professional practice perspective, these reviews are most controversial. They threaten the tradition of independent practice and raise questions about confidentiality of the practitioner-client relationship. Denials of authorization for additional treatment sessions in outpatient mental health often are based on average numbers of sessions recommended by other members of a provider network and, in the worst case, are outright attempts to reduce the number of service contacts simply based on administrative mandates to cut costs.

Service Provision Control Techniques

Service provision is often controlled by a case manager who has overall responsibility for the treatment plan and for insuring continuity of care.

Service provision control techniques require the use of the least intrusive service interventions while also doing what is necessary to enable the client to meet his or her goals for seeking help. In behavioral health this involves the issue of the least restrictive alternative — usually a noninstitutional solution. This strategy has often been interpreted as the least expensive care alternative, though better managed care companies have come to realize that the least expensive approach might be penny-wise and pound foolish over the long term. For example, shortened duration of psychiatric hospital stays, denying clinicians enough time to resolve patient situations, may lead to increased probability of return (Segal, Akutsu, & Watson, 1998).

Service provision control strategies often limit service to the provision of "medically necessary care." Medically necessary may be defined by usual practice, though there is an emphasis on finding and utilizing outcome-driven interventions. Medically necessary may be further delimited in definition to that care that involves a cost-efficient trajectory of recovery. A cost-efficient trajectory of recovery refers to approval of service up to a point where continued treatment begins to yield diminishing or little if any improvement. Such strategies are particularly controversial in behavioral health care given the absence of good outcome data on the effectiveness, and the course of behavioral disorders and the long-term care needs of chronic patients. The latter group often requires large resource investment to achieve small changes over long periods.

ANTICIPATED CHANGES IN SOCIAL WORK PRACTICE

Social work has developed in response to public social service needs, but more importantly to market demands for skills that could be quickly obtained at a reasonable cost. In the 1960s, for example, the advent of the community mental health center in the United States created a demand for relatively inexpensive practitioners with counseling skills. The social work practitioner's two-year graduate education was a cost-effective and expedient solution to market demand.

Clinical social workers, with at least master's degree training, are now the most prevalent group of mental health practitioners in the United States. In 1995 their numbers reached 36 per 100,000 — compared to 12.5 per 100,000 for psychiatrists and 26.7 for clinical psychologists. Furthermore, they have the broadest geographic distribution of any provider group — matching or exceeding the numbers of any other mental health professional group in most states of the union (Ivey, Scheffler, & Zazzali, 1998).

Service Ideology and Allocation Principles

Social work has traditionally emphasized the uniqueness and value of each individual. Managed care principles emphasize the good of the community. Under managed care, service allocation principles shift from a clinical/medical treatment approach based on meeting individual need to a public health preventive approach based on maximizing group benefits. This shift is precisely the type of change experienced during the advent of the community mental health center movement during the 1960s and early 1970s (Feldman, 1992, 1994). The current implementation of managed care should produce results quite similar to those experienced during the 1960s and 1970s period.

The community mental health center (CMHC) movement from its initiation broadened service offerings to a healthier population. Though conceived of in a public health preventive framework, actual primary prevention efforts were a small part of the services that were actually offered. In fact, a broader population with nonchronic and less serious conditions were served. This led to significant criticism of the CMHCs' effort (Chu & Trotter, 1974) and attempts to ensure that those with more serious conditions and those who were members of high-risk groups, minorities, and the poor had access to services (The President's Commission on Mental Health, 1978). Reductions in federal support and increased mandates to serve the most seriously ill led to a reduction of popular support for the program. Today's government actions regarding managed care are directed at ensuring access to care by all qualified recipients and, therefore, are still in the stage of encouraging the expansion of the service target population. While new major efforts are directed at serving the poor covered by Medicaid, these efforts eliminate only one of the criticisms of the community mental health movement. Services, under MCOs, are being directed to a broader and healthier population of poor recipients — thus raising access questions related to long-term care of the seriously mentally ill. As the focus of care shifts to a healthier population, the processes of care will further exacerbate the exclusion of the more chronic patients.

Therapeutic processes are being adjusted to conform to a group-focused ideology, including explicit utilization review and rationing procedures. The effect is to shorten the duration of care, or the number of approved sessions covered by the MCO (Alperin & Phillips, 1997). Practitioners are encouraged to use short-term treatment techniques with very delimited goals. It must be emphasized that in a limited resource environment, extended service to one individual, whose path to recovery shows minimal change after initial efforts, is a form of rationing, i.e., since others are not being served while those under care receive extensive resource effort, often with minimal gain, to the exclusion of other needy individuals. Yet, the shift in the process of care in itself leads to a selection of patients whose needs fit the new treatments. Conversely, other individuals in need of long-term supportive care may be excluded if special provisions are not made for them.

Service outcomes are more explicitly cost driven in the MCO than in fee-for-service plans. In the past, little consideration was given to the cost of a specific intervention and its relation to a projected outcome. Effort was made to meet needs. The group-focused model is a model based on efficient use of resources and the specification of the relation of these resources to specified outcomes. Given that most of the savings that can be had in the treatment of the seriously mentally ill come from the avoidance of hospitalization, MCOs concentrate much of their effort in serving the seriously mentally ill toward this end. The difficulty in obtaining measurable changes in this population in brief treatment periods is leading to the denial of service to this population on the basis of poor recovery trajectories. Further, the difficulty of demonstrating actual relationships with changes in the client condition (a matter discussed elsewhere; cf. Segal, 1997) has led to greater reliance on measures of client satisfaction in MCOs. Since such satisfaction is often more in evidence with less disturbed individuals, we may expect further pressures to cater to this less disturbed group.

How the principle of medical necessity is employed in practice will be a major factor in how the system will deliver service. A mental health plan, for example, may allow 30 visits, but in practice see a medical necessity for only 4. In a worst case scenario, the plan has taken the credit for its liberal benefits and has carefully chosen its provider network so that it has excluded those likely to actually advocate for the covered number of visits. This type of choice is made easier with the presence of information systems that allow for complete documentation of a provider's treatment strategy. Further, given a behavioral perspective, providers' performance and practice strategies are to some extent shaped by the feedback they receive as to colleagues' practices. In a tight market, where provider membership in a network is contingent on performance, that is, consistent with organizational goals, the new type of treatments and objectives are internalized as part of practice ideology and the need for utilization review eliminated.

In a best case scenario, practice is more outcome driven, clients receive the help they need and nothing more, service provision is extended to a larger client group, and clients are subset according to chronicity and the need for long-term supportive and preventive care as part of the MCO's protocols. The MCO is able to use its resources more flexibly and, in so doing, finds that its supportive care programs are preventive of expensive hospitalizations. Utilization review in turn becomes an initial procedure that is curtailed as the protocols produce desired outcomes. Medical necessity is interpreted in a manner that brings needed care to all members of the covered group.

ROLE OF GOVERNMENT

The role of government has shifted during the past 23 years from regulation and control strategies initiated by political action to deregulation and promotion of a market-based system of care. The combination of the Employment Retirement Income Security Act of 1975 (ERISA) and the 1985 U.S. Supreme Court decision in *Metropolitan Insurance v. Massachusetts* limited the power of the states to regulate health plans and effectively shifted the regulation of health care from the public to the private sector, i.e., to the competitive marketplace. Most importantly, these federal actions made health and mental health coverage a matter of negotiation between employers and their employees. Since 85% of the American public have insurance coverage through employment or some government program, the government was effectively taken out of the regulation picture by these actions (Stone, 1998).

In considering mental health care for the poor, the trend has been one of decreasing state allocations. Unable to fund increases in services without politically unpopular tax increases, states have tried to gain control of budget increases by shifting responsibility for all but the oversight of services to the local or county level of government and by capping expenditures. In efforts to provide mental health and health services to more of the poor, especially those working poor who remain uninsured, local jurisdictions have attempted to shift costs to Medicaid, a federal entitlement program. Funding a service under Medicaid, however, obligates the state to pay 50% of the costs of care. Unfortunately, until very recently, state Medicaid costs have been rapidly increasing, well outpacing revenue growth, and approaching 20% of state expenditures. To curb what to some is an uncontrolled bleeding of state general funds, states have adopted a managed care strategy. Obtaining waivers from the Health Care Financing Administration (HCFA), states have suspended some of the major provisions of the Medicaid law, particularly freedom of provider choice and "statewideness." The former allows the locality to force Medicaid recipients to accept services from a health maintenance organization's designated network of providers; the latter allows the nature of services to differ from area to area — thus allowing for significant experimentation (Frank & Gaynor, 1993, 1994). Given these changes in the Medicaid requirements, departments of mental health at both the state and county levels are divesting responsibility for service delivery in favor of an oversight role. They are becoming contractors rather than providers by seeking cost-effective arrangements in the form of *public-private partnerships* and subcontracts to *for-profit organizations*.

Organization of Services

Services will more frequently involve the use of restricted panels or networks of providers. This can happen either in a carve-out (i.e., a specialty mental health organization or, more likely, a specialty behavioral health care organization that provides both mental health and substance abuse service) or in a carve-in format. The carve-in covers all health care services as part of a general health care plan.

Provider networks are likely to be recruited as independent contractors who will have to conform to plan requirements to continue their membership. Who the client belongs to is a point of contention, though plans demand access to records.

In short, an HMO, often a former public mental health authority, will offer a *single point of entry* for access monitoring, control, and referral within a closed *provider network*. Priority will be given to outpatient versus inpatient care. *Flexible service* provision with blurred professional roles and reliance on self-help will be emphasized. *Professional providers* for networks will be sought on the basis of accepted credentials and skills, with the preference going to the least expensive yet competent personnel. *Integrated services* based on the provider's acceptance of responsibility for total care provision will be negotiated.

Financing

In the past, under fee for service, the client chose the provider he or she wanted and the insurance company paid. There were millions of clients (buyers) and a few hundred thousand providers (sellers). HMOs or prepaid health plans, by virtue of signing up most potential clients and limiting their choice to a closed network of providers, have themselves become the buyers — thus drastically reducing the effective number of buyers to a few hundred or less. Prepayment helps create a market for mental health services whereby those few buyers, who control the demand of many, have a strong position in negotiating prices for care from a large number of sellers (i.e., providers). With the advent of HMO or prepaid plan networks that restrict freedom of provider choice to their own network, the demand of the millions of buyers is expressed in the market as the demand of a few buyers negotiating prices with a large number of providers. This phenomenon has lowered the price of care to the cost of the least expensive credentialed practitioner. It has further led to payment for services based on the minimum cost for the service. This market discipline has for the moment given social work an edge.

Social work has always emphasized in its philosophy the need to help people to help themselves and to not do for people what they can do for themselves. These basic principles of social work, more stated perhaps than practiced, recognize one of the key components addressed in managed care financing schemes — the risk of moral hazard and the need to avoid it by the sharing of financial risk by the client. Services offered at no cost to the client are often overused and undervalued. Payment arrangements under managed care usually involve *shared financial risk* with the client and the provider. Copayments are typical and place a value on service. From a social work perspective in dealing with the very poor, such payments might be minimal or in kind, but still add value to the service offered. Risk is distributed to providers via contracts involving *capitation* or *case rate* methodologies.

Provider–Client Relationship

Combining of the fiscal and treatment functions changes the nature of the service. The social work practitioner has always had a dual role of social control and social service. He or she has always served two masters. Now the social worker internalizes a rationing ideology to benefit the social group as well as serve the individual. To the extent that it is the benefit of the social group rather than exploitation of the individual in service of profit, this role seems consistent with past social work performance.

In a fee-for-service plan the incentive is for the provider to offer as much service as possible to each individual. In effect, given the limitation of agency budgets, this is a form of rationing based on offering all you can to the individual being helped and ignoring the needs of those not in attendance. A capitation or case rate methodology has been criticized for offering the perverse incentive to provide as little service as possible. This strategy does, however, make the organization responsible for the entire population. In offering too little service the organization remains the responsible party (though most such organizations have been made immune to malpractice suits). Further, since the reimbursement is paid up front and not tied to a specific service, the provider has a greater flexibility in the type of service provision than in a fee-for-service system. The fee-for-service system reimburses for limited and specified services, often not needed or inappropriate to the patient. It also often fails to provide for other services that the patient requires.

Clients and their families get *flexibility and diversity* of service in return for *shared risks and burdens*. Client satisfaction is taken as a major outcome for evaluating program results. Access becomes contingent on *medical necessity* and the *cost of treatment*.

DISAPPEARING DISTINCTIONS IN CORE SOCIAL WELFARE PRACTICE AREAS

Agency-Based and Independent Practice

Social work has been an agency-based profession largely confined to public social and health service organizations and private nonprofit organizations. The role of social workers as independent private practice providers has largely been confined to the United States. Even there, this role has been a source of some conflict and concern deriving from the belief that those who have entered the private practice market had in some way been unfaithful to the profession's commitment to serve the most needy in public service organizations (Specht & Courtney, 1994). The lure of a better income and working conditions have in fact attracted some of the most talented members of the profession to private independent practice. By changing the role of public health and mental health organizations from that of service provider to that of a contractor and insurer that relies on networks of independent providers to offer services, the managed care approach has eliminated the distinction between agency-based practice and independent practice. Independent practitioners, by virtue of their enrollment in provider networks, are drawn back into the service of public health and mental health service clientele.

Public and Private Practice

The distinction between public and private practice has been evaporating with the increasing reliance of the public social services on contracting to private nonprofits and the increasing dependence of the latter on such contracts to stay in business. Managed care strategies, in their reliance on contracting and provider networks, take this process a step further by eliminating this distinction at the practitioner level.

"Any willing provider" laws mandate the inclusion of licensed and qualified providers from a variety of fields in the provider networks of MCOs. Such providers, many of whom are private practice social workers, are increasingly finding employment in these provider networks (Anderson & Berlant, 1995) serving public clients. Today's managed care environment has created a demand for credentialed practitioners in behavioral health care who are willing to contract with MCOs at a discounted fee. Mental health practice patterns typically evidence overlapping roles and functions among the major provider groups within mental health organizations (Madenlian, Patison, & Saxon, 1980). These practitioners must be skilled and available at a reasonable cost, i.e., competitive in the provider market. They must have flexible skills in community work and be able to work with bureaucratic mandates. While the three major mental health professions (psychiatrists, psychologists, and social workers) are likely to see their skills as fairly distinct, this perception is not shared by purchasers and clients (Murstein & Fontaine, 1993). Further, a recent study of outcomes of psychotherapeutic interventions failed to distinguish between the efforts of the three major professions, while showing that all three outperformed other professional groups, e.g., marriage and family counselors, and other lesser trained practitioners (Consumer Reports, 1995; Kotkin, Daviet, & Gurin, 1996).

Social workers, costing less than psychologists and doing similar work, with the exception of extensive testing, are better trained in community-based practice than psychologists and are more used to dealing with large bureaucracies than the latter group. They are trained with greater speed, and evaluative studies of therapeutic outcomes, as noted, show no significant distinctions between the professions. Social workers do, however, show better client outcomes than marriage and family counselors and other lesser trained practitioner groups (Consumer Reports, 1995; Kotkin et al., 1996). The result has been a shift of managed care organizations toward the employ of larger groups of social work practitioners (Ivey, 1997). This shift is creating a new demand environment for social workers. Social work practice and social work practice settings are changing to adapt to this new demand environment featuring managed care strategies. On the downside, social workers must maintain their flexibility and adaptability lest they be challenged by less expensive professionals or consumer providers. Social work credentialing must be guarded to defend the field against deprofessionalization. Yet no amount of guarding will achieve such a defense if the profession does not adapt proactively to the needs of the market.

For Profit and Not for Profit

The distinction between for-profit and not-for-profit practice is eliminated at the practice level, since the risk — i.e., the responsibility for the cost of the intervention — is shared by the provider and the client. This creates a burden for the provider because the provision of service in both the nonprofit and the for-profit setting is carried out with consideration of costs as a factor in the clinical decision making. In the nonprofit MCO, the clinician is working with the awareness that he or she must provide services under the constraints of a fixed fee. Services costing more than the fixed fee will have to be absorbed by the organization budget. This could mean a loss of bonuses at the end of the year, a need to take a reduction in salary, or a direct charge against profit, in the case of the independent practitioner. The MCO gets paid whether or not the client shows up, and each service offered is a direct charge against the balance that the provider goes home with at the end of the day.

What remains of the distinction between not for profit and for profit is who takes the profit. In the not-for-profit, the savings go back into the organization to expand the service potential; in the for-profit, the profits go to the owners/shareholders. This is perhaps the greatest problem for public health and mental health organizations adopting a managed care strategy. While for some adopting such a strategy has been associated with becoming a for-profit enterprise, in fact adopting a for-profit status is in no way necessary for the switching to a managed care approach (Alameda Alliance for Health, 1995). What is necessary is the broadening of the agency role from provider to that of contractor/insurer/provider. In completing the latter transition, the public agency is in the position to capture the flexibility of the managed care organization without the shift to the demand for profit generation — a demand that often comes at the expense of service provision.

OPPORTUNITIES AND DANGERS

Flexibility of Service Delivery

In the past, a major problem in the delivery of services to the seriously mentally ill has been the inability to pay for social and material services that were not considered medical. Thus, while people could be housed in a hospital, they could not be put up in a hotel to prevent deterioration that might follow from being released to a homeless status. Often the time involved in transporting a patient to work could not be covered on a fee-for-service payment schedule. Homemaker support, necessary to keep the patient in his or her apartment, could not be paid. A capitated fee allows the service to spend the money as seen necessary and allows for the maintenance of the patient in the community.

Avoidance of High Cost of Treatment

The only way that the flexibility and expansion of services to a broader but still needy population can be achieved is the avoidance of inpatient care or other high-cost treatments. Since that is where the money is currently invested and no managed care advocates are talking about increases in budgets — they are promising expanded service within current budget constraints — the consequence is the avoidance and shortening of hospital stays, perhaps inappropriately (Segal et al., 1998).

Taxing the Practitioner

The burden of care and the provision of service are transferred to the practitioner. This in some areas is reaching a point where practitioners are leaving the field. They not only have the risk of care, but are now also being asked to shoulder the responsibility of "economic advocacy," i.e., the responsibility to appeal adverse decisions on reimbursement made by an MCO that may harm the patient — and maintain a standard of care acceptable within the profession — regardless of the payment decisions of the employing MCO (Phillips, 1997).

Insuring Quality of Care and an Outcome Orientation

The mental health organization is supposed to provide the oversight to ensure quality of care and to produce the data systems to yield a service based on an outcome orientation. This is truly a difficult task in behavioral health care when the interventions are not closely tied to the outcomes. Further, the current reliance on the clinical trial for the evaluation of service programs has produced little by way of results other than "no difference." In fact, planning in the mental health field is often based on a lack of findings of differences between the more and less expensive conditions. The latter findings are, however, often obtained as a result of naive research approaches with poor measurement applied to chronic problems that have little probability of change in the course of the time allotted for the clinical trial.

Buying the Positive Outcomes

Getting lost in the search for profits is a big problem for well-meaning MCOs. No matter how idealistic and effective the managed care arrangement, if it can be bought to satisfy profit-seeking objectives, the flexibility and the benefits gained in a managed care approach can easily be subverted. Thus, a poor MCO buys a good one for the sake of buying the product name and not for the sake of maintaining good practice.

Abandoning of Chronic Care

The shift to a public health model has the potential to sacrifice the needs of the chronic client for the needs of the general community. This is a value commitment that needs to be carefully monitored along with the strategies that bring flexibility and responsibility to the practitioner.

Avoidance of Nonprofitable Markets

Having rushed into the service of the poor, many MCOs are now abandoning rural and other nonprofitable markets — usually markets where their negotiating positions are less powerful. Some HMOs are retreating to the selling of administrative support services to public systems, e.g., management information systems, rather than taking on the responsibility of developing service networks or becoming the insurer of these poor populations.

CONCLUSION

A managed care strategy offers social work the opportunity to return to its basic principles — i.e., helping people to help themselves and not doing for people what they can do for themselves. It has the potential to offer tremendous opportunities with respect to employment. Demand for social workers is likely to increase under managed care because they are relatively inexpensive professionals, quickly trained, and trained in the use of community resources and the implementation of a flexible and pragmatic approach to service. While social workers should not embrace the strategy of managed care, they should not run from it or blindly oppose it. They need to aggressively pursue it, fighting its major drawbacks (the for-profit management, the possible abandonment of the chronic patient) while adapting to a competitive marketplace. Social work is a profession that is now in the right place, at the right time, and available at the right price (an improved income if current practice in HMOs continues). Managed care has given the field the opportunity to bridge the gap between private and public practice, allowing social workers who have pursued private practice careers to now offer their services to social work's traditional clientele. It can be a launching platform for flexible and innovative service. Yet, the market can be cruel, and a totally defensive stance to managed care approaches, given the momentum they have already obtained, could be very costly to social work in terms of its long-term position as a provider of health and mental health services.

REFERENCES

Alameda Alliance for Health. (1995, October 2). Client Handout. San Leandro, CA: Alameda County Health Care Services Agency.

Alperin, R.M. & Phillips, D.G. (1997). *The impact of managed care on the practices of psychotherapy*. New York: Brunner/Mazel.

Anderson, D. & Berlant, J. (1995) Managed mental health and substance abuse services. In P. Kongstvedt (Ed.), *Essentials of managed health care*. Gathersberg, MD: Aspen.

Barry, D. (1998, May 16). Giuliani plan cuts agency for homeless. *New York Times*, p. A12(N).

Bickman, L., Summerfelt, W.T., & Noser, K. (1997). Comparative outcomes of emotionally disturbed children and adolescents in a system of services and usual care. *Psychiatric Services*, 48,1543–1548.

Chu, F.D. & Trotter, S. (1974). *The madness establishment*. New York: Grossman.

Consumer Reports. (1995, November). *Mental health: does therapy help?* (pp. 734–739). Author.

Feldman, S. (1992). *Managed mental health care*. Springfield, IL: Charles C. Thomas.

Feldman, S. (1994). Managed mental health: community mental health revisited? *Managed Care Quarterly, 2*, 13–18.

Frank, R.G. & Gaynor, M. (1993). State government choice of organizational structure for local mental health systems: an exploratory analysis. *Health Economics and Health Services Research, 14*, 181–196.

Frank, R.G. & Gaynor, M. (1994). Fiscal decentralization of public mental health care and the Robert Wood Johnson Foundation Program on chronic mental illness. *Milbank Quarterly, 72*, 81–104.

Ivey, S.L. (1997, April 5). *Managed care incentives for collaboration in the delivery of mental health services.* Presentation for the California Psychological Association, San Jose, CA.

Ivey, S.L., Scheffler, R., & Zazzali, J.L. (1998). Supply dynamics of the mental health workforce: implications for health policy. *Milbank Quarterly, 76* (1), 1988, pp. 25–58.

Kilborn, P.T. (1998, July 6). Largest H.M.O.'s cutting the poor and the elderly; a managed-care retreat; insurers cite losses and low government payments in Medicaid and Medicare. *New York Times*, pp. A1(N), A1(L).

Kotkin, M., Daviet, C., & Gurin, J. (1996). The Consumer Reports mental health survey. *American Psychologist, 51*, 1080–1082.

Madenlian, R.M., Patison, M., & Saxon, S. (1980). Economic viability of the mental health worker. *Hospital and Community Psychiatry, 31*, 328–331.

Murstein, B.I. & Fontaine, P.A. (1993). The public's knowledge about psychologists and other mental health professionals. *American Psychologist, 48*, 839–845.

Phillips, D.G. (1997). Legal and ethical issues in the era of managed care (pp. 171–184). In R.M. Alperin & D.G. Phillips, *The impact of managed care on the practices of psychotherapy*. New York: Brunner/Mazel.

The President's Commission on Mental Health. (1978). *Report to the president: the President's Commission on Mental Health*, Vol. 1.

Segal, S.P. (1997). Outcome measurement systems in mental health: a program perspective. In E.J. Mullen and J.L. Magnabosco (Eds.), *Outcomes measurement in the human services*, pp. 149–159. Washington, DC: National Association of Social Workers.

Segal, S.P., Watson, M., & Akutsu, P. (1998). Factors associated with involuntary return to a psychiatric emergency service within twelve months. *Psychiatric Services, 49* (9), 1212–1217.

Shichor, D. (1995). *Punishment for profit: private prisons/public concerns.* Thousand Oaks, CA: Sage Publications.

Specht, H. & Courtney, M.E. (1994). *Unfaithful angels: how social work has abandoned its mission.* New York: Free Press.

Stone, A.A. (1998). Paradigms, preemptions, and stages: understanding the transformation of American psychiatry by managed care. In J.A. Lazarus & S.S. Sharfstein (Eds.), *New roles for psychiatrists in organized systems of care* (pp. 187–238). Washington, DC: American Psychiatric Press.

Tischler, G.L. (1990). Utilization management of mental health services by private third parties. *American Journal of Psychiatry, 147*, 967–973.

Washington Post. (1998, February 17). Managing care for the poor (enrollment of Medicaid patients in managed care plans is on the rise) (Illustration). *Washington Post*, p. WH5.

Winegar, N. (Ed.). (1996). *The clinician's guide to managed mental health care.* Binghamton, NY: The Haworth Press.

18

NETWORKS AND ORGANIZATIONAL IDENTITY
On the Front Lines of Behavioral Health

DEBRA ANDERSON AND GARY MARSHALL

Networks are the medium through which we exchange information, resources, and influence with each other; they have momentous consequences on our lives. They enable us to transcend individual limitations by joining with others to solve common problems and develop innovations. Conversely, networks make us more vulnerable to intended and unintended actions of others; they can amplify, distort, and accelerate the consequences of our interactions, thus making the world far more uncertain and dangerous (Cummings, as cited in Chisholm, 1998, p. xvii).

INTRODUCTION

Since the mid-1990s there has been a proliferation of writing about the network model of organization. Networks, proponents claim, are more effective than single organizations in delivering behavioral health services because they require public and private organizations to coordinate and integrate the funding, service delivery, and regulation of services (Scott, 1985; Provan & Milward, 1995). As a result, fragmentation and duplication are assumed to decrease, while client outcomes increase through improved accessibility and continuity of service delivery (Rosenheck et al., 1998).

At a theoretical level, the rising interest in interorganizational relationships coincides with a "shift of focus in organizational theory from intra- to inter-organizational issues" (Reitan, 1998, p. 285). In other words, managers are encouraged to attend as much to the demands and conditions of the external environment as to their internal operations (Scott, 1985). In the behavioral health sector, these demands and conditions take the form of legislation, grants, and contracts with community agencies and federal, state, and local governments, not to mention the indirect influence exerted by manufacturers of psychopharmacological agents, educational institutions that train mental health personnel, mental health advocacy organizations, and financing and regulatory bodies (Scott, 1985).

Given the increased competition for funding combined with the desire to improve client outcomes, it is not a surprise that behavioral health organizations have sought to coordinate service delivery across organizational boundaries. By emphasizing service integration and coordination between organizations, however, have organizational practitioners and theorists neglected the experience of individuals working in networked organizations? Our fieldwork with a mental health delivery system in a midwestern state in the United States prompted us to ask: What happens to one's personal and professional identity in a networked organization? How do people get connected and relate to one another?

This chapter addresses these questions by shifting the unit of analysis away from organizational networks and back to the individual. The first part describes the key aspects of organizational networks. In the second part, studies that measure network effectiveness are reviewed. Notable in this section is the lack of attention paid to individuals who work in networked organizations. The third part comprises the bulk of the chapter. Here, the issues facing one behavioral health network are discussed, with an emphasis on exploring the ways they may compromise individual identity. Finally, the last section indicates paths for future research.

ORGANIZATIONAL NETWORKS, DEFINED

Organizational networks are defined as "the basic social form that permits interorganizational interactions of exchange, concerted action, and joint production. Networks are unbounded or bounded clusters of organizations that, by definition, are nonhierarchical collectives of legally separate units" (Alter & Hage, 1993, p. 46). As noted here, two overriding characteristics of the network model are an emphasis on horizontal rather than hierarchical relationships and on exchange-based assumptions about human behavior. The network model creates the possibility for reduced layers of communication, ease of information flow, and, ideally, better access to services. The value of such a model is the optimization of resources, including human resources. On the whole, the network is thought of as a system and the unit of analysis is precisely that, the system. Indeed, systems models have been credited, in part, with this shift from intraorganizational issues to interorganizational dynamics in the mental health sector (Scott, 1985).

In addition to systems models, network theory has evolved from transactions cost economics, principal-agent theory, resource dependency theory, strategic choice, organizational learning, and institutional theory (Barringer & Harrison, as cited in Meyer, 2000; Reitan, 1998). In simple terms, these theories argue that each actor possesses an asset another actor needs, and this interdependence spurs an exchange; that leaders establish the terms of exchange with other actors whose cooperation is important for achieving goals; and that both parties of the exchange (principals and agents) are opportunistic, seeking to maximize their gains. The principal's primary task is to monitor the agent closely to ensure compliance and cooperation (Reitan, 1998). In the behavioral health sector, rules, regulations, policies, and contracts are the instruments used to assess compliance (Scott, 1985).

The recognition of the role of the individual in relation to the organization is primarily framed in terms of altruism and trust (Alter & Hage, 1993). The basic assumption is that organizational trust reduces the transaction costs. However, the ways in which trust develops among those who perform direct service work is not examined. In general, the individual and his or her behavior are understood as variables to be managed. As such, the individual remains a secondary or partial factor in the analysis of the network model. In the current public sector environment, the emphasis remains on effecting coordination between units to optimize resources, outcomes, integration, and the like.

EVALUATING NETWORK EFFECTIVENESS

Provan and Milward (1995, 2001) have addressed the need to evaluate the effectiveness of organizational networks. They suggest that networks be evaluated at three levels: the community, the network, and the organization/network participant. The key criteria that operate at each of these three levels are summarized below.

At the community level, the network is understood to be an agent of the community. That is, the network, if effective, will provide distinct benefits to the larger community relative to the problems that the community seeks to address. The criteria at this level are the contribution the network makes to the community, the aggregate outcomes for clients, and overall costs of treatment for a client group.

At the network level, Provan and Milward consider a broader set of criteria. As they suggest, "a network is not simply one more community provider organization; it is a collection of programs and services that span a broad range of cooperating but legally autonomous organizations" (2001 p. 5). Effectiveness is determined by assessing the central organizing entity of the network: the Network Administrative Organization (NAO). The growth and maturity of the network is measured by its level of enrollment, turnover or stability, and the quality and range of services delivered. More specifically, what are evaluated include administrative structure, costs, strength of relationships, and services delivered.

The third level of evaluation proposed by Provan and Milward is the organizational level. That is, how effective are the member organizations of the network? Assessed from the perspective of the agency director or manager, the question is: Can involvement in a network help the agency achieve its objectives? Will participation in a network help the agency survive? Four criteria are proposed to determine effectiveness at this level: legitimacy, cost, resource acquisition, and client outcomes. Each of these is concerned with status, competition, power, and influence incurred by participating organizations.

In sum, research on network effectiveness in behavioral health services has primarily focused on measuring system integration and accessibility, client outcomes, service delivery structure, and financial costs and resources (Rosenheck et al., 1998; Provan & Milward, 1995). Results of such studies have been mixed, with some finding that system integration and accessibility are critical to client outcomes, but only for specific types of services (Rosenheck et al., 1998). Others have found that the most effective networks are those that are centrally controlled, integrated, and stable, possessing relatively munificent environmental resources (Provan & Milward, 1995).

To date, research has neglected the impact of networks on the individuals who work in them. Understanding the effect of the network on individuals requires some knowledge about the relationship between individual and organizational identity. It is to this issue that we now turn.

INDIVIDUAL IDENTITY IN A NETWORKED ORGANIZATION

According to Andrew Brown (2001), the "issue of identity is central to our understanding of how individuals relate to the groups and organizations in which they are participants" (p. 114). If we understand how individuals relate to their immediate work groups and organizations, we might speculate about how they make sense of, relate to, and work with organizational networks. Implicit in this notion is the belief that the construction of identity is an iterative and dynamic process that occurs between and among individuals, groups, and organizations.

Symbolic interactionists argue that one's identity is formed by a process of social comparison and reflection, fueled by the drive for self-esteem (Hatch & Schultz, 2002; Bartel, 2001; Giddens, 1991). This process of social comparison involves interactions and interrelationships between organizational members and their peers, as well as organizational members and stakeholders (Bartel, 2001; Gioia, 2000).

The individual worker's identity is formed, maintained, and challenged by network partners as well. If the worker aligns herself with clients or citizen groups, she may emphasize her role of providing mental health treatment. If, on the other hand, she works primarily with law enforcement, she may view herself as an advocate for community safety, thereby reinforcing a legalistic, as opposed to therapeutic, identity. Either perspective could influence the worker's willingness (or unwillingness) to cooperate with network colleagues.

Equally important to how one views oneself is one's perception of how he or she is viewed by others. This "inside perception of outsider impressions" (Gioia, 2000) is particularly relevant to identity formation and maintenance. Put simply, my identity is a synthesis of how I see myself and how I believe others see me, or rather, what I think you think about me (Hatch & Schultz, 2002; Gioia, 2000; Weick, 1995). If a client is appreciative of a case manager's help, for example, that case manager's identity as a professional helper may be reinforced. If a colleague in another program is critical of the case manager's intervention with the client, however, the case manager's identity as a professional may be negatively affected. Embedded in this example are the issues of status and power. Those perceived to have more status and power may have a greater influence on one's identity than those perceived to have less power (Gioia, 2000).

This process of identity formation and maintenance is assumed to continue in much the same way as one moves up and down the network. However, because an individual has different kinds of relationships with clients, co-workers, supervisors, board members, and community partners, Michael Pratt and Peter Foreman (2000) argue that multiple roles can lead to complex individual and organizational identities, some cooperative and others conflicted.

ORGANIZATIONAL NETWORKS AND IDENTITY: A CASE STUDY

Whether a network system or a more traditional model of organization, our contention is that the central dynamic between the individual and the organization is the same. That is, as Rashford and Coghlan (1994) argue, there is a bonding relationship. Our thesis, however, is that in a network system the social fabric that binds employees to one another and to the network is both more fragile and complex than in a single organization. It is more fragile because members may not have opportunities for the repetitive, face-to-face contacts necessary for forming attachments. The bonds may be more complex due to the wide range of client populations, breadth of client problems/needs, differences in service delivery philosophies, variations in funding sources, and types of stakeholder demands. The results of fieldwork in a behavioral health network are presented here to increase awareness of the issues facing one network and the effects on individual identity.

Behavioral Health Network

In the midwestern state where this fieldwork occurred, mental health and substance abuse services to children and adults are delivered through six geographical regions. Local units of government, referred to as regional governing boards, administer each region. The six behavioral health regions, along with the Department of Health and Human Services; the

Office of Mental Health, Substance Abuse, and Addiction Services; and the state hospitals, work as partners to deliver behavioral health services throughout the state.

Each regional governing board is responsible for locating funding for the respective region. In addition to contracting for federal and state funds, counties provide matching funds. These funds are used to manage a network of behavioral health providers, provide care coordination for children and adolescents with serious emotional disorders and their families, and ensure the provision of mental health and substance abuse prevention, treatment, rehabilitation, and support.

Within the Network Administrative Organization (NAO) there are two primary programs. The first program, referred to as the Wraparound Program, delivers intensive therapeutic case management to families who have children with serious emotional disorders, and is based upon the wraparound philosophy to service delivery. The wraparound philosophy cultivates natural support systems in the client's community, individualizes treatment for each client, builds on family strengths, and emphasizes cultural competency in service delivery. The second program, referred to as the Comprehensive Care Program, delivers a comprehensive system of care for children and adolescents with serious emotional disorders. The services provided by Comprehensive Care are similar to those of the Wraparound Program, although the former focuses on working with children and adolescents needing more intensive services. Workers in the Comprehensive Care Program carry smaller caseloads to enable them to provide the level of services needed. Wraparound Program workers are based in the various counties in which their clients reside, while Comprehensive Care workers are centrally located in the child welfare division of the Department of Health and Human Services.

Issues Facing the Behavioral Health Network

A qualitative study of the behavioral health network, with a focus on the NAO, included the following data: written information provided by stakeholders, employees, and the NAO leadership team, along with the field experiences of the authors consulting to the organization. Data analysis occurred in conjunction with the leadership team, identifying the strengths and weaknesses of the network and NAO, and then addressing priority areas. Primary among the strengths is the support the network receives from clients, stakeholders, and employees.

Other strengths include the network's responsiveness to external influences, particularly legislative initiatives related to behavioral health reform, adaptability in modifying policy and program direction as legislative mandates change, and promotion of excellence, demonstrated by efforts to develop state-of-the-art interventions. However, four issues challenge the NAO and larger network: sustainability, resource development, decision making, and employee/organizational health. Although single organizations face many of these same challenges, the focus here is on how they affect the individuals within a behavioral health network.

Network Sustainability and Behavioral Health Reform

For any organization providing behavioral health services, the ability to sustain daily operations is an ongoing challenge. Developing a positive image, raising funds, and meeting client needs are necessary to survival. For a behavioral health network, however, sustainability refers to more than survival; it is about developing a system that is not only responsive to the communities it serves, but also to the citizens whose tax dollars support it and the policy makers who entrust it with federal, state, and local funds. To that end, sustainability also refers to the network's ability to develop positive working relationships with client advocacy groups, the state legislature, state departments such as the Department of Health and Human Services, state hospitals, law enforcement agencies, court systems, and the general public.

Sustainability also refers to the network's willingness to adapt to environmental changes so that programs and services remain current and in demand. In recent years, the wraparound philosophy has been implemented by the network, emphasizing a holistic assessment of mental health issues combined with individualized, family-based, culturally competent treatment. This philosophy is promulgated throughout the network despite the fact that caseload sizes and workload demands detract from its full actualization.

Sustainability and Identity

Just as the network must be adaptive and flexible to changes, so too must members of the network be able to adapt and change. However, one complaint voiced by employees of the NAO is the demand to complete tasks on short notice or adapt their work schedules according to larger system changes. Direct service workers are particularly vulnerable to changes in service delivery philosophies and methods, which — in the case of behavioral health reform — places demands on them to change intake procedures, increase caseload sizes, or introduce new methods of intervention (more community-based services, for example).

While some employees view network and program changes as simply the nature of the work, others express feelings of being "stretched too thin" by the requirements that come with sustaining the network. In a network where contracts, rules, and regulations dictate the way individuals relate to one another, their clients, and the larger system, the tension between maintaining one's sense of professional self while also sustaining the network is significant. Operating under such tension, workers are at risk of losing interest in their work as the inability to innovate or control their work contributes to stress and burnout (Scheid, Fayram, & Littlefield, 1998).

Resource Development

Directly related to sustainability is the need for ongoing funding for programs and services. Many behavioral health network programs are funded through federal and state grants and appropriations; therefore, funding stability is a continuous challenge as laws, policies, and program priorities change. While seeking and sustaining funds are not unique to organizational networks, this behavioral health network, similar to others (Alter & Hage, 1993), is vertically linked and resource dependent upon the state health and human service agency. Although the NAO is accountable for allocated monies, it lacks a certain degree of autonomy and authority in resource solicitation and implementation.

Direct service employees within the NAO and behavioral health network generally are not fully knowledgeable about the types of funds the network receives for the various programs. However, most are aware that those who work in grant-funded programs are at risk of losing their jobs. For example, the Wraparound Program must continually seek funding, as several of its grants have expired. Therefore, resource dependence has led to emotional dependence as wraparound case managers project their worries about job security upon the leadership team with expectations that the team will secure funds to sustain the program. While the NAO has formed a grant team whose purpose is to search for and apply for funding, these duties are added to employees' full work schedules, resulting in limited success.

Resource Development and Identity

Because social identity is driven by a need for self-esteem, and because network members project some of their self-esteem needs into the work group, individual identity is intertwined with the success of the program, department, and network, such that one experiences its accomplishments and failures vicariously (Bartel, 2001). In the case of the network's resource development needs, the loss of funding is experienced as a failure by individuals working within the grant-funded program, the grant team that has been unsuccessful in obtaining funds, and the larger network that must discontinue the program if funding is not secured. Carried further, clients and their families ultimately fail if services and programs are not available.

Employees within the NAO attempt to protect themselves from threats such as funding losses because such threats are perceived to be attacks against individual self-esteem, the program, the NAO, and the network (Brown, 2001). Defensive behaviors frequently include projecting blame about losses onto the leadership team (for failing to secure new funds), the community (for failing to support the program), and the legislature (for failing to recognize the value of the program). Additionally, direct service workers may project blame onto clients and their families for not working harder or improving sooner.

Decision-Making Processes within a Networked Environment

One defining element of an organizational network is joint decision making and problem solving among the member organizations (Alter & Hage, 1993, p. 78). In efforts to coordinate lateral linkages — specifically with the Department of Health and Human Services and local law enforcement agencies — the behavioral health network has excelled. However, it has only recently adopted a formal decision-making process for programs within the NAO. Lack of clarity about decision-making authority and autonomy has resulted in frustration and stress for NAO members, as it has led to miscommunication between members, loss of time in taking action, and a perception of work overload for certain members within the NAO. In an effort to decentralize decision making, the leadership team and the direct service staff formalized a decision-making model for the NAO.

Interestingly, this change has had both positive and negative effects. On a positive note, employees report more opportunities for decision making about their work, departmental operations, and NAO policies. Contrarily, they express less opportunity to provide feedback and input into decisions made by the leadership team. Some direct service employees report great variations among supervisors and members of the leadership team with regard to the level of input sought.

Decision Making and Identity

Just as organizations seek to protect their autonomy, so too do individuals desire the ability to independently exercise choice and make decisions about their work lives. However, Dillon (1990) reports that because social workers in the mental health field lack control over who they see, the nature and length of client contacts, the range of duties they are expected to carry out, and the value placed by others on their work, their autonomy is decreasing while their stress levels are increasing. Moreover, they can expect to experience continued conflict as they struggle to reconcile the demands placed on them in the form of rules and regulations for compliance and their own expectations for professional autonomy (Lloyd, King, & Chenoweth, 2002; Scott, 1985). In order to enhance an employee's commitment to an organization, he or she needs opportunities to make decisions about issues that affect job performance. For when rules and regulations are used to control workers' decisions and behaviors, their sense of efficacy decreases, thus increasing the risk for burnout (Scheid, Fayram, & Littlefield, 1998; Jayartne & Chess, 1984).

Valuing Employees/Organizational Health

Alter and Hage (1993, p. 17) argue that one reason people are more willing to participate in networks is due to the development of cooperative cultures built upon social ties and trust. However, if behavioral health network employees do not have opportunities for socialization due to different office locations, workload demands, types of clients served, or services delivered, then employees are more likely to note their differences than their similarities. Interestingly, in the behavioral health network studied, cooperative relationships among member organizations were viewed as positive, affirming, and supportive, while relationships among employees within the NAO were troubled by a lack of communication and signs of disrespect.

Many employees within the NAO do not know one another. The Comprehensive Care workers located at the Department of Health and Human Services are more familiar with DHHS policies and acculturated into that environment than to the policies and culture of the NAO. Similarly, workers located in satellite offices have little contact with central office employees and managers, and thus are more likely to make decisions based on situational imperatives (Wilson, 1989) rather than rely on network policies and practices.

Additionally, few members understand the connections between programs. Many lack understanding of the scope of their co-workers' responsibilities beyond a superficial awareness of the other programs. As a result, employees complain that caseloads are unfairly distributed, miscommunication and lack of respect are pervasive, and territorialism about program expertise impedes coordination of services. Ultimately, the network employee's identity as a professional and as a member of the network may be compromised as well.

Valuing Employees/Organizational Health and Identity

Individuals in organizations seek cohesiveness and support from their co-workers. The sense of belonging is what connects the individual to the group and organization and what may provide security during times of stress and change. Indeed, Gary Koeske and Randi Daimon Koeske (1989) report that social support from co-workers is more effective than supervisory support in buffering against work stress. However, as organizational coordination becomes optimized in networks, fewer opportunities for socialization exist. As a result, the potential to develop a shared culture through which members of the network share some common sense of mission, organizational responsibility, and commitment diminishes. As an example, despite the similarities in the Wraparound and Comprehensive Care Programs, the relationships between the workers are characterized by a lack of respect.

Additionally, the multiplicity of professions and organizations that make up a behavioral health network, combined with the demands placed upon worker performance, suggests that workers may be hard-pressed to provide support to one another. Because professional status is a source of group identity, social workers may seek to protect the domains of practice they believe belong to them (Scheid, Fayram, & Littlefield, 1998; Jayartne & Chess, 1984). However, for social workers in a behavioral health network, the lack of clear consensus about what they do suggests that their rank may be lower than that of law enforcement or medicine, professions assumed to be more clearly understood by most people. Therefore, rather than work cooperatively, as is assumed in the organizational network literature, professionals may highlight their differences rather than their similarities.

PATHS FOR FUTURE RESEARCH

In this study of a behavioral health network, four issues were addressed: network sustainability, resource development, decision making, and valuing employees/organizational health. Are these issues unique to networked organizations? Of course not. Both traditional and networked organizations are challenged by demands to remain sustainable in the wake of multiple stakeholders who differentially value their services, hold contradictory philosophies about service delivery, and wield high degrees of power, influence, and resources. Both must continually secure funds and staff, while promoting state-of-the-art interventions that not only maintain but extend programs and services. Both seek ways to include employees at all levels of decision making in order to promote ownership and self-efficacy at work. Finally, both are concerned with enhancing individual and organizational health by encouraging mutual communication, respect, and coordination among employees and programs.

However, our purpose was not to compare traditional and networked organizations, but rather to examine the ways that networks affect the individuals who work within them. Here we attempted to show that while organizational networks purport to transcend instrumental rationality by dissolving boundaries and striving for coordination and cooperation, the very people needed to build cooperative trusting relationships have been neglected in the shuffle to create the most effective and efficient network. Future research about organizational networks need not neglect measures of efficiency and effectiveness, but certainly ought to consider the identity and growth needs of the organizational members who constitute these networks.

Our study indicates that network sustainability is an ongoing challenge; it also suggests that continuous policy changes inhibit creativity and innovative interventions. How much change is the right amount for workers in behavioral health networks? Are there ways for workers to be creative within the parameters of externally imposed mandates? Can employees maintain a consistent and enduring sense of self in the wake of continual policy and program changes?

Second, securing stable funding for programs and services is an ongoing and necessary preoccupation for organizational networks. Research is needed to explore whether loss of funding is experienced as an injury to network members' self-esteem. Do employees, for example, blame clients who, in effect, "use up" the limited resources available? Are funds expected to be magically obtained by administrators or grant teams?

Laws, rules, and regulations influence the autonomy, authority, and responsibility of networked organizations. If we agree that members of organizational networks need to exercise choices about their work in order to experience a sense of professional efficacy, research is needed to determine the degree of decentralization that ought to occur in networked organizations. Do employees want to participate in decisions? What types are most important to preventing stress and improving job satisfaction?

Finally, and arguably most pressing, research is needed to determine whether employees' sense of belonging with co-workers is diffused in an organizational network due to differences in office locations, variations in workload demands, diversity among client populations, and conflicts in service delivery philosophy. Given the multiplicity of roles assumed and relationships managed, are social bonds enhanced because of the greater number of opportunities to develop relationships with members throughout the network, or are they more fragile and complex, as argued in this paper? Future research might focus on exploring these constructs in more detail, comparing the similarities and differences between traditional and networked organizations, to determine if workers indeed are constrained by rules and regulations, with less ability to exercise decision making and action congruent with practice wisdom; or if, in the absence of direct knowledge about their practice, workers operate according to situational imperatives. In other words, in the absence of clear responsibility and authority, do workers simply do what they think needs to be done? And if so, does this enhance or hinder their personal growth and professional identity?

The issues uncovered in this study suggest that one's personal and professional identity is largely determined by relationships within one's work environment. By expanding our understanding of the experiences and needs of those who work in organizational networks, we may gain insight into creating organizational structures that are measured not only by the standards of efficiency and effectiveness, but more importantly, by whether or not they grant primacy to the growth and identity of the individual (Denhardt, 1981).

REFERENCES

Alter, C. & Hage, J. (1993). *Organizations working together*. Newbury Park, CA: Sage Library of Social Research 191.

Bartel, C.A. (2001). Social comparisons in boundary-spanning work: effects of community outreach on members' organizational identity and identification. *Administrative Science Quarterly, 46*, 379–414.

Brown, A.D. (2001). Organization studies and identity: towards a research agenda. *Human Relations, 54*, 113–121.

Chisholm, R.F. (1998) *Developing network organizations: learning from practice and theory*. Reading, MA: Addison-Wesley.

Denhardt, R.B. (1981). *In the shadow of organization*. Lawrence, KS: Regents Press of Kansas.

Dillon, C. (1990). Managing stress in health social work roles today. *Social Work in Health Care, 14*, 91–108.

Giddens, A. (1991). *The consequences of modernity*. Stanford, CA: Stanford University Press.

Gioia, D.A. (2000). Organizational identity, image, and adaptive instability. *Academy of Management Review, 25*, 63–82.

Hatch, M.J. & Schultz, M. (2002). The dynamics of organizational identity. *Human Relations, 55*, 989–1018.

Jayartne, S. & Chess, W. (1984). Job satisfaction, burnout, and turnover: a national study. *Social Work, 29*, 448–453.

Koeske, G.F. & Koeske, R.D. (1989). Work load and burnout: can social support and perceived accomplishment help? *Social Work, 34*, 243–248.

Lloyd, C., King, R., & Chenoweth, L. (2002). Social work, stress, and burnout: a review. *Journal of Mental Health, 11*, 255–265.

Meyer, K.P. (2000). Interorganizational networks. Unpublished manuscript.

Pratt, M.G. & Foremann, P.O. (2000). Classifying managerial responses to multiple organizational identities. *Academy of Management Review, 25*, 18–42.

Provan, K.G. & Milward, H.B. (1995). A preliminary theory of interorganizational network effectiveness: a comparative study of four community mental health systems. *Administrative Science Quarterly, 40*, 1–33.

Rashford, N.S. & Coghlan, D. (1994). *The dynamics of organizational levels: a change framework for managers and consultants*. Reading, MA: Addison-Wesley.

Reitan, T.C. (1998). Theories of interorganizational relations in the human services. *Social Service Review, 37*, 285–309.

Rosenheck, R., Morrissey, J., Lam, J., Calloway, M., Johnsen, M., Goldman, H., Randolph, F., Blasinsky, M., Fontana, A., Calsyn, R., & Teague, G. (1998). Service system integration, access to services, and housing outcomes in a program for homeless persons with severe mental illness. *American Journal of Public Health, 88*, 1610–1615.

Scheid, T.L., Fayram, E.S., & Littlefield, V. (1998). Work experiences of mental health care providers: professional and organizational determinants of burnout and satisfaction. *Research in the Sociology of Health Care, 15,* 57–82.

Scott, W.R. (1985). Systems within systems: the mental health sector. *American Behavioral Scientist, 28,* 601–618.

Weick, K. (1995). *Sensemaking in organizations.* Thousand Oaks, CA: Sage.

Wilson, J.Q. (1989). *Bureaucracy: What government agencies do and why they do it.* New York, N.Y.: Basic Books.

19

THE UNCERTAIN FUTURE OF PUBLIC MENTAL HEALTH SYSTEMS
A West Virginia Case Study
ELIZABETH RANDALL AND MARY ALDRED-CROUCH

During the past decade, the mental health (or behavioral health) treatment system in the nation has undergone dramatic changes, including the widespread use of managed care oversight, reduced state and federal funding, greater emphasis on brief treatment modalities, and restricted availability of housing and vocational supports for persons with severe and persistent mental illness (Bazelon Center, 2003). In 1999, the Office of the Surgeon General published its first comprehensive report on mental health (USDHHS, 1999) and concluded that "the efficacy of mental health treatment is well documented" (p. 13). However, this report also pointed out that the actual implementation of state-of-the-art treatment methods is quite rare in most regions of the nation. For years, unfortunately, legislative bodies have been distancing themselves from responsibility for funding comprehensive mental health services, even for those most in need (Mowbray & Holter, 2002).

According to the final report of the president's New Freedom Commission on Mental Health (2003), "for too many Americans with mental illness, the mental health services they need remain fragmented, disconnected and often inadequate, frustrating the opportunity for recovery" (p. 1). The present review is intended to help clarify how changes in public behavioral health service systems are affecting consumers in one state (West Virginia), as compared with the nation as a whole. Mental health services for children and youth, although similarly impacted, are not included in the present analysis.

FUNDING MENTAL HEALTH SERVICES

In the 1950s, mental health services were almost exclusively the responsibility of state governments. This situation continued into the era of deinstitutionalization, with the establishment of the community mental health centers in 1963 (Mowbray & Holter, 2002), which marked trends toward decentralization, and also the availability of a wider variety of federally assisted programs for consumers. Another major shift came about with the creation of Medicare and Medicaid. This federal initiative, enacted as an amendment to the Social Security Act in 1965, put more health care purchasing power into the hands of consumers, allowing them more flexibility and choice of providers, marking the beginning of the present proliferation of mental health disciplines. Another landmark event was the federal introduction of the Mental Health Block Grant (MHBG) program in 1981, which represented a shift away from categorical federal support for state mental health programs to a lump-sum approach that program directors were free to use flexibly in response to regional service needs. At the same time, however, states were generally forced to assume a higher proportion of the overall costs of public mental health care under this system, as the federal Block Grant program continued to decline, shrinking by 49% (in inflation-adjusted dollars) from 1983 to 1997 (Lutterman & Hogan, 2001).

During the 1980s, health care costs in general began spiraling out of control. According to Cummings (1996), mental health care costs were one of the most significant sources of health care cost inflation during this interval. Especially stringent cost containment measures have been applied to mental health benefits ever since, even though the particular culpability of mental health systems is a thing of the past by now (Bazelon Center, 2002).

A Growing Crisis: The Case of West Virginia

By the mid-1980s, mental health program directors were under considerable pressure to offset cuts in federal support. One way was to bill an ever-increasing variety of services to Medicaid. This strategy has been referred to as Medicaid maximization, and for a while it seemed to help, allowing community mental health centers to maintain a broad array of services in an era of shrinking federal allocations (Mowbray, Grazier, & Holter, 2002). In West Virginia, providers and program directors have borne the brunt of criticism for allowing this practice to reach crisis proportions, but choices and priorities set by state legislators were also very much involved.

By the early to mid-1990s, federal Medicaid reviewers began to disallow payments for services that did not fully satisfy eligibility and appropriateness criteria. Losing large sums from this irreplaceable source of external funding led to rapid changes, such as wholesale program cuts and staff reductions in many areas, as key services upon which these programs depended for their *raison d'etre* were declared Medicaid ineligible. By 2002, unable to respond to the ensuing chaos within the context of a deepening budget crisis, the largest public mental health center in the state, Shawnee Hills, went bankrupt and closed its doors (Davia, 2002). This was the most notorious and well-publicized failure of a state mental health agency in West Virginia during this interval, but not the only one (J. Russell, personal communication, March 17, 2003).

In the mid-1990s, federal Medicaid authorities presented the West Virginia Department of Health and Human Resources (which subsumes the Bureau for Behavioral Health) with a demand for repayment of approximately $90 million for mental health services judged to have been inappropriately billed to Medicaid over a span of several years. However, this payback could be forgiven if the state implemented managed care oversight of Medicaid-eligible services (J. Plitt, personal communication, March 19, 2003). Consequently, the state awarded a three-year contract to APS Healthcare in June 2000 to provide prior authorizations and utilization reviews of Medicaid-eligible services delivered by all the community mental health centers, and this managed care plan began during the fall of that year. As of this writing, plans were under way to include Medicaid behavioral health claims from private practitioners for processing within the APS system as well. In financial terms, the program has been a resounding success, yielding approximately 40% Medicaid cost savings within its first contractual cycle (S. Brack, personal communication, March 3, 2003), and the contract was recently renewed (with yearly reviews) for five years. However, in terms of optimal clinical outcomes and quality of life for mental health consumers, the success of this program is, arguably, much more qualified. More will be said about the clinical implications of managed care in West Virginia community mental health in a subsequent section.

Recent Trends in Mental Health Funding in West Virginia

At present, the majority of mental health centers in the public sector are partially privatized, and operate from a mixed bag of funding sources, including direct payment of fees for services, private insurance reimbursements, grant funds, limited contributions from county resources, federal funding, Medicare and Medicaid reimbursements, and state support.

A senior administrator with the Bureau for Behavioral Health acknowledged, during a recent public meeting, that the lack of a centralized and comprehensive database capable of pinpointing behavioral health expenditures from a single reference source is very much an issue at present, but that "the whole Bureau would have to stop what it's doing for two months in order to get a handle on that" (Randall, 2003a).

Nevertheless, some strong inferences may be drawn from a number of sources of information, as follows:

- On the average, state expenditures for mental health services decreased 7%, when adjusted for inflation, from 1990 to 1997 (Autry & Arons, 2001).
- In mid-2003, West Virginia was at risk of losing its federal Mental Health Block Grant, on grounds of insufficient "maintenance of effort" (i.e., reasonably comparable allocations drawn from state revenues from one fiscal year to the next). Notification of this potential funding emergency created an urgent need to revise and resubmit the state's MHBG renewal application, to address federal concerns about the possible inadequacy of ongoing state support for mental health, before the grant could be renewed (Randall, 2003a).
- West Virginia had the second lowest per capita state expenditure for mental health services ($20.54) in the United States in 1997 (Lutterman & Hogan, 2001, p. 223).
- From 1986 to 2002, expenditures for mental health services derived directly from state budget revenues were reduced from $35,206,447 to $28,690,901 in constant dollars (State of West Virginia, 1986–2003).
- Further budget cuts for West Virginia mental health in the range of 3 to 5% were projected for fiscal year (FY) 2003 (Lutterman, 2003).

Thus, converging lines of evidence all support the conclusion that financial support for public mental health services in West Virginia has been steadily eroding. There can be little doubt that this financial undermining has had a direct, negative effect on the quality and appropriateness of those services that remain in place. A review of the present status of program and services is offered in the next section.

THE PRESENT STATUS OF PROGRAMS AND SERVICES

In the literature on public mental health systems from two or three decades ago, the acronym CCMHC is often found, which stood for comprehensive community mental health center. However, according to a recent remark made by Eugenie Taylor, West Virginia's acting commissioner of behavioral health, the notion of public mental health centers offering "comprehensive" services has become anachronistic, and is unlikely to return as a meaningful descriptor in the foreseeable short term (Randall, 2003b). Instead, according to George Lilley, CEO of Valley HealthCare in Morgantown, WV, community mental health centers (CMHCs) now function mainly as programs of last resort for persons with few options. Dr. Lilley did not intend this description as an indictment of the professionalism of mental health center staff, nor as a disparagement of the quality of those services that the centers do remain authorized to provide. In so saying, however, he did seem to imply that the inadequacy of the help that is presently available for the chronically mentally ill, relative to the need, would most likely be deemed intolerable to any population not suffering from socioeconomic marginalization (G. Lilley, personal communication, April 22, 2003).

At present, one of Valley HealthCare's priorities is to serve persons who have been referred for aftercare following an emergency admission (or possibly a civil commitment) to a psychiatric hospital, often for a psychotic episode (loss of contact with objective reality). Such a client will generally receive a thorough assessment, medication management, and intermittent brief, supportive therapy. The goal of these services is to prevent relapse, leading to readmission to a psychiatric hospital. This goal is beneficial for the client, but is also motivated by strong financial incentives, as inpatient treatment remains considerably more expensive for states than outpatient care. However, the public mental health system can no longer generally afford the more ambitious goal of psychosocial rehabilitation for the severely and persistently mentally ill, which might mean the ability to live independently, and perhaps enjoy a greater degree of integration into community life. Valley HealthCare is not presently able to offer assisted living, day treatment, social skills training, or wraparound services, although many of these services were common as recently as 5 or 10 years ago (G. Lilley, personal communication, April 22, 2003).

A particular model of psychosocial rehabilitation for the chronically mentally ill that has received widespread recognition for its strong empirical support is assertive community treatment (ACT) (Scott & Dixon, 1995; Lehman, 1998). ACT is "an intensive approach to the treatment of people with serious mental illnesses that relies on provision of a comprehensive array of services in the community" (USDHHR, 1999, p. 286). While ACT is on the schedule of Medicaid-eligible services in West Virginia, Valley HealthCare does not offer this model, due to a predetermined rate of reimbursement that Dr. Lilley and other program directors in the state consider too low to cover actual costs (G. Lilley, personal communication, April 22, 2003).

At Prestera Center, the public mental health center that absorbed most of the clientele and a number of staff when Shawnee Hills went bankrupt and ceased operations in 2002, the status of services for the chronically mentally ill is much the same. According to Bob Hansen, executive director of Prestera Center, all clients who need to be seen are served in a timely manner. However, services are relatively brief and impersonal and less flexible than might be preferred, due to staff pressures to maintain economically productive ratios of billable hours in proportion to total working hours (B. Hansen, personal communication, March 10, 2003).

During the summer of 2003, the present team of investigators conducted an informal telephone survey of services presently offered by the 13 public mental health centers in West Virginia. We posed a series of four questions covering a selection of possible consumer requests for services, with an open-ended question at the end to invite comments about any other noteworthy circumstances that respondents were encountering.

In response to our first question, "Does the center administer any residential/supportive living group homes for persons with persistent and severe mental illness?" 8 of 13, or 62%, affirmed that they do offer group home support, at least to a nominal extent. However, a recent five-state study of mental health performance indicators concluded that even where housing supports were offered, only 3% of consumers were actually being served (Manderscheid, Henderson, & Brown, 2001). Therefore, the qualitative comments offered by several respondents concerning this question were illuminating. Several noted that their agencies had been offering residential services to the severely mentally ill in the recent past, but could do so no longer, due to reimbursement rates so inadequate as to threaten their financial solvency were they to continue to try. A respondent at Prestera Center noted that it is a common belief among staff at that center that four consumers in their catchment area had died in the past year due to environmental risks directly related to the closure of supportive living group homes, a belief that was reiterated by Prestera's executive director (B. Hansen, personal communication, March 10, 2003). In view of data indicating that many group home closures have been recent, and that further budget cuts and reductions in services are projected for West Virginia, a concern that additional group home closures may be imminent did not seem unrealistic. Of particular concern are data indicating that additional Medicaid restrictions are on the way (Lutterman, 2003).

Our second question asked, "Does the center offer a day treatment program for persons with persistent and severe mental illness?" This was a more frequently offered service, as 9 of 13, or 69%, responded affirmatively. However, we again found that struggles to secure reimbursement for day treatment made it difficult for CMHCs to continue to provide this service. Several CMHCs that did not provide day treatment noted that the expenditures for day treatment far exceeded reimbursement. John Mayes, clinical director of Logan-Mingo Area Mental Health, noted that his facility ceased offering day treatment six months prior to our inquiry, because reimbursement only approached 40 cents on the dollar in comparison with actual costs (J. Mayes, personal communication, June 11, 2003).

Concerning our inquiry into the availability of assertive community treatment in West Virginia, no CMHC in the state offered ACT at the time of our survey, although two were considering plans to begin doing so. By far, the most pressing reason reported to us was the reimbursement issue: the preset reimbursement schedule for ACT is simply too low to cover the cost.

Our fourth question dealt with the historical mandate for the community mental health centers to provide care for persons in acute or short-term need of treatment, but unable to pay. We used the hypothetical case of an unemployed, non-Medicaid-eligible victim of domestic violence as an example. Three CMHCs noted that they would not provide care for this hypothetical help seeker without either Medicaid or private insurance, and one stated that his agency would have to charge an up-front fee of $150 for an initial assessment in this case. Another stated that his agency had stopped providing indigent mental health care because the necessity of absorbing or "writing off" these nonreimbursable services was threatening the agency's survival. Two additional centers said that they were currently receiving about 20 to 30 cents on the dollar from state funds in comparison with actual costs of indigent care provided. Another center noted reimbursement of about half of its true costs for indigent care.

Although our informal survey of the CMHC programs and services in West Virginia is by no means all-inclusive, it does support the impression of a system in which services tend to be minimal and providers tend to be under a great deal of stress and strain. Large gaps and rents appear to have developed in the "safety net," as the public sector mental health system has often been called (Lutterman & Hogan, 2001). In the next section, the effects of managed care on public sector mental health will be reviewed.

THE EFFECTS OF MANAGED CARE ON THE CMHCS

Advantages of Managed Care

Managed care can convey several distinct advantages, leading to substantial reductions in expenditures. Managed care combats frankly fraudulent claims, as well as overbilling, by means of keeping clients enrolled in services for which they once qualified, but presently no longer need (USDHHS, 2000). However, other advantages are also possible. The need to justify each claim encourages providers to sharpen their diagnostic acumen, and program directors are pleased that staff gain knowledge and hone their professional skills in this way. Managed care also encourages adherence to evidence-based practice, which some professionals consider its most advantageous result (J. Plitt, personal communication, March 19, 2003). The managed care emphasis on brevity of contact may also motivate providers to provide treatment in a more focused and planned way, and to remain cognizant of the advantages of preplanned termination, which have been well documented in the literature on brief treatment (Wells, 1994).

Disadvantages of Managed Care

A big disadvantage of managed care is that the system interferes with the inherently relational nature of meaningful mental health work. One of the most robust and invariant findings in the literature on mental health outcomes is that success depends on the ability of the consumer and the provider to relate to one another in an authentic manner, one in which the consumer perceives the provider as a caring person, who is nonjudgmental, and in whom it is safe to confide (Truax & Mitchell, 1971; Nugent & Halvorsen, 1995).

Yet within the managed care environment, the first order of business with each new client is to establish whether there exists a "medical necessity" for the client to be seen at all. To accomplish this, an assessment form must immediately be filled out and submitted online to the managed care company (APS Healthcare, for West Virginia Medicaid clients). The form is lengthy: depending on the situation, the assessment may contain about 250 questions, some of which are typically perceived as highly personal and intrusive. This process is rote and depersonalizing for both the consumer and the provider, and runs counter to the knowledge that the relational context in which the work is performed is the single most important predictor of a positive outcome (Martin, Garske, & Davis, 2000; Barber, Connolly, Crits-Christoph, Gladis, & Siqueland, 2000). What is particularly frustrating to mental health professionals about the barriers that are thrown up during assessment interviews based on procedures such as these is the realization that both purposes *could* be served: it is entirely possible to design an assessment protocol that recognizes the interpersonal context of the interview process, allowing the consumer and the provider to connect meaningfully, yet also satisfies the requirement of ascertaining a considerable amount of objective and factual information within a reasonable time limit. Instead, mental health professionals commonly feel that crucial relational goals for early encounters with a new client appear to be dismissed as irrelevant, and that this is driven by a value orientation within the managed care environment that originates within the discipline of business and economics rather than human services. While the perceived intrusiveness of the managed care environment may be particularly problematic during the assessment phase, clinicians may also report feeling its interfering effects at numerous points throughout the course of treatment.

Other potential disadvantages of managed care may include: (1) paperwork burden; (2) threats to client confidentiality; (3) premature termination of services; (4) pressure on providers to apply invalid diagnoses, in an effort to improve consumer eligibility for services;

and (5) lost continuing education opportunities for direct service staff, due to budget woes and extreme pressures to maintain the highest possible levels of "productivity." Each of these were endorsed as problems within the managed care environment by a majority of respondents in a recent survey, undertaken by the present authors, of 300 mental health professionals in West Virginia (Randall & Aldred-Crouch, 2004).

Also, there is undoubtedly rationing of care. In some instances care is so sharply curtailed as to leave practitioners wondering whether there has been any net benefit for the consumer, who must weigh modest (and perhaps temporary) symptomatic relief against loss of hope, when further services are denied.

To the present authors, it seems that the "culture clash" of seemingly incompatible underlying values between the managed care industry and the community of mental health providers is the biggest single problem brought about by the advent of managed care. Each side in this battle is entrenched, and each could do a far better job of extending the assumption of good faith to the other and of identifying commonality of purpose. Were this to happen, the possibility of a behavioral health regulatory system that retains the significant advantages of the present managed care industry, while showing greater appreciation and respect for the essentially relational nature of all effective behavioral health work, could begin to be realized.

UNINTENDED CONSEQUENCES OF CUTBACKS IN SERVICES

Increases in Psychiatric Hospitalization

Lately in West Virginia there has been a sharp rise in emergency admissions to inpatient psychiatric facilities, particularly among persons with chronic mental illness. Limitations on consumer eligibility for services and widespread shortages of case managers have seriously undercut the flexibility and responsiveness of the outpatient system of care. Too often, clients who may be in crisis perceive no other recourse than to seek hospitalization on an emergency basis. Eugenie Taylor, acting commissioner of the Bureau for Behavioral Health, remarked in a recent presentation to the state legislature, "As we speak, we have West Virginia's two state psychiatric facilities burdened with more patients than we have beds for." Further on she added, "many of the services that helped keep folks out of the psychiatric hospitals are now not offered" (Taylor, 2003). This trend is costly and cuts into net financial gains realized through outpatient program reductions.

Increased utilization of inpatient services for crisis management is affecting general medical hospitals in West Virginia as well. According to Theresa Cox, health reporter for the *Charleston Daily Mail*, "The trend of an increasing number of patients seeking help at state psychiatric hospitals signals the reverse of a three-decades-long effort to provide services in the community so people can lead more normal lives at home." Ms. Cox went on to say that "much of the overflow of patients [from Bateman, a state hospital] is sent to the nearby, private River Park Hospital, at a higher, market-driven rate at the state's expense" (Cox, 2003).

Low Staff Morale

Another unintended consequence of cutbacks in mental health funding and programming is low staff morale. Low staff morale and high staff turnover were mentioned as factors that contribute significantly to present difficulties faced by all CMHC administrators and program directors who were interviewed during the course of this study. One program director (who asked not to be identified) noted that uncommonly high staff turnover has created a foreshortened sense of a professional future, and has seriously undercut his ability to engage in mid- to long-range planning on behalf of his behavioral health program and its clientele, since he cannot count on staff to stay in pivotal positions long enough to lend their talents and experience to the attainment of the desired goals.

Reimbursement rates and direct service salaries have been stagnant in West Virginia for a number of years. The present acting commissioner of the Bureau for Behavioral Health acknowledges that some behavioral health services in the state have not been granted rate increases for 11 years (E. Taylor, personal communication, November 12, 2004). An office manager for FMRS Health Systems, a CMHC in southern West Virginia, noted that as of the fall of 2003, there had not been an increase in reimbursement rates for services for at least five years. Under these conditions, she noted, the only way for the administration to eke out any pay increases for staff has been to cut staff while maintaining relatively constant levels of billable services. This formula obviously creates a need for increased productivity, and stories abound of staff remaining after hours to complete case management services (that may not be billable) on their own time, or to complete relentless quantities of required paperwork (often perceived as duplicative). The office manager also described the emotional breakdown of several staff resulting from grief over the closure of consumer group homes, when it was unclear where else the displaced residents were to go (M. Redmon, personal communication, September 4, 2003).

As of this writing, increased staff productivity has been a preferred solution for budget woes in many behavioral health-related agencies and programs for five years or more. While this stop-gap solution may make sense economically in the short term, it cannot be sustained over the long term, as the cumulative effects of mental fatigue and burnout will inevitably lead to drastic reductions in the quality of care.

In the current climate favoring services that are rendered in an ever briefer and more impersonal manner, the intrinsic satisfaction and meaningfulness of a job well done are steadily being eroded for mental health professionals, and it is these invisible "pay cuts" that are driving workers out of the field in increasing numbers.

Under these conditions, one wonders how much longer the distressed public mental health system in West Virginia will be able to continue doing more with less.

WHAT DOES THE FUTURE HOLD?

In West Virginia, concerned constituencies have taken steps to patch the unraveling mental health safety net as best they can. Three main initiatives can be identified: advocacy, increased use of consumer peer support networks, and integration of behavioral health care into primary health care practice. A brief summary of each of these efforts follows.

As of this writing, the political climate in the nation favors "significant increases in funding for security programs combined with dramatic reduction in the growth of discreet spending unrelated to security" (Office of Management and Budget, 2004). As a result, most states have worrisome budget woes, as they cope with shouldering an ever larger share of fiscal responsibility for the social welfare of their most vulnerable citizens. In such a climate, advocacy for increased behavioral health funding is extremely challenging. However, some concerned citizen groups continue to try. Some feel that the public is probably unaware of the seriousness of the situation. These advocates hope that improved public awareness and consciousness raising would cause a surge of public support for the faltering system of care. One such plan of action was undertaken by the West Virginia Mental Health Planning

Council and the Mental Health Consumers' Association, which conducted a series of public forums on the impending crisis in public sector mental health throughout the spring and summer of 2004. Only the future will tell whether these and other advocacy initiatives will make a significant difference in West Virginia, but many feel it is imperative to try.

A second noteworthy response to the present crisis is mobilization of additional peer support resources and networks for behavioral health consumers. Peer support models like WRAP (Wellness Recovery Action Plan) (Copeland, 1997) and the Georgia Peer Support model (Riefer, 2003) are growing in the state. This consumer-oriented recovery movement is offering peer counseling, groups, and outreach services, such as sending WRAP-trained liaisons to the state hospitals to network with consumers in need of assistance with discharge planning and aftercare. These models emphasize personal responsibility for change, and a recognition of each consumer as the true expert on what "recovery" would mean in his or her unique situation. In West Virginia, the Bureau for Behavioral Health has begun providing financial support for collaborative programs and outreach activities cosponsored by staff and peer support specialists on the premises of community mental health centers.

A third recent initiative is the integration of behavioral health services and primary health care practice. One approach is the co-location of traditional behavioral health staff within primary care facilities, but with a separate referral and appointment system. In this model, intervention is typically based on brief, focused therapy. An alternative approach places the behavioral health professional in the immediate consulting area in primary care settings. The behavioral health professional, working in tandem with the physician, provides psychoeducational treatment for clients with psychological issues that may be affecting their health, but not therapy per se. In West Virginia, some federally qualified health centers (FQHCs) are now offering behavioral health services, since the community health care system enjoys special latitude with regard to Medicaid reimbursement for this category of services (Strosahl, 2004).

In view of research indicating that no organic basis can be found for the majority of consumer complaints in primary care settings (Patterson, Peek, Heinrich, Bisehoff, & Scherger, 2002), behavioral health integration shows great promise for helping to dismantle arbitrary conceptual distinctions between *psyche* and *soma*, enabling primary care providers to provide more holistically responsive treatment. As presently conceived, however, it is not a replacement or substitute for the traditional mental health system of care. The preferred models of psychosocial treatment in integrated primary care settings are too brief and limited in scope to meet the needs of large number of behavioral health consumers, particularly those with severe and persistent mental illnesses.

WEST VIRGINIA'S RESPONSE

State officials are painfully aware of the challenges facing the public mental health system and are doing what they can to respond to the crisis despite resource limitations. Some specific steps have been taken in the short term. One recent approach has been the formation of a Task Force on Overbedding, involving consumer advocates, hospital administrators, and mental health program directors in a collaborative effort to reduce overutilization of inpatient facilities for crisis stabilization. Also, the Bureau for Behavioral Health is encouraging providers to think differently about treatment, and to give preference to evidence-based forms of care over models supported mainly by tradition or practice wisdom. This initiative has resulted in less reliance on traditional day treatment, in favor of increased utilization of community-focused treatment, a service model designed to emphasize goal-directed outcomes like skills training and enhancement of social competencies for consumers (WVDHHR, 2002). In addition, the Bureau for Behavioral Health has increased funding for charity care within the last year. Just before this chapter went to press, the authors were advised by Eugenie Taylor, acting commissioner, that we would have gotten much more positive feedback from CMHC program directors about their ability to afford acute care for uninsured, low-income citizens if we had conducted our telephone surveys a few months later than we did. Ms. Taylor also notes that a CMHC in central West Virginia recently began offering assertive community treatment, which has substantially reduced relapse rates for the severely and persistently mentally ill in its catchment area (E. Taylor, personal communication, November 12, 2004).

Over the long term, the picture of what could or should happen is less clear. Ms. Taylor believes the bureau will need to define the demographic and diagnostic parameters of the populations for whose care it is principally responsible, and to "see that they get the care they need" (E. Taylor, personal communication, November 12, 2004). This may mean that in the future, fewer consumers will be served more comprehensively. She also foresees more blended funding, with resources pooled and possibly redistributed, resulting on the whole in a more coordinated, less spotty system of care. The new plan will be consistent with the goals set forth in the final report of the president's New Freedom Commission on Mental Health, and will also honor principles of evidence-based practice throughout. At present, the bureau is awaiting bids on a request for proposals from facilitative groups invited to make recommendations for a plan that would do the most to meet these goals within the probable limitations on resources. However, as Ms. Taylor acknowledged, "the devil is in the details" (E. Taylor, personal communication, November 12, 2004), and what role the present community mental health system would play in this future system of care is presently unknown.

SUMMARY

In West Virginia, as in many states, public mental health facilities are struggling to stay afloat and minimally serve consumers as they cope with reduced governmental responsibility for the humane maintenance of the mentally ill. In 2000, managed care was implemented in an effort to curtail runaway costs thought to result from a lack of sufficient provider accountability. From a business standpoint, this system of utilization review has been a noteworthy success. However, it has also contributed to consumer frustration with a system perceived as bureaucratic and uncaring, rationing of care, overreliance on hospitalization for patients in crisis, a "culture clash" between managed care personnel and mental health providers, and low morale and high turnover among direct service staff. These factors, in turn, lead to compromised continuity of care and, in many instances, consumer disillusionment and fading hope (New Freedom Commission on Mental Health, 2002).

Planning is in progress to reallocate state support for behavioral health in a more concentrated way. The role of the present community mental health system within the new plan is not clear, and some mental health administrators have expressed the opinion that continuing to provide significant support for the CMHCs may not be the best use of state resources in the future (Majic, 2004). In one hypothetical future, the Bureau for Behavioral Health will be supporting more effective services, but to fewer consumers. However, movement in this direction could create an expanded population of persons who (1) lack insurance, (2) do not fit newer and narrower definitions of "most in need," (3) cannot pay out-of-pocket costs for behavioral health care, and (4) have needs that extend beyond the scope of behavioral health integration in primary care. A limited number of faith-based and grant-funded agencies in West Virginia provide low-cost or no-cost mental health care, but these resources are entirely inadequate to meet the full extent of the need. If the present community mental health system were unable to develop alternative funding sources to serve those unable to access the charitable system of care, then increasing numbers of persons would fall through the gaps in the safety net, unnecessarily increasing the epidemiology of a variety of social ills, including (but not limited to) their own personal suffering.

In summary, healthcare rationing is a reality. It can happen as a deliberate, thoughtful strategy, or it can be dictated by the vagaries of market forces and the economy's changing climate. The community mental health centers' original mandate to provide comprehensive, community-based mental health services is more critical now than ever. And yet many of these centers find themselves on the precipice of extinction. Their fate lies in the hands of federal and state policy makers. So does the well-being of millions of Americans who rely on the safety net that community mental health centers provide (National Council for Community Behavioral Health Care, 2003, p. 17).

REFERENCES

Autry, J.H. & Arons, B.S. (2001). Executive summary. In R.W. Manderscheid & M.J. Henderson (Eds.), *Mental health, United States, 2000* (DHHS Publication SMA 01-3537, pp. iii–xv). Washington, DC: U.S. Government Printing Office.

Barber, J.P., Connolly, M.B., Crits-Christoph, P., Gladis, L., & Siqueland, L. (2000). Alliance predicts patients' outcome beyond in-treatment change in symptoms. *Journal of Consulting and Clinical Psychology, 68,* 1027–1032.

Bazelon Center for Mental Health Law. (2002). *An act providing a right to mental health services and supports: a model law.* Washington, DC: Author.

Bazelon Center for Mental Health Law. (2003). *Criminalization of people with mental illnesses: the role of mental health courts in system reform.* Washington, DC: Author.

Copeland, M.E. (1997). *Wellness recovery action plan.* West Dummerston, VT: Peach Press.

Cox, T. (2003, October 3). Psychiatric patients put strain on area hospitals. *Charleston Daily Mail,* p. 11A.

Cummings, N.A. (1996). Does managed care offset costs related to medical treatment? In A. Lazarus (Ed.), *Controversies in managed mental health care* (pp. 213–227). Washington, DC: American Psychiatric Press.

Davia, J. (2002, May 1). Shawnee Hills down for the count. *Charleston Gazette,* p. 1.

Lehman, A.F. (1998). Public health policy, community services, and outcomes for patients with schizophrenia. *Psychiatric Clinics of North America, 21,* 221–231.

Lutterman, T. (2003). *State mental health budget shortages: FY '03 & 04.* Alexandria, VA: National Association of State Mental Health Program Directors Research Institute.

Lutterman, T. & Hogan, M. (2001). State mental health agency controlled expenditures and revenues for mental health services, FY 1981 to FT 1997. In R.W. Manderscheid & M.J. Henderson (Eds.), *Mental health, United States, 2000* (DHHS Publication SMA 01-3537, pp. 218–230). Washington, DC: U.S. Government Printing Office.

Majic, D. (2004, October 7). *Overview of children's mental health services.* Presentation to the Governor's Citizen's Advisory Council on Children and Families, Charleston, West Virginia.

Manderscheid, R.W., Henderson, M.J., & Brown, D.Y. (2001). Status of national accountability efforts at the millenium. In R.W. Manderscheid & M.J. Henderson (Eds.), *Mental health, United States, 2000* (DHHS Publication SMA 01-3537, pp. 43–63). Washington, DC: U.S. Government Printing Office.

Martin, D.J., Garske, J.P., & Davis, M.K. (2000). Relation of the therapeutic alliance with outcome and other variables: ameta-analytic view. *Journal of Consulting and Clinical Psychology, 68,* 438–450.

Mowbray, C.T., Grazier, K.L., & Holter, M. (2002). Managed behavioral health care in the public sector: will it become the third shame of the states? *Psychiatric Services, 53*, 157–170.

Mowbray, C.T. & Holter, M.C. (2002). Mental health and mental illness: out of the closet? *Social Service Review, 76*, 135–179.

National Council for Community Behavioral Health Care. (2003). *Celebrating forty years: community mental health centers at the 40-year mark: the quest for survival.* Rockville, MD: Author.

New Freedom Commission Mental Health. (2002). *Interim report of the President's New Freedom Commission on Mental Health.* Available from http://www.mentalhealthcommission.gov/reports/Interim_Report.htm

New Freedom Commission on Mental Health. (2003). *Achieving the promise: transforming mental health care in America. Final report* (DHHS Publication SMA-03-3832). Rockville, MD: Author. Available from http://www.mentalhealthcommission.gov

Nugent, W.R. & Halvorsen, H. (1995). Testing the effects of active listening. *Research on Social Work Practice, 5*, 152–175.

Office of Management and Budget. (2004). *Overview of the president's 2005 budget.* Washington, DC: The Executive Office of the President, Office of Management and Budget. Available from http://www.whitehouse.gov/omb/budget/fy2005/overview.html

Patterson, J., Peek, C.J., Heinrich, R., Bisehoff, R., & Scherger, J. (2002). *Mental health professionals in medical settings.* New York: Norton.

Randall, E.J. (2003a, July 16). Notes. WV Bureau of Behavioral Health, Behavioral Health Advisory Council Meeting.

Randall, E.J. (2003b, October 15). Notes. WV Bureau of Behavioral Health, Behavioral Health Advisory Council Meeting.

Randall, E.J. & Aldred-Crouch, M. (2004). Is Managed Care Affecting Your Practice? Unpublished manuscript.

Riefer, M. (2003). *Georgia's consumer-driven road to recovery.* Atlanta, GA: Georgia Department of Human Resources, Division of Mental Health, Developmental Disabilities, and Addictive Diseases, Office of Consumer Relations. Available from http://www.gacps.org/ConsumerManual.html

Scott, J. & Dixon, L.B. (1995). Assertive community treatment and case management for schizophrenia. *Schizophrenia Bulletin, 21*, 657–668.

State of West Virginia. (1986). Executive Budget, Fiscal Year 1987. Charleston, WV: Author.

State of West Virginia. (1987). Executive Budget, Fiscal Year 1988. Charleston, WV: Author.

State of West Virginia. (1988). Executive Budget, Fiscal Year 1989. Charleston, WV: Author.

State of West Virginia. (1989). Executive Budget, Fiscal Year 1990. Charleston, WV: Author.

State of West Virginia. (1990). Executive Budget, Fiscal Year 1991. Charleston, WV: Author.

State of West Virginia. (1991). Executive Budget, Fiscal Year 1992. Charleston, WV: Author.

State of West Virginia. (1992). Executive Budget, Fiscal Year 1993. Charleston, WV: Author.

State of West Virginia. (1993). Executive Budget, Fiscal Year 1994. Charleston, WV: Author.

State of West Virginia. (1994). Executive Budget, Fiscal Year 1995. Charleston, WV: Author.

State of West Virginia. (1995). Executive Budget, Fiscal Year 1996, Budget Detail. Charleston, WV: Author.

State of West Virginia. (1996). Executive Budget, Operating Detail, Fiscal Year 1997. Charleston, WV: Author.

State of West Virginia. (1997). Executive Budget, Operating Detail, Fiscal Year 1998. Charleston, WV: Author.

State of West Virginia. (1997). Executive Budget, Vol. II, Fiscal Year 1998. Charleston, WV: Author.

State of West Virginia. (1998). Executive Budget, Vol. II, Fiscal Year 1999. Charleston, WV: Author.

State of West Virginia. (1999). Executive Budget, Vol. II, Fiscal Year 2000. Charleston, WV: Author.

State of West Virginia. (2000). Executive Budget, Vol. II, Fiscal Year 2001. Charleston, WV: Author.

State of West Virginia. (2001). Executive Budget, Vol. II, Operating Detail, Fiscal Year 2002. Charleston, WV: Author.

State of West Virginia. (2002). Executive Budget, Vol. II, Operating Detail, Fiscal Year 2003. Charleston, WV: Author.

State of West Virginia. (2003). Executive Budget, Vol. II, Operating Detail, Fiscal Year 2004. Charleston, WV: Author.

Strosahl, K. (2004, November). *How to design and implement your primary care behavioral health service.* Slide presentation given at the 2004 Annual Clinical Regional Advisory Network Region III HealthCare Program, Linthicum Heights, MD.

Taylor, E. (2003). Presentation: October 2003 Interims, Legislative Oversight Commission on Health and Human Resources Accountability (Report). Charleston, WV: Department of Health and Human Resources, Bureau for Behavioral Health and Health Facilities.

Truax, C.B. & Mitchell, K.M. (1971). Research on certain therapist skills in relation to process and outcome. In A.E. Bergin & S.L. Garfield (Eds.*), Handbook of psychotherapy and behavior change* (pp. 299–344). New York: Wiley.

U.S. Department of Health and Human Services (USDHHS). (1999). *Mental health: a report of the surgeon general.* Rockville, MD: U.S. Department of Health and Human Services, Substance Abuse and Mental Health Services Administration, Center for Mental Health Services, National Institutes of Health, National Institute of Mental Health.

U.S. Department of Health and Human Services (USDHHS), Office of the Inspector General. (2000). *Mandatory managed care: changes in Medicaid mental health services* (OEI-04-97-00340). Washington, DC: Author.

Wells, R.A. (1994). *Planned short-term treatment* (2nd ed.). New York: The Free Press.

West Virginia Department of Health and Human Resources (WVDHHR). (2002). *Medicaid regulations*, Chapter 500, *Community focused treatment.* Charleston, WV: WVDHHR, Bureau for Medical Services.

20

MENTAL HEALTH LEADERSHIP IN A TURBULENT WORLD

W. PATRICK SULLIVAN

Much has changed in community mental health since the program was launched in 1963. Indeed, the past two decades have been particularly tumultuous. It is now widely accepted that the community is the preferred locus of care for even the most severely compromised individuals, and as a result, there has been a significant expansion in services geared to serve this population. By the 1990s the specter of managed behavioral health care sent shock waves through the system, and ready or not, providers were forced to learn a new lexicon, and firmly and explicitly merge the worlds of clinical care and finances like never before. New realities forced the acquisition of serviceable management information systems, reliable actuaries, and the skills needed to manage fiscal risk. Additionally, increased accountability demands and the recent rise of evidence-based practice have reshaped the service landscape and directly challenged some widely held beliefs and practices of mental health professionals.

All change is difficult, but in this case, where seemingly diverse goals of care and businesses collided, greater demands were — and continue to be — placed on those who hold significant leadership positions. No longer is a distinguished clinical career viewed as adequate preparation to lead in contemporary mental health. Yet, the reverse is also true: businesses acumen, minus the needed clinical sensitivities and sensibilities, can lead to equally ineffective stewardship (Culbertson, 2000; Eilenberg, Townsend, & Oudens, 2000; Feldman, 1981; Gabel, 1998). In essence, it has become increasingly clear that the modern leader in community mental health must possess a range of diverse skills in both the clinical and business world, or at a minimum, recruit a well-functioning team that can address the wide-ranging demands of key stakeholders.

This chapter will explore the issues and trends that have shaped the day-to-day life of community mental health practice with an eye toward how the ever-changing environment alters the task and responsibilities of leaders. To augment this analysis, the impressions of 12 veteran mental health leaders, all from the state of Indiana, will be drawn upon. Ten of the informants hold the position of executive director in a community mental health center (CMHC) — one serves as the vice president of behavioral services — with additional insights offered by the CEO of the Indiana Council of Community Mental Health Centers.

The directors, representing one-third of Indiana's CMHCs, serve in both rural and urban areas and represent a geographical cross section of the state. On average, the respondents have worked in the field of mental health for 29.5 years and have served in a leadership position for nearly 22 years. These statewide leaders were asked three basic open-ended questions: (1) How has your job changed over time? (2) What are some of the key challenges you face today? (3) What critical trends will shape the field in the future?

THE EVOLUTION OF COMMUNITY MENTAL HEALTH

Community mental health centers have struggled to gain a steady foothold in the landscape of American health care for over four decades. The dedicated work of individuals like Dr. Jack Ewalt and Dr. Robert Felix, along with key support from well-positioned legislators and philanthropists, culminated with the signing of the Mental Retardation Facilities and Community Mental Health Centers Construction Act of 1963. Two years later an important amendment to the original act, commonly referred to as staffing grants, provided the necessary mechanism needed to recruit professionals to serve in this new public utility (Foley & Sharfstein, 1983).

Clearly, the initiation of a national community mental health program required unwavering individuals adept at the political arts and a president who was fully committed to the plan. Yet, to survive to this day, community mental health has weathered an attempt by the Nixon administration to withdraw federal support, the Block Grant formula enacted by Ronald Reagan, and the challenging fiscal landscape ushered in by managed care and the rise of proprietary behavioral health care organizations.

Naturally, these same developments, viewed from a national perspective, had a dramatic impact on the community mental health system in Indiana. All states configure mental health services differently. Yet, the basic pressure to provide quality service to an expanding numbers of clients while simultaneously controlling costs is a universal challenge experienced across the nation.

A decade ago, Indiana's mental health system was under siege. A major state hospital had been closed amid scandal and controversy, and through great effort and compromise, key mental health officials and advocates had worked together to successfully pass reform legislation that laid the groundwork for a sweeping series of changes known as the Hoosier Assurance Plan (McGrew, 1999). The Hoosier Assurance Plan resulted in a series of key modifications in the system, all geared to create a public model of managed care. As managed care began to change the shape of behavioral health care across the land, many were concerned that a commitment to the most seriously mentally ill, and the provider network in place to serve them, would wither away. Accordingly, efforts were undertaken to mimic key features of managed care and ultimately prepare the universe of mental health and addictions providers to be well positioned to survive if and when full-scale managed care reached the state. Key activities included the introduction of common assessments for purposes of enrollment, the creation of enrollment rates and concurrently the implementation of a form of risk-based contracting, the elimination of catchment areas leading to managed competition, formal gatekeeping and bed allocation to control state psychiatric hospital use, and the designation of clear priority populations for state funding, including the seriously mentally ill, severely emotional disturbed children, the chronically addicted, and persons in crisis. Alteration in fiscal policy also had a dramatic impact on community mental health services. The initiation of the Medicaid rehabilitation option alone, by creating a funding mechanism for case management, influenced hiring practices and the inventory of programs offered to consumers in a predictable manner, with outreach services quickly supplanting traditional therapy for the most disabled.

The specifics of the Indiana experience are less important than an appreciation that these changes, in part or parcel, mirrored the revolution in public mental health experienced elsewhere. In synch with the movement toward new public management, introduced in part by David Osborne and Ted Gaebler in *Reinventing Government* (1992), and consistent with increased concerns about rising health care spending, human services at all levels faced greater scrutiny while state policy makers scrambled to adopt insurance and market-based models to fulfill their responsibilities (Buck, 2003; Durst & Newell, 2001; Eikenberry & Kulver, 2004; Ryan, 1999). The new world of managed care, even if simply a threat over the horizon, forced everyone in the mental health and addiction world to change the way business was conducted.

THE EVOLVING CHALLENGE OF LEADERSHIP IN COMMUNITY MENTAL HEALTH

In spite of the excitement that surrounded the initiation of community mental health, aside from general agreement on a set of key required services, many programs began as a blank sheet of paper. In time it became clear that most everything about community mental health would remain fluid, and consistent with the job description, leaders are often asked to create order in the midst of chaos. Reflecting on his first days as an executive director of a CMHC in Chicago, Norman J. Groetzinger said:

> I was the executive director, I was also the chief financial officer; I did all the financial work. I didn't have a bookkeeper, let alone a controller. I was the human resource manager, and I was the development officer. Because of the size I was even the backup receptionist, and I was the guy who, when there was a broken lock, I fixed the lock! (Gumz, 2004, p. 364)

Groetzinger's experience matches that of Don Aronoff, who has spent 28 years as a mental health director, serving in that capacity in rural Indiana:

> When I started in 1976, my role as center director was to provide organization and structure to the center. Community mental health services were not well organized at that time, and I remember spending a great deal of time trying to create some structure and logic to our systems. We also spent a lot of energy trying to educate staff about the necessity of goal-oriented treatment through structured treatment plans. We were still working with staff who had been educated in the 1950s and 1960s who thought that treatment consisted of assessment and diagnosis. They were good at identifying problems but often didn't know how to treat them.

In a similar vein, Bob Dunbar, who has spent 30 years as a mental health leader and currently leads a CMHC in greater Indianapolis, agrees that in his early years, the bulk of his efforts focused on developing a working infrastructure for the delivery of services:

> When I first became a CEO of a community mental health center, the center was in the early stages of development, had very few administrative staff, hired mostly licensed degreed professionals, and was deficit financed. I devoted a considerable amount of time drafting policies for board review and approval, expanding and developing clinical services funded exclusively by the Division of Mental Health,

hiring staff, and promoting the CMHC within our exclusive catchment area. My time was primarily spent on internal operations and community relations.

In today's competitive environment it would be easy for the modern mental health administrator to reflect on the past with fondness, yet as Thomas Kane (1993) noted some years ago, "reality forces me to acknowledge that 'the good old days' weren't always that good" (p. 101). A part of the frustration involved simply trying to discern how services could be improved in the face of mounting pressures to be accountable. Ann Borders, who has spent 28 years in a leadership position in mental health, 11 as the CEO of a CMHC, remembers the 1970s well:

> In the 1970s, it often seemed as if we operated by the seat of our pants. We did not have the benefit of readily available scientific research; there were no "tool kits" that allowed for easy implementation of evidence-based practices. Few medications were effective and we were frustrated — and sometimes devastated — by the resulting human toll. It was the job of organizational leaders to set expectations for service delivery. There were no outcome measures, so we couldn't demonstrate the effectiveness of one approach over another.... "Try another way" was the mantra.

As community mental health matured, demand increased for services from a variety of fronts. On one hand, mental health services were often criticized for not addressing the needs of the most seriously ill, a population that once was almost exclusively served in state psychiatric hospitals. Yet, as the stigma of mental health issues began to subside, the press for services from people with a wide range of challenges continued to test the ability of CMHCs to respond. By the late 1970s and early 1980s, specialized services for those with serious mental illnesses began to proliferate, and as the sheer size of organizations began to grow, they became, by definition, more complex. Leaders in such organizations could no longer afford to be a Jack or Jill of all trades, but instead had to marshal the forces of a wide range of actors to get the job done. Bob Krumweid leads a CMHC in the shadow of Chicago and notes that in comparison to 15 years ago, he "feels more like a conductor of an orchestra today, where I used to feel like the front man of a four-member band."

Leaders in CMHCs, particularly those who still had a foot in clinical care and with a natural penchant for being hands-on, suddenly had to utilize a new set of skills to be successful. Planning, policy making, and oversight became key features of the job description, and issues of productivity and accountability also came to the fore (Gumz, 2004). Don Aronoff remembers that "it took a good number of years to help staff understand that it was not sufficient to do good, but the amount of good we did, and the amount of time we spent on clients was a necessary expectation of our efforts." In addition, more and more external regulations in the form or accreditation standards, rules, and responsibilities to third-party billing agents added additional layers of responsibility to the job description of key administrators. Where Ann Borders lamented the lack of precision in clinical care in past years, the issues she faces today are equally daunting:

> The challenge today is to somehow manage to deliver good care while maneuvering through a seemingly impenetrable maze of external laws, regulations, and requirements governing behavioral health care. Today, the job of the behavioral health leader is twofold. First, they must devote a significant amount of their time to organizational risk management, ensuring that accreditation, fraud and abuse, antitrust, local/state/federal contracts, human resources, HIPPA, and other state and federal laws and requirements are met. Second, leaders must somehow create

a culture that puts principles, purpose, and guiding beliefs of the organization first. When the legal-regulatory axe is at the neck, it is very easy for an organization to develop a culture where rules become the end.

Terry Stawar, at six years on the job as a CEO in southern Indiana, is a relative new-comer among his peers, yet two decades in the field have provided him with an opportunity to see how the field of mental health administration has evolved, noting that "the emphasis has changed from clinical leadership and entrepreneurial activity."

The job a mental health leader faces in today's world has been shaped by a range of forces largely outside of his or her control (Culbertson, 2000; Gabel, 1998; Ryan, 1999). Language can be deceivingly simple; thus, words like *efficiency*, *accountability*, and *effectiveness* evoke positive responses. In terms of mental health practice, citizens rightfully demand improvements in these keystone areas, particularly in a public or quasi-public system. However, signaled strongly by the managed care movement and the rise of proprietary behavioral health care, the language of the market, a focus on entrepreneurship, and a more explicit concern with the bottom line caused some to ponder if the mission of community mental health is in jeopardy (Eikenberry & Kulver, 2004).

Ryan (1999) suggests that when for-profit enterprises began to enter into the world of social services, and governmental authorities demonstrated a willingness to partner with them, the viability and survivability of the traditional provider network was immediately threatened. Certainly, any organization threatened with survival must take action, but as Ryan (1999) notes, "the danger is that in their struggle to become more viable competitors in the short term, nonprofit organizations will be forced to compromise the very assets that made them so vital to society in the first place" (p. 128). Eikenberry and Kulver (2004) argue that nonprofit organizations make a viable contribution to society by serving as value guardians, providing service and advocacy, and helping to build social capital, all notions that could be deemed superfluous in an arena where the market alone reigns supreme.

Kane (1993) lamented some of these changes in community mental health over a decade ago — signified in part by the abandonment of the public health model, a guiding principle embraced by those who framed this new approach to care, and by focusing the lion's share of attention on those with serious mental illnesses. The headache for administrators, according to Kane (1993), is that the public still expects the CMHC to deliver a public health model marked by easy accessibility and services for the entire population. In the end, the public may "vent their frustration toward community mental health administrators who say, 'We just can't do it'" (Kane, 1993, p. 102). In some respects, vigilant leaders should anticipate this kind of pressure and dissonance as they work to move their organizations into the unfamiliar territory guided by values and goals of business and the free market. This is particularly so when the changes faced are measured against professional norms and values held by self, and those whom administrators are entrusted to lead (Gabel, 1998; Perlmutter, Netting, & Bailey, 2001).

Today, leaders must somehow take the pragmatic steps necessary for survival without compromising the central values that have traditionally defined community mental health. Central to this task is the ability to articulate and enact a viable vision of the future. But more is also needed, for as Gabel (1998, p. 5) offers:

> Risk taking, aggressively seeking opportunities, nurturing members and maintaining a task orientation are all involved in leadership. Effective leaders accurately perceive the reality of their organizations and the place of their organization in larger contexts; they are active, energetic, oriented to action, eager to set and achieve goals, able to set priorities and to serve as an example to others.

History shows that community mental health services are in a constant state of flux and peril. In the next section some of the current issues and opportunities that lie ahead will be explored.

MENTAL HEALTH LEADERSHIP: THE NEXT GENERATION OF PROMISES AND PITFALLS

Managed care, or at least associated methods of this model, along with a robust economy helped curb health care spending in the early 1990s, albeit in the face of continual criticisms from both consumers and providers. While managed care extensively penetrated the world of general health care, the impress of this model in behavioral health care, while significant, was more tempered. The unpredictability in the course and treatment of mental illnesses and addictions adds to the pool of risk a vendor must accept when considering including behavioral health care in the scope of a contract. In fact, we have seen a decline in Medicaid managed care plans especially for disabled populations (Landon, Schneider, Tobias, & Epstein, 2004).

Nonetheless, Medicaid and general health care spending is again on the rise, with much of the growth in the Medicaid rolls comprised of those with disabilities (Boyd, 2003; Reinhardt, Hussey, & Anderson; 2004; Vladeck, 2003). It is easy to predict that there will be mounting pressure to curb this growth and further attempts to bring the world of primary health care and behavioral health care into alignment.

These trends create real dilemmas for mental health organizations that rely heavily on Medicaid revenues, and many have essentially built their infrastructure based on this funding stream. With this strategy comes risk, for by setting aside considerable portions of the budget to provide for the matching funds necessary to leverage Medicaid dollars, the system, at the state or provider level, becomes less flexible (Frank, Goldman, & Hogan, 2003). This, plus the impetus for state officials to target funds to the most disabled, allows few degrees of freedom to serve those who have less serious but vexing problems, including many of the working poor. Jim Jones has spent 40 years in Indiana's mental health system and now heads the trade organization that advocates on behalf of CMHCs. To his dismay, he feels that providers are now forced to "choose to focus their mission away from being a comprehensive safety net for all and either provide less service to all, or exclude some in favor of not compromising quality." Buck (2003) suggests that emphasizing the insurance model "means that providers have considerably less discretion about the amount and nature of services and who may receive them. Instead, services are determined by the benefit coverage, network policies and utilization management practices of the health plan, primarily Medicaid" (p. 972).

Within this context several tasks confront today's mental health leader. In order to survive, the organization must now capture and consolidate diverse funding streams. Increasingly, it is now Medicaid, not the state mental health authority, who is the most important player driving care at the community level. Second, in order to continue to offer uncompensated care, providers must attract a diverse clientele either through offering special boutique services (often in locations with a different name) or capturing outside contracts with other branches of government and business and industry. All of this results in complicated regulations, differing but important accountability requirements, and an increased reliance on management information data that can report on activities, costs, revenues, and outcomes. Galen Goode, who oversees an expansive set of community mental health services from his Terre Haute office, observes that:

Thirty-five years ago all of the funding was state dollars, so in many ways the system was easier to influence and less complicated. Today our revenue streams are multiple and we have to balance programs that make a profit with those where we donate services so as to cover total expenses and have enough money for program expansion. With multiple payer sources come multiple expectations and audits.

"Our industry is going through revolutionary change," says Larry Burch, who is heading towards his silver anniversary as a mental health director. "An organization must be able to make market adjustments without compromising its mission. Likewise, setting the moral/ethical climate for the organization is most critical. The emphasis on corporate compliance and corporate integrity is a part of the brave new world."

Most mental health administrators will begin and end a discussion on current struggles with a conversation about funding. Indiana's leaders are no different. Charles Clark, who has served as the director of business operations in community mental health, acknowledges that providers are simply forced to do more with less — "less staff, less money, and less resources with a patient population that is very dependent upon our services. A major challenge I am facing is how to redesign services to be more cost-effective and still be staff and consumer friendly." Paul Wilson, who heads the local CMHC in Fort Wayne, has worked with his staff to be more effective and efficient, but in spite of "increasing productivity 20% each of the last few years, the direct service revenues are barely enough to offset state decreases." Terry Stawar also recognizes that competition now comes from new sources as "managed care has squeezed the market to make Medicaid and Medicare reimbursement and state service contracts more attractive to entities that previously went after private insurance and self-pay."

In a nutshell, mental health leadership has become an increasingly complex job that requires fiscal savvy, skills in the political arts, and the ability to perform public relations functions and continue to gain and hold the confidence of staff and key stakeholders. In many ways these leaders are vital to the ultimate ability of community-based services to survive and thrive. To ensure success, what must these leaders do?

One of the great strengths of proprietary managed care companies is the power of their management information systems — community mental health was forced to play a game of catch-up. Larry Burch believes that "any health care organization that is going to survive in the future must make a commitment to electronic technology. This must take place on the clinical as well as business side of the organization." In some instances the nonprofit world has caught up with its peers in the proprietary world, but now the avalanche of data requires a sifting process to reveal what is useful and meaningful. Ann Borders admits that:

> We now have outcome data of every stripe. We have the capacity to quickly mine the knowledge of colleagues across the country, and even internationally. Yet, we are also bombarded with data, e-mails, websites, and research updates to the extent that leaders are challenged to help staff manage the information overload.

One of the goals of capturing outcome data is to offer services that work, and ideally work with the least expenditure of time and money. Some foresee a day where reimbursement will be directed only to interventions that are unquestionably deemed to be efficacious, but even short of this dramatic step, key stakeholders are increasingly requiring reassurance that their investment makes a difference. Bob Williams, who has spent a quarter century in the field of mental health and a dozen years at the helm of a CMHC based in Columbus,

IN, feels that this trend will not abate, noting that "accountability has moved from being an abstraction to a daily imperative."

Therefore, among a vocal subset of Indiana leaders, there is strong sentiment that providers must adopt evidence-based treatments to keep pace with the demands of funders. It is also acknowledged that there are times when the use of evidence-based practice runs counter to the desires of consumers, requiring, according to Larry Burch, "providers to walk a fine line, at least in the distant future." On this front, however, the future looks bright, particularly in light of improved medications and continued scientific breakthroughs that point to the relationship between the brain and behavior. "I believe we are on the verge of a major paradigm shift," says Bob Williams. "With the implementation of assertive community treatment, dialectical behavior therapy, strengths-based case management, affirmative employment, and other proven interventions, there is less need for inpatient services, supervised residential services, and even day treatment programs."

In the attempt to diversify funding streams, create opportunities, and reduce costs by merging various administrative functions, mental health providers have formed partnerships or network alliances among themselves, and often with a new set of community partners. Managed competition has reportedly reduced former levels of cooperation among some providers, who now fight for turf and clients, and even community relations have taken a different turn. According to Galen Goode:

> At the local level each of our service locations now have multiple community partners. In my early years we had informal partners that operated on verbal agreements and we worked through problems using our relationship as the basis for common involvement. Today our relationships are much more formal, at times competitive, and in many cases void of relationship building. People are more guarded in what they share, look out for what is best for themselves rather than consumers, and are not supportive of one another outside of the formal relationship.

Paul Wilson feels that the trick is to sort those opportunities that can be self-supporting from those that will simply sap the organization's time and resources. Nonetheless, he views these relationships as essential to a stated goal "to make Fort Wayne the best place in America to have a mental illness." The level of community involvement discussed here seems consistent with the early impulse of community mental health, yet these activities, which consume a considerable portion of a leader's time, are now caste in a new contextual framework, revealed in Bob Dunbar's comment that he spends "much more time developing and nurturing a number of strategic alliances formed as a result of public managed care and increased competition."

Forces outside the walls of an organization always reverberate internally, and an obvious task of a leader is to shape and nurture organizational culture and help deflect activities in the general direction of the guiding mission. Larry Ulrich came to the human services to make a difference, serving first as a pharmacist on a reservation in northern Minnesota. He senses a change in the modern workforce, where more employees "view the job as a means to an end. They do not seem as motivated to solve the world's problems as in the past." According to Bob Williams, his workforce needs to feel as if they are engaged in meaningful work, and "if they are provided with the latest training and the best in supervision, they will probably continue to work for us. With reduced turnover and happier staff come better revenues and a growing business." Then again, recruiting the right staff with the right skills is routinely viewed as an ongoing challenge among this sample of leaders.

LEADERSHIP THEORY AND THE CHALLENGE OF TOMORROW

While it is customary to underscore the differences between human service organizations and the world of business, in terms of form and function we appear to be in an era of convergence. Business and industry learned that in the modern world, an autocratic style of leadership that was devoid of an understanding of the needs and desires of employees was doomed to fail. For help, many turned to the social sciences. In the 21st century it has become equally clear that human service agencies in all shapes and colors can no longer afford to ignore the bottom line. The socialization of mental health professionals underscores the ethic of care — and many in the field feel a deep obligation to do everything possible for the betterment of consumers. Enrollment rates, utilization reviews, and notions of maximum feasible benefit are not terms that such professionals routinely use. It is as if a stranger has crept into one's house and rearranged the furniture: everything is in place, but it is clear that something has changed.

Regardless of the frustrations and protestations of professional staff, no one benefits if human service organizations fail to survive. Mental health leaders are left with the task of melding seemingly conflicting paradigms together in a meaningful way, and to do so, curiously enough, they rely on the same leadership trends that are extant in business and industry. These leaders must endeavor to couple all the agencies' activities around a firmly embraced mission, offer an exciting vision for the future, and nurture a culture that is customer-friendly. Ann Borders notes:

> Today's behavioral health leader must develop an organization that maintains its focus on the mission, vision, and values of the organization while continuously "moving to the next level" in terms of implementing clinical and business best practices. The leadership challenge is to develop the passion, the energy, and the creativity necessary to unleash the potential of the people who will be moving the organization forward. Since the demands of the current behavioral health environment constantly pull in the opposite direction, leaders are challenged to help create time for staff to think "big picture," to stimulate creative discussions within the organization, and to cultivate the passion necessary to serve our communities well.

For those preparing to enter community mental health practice, the range of behaviors and responsibilities faced by leaders can appear to be overwhelming — and at times they are. After sharing the various aspects of his job, Galen Goode was forced to comment that "now that I think about it, no wonder we are all tired at the end of the day and fall asleep when the game is half over." What was true yesterday, however, is equally true today. Good leadership begins with a bedrock commitment to what you are doing and the people you serve, and leaders must secure that same level of commitment from others. When considering the nature of the leadership challenge he faces today, Bob Williams offered this insightful comment:

> Let me start with how my job has not changed: I still need the same basic tool kit I needed 20 years ago: enthusiasm for our line of work, enthusiasm for learning new things, an appreciation for the superiority of decisions made by an interactive team with good data, negotiation skills based on a "win-win" or "no deal" philosophy, an innate optimism about the future, an entrepreneurial spirit, and persistence in creating a shared vision.

SUMMARY

There was a time when many mental health leaders moved to the front office after distinguished clinical careers. Their years of practice helped them offer support and guidance to a new generation of practitioners who struggled with the emotions and challenges that are endemic to direct practice. Serving as master supervisors, these leaders helped the organization remain focused on a basic mission to help those in their communities who faced distressing conditions. There were few real competitors, as mental health practice was rarely seen as a lucrative enterprise. While policy shifts always kept leaders on edge, there were only a handful of funding streams to consider, and clinical discretion was rarely challenged by third parties.

The world has dramatically altered. The pace of change in all aspects of life is dizzying, and the world of behavioral health care has been turned on its head in the past two decades. Today's leader in community mental health must still lead with vision, but the world of law, finance, policy, electronic technology, and pure business is no longer foreign territory, but part and parcel of daily life. Preparation for executive positions has become equally complicated as well given the multiple roles leaders must now play. Wise leaders also fill those gaps in the existing talent pool in areas where the organization is most vulnerable and harness the energies of these diverse individuals to pull in one direction. While the success or failure of an individual leader may rest with his or her ability to meet these challenges, much more is at stake. Indeed, effective leadership may well hold the key to the ultimate survival of community mental health.

REFERENCES

Boyd, D. (2003). The bursting state fiscal bubble and state Medicaid budgets. *Health Affairs, 22,* 46–59.

Buck, J. (2003). Medicaid, health care financing trends, and the future of state-based public mental health services. *Psychiatric Services, 54,* 969–975.

Culbertson, R. (2000). The changing face of the leader. *Administration and Policy in Mental Health, 27,* 269–286.

Durst, S. & Newell, C. (2001). The who, why, and how of reinvention in nonprofit organizations. *Nonprofit Management and Leadership, 11,* 443–457.

Eikenberry, A. & Kulver, J. (2004). The marketization of the nonprofit center: civil society at risk? *Public Administration Review, 64,* 132–140.

Eilenberg, J., Townsend, E., & Oudens, E. (2000). Who's in charge anyway? Managing the management split in mental health organizations. *Administration and Policy in Mental Health, 27,* 287–297.

Feldman, S. (1981). Leadership in mental health: changing of the guard for the 1980's. *The American Journal of Psychiatry, 138,* 1147–1153.

Foley, H. & Sharfstein, S. (1983). *Madness and government.* Washington, DC: American Psychiatric Press.

Frank, R., Goldman, H., & Hogan, M. (2003). Medicaid and mental health: be careful what you ask for. *Health Affairs, 22,* 101–113.

Gabel, S. (1998). Leadership in the managed care era: challenges, conflict, ambivalence. *Administration and Policy in Mental Health, 26,* 3–19.

Gumz, E. (2004). An administrator's perspective of trends in community mental health: an interview with Norman J. Groetzinger. *Families in Society, 85,* 363–370.

Kane, T. (1993). Reflections on the community mental health movement: implications for the administrator. *Administration and Policy in Mental Health, 21,* 101–105.

Landon, B., Schneider, E., Tobias, C., & Epstein, A. (2004). The evolution of quality management in Medicaid managed care. *Health Affairs, 23,* 245–254.

McGrew, J. (Ed.). (1999). Multiple perspectives on the closing of a state hospital. *The Journal of Behavioral Health Services and Research, 26.*

Osborne, D. & Gaebler, T. (1992). *Reinventing government.* Reading, MA: Addison-Wesley.

Perlmutter, F., Netting, E., & Bailey, D. (2001). Managerial tensions: personal insecurity vs. professional responsibility. *Administration and Social Work, 25,* 1–15.

Reinhardt, U., Hussey, P., & Anderson, G. (2004). U.S. health spending in an international context. *Health Affairs, 23,* 10–25.

Ryan, W. (1999, January/February). The new landscape for nonprofits. *Harvard Business Review,* pp. 127–136.

Vladeck, B. (2003). Where the action really is: Medicaid and the disabled. *Health Affairs, 22,* 90–100.

SUGGESTED READINGS

Bargal, D. & Schmid, H. (1989). Recent themes in theory and research on leadership and their implications for management of the human services. *Administration in Social Work, 13,* 37–54.

Buck, J. (2003). Medicaid, health care financing trends, and the future of state-based public mental health services. *Psychiatric Services, 54,* 969–975.

Collins, J. (2001). *Good to great.* New York: Harper Collins.

Collins, J. & Porras, J. (2002). *Built to last.* New York: HarperBusiness Essentials.

Foley, H. & Sharfstein, S. (1983). *Madness and government.* Washington, DC: American Psychiatric Press.

Gardner, J. (1990). *On leadership.* New York: The Free Press.

Hasenfeld, Y. (Ed.). (1992). *Human services as complex organizations.* Newbury Park, CA: Sage Publications.

Joint Commission on Mental Illness and Health. (1961). *Action for mental health.* New York: Basic Books.

Mechanic, D. (1999). *Mental health and social policy.* Boston: Allyn and Bacon.

Peters, T. (1982). *In search of excellence.* New York: Harper & Row.

Rapp, C. & Poertner, J. (1992). *Social administration: a client centered approach.* White Plains, NY: Longman.

GLOSSARY

Advocacy groups — Groups dedicated to addressing social problems and advocating for change.

Antidepressant — Medication designed to address and treat depressive symptoms.

Antipsychotic — Medication designed to stabilize and reduce psychotic symptoms.

Assertive community treatment — Interdisciplinary teams that manage consumers outside in the community and provide a wide variety of psychiatric and psychosocial support.

Asylum — An institution for the care of the seriously mentally ill. Many persons with severe mental illness lived the majority of their lives in asylums in the years preceding deinstitutionalization. Such persons often received minimal treatment.

Biopsychosocial — A framework to assess and support functioning that addresses needs and resources at a biological, psychological, and social level.

Bipolar disorder — Major mental illness characterized by a disturbance in mood. Symptoms can include mania and psychotic depression.

Capitation — A method for asserting financial control for health care services. A capitation strategy asks the organization to provide a specified service package to a target population and pays a prearranged fee for each member of the population regardless of whether or not they use the services.

Case management — Treatment programs that utilize outreach services and may include working with clients in their homes or on the streets. Services typically provided include housing assistance, financial entitlements, linkages with general health care and social services providers, and transportation to community services or meetings.

Clinical case management — Case management that includes counseling and psychodynamic therapy. Services provided by a case manager who is trained as a therapist.

Clinician bias — Personal opinions and attitudes held by clinicians that interfere with being able to refrain from judgments. Nonscientific and subjective perceptions about a client.

Coercive — To be forced to do something against one's will. Persons with serious mental illness who are hospitalized involuntarily are coerced.

Cognitive-behavioral training — A treatment approach wherein cognitive techniques to modify problematic behaviors.

Community aftercare — Community treatment provided to persons with serious mental illness postdischarge from an inpatient unit.

Community-based services — Services provided in the community and designed to support successful adaptation to community life.

Community housing — Residences in the community that provide a variety of living arrangements and services for the seriously mentally ill; can include supported living, community residences, group homes, and independent living apartments.

Community Mental Health Act of 1963 — Legislation that provided for funding for the development of community-based mental health care programs. The act called for a shift from an institution-based public mental health system to a community-based system and ushered in the period of deinstitutionalization.

Community mental health centers — Entities that address mental health needs that are located in neighborhoods and counties and provide services to the local population.

Consumer-operated services — Therapeutic or social services run by consumers.

Consumers — Persons who both utilize and often participate in treatment provision for the seriously mentally ill. The term *consumers* represents a philosophical shift from a traditional medical model, which views the mentally ill as patients, to a perspective based on principles of empowerment and treatment collaboration.

Continuous treatment teams — Often considered a variation of ACT teams, the use of a multidisciplinary team approach to serving the seriously mentally ill, and is generally used to treat the client in his or her community.

Co-occurring mental and substance disorders — Consumers who are dually diagnosed with mental illness and substance abuse. Such persons are often referred to as mentally ill chemical abusers (MICA).

Culturally competent — An approach wherein an understanding of the client's background (cultural, gender, sexual orientation, etc.) informs the therapeutic relationship and treatment.

Deinstitutionalization — The large-scale discharge of persons with severe mental illness to the community, and emphasizing the use of the least restrictive treatment settings and rehabilitation programs in the community. Deinstitutionalization has often been criticized as falling short of its promise to provide adequate community services.

DSM-IV-TR — *The Diagnostic and Statistical Manual.* The standard classification of psychiatric disorders.

Empowerment — A key concept of the recovery model, empowerment emphasizes the consumer's self-determination in treatment and lifestyle choices.

Environmental barriers — Barriers in the environment, such as lack of adequate housing, that impede successful community adaptation.

Eurocentric — A perspective that interprets reality and history solely from the experience of European civilization.

Evidence-based practice — Treatment that is based on research that demonstrates its efficacy.

Fee for service — A system of payment for services based on individual visits.

Fountain House — A clubhouse in New York City for persons with serious mental illness, Fountain House is one of the earliest programs dedicated to the recovery of men and women with mental illness by providing opportunities for its members to live, work, and learn, while contributing their talents through a community of mutual support.

Gender stereotyping — Myths and stereotypes based on gender.

Illness-based management — Treatment based on the premise that persons with serious mental illness are "sick."

Intensive case management (ICM) — A case management approach that typically has a low caseload ratio of 10:1 or 15:1. It has many of the same admission criteria and goals as ACT, but is less clearly defined and often operationalized differently across programs. It typically does not use a shared-client team approach.

Internalized oppression — The process of adopting negative attitudes perpetuated in the dominant culture. For example, persons of color who adopt racist stereotypes and internalize oppressive attitudes.

Labeling — Assigning characteristics to persons based on stereotypes and without taking into account individual variation.

Major depression — Mental illness characterized by severe depressive episodes.

Managed care — Refers to a variety of techniques packaged as unique strategies aimed at marshaling appropriate clinical and financial resources to ensure needed care.

Measures of fidelity — Methodologies that replicate an original research design.

Medical necessity — Access to treatment is based on medical considerations and restricted. Often the condition has to be deemed sufficiently serious for treatment to be provided, and generally excludes emotional and psychological factors.

Mood stabilizers — Medication designed to address mood disorders, such as bipolar disorder.

Motivational interviewing — Interventions such as motivational interviewing are intended to assist clients in understanding the impacts of their illness and drugs and alcohol on their lives. Techniques are utilized to help the client identify discrepancies between current behaviors and future goals, and to develop strategies to begin to achieve them.

National Alliance for the Mentally Ill (NAMI) — Founded in 1979, NAMI is a nonprofit, grassroots, self-help, support and advocacy organization of consumers, families, and friends of people with severe mental illnesses.

National Committee on Mental Hygiene — Founded in 1909 by Clifford Beers, the National Committee for Mental Hygiene, the precursor to today's National Mental Health Association, was dedicated to improving mental health care and combating stigma. Often called the founder of the modern mental health movement, Clifford Beers himself struggled with major mental illness and subsequently devoted his life's work to advocacy on behalf of persons with mental illness.

Neuropsychiatric — A medical framework that incorporates both neurology and psychiatry.

Neurotransmitters — A substance in the brain that transmits nerve impulses across a synapse.

Not-for-profit organizations — Although the distinction between private and not for profit (voluntary agencies) is increasingly blurred, traditionally not-for-profit agencies do not seek to make a profit and are supported by public funding.

Organizational networks — Social structures that allow organizations to interact, exchange information, and work together on joint projects and plan regional service.

Outcomes evaluation — An increasingly popular focus on evaluating efficacy of treatment approaches through systematic review of outcomes.

Partnership model — Sometimes used to describe peer or group support in which people with a common concern voluntarily come together to help one another.

Peer case management services — The practice of peers (or consumers) who function as case management providers for persons with serious mental illness.

Peer support — An increasingly popular treatment model, the use of peers to provide therapeutic and social support.

Pharmacotherapy — Treatment of mental illness using medication.

Psychosocial rehabilitation — A recovery model based on stages of consumer development toward independent living and productive social functioning.

Psychotic disorders — Mental illness characterized by psychosis, including schizophrenia and bipolar illness.

Recidivism — A tendency to relapse, to return to a previous condition of illness.

Recovery — A treatment philosophy based on wellness and recovery as opposed to support groups, groups wherein persons with a common condition or problem come together for support. Often such groups may be self-help maintenance and psychiatric stability.

Schizoaffective disorder — Major mental illness characterized by both a disturbance in thinking and a disturbance in mood. Often one of the most severe forms of mental illness.

Schizophrenia — A major mental illness characterized by severe thought disorders, including delusions and psychosis.

Scientific racism — Epidemiological studies that reflect and perpetuate racism. For example, studies that served to provide a rationale and justification for slavery and discrimination against blacks after emancipation.

Self-determination — A central concept of the recovery model, self-determination emphasizes the consumer's ability and right to fully participate in treatment planning.

Self-stigma — The process of internalizing negative social stereotypes. For example, gays and lesbians identifying with homophobic attitudes.

Sheltered workshops — A vocational rehabilitation where persons with serious mental illness were trained to perform simple functions, such as mailroom and stock.

Social integration — To integrate oneself into the community and into social groupings.

Staff downsizing — A pattern of reducing employment in agencies. Often a response to funding restrictions.

Stigma — The assignment of negative characteristics to individuals based on nonobjective and unscientific criteria.

Supported employment — A component of the psychosocial rehabilitation model, an intervention designed to assist consumers in successfully navigating the world of work.

Symptomatically — Presenting with the characteristics (symptoms) of an illness.

Synapses — The point at which a nervous impulse passes from neuron to neuron.

Telepsychiatry — The practice of utilizing secure computer and video linkages to enable interviews and treatment between clients and psychiatrists who are geographically separate.

Total institution — These facilities "warehoused" persons with serious mental illness, divorcing them from contact with the "outside" world and providing for all their daily needs.

Transinstitutionalization — The process of going from one institution to another. For example, a psychiatric inpatient who is transferred to a prison.

Voluntary — To engage in willingly and by choice.

WANA (We Are Not Alone) — In the 1940s, a group of former mental health patients formed WANA. Their goal was to help others make the transition from inpatient hospitalization to community living. These efforts led to the establishment of Fountain House.

Wellness-based management — Part of the recovery philosophy, emphasizing the consumer's strengths and potential for wellness.

CONTRIBUTORS

Gregory Acevedo, Ph.D., attained his Ph.D. in social work from Bryn Mawr College. Previously, he worked in various mental health settings, and children and family agencies in Philadelphia, Pennsylvania, including the Philadelphia Child Guidance Center. He is currently an assistant professor of social work in the Fordham University Graduate School of Social Service. Dr. Acevedo has held previous positions as an assistant professor of social work at the Temple University School of Social Administration and in Puerto Rican/Latino Studies at the University of Connecticut School of Social Work.

Mary Aldred-Crouch, MSW, is a recent graduate of the West Virginia University Division of Social Work, currently holding the position of behavioral health professional in a rural primary health care center in which behavioral health services are provided using an integrated practice model. She also has training in speech pathology, as well as considerable experience as a research assistant in a variety of academic settings. Ms. Aldred-Crouch has particular interest in the clinical management of chronic pain, behavioral health integration, and brief therapy.

Debra Anderson, Ph.D., is an assistant professor of social work at the University of Nebraska at Omaha, where she teaches courses on social policy, program planning, and supervision and personnel administration. She holds a Ph.D. in public administration from the University of Nebraska at Omaha, and her areas of research include organizational theory, organizational change, and psychoanalysis. She maintains a consulting practice dedicated to developing change strategies with private, public, and not-for-profit organizations. Examples of her work can be found in the *American Review of Public Administration*, *Journal of Teaching in Social Work*, and *Journal of Social Work Education*.

David E. Biegel, Ph.D., is the Henry Zucker Professor of Social Work Practice and professor of psychiatry and sociology at the Mandel School of Applied Social Sciences, Case Western Reserve University. Currently, he serves as co-director of the Mandel School's Center on Substance Abuse and Mental Illness. Dr. Biegel's recent research activities have focused on family caregiving, support systems for persons with severe and persistent mental illness and substance abuse, and mental health and aging. He is the author of 11 books and over 80 journal articles and book chapters about aging, caregiving, mental health, self-help, and social networks and social support.

Joel Blau, DSW, is professor of social policy and director of the Ph.D. program at the School of Social Welfare, Stony Brook University. He is the author of many articles and three books on social policy: *The Visible Poor: Homelessness in the United States*, which won a Choice Award as one of the outstanding sociology books of 1992; *Illusions of Prosperity: America's Working Families in an Age of Economic Insecurity*; and with Mimi Abramovitz, a new social welfare policy text, *The Dynamics of Social Welfare Policy* (2004).

Eric J. Bruns, Ph.D., is assistant professor in the Department of Psychiatry, University of Washington School of Medicine. Dr. Bruns's major research focus has been developing, evaluating, and disseminating processes for delivering community-based services and supports for children with intensive needs and their families. Currently he is engaged in research on the "wraparound process," an approach to planning and implementing care for these families. In addition, Dr. Bruns also conducts research on school-based mental health services, theory-based evaluation of comprehensive community-based initiatives, and neighborhood effects research using data derived from administrative data sets.

James W. Callicutt, Ph.D., is professor of social work at the University of Texas at Arlington. After receiving his MSSW degree, he worked in mental health settings in Tennessee and Massachusetts. Following his doctoral studies at Brandeis University, he began his long association with the University of Texas at Arlington, where he has served as associate dean, interim dean, and professor. As a consultant for community mental health centers in Maine and Texas, he obtained federal funds for mental health and substance abuse services. His numerous publications, including *Mental Health Policy and Practice Today* [coauthored with Ted Watkins], reflect his commitment to mental health studies.

Alma J. Carten, Ph.D., is an associate professor of social work at New York University. She has held a number of faculty appointments, including director and chair of a CSWE-accredited undergraduate social work program, adjunct professor for the Hunter College School of Social Work, teaching in the school's distance learning program for city employees, and visiting professor with the Behavior Science Department of the New York City Police Academy. She has conducted research and published on family preservation programs, maternal substance abuse, child survivors of HIV/AIDS, independent living services for adolescents, child maltreatment and Caribbean families, and neighborhood-based services. She is immediate past president of the New York City Chapter of NASW.

Jennifer Reicher Gholston is a graduate of Rollins College in Winter Park, Florida, and received her master's degree in social work from the Columbia University School of Social Work in New York. She has been working with the homeless since 1993. Since 1998, she has been a clinical team member at Project HELP, working with and assessing dangerousness levels of homeless mentally ill patients on the streets of New York City.

Manny John González, Ph.D., is an associate professor and chair of the clinical concentration area at Fordham University Graduate School of Social Service, Lincoln Center Campus. He teaches courses in clinical practice, psychopathology, and the treatment of children. Dr. González also teaches courses in practice theory and research issues in mental health and services to children and families in the school's Ph.D. program. He has published manuscripts in the following areas: mental health practice with Hispanic immigrants and refugees, Hispanics and community health outreach, urban children, cross-cultural practice, and evidence-based practice. Dr. González maintains a private practice in New York City.

Christian Huygen, Ph.D., has served as director of the Rainbow Heights Club, a project of the Heights-Hill Mental Health Service Community Advisory Board, since 2002. He received his doctorate from the graduate faculty of the New School for Social Research, where his research in the cognitive science lab examined group identifications, social remembering, social context, and autobiographical memory. His current focus is the provision of culturally affirming mental health services to marginalized populations. He frequently lectures on the provision of culturally competent treatment to lesbian, gay, bisexual, and transgendered (LGBT) consumers, and writes an ongoing column on LGBT mental health issues for *New York City Voices.*

Eileen Klein, Ph.D., LCSW, has been working in public mental health as an administrator and supervisor for over 25 years. She has extensive experience with mentally ill consumers, both in clinical treatment and in social policy. She has been extensively involved in program planning, grant writing, and development for a variety of patient populations throughout her career. In addition, she is an adjunct professor at New York University and Long Island University in their master of social work programs. Dr. Klein specializes in teaching issues related to community mental health.

Lenore A. Kola, Ph.D., is an associate professor of social work at the Mandel School of Applied Social Sciences and former dean, School of Graduate Studies, at Case Western Reserve University in Cleveland, Ohio. Her professional focus has been on the development and implementation of training programs in mental and substance use disorders for faculty, graduate students, and community practitioners, supported by federal, state, as well as foundation funding. She is currently the co-director of the Ohio Substance Abuse and Mental Illness Coordinating Center at Case. She was the founding chair of the National Association of Social Workers' Section on Alcohol, Tobacco, and Other Drugs.

Winnie W. Kung, Ph.D., is associate professor at Fordham University Graduate School of Social Service. Her research interests include mental health and families, with an emphasis on cultural impacts. Her recent publications include Chinese American caregivers' burden and causal attributions of schizophrenia, Chinese Americans' help-seeking behaviors and barriers to mental health treatment, integration of primary care and mental health services, and the sociocultural contexts in shaping divorced women's stress and coping in Hong Kong. She is currently developing an ethnic-sensitive family intervention for Chinese American caregivers of patients suffering from schizophrenia. She teaches graduate practice courses with individuals and families.

Michael A. Mancini, Ph.D., is an assistant professor in the School of Social Work at St. Louis University. He has practice, teaching, and research experience in the area of mental health, particularly with individuals diagnosed with serious psychiatric disabilities, and he has expertise in the use of qualitative methods. Dr. Mancini teaches graduate-level mental health assessment and treatment practice courses as well as undergraduate research methods at St. Louis University. Dr. Mancini's practice experience consists of being chief of mental health services for a large, maximum security prison, as well as a program specialist for the New York State Office of Mental Health.

Gary Marshall, Ph.D., is an associate professor of public administration at the University of Nebraska at Omaha. He holds a Ph.D. in public administration from Virginia Tech's Center for Public Administration and Policy. Professor Marshall teaches in the areas of public administration theory, organization theory and behavior, organization development, and public policy mediation. His work has been published in leading academic journals such as *Public Administration Review*, the *American Review of Public Administration*, and *The American Behavioral Scientist*.

Steven Miccio is the executive director of People, Inc., in Poughkeepsie, New York, a consumer-operated mental health advocacy organization. A consumer leader, Steve has recently been developing a white paper authorized by over 200 consumers in New York State that demands quality services and renewed values in mental health services. Steve was diagnosed with bipolar disorder in the 1990s and has been an advocate for eliminating stigma and discrimination for many years.

Jaimie Page, MSW, Ph.D., is an assistant professor at the University of Texas at Arlington, School of Social Work. Dr. Page worked more than 10 years in the field of homeless health and mental health in street- and shelter-based clinical and administrative capacities before entering academia. She continues her research in barriers to transferring client care from street-based programs to community mental health systems, and in nontraditional treatment approaches with marginalized populations. Dr. Page's other research and policy activities involve harm reduction, drug policy, and health care issues.

Richard T. Pulice, Ph.D., has had over 25 years of experience in mental health working for state and local governments, not-for-profit agencies, and in private practice. He has published many articles regarding services for the seriously mentally ill in both the popular press and professional journals, and is a frequent speaker at state, national, and international conferences, advocating for persons with a mental illness. Formerly a professor at SUNY Albany and SUNY Empire State College, he is now an associate professor of social work and field coordinator in the School of Math and Sciences, Social Work Department, at the College of St. Rose, Albany, New York.

Elizabeth Randall, Ph.D., LICSW, has 20 years of experience in clinical social work, including inpatient experience, but concentrated mainly within the rural community mental health system in the southern region of the nation. She currently holds the position of associate professor with the Division of Social Work at West Virginia University. She also maintains a limited private practice, including consulting and clinical supervision for the Veteran's Administration and the Federally Qualified Health Center system within the state.

Robert J. Ronis, M.D., MPH, L. Douglas Lenosky Professor of Psychiatry is interim chair, Department of Psychiatry and co-director of the Ohio SAMI Coordinating Center of Excellence (CCOE) at Case Western Reserve University. A graduate of the CASE School of Medicine, Dr. Ronis received his master's in public health from Ohio State University in 1995. He is a diplomate of the American Board of Psychiatry and Neurology, with added qualifications in addiction psychiatry, and was named a distinguished fellow of the American Psychiatric Association. His areas of expertise include serious and persistent psychiatric disorders, addiction psychiatry, co-occurring mental and substance use disorders, and community mental health issues.

Jenny Ross, CSW, is the director of Project HELP, a program of Gouverneur Hospital, New York City, where she has worked for the past 12 years — for 6 years as a Project HELP team member and 6 years as director. Other programs she supervises are the Gouverneur Mobile Crisis Team, Project Liberty, and the Citywide Assistance Team (CAT). She is a graduate of NIP's (National Institute for the Psychotherapies, Inc.) four-year psychoanalytic training program. She holds a master's degree in social work from New York University. She maintains a private practice in Manhattan and is a board member of the Ericksonian Institute for Hypnotherapy.

Steven P. Segal, Ph.D., is a professor in the Schools of Social Welfare and Public Health, University of California, Berkeley. He is the director of the Mental Health and Social Welfare Research Group, School of Social Welfare, University of California, Berkeley, and the director of the Center for Self Help Research. Dr. Segal is the winner of the 2003 Distinguished Achievement Award from the Society for Social Work and Research. He has been the recipient of senior Fulbright research and lecture awards in Australia, the United Kingdom, and Italy. He has worked on mental health services research related to long-term community and residential care, civil commitment, the assessment of dangerousness and quality of psychiatric emergency care in general hospital psychiatric emergency rooms, and consumer roles in mental health services provision.

Lynda R. Sowbel, BCD, assistant professor of social work at Hood College in Frederick, Maryland, is currently working on a doctorate at the University of Maryland. Articles addressing aging enrichment in social work will be forthcoming in the *Journal of Gerontological Social Work* and the *Journal of Baccalaureate Social Work*. Ms. Sowbel has practiced psychiatric social work for over 20 years.

Wendy Starnes, OTR/L, is an occupational therapist who has designed and implemented training programs for professional interns in mental health programs. She is currently the associate director of the National Board for Certification in Occupational Therapy.

W. Patrick Sullivan, Ph.D., serves as professor at the Indiana University School of Social Work. He also served as director of the Indiana Division of Mental Health and Addiction from 1994 to 1998. While earning a Ph.D. at the University of Kansas, Sullivan helped develop the strengths model of social work practice, and has extended the model in mental health and addictions treatment. He has over 50 professional publications on a diverse range of topics. He received the Distinguished Hoosier Award from Governor Frank O'Bannon in 1997, and earned the Sagamore of the Wabash from Governor Joseph Kernan in 2004.

Melissa Floyd Taylor, Ph.D., LCSW, is an assistant professor of social work at the University of North Carolina, Greensboro. She completed her doctoral work at Virginia Commonwealth University (VCU) in 2002 after receiving her MSW from VCU in 1994. She received her undergraduate degrees in psychology and political science from Miami University in Oxford, Ohio. Throughout her practice career, she worked in direct service settings, primarily with persons who have serious mental illness, substance abuse issues, or both. She has recently published articles related to social work values in practice and the implications of conceptualizations in mental health of brain disease and behavioral health. Additionally, she is pursuing current research into creative, consumer-driven alternatives to involuntary mental health interventions, jail diversion, and family and substance abuse.

Philip Thomas, LCSW, ACSW, is a supervisory social worker and the coordinator of the Community Rehabilitation Section of Psychiatry Service, Roudebush VA Medical Center, Indianapolis, Indiana.

Yi-Fen Tseng, MA, graduated from Chingchi University Department of Sociology in Taiwan and is a doctoral student at Fordham University Graduate School of Social Service. Her research interests include mental health and families, especially on women and children, with an emphasis on cultural comparison. In Taiwan, she had experiences working with disadvantaged women and teenagers in both private agencies and the public sector. She also implemented a national project in Taiwan on the adjustment outcomes of children from divorced families. Cultural adjustment and impact on sensitive issues like mental health and teenage pregnancy are her current foci in her doctoral training.

Janet S. Walker, Ph.D., is director of research and dissemination at the Research and Training Center on Family Support and Children's Mental Health at Portland State University in Portland, Oregon. She received her doctorate from the University of Chicago in 1997. Dr. Walker's research focuses on how individuals and organizations acquire the capacity to implement and sustain high-quality practice in human service settings. Recently, she has studied the practice of *wraparound* — a team-based planning process for children with intensive needs. Her research has examined teamwork and effectiveness within wraparound, as well as the organizational and system-level conditions that are required for high-quality teamwork to occur. Together with Dr. Bruns, Dr. Walker coordinates the National Wraparound Initiative, a model development and consensus-building project.

William H. Wilson, M.D., is professor of psychiatry and director of inpatient psychiatric services at the Oregon Health and Science University, in Portland. Dr. Wilson received his undergraduate degree from Brown University in Rhode Island, attended medical school at the University of Pennsylvania, and completed his specialty training in psychiatry at the University of Wisconsin–Madison. He twice received the Exemplary Psychiatrist Award from the National Alliance for the Mentally Ill, and was awarded the State of Oregon's 2000 Mental Health Award for Excellence. He is a distinguished fellow of the American Psychiatric Association.

INDEX

A

Abstinence, 65-67; *see also* Relapse prevention

ACCESS (Access to Community-Care and Effective Services Supports) project, 185, 190–191

Accessibility/appropriateness, of services, 109, 133, 134, 145

Access to Community Care and Effective Services Supports (ACCESS) project, 185, 190–191

Access/utilization control techniques, in managed care organizations (MCOs), 211, 214; *see also* Accessibility/appropriateness, of services

Acculturation, 144

Addiction intervention, 63; *see also* Integrated treatment programs

Addictive disorders, 61–62; *see also* Co-occurring mental/substance disorders

Advanced mental health directives, 79–80

Advocacy groups, 10, 12, 28, 50, 110–111; *see also* Consumer movement

Affective disorders, 132

African Americans; *see also* Oppressed groups, public mental health and
  barriers, access, and service utilization, 133–136
  current status of, 131
  defining concepts, 129–130
    of the black cultural experience, 129–130
    of mental health and mental illness, 129
    of race, ethnicity, and culture, 129
  empowerment theories and, 28
  historical context of mental health services for, 126–127
  introduction on, 125–126
  neuropsychiatry and, 96
  prevalence/need for service for, 131–133
  protective/risk factors of, 130–131
  scientific racism and, 127–128
  summary/conclusion on, 136–137

Aftercare services, 35, 64; *see also* Outpatient treatment needs

Agency-based practice, 216

Agoraphobia, 90

Alaska Natives, 107

Alaska Youth Initiative, 49

Alcohol, drug, or mental health problems (ADM) problems, 181, 182, 189, 191; *see also* Co-occurring mental/substance disorders

Alcoholics Anonymous (AA), 65

Alcove Childcare Center, 176–177

Alternative treatments, 12, 20, 211

Alzheimer's dementia, 92, 133

American Psychiatric Association (APA), 85, 128

Amphetamine abuse, 92

Annette G. Strauss Family Gateway Center, 172–174, 178

Anticholinesterase medications, 92

Antidepressants, 86, 89

Anti-Insane Asylum Society, 8

Antipsychiatry movement, 9, 10, 98

Antipsychotics, 86, 87, 89, 91

Anxiety disorders, 90–91

Approaches, defining, 184

Arlington Life Shelter, 170–172, 177, 178

Asian Americans; *see also* Oppressed groups, public mental health and
  culturally responsive service delivery models for, 144–146
  culturally sensitive clinical practice with, 146–149
  help-seeking behaviors of, 142–144
  introduction on, 107, 141
  summary/conclusion on, 149–150

Assertive case management, 25